Hiram Woodruff

Engraved by G. R. Hall from a portrait by C. A. Koster.
EXPRESSLY FOR THE "TROTTING HORSE OF AMERICA."

THE

TROTTING HORSE OF AMERICA:

HOW TO TRAIN AND DRIVE HIM.

WITH

REMINISCENCES OF THE TROTTING TURF.

BY

HIRAM WOODRUFF.

EDITED BY CHARLES J. FOSTER
OF "WILKES' SPIRIT OF THE TIMES."

INCLUDING AN INTRODUCTORY NOTICE BY GEORGE WILKES, AND
A BIOGRAPHICAL SKETCH BY THE EDITOR.

NEW YORK:
J. B. FORD AND COMPANY.
1871.

UNIVERSITY PRESS: WELCH, BIGELOW, & Co.,
CAMBRIDGE.

IN

CONFORMITY WITH THE INTENTION AND DIRECTION

OF

THE AUTHOR,

AND

MUCH TO THE GRATIFICATION OF THE EDITOR,

THIS WORK

IS, BY PERMISSION, RESPECTFULLY INSCRIBED TO

ROBERT BONNER, ESQ.,

BY WHOM ITS COMPOSITION WAS

FIRST SUGGESTED.

EDITOR'S PREFACE.

THE composition of this work was first suggested by Mr. ROBERT BONNER, who fully appreciated the original views and vast experience of HIRAM WOODRUFF in all matters pertaining to the art of training and driving the trotting-horse. At the earnest solicitation of Mr. GEORGE WILKES (the editor of "The Spirit of the Times"), and of some other of his friends, HIRAM agreed to undertake it. They believed, and their arguments induced him to believe, that such a work from him would be a public benefit to the owners of horses, and a service to the horse himself. From the nature of the avocations to which he had devoted himself with unparalleled success for forty years, HIRAM WOODRUFF was not a ready penman; and therefore it was not until the writer of this introductory preface had promised to act as his amanuensis, and to edit the work, that he consented to go on with it. Its reception, when some chapters had been published, was such as to establish its value; and all those who had been long acquainted with the author clearly recognized his strong, original turn of thought, and painstaking anxiety to make it eminently practical and useful. During its composition, there were some delays caused by the great application necessary on the part of the author to his business as trainer and driver of horses. He had sometimes as many as twenty in his charge; and he felt that at such periods he could not, with justice to the work itself and to them, continue its composition.

To suggestions that the public was eager for the book, and wanted it completed early, he commonly replied that *he* wanted it completed *well*. There was, he said, no more reason for hurrying out this, his only work, than there would be in his hurrying on the education of a horse that he deemed certain to make a trotter. He was no believer in the "forcing" process, and always contended that the book would be all the better for the extra time he had resolved to devote to it. Nothing could exceed his anxiety to avoid any thing that by misapplication might be mischievous. He was eminently a man of clear, strong views, and of few, terse words. Many of the most valuable and well-tried conclusions of his genius and experience will be found set down in his literal words in a very few lines. I have never met with a man who was so quick and direct in coming at the kernel of a question, and who threw away the husk and shell so promptly as utterly worthless.

Just before his last illness, the materials for the completion of the book were all arranged, and I received his directions to that end. During the progress of the work, I had some hundreds of interviews with him, during which he dictated the matter now presented to the reader in this volume. It was his custom to read carefully every chapter as it appeared in "The Spirit of the Times," and he gave a few directions for emendations. These have been strictly followed. His memory was marvellous, not only of events, but of the little details connected with them; and he had such a graphic way of describing matters and things, that his hearers and his readers were carried to the scene and time, and virtually made spectators of the things themselves. He was utterly intolerant of quackery in any shape; and his readers may rely upon it that the only way to develop the gifts and capabilities of the trotting-horse is to employ those elements which HIRAM WOODRUFF brought to the composition of this work,—judgment, conscientious painstaking to be right, and much perseverance.

CONTENTS.

XII.

XIII.

XIV.

XV.

XVI.

XVII.

XVIII.

XIX.

XX.

XXI.

XXII.

XXIII.

XXIV.

XXV.

XXVI.

XXVII.

XXVIII.

XXIX.

XXX.

XXXI.

XXXII.

XLI.

XLII.

XLIII.

XLIV.

XLV.

XLVI.

XLVII.

HIRAM WOODRUFF.

IT has been remarked by philosophers, that the progress of the human race is to be traced more distinctly in the individual history of its great men, than by any other process known to the human observation. It has even been held by some writers, and among them by Napoleon the Third, that the most familiar method by which Providence confers his greatest benefits upon mankind is in the raising up of favored men at certain periods, who, being imbued with the new principles which are to advance the fortunes of their era, are enabled "to stamp the age with the seal of their genius, and to accomplish in a few years the labor of many centuries." If this agreeable theory is correct, the humble trainer and driver who departed this life at Jamaica Plains, Long Island, on the morning of the 15th of March, 1867, may fairly rank among the great men of his period, and be frankly awarded a full share of the honors which are due to those who have been benefactors to their country. We measure genius, not merely by a man's social status, but by "the empire of his ideas," the results which they enforce, and the benefits which inure through them to the world. To bring this principle to its test for the purposes of our theme, we find that there are but two nations of the earth which possess a race of animals known as the trotting-horse. One of these nations is Russia; the other, the United States. In the first-named country, we find an animal proceeding from the Arabian fountain, fused, it is said, upon the Flanders stock, which is called the Orloff trotter; but this breed, though bending the knee when striding, and though having in other respects the trotting action, is considered by good judges as being only half-developed. In this country, on the other hand, we have "a paragon of animals," which is already the wonder of the world; and which, from the familiar, affectionate, and almost universal use made of him on this continent, and from the growing demand which is made for him in other countries, has already become an American commercial product, of vast importance and proportions. It is certain that this animal is an American production; as much so, in fact, as the thorough-bred horse, which disdainfully gives weight at Goodwood and Ascot to the purer descendants of his Arabian ancestry, is a creation of the English breeding-stable and the English race-course. And it is also certain, that the development of the American trotter to its present marvellous pre-eminence over all other breeds of horses used for harness and road purposes is more due to Hiram Woodruff than to any, if not than to all other men who ever lived. Those who know the history of trotting in this country, and who recall to mind the average speed of the fast harness-horse when Hiram identified himself with its advancement, will not hesitate to say, that he doubled the value of the original element on which he worked, and, at the end of a few years, gave a *great* animal to the country, in place of what had been only a *good* animal before.

It is recognized by those who are versed in the origin and characteristics of the American trotter, that the highest type of that invaluable breed descends from the English thorough-bred horse Messenger, which was imported into this country in the latter part of the last century. Indeed, so widely is this fact acknowledged, that breeders of experience, in view of the excellence of which he was the founder, and of the vast extent of the interest which has proceeded from his loins, have been heard to declare, that, when that old gray came charging down the gang-plank of the ship which brought him over, the value of not less than one hundred millions of dollars struck our soil. If that be true, the man who developed Messenger's value through his progeny can hardly be regarded as less than a genius, as well as a public benefactor. It cannot be doubted, therefore, that HIRAM WOODRUFF was the man of his period for the development of the interest with which he identified himself; and in proportion to the importance of that interest will his merits be valued by posterity. In all the future of our particular turf-history, his figure will loom up to the contemplation of its followers, as the sole great man who had been produced, in connection with that interest, down to the day of his decease.

But HIRAM WOODRUFF brought something more to his vocation than a mere intuitive perception of the new principles by which the trotter was to be improved. He brought a generous, cheerful, kindly nature; and his faculties were insensibly buoyed and sustained by that invariable accompaniment of true genius, — a good heart. He had, moreover, one of those happy dispositions of mixed simplicity and candor, which commands at once the confidence of men, and which, when its influences are applied to the secondary animals, fascinates and subjects them completely to the owner's will. There is nothing which recognizes the subtle instincts of affection so quickly, and which knows them so unmistakably, as a horse; and much of HIRAM'S facility of communicating his purpose to the animal he rode or drove or trained proceeded from his power of making it love him. Like RAREY, his doctrine was kindness; and, when he walked through his stables, the undoubted accord which he had established with its glossy inmates was at once evinced by the low whinnies of welcome which would greet his kindly presence as he went from stall to stall. They knew him for the friend who mixed among them, almost as if he were an equal, and who never ceased to talk to them as if they were his equals when he took them out for their exercise, or even when he encouraged them during the strife of the arena. What would they not do for that man, which he could make them understand? and how could they fail to know his wish, when, inspiring them with his chirrup, and shaking the bit in their mouths, he "lifted" them, as it were, and sent them whirling with an unknown velocity along the course? Perhaps Flora Temple was the most remarkable instance of the great horseman's conquest over animal affection during his career. She loved him with an unmistakable cordiality; and when he and she were engaged in some of their most notable struggles, the man and horse seemed to be but parts of the same creature, animated by the fury of a common purpose. Many drivers have been heard to wonder how it was that HIRAM obtained such a mysterious mastery over his horses on all occasions; but the secret was, that he gained their confidence through their affections; and, after that, every thing was easy. The reason why women so easily fascinate a horse is because of the tenderness of their approach; and, so far as gentleness went, HIRAM WOODRUFF had the nature of a woman.

Commanding the horse, therefore, to the absolute extent he did, there is no reason for wonder that he made his steed understand himself, as well as know his master. One half of a horse's speed is in the mind of his rider or driver. When it is known to the world that a horse has made a mile a second or half-second faster than it was ever made before, some rider of some other horse, nerving himself with the knowledge of the fact, and infusing that knowledge into his horse by dint of his own enthusiasm, sends *him* a second or two faster still; and the result of the mental emulation is a permanent improvement which never is retraced. HIRAM WOODRUFF was the first to take this mental grip of the powers of the trotting-horse; and the result, in his case, was, that, by dint of his own mind, he carried him triumphantly over the gap which lies between 2.40 and 2.18.

There are yet other characteristics of HIRAM WOODRUFF, which, in bidding him farewell, we are called upon to notice. Viewed in connection with his peculiar walk in life, these traits are, if possible, more remarkable than his genius; and they arrest the attention as matters of surprise. We allude to his incorruptible personal integrity under the usual temptations of his station. It is not enough, therefore, to say that HIRAM WOODRUFF was an honest man. He was more than that; for he was utterly incapable even of sharp practices, or meannesses of any kind. Happen what might, he would not conceal any of his opinions from an employer, or retain an employment by misrepresenting the merits of an animal intrusted to his care. And, when he brought his horse to the arena, it was certain he would be honestly driven, however the money might be on. The most abandoned men who frequent the trotting-tracks dared not, even after he had been on the turf but a short time, venture to approach him with a dishonorable proposition; for they had discovered his invincible integrity, and felt, that, in such case, their exposure was inevitable. In this respect, and taking all things together, HIRAM WOODRUFF may be regarded as a phenomenon. Here is a man, born, as it were, in the very dregs of the stable, thrown constantly among the vicious and depraved, and frequently tempted by the most alluring opportunities of profit, who preserves his integrity intact, in the midst of a general society largely tainted with corruption, and during a period in which the honesty of almost every public officer is touched with suspicion. It is not singular, therefore, that no trainer or driver ever envied HIRAM his business or disputed his superiority.

His virtues were above the aim of jealousy; and his mission was as much to prove to bad men the value of leading a good life, as to improve the condition of the horse. He was a boon not only to those of his own order, but to society at large. He never betrayed his trust; never was suspected of a lie; and, if good deeds can charter a man to be regarded as a Christian, HIRAM WOODRUFF certainly was one.

On the 22d of February, he celebrated his fiftieth birthday with his friends at home; and he exhibited on that occasion, while alluding to the "events" for which he stood engaged, the same cheerful confidence which marked all his expectations. He now lies on that slope of Cypress Hill which looks toward the course on which he has earned so much of his renown.

Many a throng which will gather during the coming seasons to witness the contests of the horses he had in part prepared will turn gloomily to that cold hill; and there will be none among them who will not feel that there is a great void in their midst, and that the Master has gone.

GEORGE WILKES.

BIOGRAPHICAL SKETCH OF THE AUTHOR.

BY CHARLES J. FOSTER

> "He was a man! take him for all in all,
> I shall not look upon his like again!"

OUR dear, esteemed friend, Hiram Woodruff, died on the morning of Friday, March 15, 1867, and was buried on the following Sunday, in the Cypress-hills Cemetery, between East New York and the house he kept so long. It has become our mournful duty to sketch, as nearly as we may, some incidents of his life, and to show what manner of man he was. Hiram Washington Woodruff was born on the 22d of February, 1817; and consequently, at the time of his death, he was fifty years and twenty-one days old. His father, John Woodruff, afterwards called by his friends and familiar acquaintances "Colonel Ogden," lived at Birmingham, a small place near Flemington, in Huntington County, New Jersey, where his wife bore him his second son, Hiram. The eldest son was Isaac, and the youngest William. These brothers, with their sister Margaret (Mrs. Nelson), still survive. The Woodruffs were a family of horsemen. The old colonel was noted as a trainer. His brother, George Woodruff, was still more famous in that capacity, and was without an equal perhaps, except Peter Whelan, as a rider of trotting-horses, until his nephew appeared, and surpassed them both. It was at one time intended that Hiram should learn a trade, and that of a hatter was thought suitable. But in him, boy as he was, the call "to horse" was already like that of the trumpet to the trooper when it sounds "boots and saddle." Very early in life he began to ride; and the foundation of his future immense and accurate knowledge of horsemanship, in all its branches and in all their details, was laid while he was a little boy. He was but fifty years old at the time of his death; and, forty years before, he had ridden the famous trotting-horse Topgallant—a son of imported Messenger—at his exercise. Thus the first horse with whom we can certainly associate this most celebrated of trainers, riders, and drivers, was one worthy of his own high renown. Upon the merits of this game old horse, who was spavined in both hind-legs, and yet in his twenty-fourth year beat Whalebone three-mile heats, Hiram loved to dwell.

Top-Gallant was one of a lot of famous horses in the stable of George Woodruff, and Hiram learned his first regular lessons in horsemanship from his uncle. His first race was ridden at the Hunting-park Course, Philadelphia, where George had Top-gallant, Whalebone, Columbus, and others of great note, in training. The gentlemen who frequented the ground one afternoon offered a purse, to be trotted for by any horses that the boys could pick up. Young Hiram (he was then fourteen years old) knew that there was at plough in a field hard by a horse called Shaking Quaker, that had trotted on Long Island. This horse he got, and with him he won the purse. In two or three weeks it was followed by another race for a larger amount, Mr. F. Duffy having backed his mare Lady Kate to trot fifteen miles an hour. He selected Hiram and another boy to ride, never imagining that one of them could ride a fast trotter a whole hour without a rest. Duffy, in fact, played a keen game; for he led the mare up and down by the bridle, with a heavy saddle on, and induced the backers of time to believe that he was going to ride her himself. His money was well laid, and the time for the start was near, when the backers of the watch, to their surprise and confusion, saw little Hiram come out of the bushes, with his light saddle on his arm, to ride the mare. She trotted sixteen miles in a trifle less than fifty-seven minutes, and Hiram rode her eight-miles and three quarters only.

Two years later he rode in another time-match, and acquired still higher distinction. His father was then keeping the Harlem-park Course; and there Mr. William Niblo had in training, under his own supervision, a gray gelding called Paul Pry, a grandson of imported Messenger. This horse was matched for two thousand dollars a side, to trot sixteen miles an hour, with two hundred and fifty dollars a side on every quarter over that distance up to seventeen and three-quarter miles. Hiram rode Paul Pry at his work, and was chosen to steer him in his race on the Union Course. The confidence Mr. Niblo had in the strength, endurance, and judgment of the lad of sixteen was signally justified by the event. Hiram rode the horse eighteen miles in a fraction less than fifty-nine minutes, and the last quarter was jogged out at that. Considering the great difficulty there is in riding fast trotters many miles at a time, and recollecting the fact that Paul Pry was a puller, this was a very remarkable feat; and those among the trainers and amateurs who looked ahead must have concluded that in this lad there was the stuff of which great men are made. Some have said that Hiram Woodruff first distinguished himself by riding Dutchman; but it is an error. He was famous before Dutchman had left the string-team which hauled the brick-cart.

At this time, and for many years afterwards, Hiram was a model of strength, grace, activity, and suppleness. He was a swift runner and a mighty jumper and leaper, as well as a bold and skilful rider; and his stamina was afterwards found to be such, that Jack Harrison, a noted matchmaker of those days, publicly offered to back him to ride different horses a hundred miles in five hours. The offer was not accepted; for the sportsmen had already learned, that, with uncommon fine constitutional stamina, young Woodruff possessed sinews of steel, nerves that could not be shaken, and an intuitive sagacity which made him master of almost any situation, and capable of accomplishing almost any feat. All this, too, was accompanied by a cheerful modesty of disposition, which endeared him to his associates, and a high rectitude of principle, which his friends can now justly boast was never in his whole life impaired. His integrity, indeed, through life, has been of that adamantine and obstinate degree that it never took the seeming of a flaw. It was of that high quality which may be compared to the constancy and courage of a bull-dog of true English breed, which may be cut up piecemeal, but can never be subdued.

It was while here at Harlem that Hiram was fortunate enough to win the affections of Miss Sarah Ann Howe, a young lady of great personal beauty and much sweetness of disposition. His father soon moved to the old Centreville House, near the Centreville Course; and Hiram went with him. On Christmas Day, 1836, and therefore before he had quite arrived at his twentieth birthday, Hiram Woodruff was married to Sarah Ann Howe, at Jamaica. He took his young bride home with him to his father's; and now, over his grave, after his more than thirty years of wedded life have ended, his friends can truly say that never was man more blessed in an excellent wife than he, in her he loved so well, and has left to mourn behind him.

It was not long after his marriage when Dutchman came into his hands. The first race he won with him was against Lady Suffolk and Rattler. The latter was trained and ridden by William Whelan, brother of Peter of famous memory, and himself now survivor of his old and valued friend Hiram. Out of this race grew that at three-mile heats between Dutchman and Rattler, which was won by the former in four heats. The two friends latterly, in their reviews of what happened thirty years ago, used to ride this race again. Hiram would show how it was won; and Whelan argue that it was lost because Rattler was a poor feeder, and so, at that time, not quite equal to Dutchman in lasting qualities. These young riders and trainers were now "the coming men." George Woodruff and Peter Whelan were to have successors as great, if not greater, than themselves. The seas soon separated the young men. Whelan went to England with Rattler, where he beat everything with ridiculous ease, and issued a challenge to the world. Thereupon an English merchant of New York sounded Hiram Woodruff, to ascertain whether he would go to England to train and ride Dutchman if the horse were purchased. Hiram was not very anxious to leave his home and his young wife; but his confidence was great in Dutchman, and he consented to go. But the bargain for the horse went off. His owners were offered two thousand seven hundred dollars and a black mare, then in Hiram's hands, for him. They wanted three thousand dollars and the mare. Whelan thinks that Rattler might have defeated Dutchman in England, as the former had got to feeding strong there. But Hiram has often told us that the probabilities were all the other way, as Dutchman's great speed was only just coming to him when he beat Rattler in the race of four heats. In Hiram's hands, Dutchman performed three great feats. The first was the defeat of Rattler in the great race of four three-mile heats.

The second was the distancing of Awful, three miles in harness, in 7m. 41s. The third was the time-match, three miles, in which the mark, still standing at the head of the record, 7m. 32½s., was made. Hiram has always maintained, and no doubt with good reason, that Dutchman could have greatly surpassed this. In the second mile, which was trotted in 2m. 28s., Isaac Woodruff, who was on the running companion, conceived that Hiram was going too fast, and called to him to pull. The third mile was in 2m. 30s., and Dutchman was pulled all the way. It was Hiram's conviction that he could have trotted this in 2m. 26s. This very remarkable horse was not coarse, as many suppose him to have been. He showed brëeding in form as well as bottom, and was savage in disposition. After his time-match he went to Philadelphia, and Hiram beat him two or three times with Washington. But he returned into Hiram's hands, and trotted his famous races with Americus under his direction.

Hiram Woodruff had then just reached his twenty-sixth year, and had fully entered upon that career of hard work and usefulness which was increasing in importance every day, which finally made him one of the best known and most renowned men in America, and in which his genius, his faithfulness, and his sagacity enabled him to do his country weighty and honorable service. The greatest nations, and many of the greatest men that have existed in the world, have held, that, next to the improvement and culture of mankind itself, the improvement and cultivation of the horse is one of the best and mightiest of tasks. Our country is distinguished abroad, as well as at home, for having effected the greatest and most surprising improvement in the horse of daily use, the trotter, that is mentioned in the annals of horsemanship, from the period of the misty fables of Castor, Pollux, and Chiron the Centaur, down to this day. Now, for this improvement the country is more indebted to Hiram Woodruff than to any other man — or any ten men. Nobody with any character for sense and veracity will dispute this.

Before he had done with Dutchman on the turf, Ripton had come to Hiram Woodruff; and this "white-legged pony" soon became as great a favorite with him, as great a prodigy with the public, and as great a scourge to those who stood against him, as Dutchman had been. He it was that first made two miles in 5m. 7s., in harness, going against Lady Suffolk; and he finally became such a thorn in Bryan's side, that he declared the mare should not trot against him any more, unless it was under saddle. It was in driving Ripton against Americus, that Hiram displayed one of his finest exhibitions of coolness, craft, and science. He won the race against Americus when a hundred to five had been laid on the latter horse. Ripton was one of Hiram's prime favorites. His fine speed, his stoutness, his grand action, his turbulent spirits, and indomitable game, were themes that Hiram never tired of when he had once begun. To hear him and Dan Pfifer, who took care of the "white-legged pony," go on about him, with Sim Hoagland and Whelan to drop in suggestive and sage remarks here and there, was a treat indeed. The "white-legged pony" was also a prime favorite with Hiram's devoted friend Oliver Marshall. Friends! when shall we truly realize that the tongue which spoke with such wisdom, enthusiasm, and terse eloquence, at these, our well-remembered sittings, is silent now forever?

It is beyond the scope of this sketch, even to mention by name all the horses which Hiram trained, rode, and drove. His own work (which follows) may be referred to as regards those of most renown who preceded the era of Flora Temple. He was always fond of the Messenger blood. Beginning with old Topgallant, and coming along down with Paul Pry, grandson of Messenger; Lady Suffolk, his granddaughter; Ajax and Hector, sons of Abdallah; and then to the Hambletonians, of whom he made the wonder, Dexter, — what famous horses of that famous strain came to his hands to have their excellencies made manifest! Flora herself has a dash of the blood; and she, too, was the work of Hiram's strong, patient, and cunning hand. When he was twenty-eight years old, Hiram removed to Harlem, and became proprietor of the track there which his father had had. He kept it two years, and then removed to Boston, where he was proprietor of the Cambridge Course from 1847 to 1850. When he returned to New York, he went into business in the Union Saloon, Broadway; which he kept in partnership with Albert Losee. But the City was not by any means the place for Hiram. His was a spirit which delighted in the country, by hill and stream, and where, with hand upon the shoulder of his horse, he could hear the booming of the wild waves on the beach. So, near "old Long Island's sea-girt shore," in the spring of 1851, he took the house at the foot of the hill, on the Jamaica Road, between East New York and the Corners; and this was known far and wide for two or three years as "Hiram Woodruff's." When he left that, it was to remove to the house in which he died; and here his friends of late years were wont to assemble in great numbers around him. He had now reached his prime, and gained a station and esteem with the world at large such as no other man in the like capacity had ever attained to. Hundreds of thousands who had never seen the man held him in regard; and all through the regions of the West his name was in their mouths, familiar as a household word. In the Eastern States, too, he was very much respected and beloved. He often visited Boston and Providence, and these trips were his great holidays. His arrival at these places was the signal for general rejoicing. Troops of friends crowded round him to express their satisfaction, and manifest their attachment. When thus away from home, the deep and abiding love he cherished for his wife was seen by his nearest friends in his behavior. She was never out of his thought; and when his friends got him to stay a day or two longer, he always sent despatches home. He loved music; and one there was in the Eastern States who used to sing a song called "My Sarah." This never failed to move Hiram to tears.

One other recreation he greatly enjoyed. It was his custom to go down upon the shores of Jamaica Bay, in the summer time, and there, camping out in a shady grove with a few friends, spend the days in fishing. Oliver Marshal and Henry Collins were commonly his associates in these excursions. Dan Pfifer was often there; and Sim Hoagland drove over to the camp most days. Hiram and Dan had matches at fishing as they had at training and driving. Hiram took great catches of blue-fish when they were running; but in spite of all his delicate manipulations of the line, — and he had a finger as true as that of a player on a harp-string, — he could never catch a sheep's-head. Pfifer caught a few; but there was another of their friends who beat them both, far and away, in catching this delectable and noble fish. It was William Shaw, another fine horseman, whose youth and manhood had been mostly passed in training runners. His death, some time ago, was suitably noticed. He went home ill from a party at Hiram's, given to celebrate the wedding of his daughter to young Hiram Howe, and never left his bed alive. He died of a relapse of fever, contracted in the service of his country at New Orleans during the great war. Henry Collins was always on the fishing-excursions, and amused the others by his sallies of dry, quaint wit. His death was not long after that of Mr. Shaw; and it was a heavy blow to Hiram, Collins had been such a loving, faithful friend and companion. It is, indeed, to be especially remarked, that Hiram Woodruff had, above most men, the gift of inspiring true affection. It was the pure sincerity and simplicity of his nature which effected this. He was as open and frank as a child: he could not even *think* a rascality; and rascals as well as honest men knew it. Then his kindliness of disposition, and generosity, won the heart at once. If a neighbor wanted any thing, — if the poor, the sick, the aged, or the feeble wanted aid, — he gave it; not patronizingly or pompously, but just as though he was paying them something that he owed. Alas! we have looked our last upon this great, loving, charitable, child-like man.

He was not of a demonstrative nature, except among his cherished and trusted friends; but the least sign of suffering, or need of sympathy, in any one, opened the flood-gates of his heart. His face was square, with immense firmness about the jaw. His forehead was broad and lofty; his eye, a deep, dark gray. It was eminently a thoughtful face; and there was a sweetness in his smile which will not be forgotten. Of late years the writer of this has been closely intimate with Hiram, and has often pondered over his virtues and great parts. His scrupulous regard for the feelings of others was always shown when he mentioned other trainers and drivers. In the composition of his book he carefully avoided any thing that could by possibility wound or injure any of them. It was, too, his pleasure to mention them individually, so that he might leave a testimony to their capacity and worth. This was so like the man! He would do good by stealth. He began his work on the American Trotter at the earnest solicitation of Mr. Wilkes and other friends, who felt convinced, and at last convinced him, that, out of his vast store of wisdom and experience in relation to trotting-horses, he might set down much that would be of value to the world. It was highly appreciated. The people hailed it all over the country. English papers copied chapter after chapter at length; and his old horsemen friends harangued each other about it, declaring, "It's capital, I tell you; and every word *jest like Hiram!* I didn't know that he could write any thing more than a letter; but, in writing about horses, he can beat 'em all!" Hiram himself took pride and interest in it; and herein again he manifested another trait in regard to his wife. As soon as the paper arrived, containing his latest chapter, he peremptorily ordered it to be taken up to Mrs. Woodruff. "For," said he to us, "she reads it out to the ladies that call upon her; and, between you and me, she thinks it good!" Poor friend! he had great and just confidence in his wife's capacity; but when ordering "The Spirit" up-stairs, as soon as it arrived, much to the dissatisfaction of some who wanted to read it down-stairs, it never occurred to him that he could have as many copies as he pleased. His uncle George and Crepe Collins were much pleased with the work as it progressed; so were Oliver Marshall and Sim Hoagland. Some fools thought he was not the author of it; as if any other living man but he, no matter what might be that man's capacity, could have produced it.

His opinions about horses and horse-matters were decided when once formed; but he was far-seeing and cautious in the making of them. Mr. Bonner's gray mare, Peerless, was at the very top of his esteem,—his model of a fast and lasting trotter. Like Ripton, Kemble Jackson, Flora Temple, and so many others, she was formed by him. Dexter stood as high as any for racing-purposes. Hiram amazed us when, early in that famous horse's career, he predicted that he would beat the world. Many thought him almost crazy to match Dexter against Stonewall Jackson of Hartford, three-mile heats. Dexter's two greatest races in his hands were the two-mile heats to wagons; in which he beat Butler the second heat in 4m. 56¼s.; and the mile heats, three in five, in harness, in which he beat Butler and Vanderbilt in five heats. Butler won the first and second heats, and Eoff considered that he had the money in his pocket. Odds of ten to one were laid upon the black horse, and great sums were pending. Dexter was sore and lame. Nothing but a mighty effort could save the race; but the great master of the art, the King of American Horsemen, was behind the brown gelding, and he now displayed one more of his grand masterpieces. He won the third heat. The fourth he won in the unprecedented time of 2m. 24½s.; and Vanderbilt was distanced. The backers of the Contraband stood aghast. The men from the South Side gave a roar that might have been heard at Jamaica Bay. "We have got you," they cried to the friends of Butler: "Eoff is a captain, but this is the Old Field-Marshal here behind Dexter!" Thousands were present; but there was not a sound to be heard, save the tramp of these famous horses, as their more famous drivers brought them along, in scoring for the deciding heat. Eoff drove with immense resolution and skill; but the hand of the great master was upon the reins of Dexter, and he won the fifth heat in the marvellous time of 2m. 24¼s. "Now, I'll tell you what it is," said a gentleman who had lost heavily on the race: "it is twenty or thirty per cent. in favor of any horse that Hiram Woodruff drives, — I don't care who drives the other! I've paid dear enough for that opinion; and it's mine!"

Lady Emma was another held very high in the judgment of Hiram, and her owner was fast in his dearest esteem; but, at the end of the last season that the great trainer and driver was ever to see, the horse of his heart was Mr. Bonner's chestnut, the famous Auburn Horse. Very late last fall we took one of our accustomed drives over to Hiram's, and found all about the place in a sort of pleasant commotion. Hiram Howe, Pelham John, Long Tom Farrell, Dan Delahay, and several others, were full of what the Auburn Horse had done that morning. Nothing was ever seen like it, they averred, since old Pocahontas the pacer distanced Hero in 2m. 17½s. The horse had, unquestionably, come up the stretch with such an electric burst of speed as had amazed the spectators. It never was Hiram's practice to talk about his horses to Mrs. Woodruff; but, on this occasion, he had no sooner returned from the course, than he went in, and told her that he had never ridden so fast behind a trotter in his life as on that morning. This we had from Mrs. Woodruff the same day. When we reached Hiram, in the stable-yard, he made use of the very same expression. While we were talking, Mr. Bonner drove up. We all three went to the box, and Hiram stripped the chestnut. "He is," said he, "the best balanced big horse in America!" Afterwards, we all three stood in the autumn sun, by the garden-gate, and a conversation ensued. Hiram said, "I rode faster behind him this morning than ever I rode in my life."

Mr. Bonner was silent; and, it being our custom to stand up for the absent, we determined to put in a word or two for the gallant gray. So we said, "Now, look here, Hiram: you rode at the rate of two minutes to the mile behind Peerless for a quarter. Capt. Moore will swear to it. Do you mean to say that you rode faster behind the Auburn Horse than behind the gray mare?"

"Faster than behind the gray mare? Faster than I ever rode behind *any* horse!" said he, with his resolute eye and grave smile.

Mr. Bonner was silent as Hiram said this with his hand upraised; but we determined to have another word, so we at it again argumentatively. Hiram looked over toward the sea, where the sun was shining in the southern board; and he said, "If the weather holds good a few days longer, and there is a fair day and track next week, something will be done!"

"What do you think it will be?"

He smiled and said, "Mr. Bonner wants to know what I think, no doubt; and I don't mind telling you what I expect, because you never blow things."

"Yes, yes: now, what do you expect?"

"To wipe out all that has ever been done on this island."

"You mean all that has ever been done in harness?"

"All that has ever been done at all. Listen, now: I am not given to exaggeration, and I want to keep within limits. I am confident that I can drive that horse the first half-mile in 1m. 8s. If I can't bring him home the other half in 1m. 10s. I ought to be horsewhipped. That will be 2m. 18s."

It happened that the weather got cold and bleak immediately after that delicious afternoon, and the course was not in order again; so the great trial never came off. Knowing the care, knowledge, and vast experience which Hiram brought to the making up of his opinions, and having witnessed the gravity and earnestness with which he advanced this as his settled conviction, we fully believe, that, under favorable circumstances, the chestnut could have done what he said. Therefore, we say that the Auburn Horse filled his eye at the last moment when there was great ambition and speculation in it; and was the last, as well as the greatest, in point of speed, of those world-renowned trotters which were stabled in Hiram Woodruff's vast brain and mighty heart.

During the winter, Hiram's health had not been good. He had several attacks of illness; and when he got a little better, he would get up and go about as though he had not been sick. This made strong calls upon his constitutional stamina, which had once been as good and perfect as his honesty and pluck. At his birthday, on the 22d of February, he was well, and singularly happy and genial. He dined with his friends; consented to the wish of Mr. Parkes, of Brooklyn, to sit for his portrait, to be presented to his wife; and, finally, had the pony (the fifty-miler), brought into the parlor, among his friends, in order that he might expatiate upon his rare merits. Six days after that we saw Hiram for the last time, a fortnight before his death; and never, since our friendship began, did we see him more cheerful, bright, and genial than he was upon that day. It was a spring day, light and mild: we found Hiram in the yard, and he hailed us with a cheery halloa, "I'm glad you've come: I'm getting ready for the next campaign! First of all, come and look at Quicksilver and Rosamond."

We answered that we were impatient to look at Pocahontas and Strideaway. He said, "Time enough." We looked at the horses. We looked at his hogs. We surveyed the renowned mare and her son. He never was more happy, never more pleasant and wise. We said how we rejoiced to find him looking and feeling so well. He put his hand upon our shoulder; and, with the smile we all knew and loved so well, he said, "I am not as well as I look, but I am better than I was most of the winter."

We then went and looked over his wagons and sulkies, which had all been painted and put in order for the season he was never to see. We talked about his book, and the plan of its conclusion was settled. "You must come here often," said he: "I want to see you very often."

We replied, that, when the roads got good, we would often drive over: but he replied that there was no need to wait for the roads. He had a plan to meet that difficulty: it was, that he would get a saddle and bridle, and we must ride over on horseback. "You can jump up and slip over here any time on horseback; and I'll see about the saddle and bridle to-morrow."

It is in some sort a consolation, that, at our last parting from this valued friend, he felt so happy, and was so kindly disposed to us. On the Sunday week following, he was taken sick with bilious vomiting in the middle of the night. Andrew Howe, his relative and confidential steward, was lying in the house sick, and died the next day. Hiram got worse; and a despatch was sent for his friend Mr. Marshall, who arrived on Thursday morning at daylight. Sim Hoagland had been constant in his attentions to his friend. Mrs. Woodruff was, of course, in sore distress, but still hopeful. The doctor, as Mr. Marshall entered, declared that a change had taken place, and that he had great hopes. But this was fallacious. Even then the

"Single warrior, in sombre harness mailed,
Dreaded of man, and surnamed the Destroyer,
The rampart wall had scaled."

Hiram was anxious to talk then, but Mr. Marshall wanted him to keep quiet; so he left him with Mrs. Woodruff, who had made him some beef-tea. Towards night he grew weaker and weaker. Through the long, sad watches of that mournful night he failed gradually, but retained his consciousness. Fondly pressing the hand of his dear wife, and with many a look of affection cast upon the brother of his heart, Marshall, and Hiram Howe, he gradually sank away, and died without a groan or pang, as a baby falls to sleep. It was ten minutes to four o'clock in the morning when he died; and the last clearly articulate word that he spoke was "HORSE!"

The news of his death caused an extraordinary sensation. Thousands who had never seen him — business men, professional men, and idlers — spoke of it as the event of the time, and always with kindness and regret. It was the same all over the country, for there was not a man in America, except perhaps General Grant, esteemed by a greater number of people than Hiram Woodruff.

The funeral was held on Sunday, in the afternoon. The weather was terrible for the season; and the roads so bad, that it was only by work like that with which pioneers precede an army, that the house of mourning was reached by many from a distance. The snow lay thick and deep, and fell all day. The wind howled from the east. White-bearded Winter had come back to shiver over the grave of this great, honest man. Nevertheless, there was a great concourse of people at the funeral. Full of attachment and regret, they had come from all parts to pay the last tribute of love and respect to their friend. The place was crowded in every part. About a hundred and fifty carriages and large sleighs were under the sheds all about. Some of them had been drawn by four horses; and this was a wise forethought on the part of their owners. Hiram lay in the parlor, in a handsome coffin of rosewood with silver-plated furniture. We say HIRAM, because, as he lay there, he looked so natural and composed, that he seemed no cold corpse, but a composition that still had life in it, and might awake and speak at any instant. The scene was very affecting. The country people, who knew and loved Hiram well, had come from their farms and villages. When these stout yeoman looked upon his calm, quiet face, with its sweet smile, they broke down at once; and "eyes albeit unused to the melting mood" swam over with tears. Some few, including Dan Pfifer, could not trust themselves to meet him face to face. All the trainers and drivers were there, with most of the eminent owners of fast horses. The ladies were there in great numbers; and this was truly fitting, for Hiram was always distinguished for his ceremonious politeness to them. He was, in fact, when seen at his best, in person, in dress, in manners, and in mind, a thorough gentleman. The service was performed by the Rev. Mr. Munn, of East New York, in an impressive manner. And then the procession, with its mourners, and Oliver Marshall, Simeon D. Hoagland, William Whelan, Joseph Crocheron, John Crooks, John I. Snedeker, and Wellington Simonson as pall-bearers, streamed along through the snow, to the cemetery-gate, and wound its way up the hillside, and past the lofty monument, to the grave. It was a long time ere the most had reached the place; and many, indeed, never got there at all until after the clods from the spade fell on the coffin, and smote upon our ears all mortal fate. Hiram Woodruff lies near the summit of a lofty hill, which overlooks the south side of the Island and the great waters upon which he loved to sail. The beauties and the grandeur of nature are all about his last resting-place. When it is bleak and stormy, as it was that day, the sough of the wind seems to bear with it the deep roar of the majestic ocean. When it is fine, there is no lovelier spot on all the Island; and, standing near his place of rest, one can look out far and away over a world of life and fertile land and busy waters. Peace to him who sleeps on that hallowed summit!

THE TROTTING-HORSE OF AMERICA.

I.

Reason for writing the Book. — Necessity for Practical Experience in Training. — The Author's Experience. — Improvement in Tracks and Vehicles. — Causes of Improvement in Time. — Originality of the American System. — Its great Superiority to the English System. — Rules as to Breaking from the Trot.

I HAVE often had applications from gentlemen in various parts of the country for advice and instruction in regard to the treatment of their horses, to which I have been unable to make satisfactory replies. My time has been too much taken up in training and driving the large number of horses placed in my care to admit of my writing letters, though I have always been willing to give such information as I could to those who sought it of me. In the course of the work I have now undertaken, the gentlemen who have applied to me, and those who might wish to do so, but yet, knowing my constant occupation, have refrained, will find all that it is in my power to communicate in regard to the management of trotting-horses. The persuasions and assurances of some of my friends have induced me to believe that the results of my thoughts and experiences, plainly set down, and illustrated here and there by such anecdotes and recollections of our famous trotters as, being in point, may most readily present themselves to my mind, will be interesting to the readers of this my work, and useful to the vast number of persons who now keep good road-horses, if not fast trotters. It was not without some hesitation that I agreed to devote a whole winter to the work I have begun. I found, upon reflection, that it would not be very easy for me to convey in print my own ideas upon the subject of training and driving; and my own experience with some hundreds of trotting-horses has convinced me, that any hope of teaching a man how to put a horse in condition by rule would be entirely fallacious.

I say, then, at the outset, that this work is to be taken more as a guide and finger-post, showing the way to practical experience, than as a substitute for experience itself. Such general method as I have pursued with good results, I shall communicate; but I cannot undertake to relate the circumstances constantly arising among horses in training, which have called, and always will call, for varied applications and abatements of the rule. Of these, the man in charge of the horse must be the judge as they present themselves; and, if he is not able to determine how far the general method may be intensified or relaxed in the case in hand, it is safe to say, that it will be more a lucky accident than any thing else if the trotter is fit when he comes to the post. I say, without any qualification, that a man can no more train horses by means of rules ascertained beforehand by other people than one can cure the complaints the human frame is subject to by books written by the most learned of the faculty. It would be a great deal easier for a clever man to write a good book upon a given complaint than to cure a case of it; and, if the writer was taken with the disorder himself, I have no doubt he would pitch his book on one side, and send for a practising physician. The fact that the man who is his own attorney has a fool for a client has passed into a proverb; and this is another instance of worthlessness of book-learning, taken by itself.

Yet books are very necessary for the making of doctors and instruction of lawyers; and so, when I say that the work

I am going to produce is only calculated to be useful when used as a stepping-stone to experience, I do not really undervalue it, as some may think. Besides, I intend to make it interesting to the general reader, as well as to him who is in quest of the rules and maxims of the trainer's art. I also wish it to be understood at the outset, that very many clever horsemen will differ with me in regard to some of the things I shall lay down as proper to be pursued. I know it will be very often said by some of my associates of years gone by, as they read these pages, "'Old Blocks' is wrong in regard to so-and-so;" but I can assure the reader that I shall recommend nothing but what I have tried, and in a measure proved myself.

It is more than thirty years since I began to handle trotting-horses, and more than five-and-twenty since I had charge of Dutchman, the best, take him for all in all, of the old-time trotters. Some things are done differently now from what they were then; yet there has not been any great change in the method we then pursued, nor has there been, in my opinion, as much change and improvement in our horses as some imagine. It is true that there are more fast trotters now than there ever were before, that the best time has been much cut down of late years, and that the driving on the road is a deal more rapid now than it was then. But then it is to be remembered that the tracks are now much better ordered than they were in former times, that the vehicles for trotting have been much lightened and improved, and that a corresponding improvement in roads and road-wagons has taken place. Besides, there are hundreds of horses trained nowadays to one that was handled by a really competent man then; and thus a greater amount of speed is developed in the multitude. And though it is not altogether clear why it should be so, there is no doubt in my mind about this, viz., that, as the excellence of the multitude increases, the excellence of the best among them will reach a higher standard. Except in exceptional cases, it is easier to be the best among a few than the best among many; for the reason that among the many the mark necessary to be attained will generally be higher and more difficult. The improvement in the time of our trotters is, then, to be laid to the account of several causes; which include improvement in courses, vehicles, methods of training, style of driving, and in the trotting-horse himself.

The system of teaching, training, driving, and riding the trotting-horse of this country has long been an art of itself, quite different, as far as I have heard, from that pursued in other countries. I look upon the English as a nation of horsemen, and their success with hunters and racers has been very great: but, ever since I can remember, we have been as much superior to them in handling the fast trotter as we are now. When Rattler was taken over there, twenty-five years ago, the gentleman who had the horse took good care to take William Whelan along to steer him; and, when the party got above themselves, and challenged the world, it was not resolved to buy Dutchman, and carry him across the water to clip their combs, until, after much pressing, I had agreed to go, too, to drive him. A difference of only three hundred dollars in the price of Dutchman prevented our voyage to England. The gentleman — he was English, but had lived some years in this country — offered twenty-seven hundred dollars, and a black mare I then had in charge, for the horse. The Philadelphia party wanted three thousand dollars and the black mare; and so the deal fell through. If it had been consummated, the challengers in England, with Whelan and Rattler, would soon have found Woodruff and the Dutchman in the little island, come to take it up. So there we should have been, — a real American party, — disputing across the Atlantic, in the land of our ancestors, for pre-eminence in the sport our own country had already exalted and dignified at home. The handling of the English trotting-horses at that time was as much inferior to the American system as their horses were to ours; and, though I say it myself, who belong to the profession, it is not unfit to be said, that the American system of breaking, training, and driving, has mainly made our trotters what they are. The English had the stock all along, just as much as we had; and it is our method of cultivation and perseverance that has made the difference between their fast trotter of a mile in three minutes and ours of two minutes and twenty-five seconds, or thereabouts.

According to the best information at my command now, I find that a three-minute trotter in England is about as scarce an article as a two-thirty horse is here. This is the result of our method of breeding, training, and driving the trotting-horse in this country, aided by the enterprise and ingenuity which provide vehicles, harness, and all the paraphernalia of that combination of lightness with strength which is upon the plan of the best trotting-horse himself. It is, however, only fair to observe, that the English have had some rules in their match-trotting which probably acted as a hinderance to the making of the best time of which their horses were capable. The penalty of a break was such that the rider or driver would be afraid to push his horse up to the top of his speed. If it was a harness or wagon race, the driver was compelled to pull up, and back the wheels when his horse broke. Ever so little backing of the wheels would do; but he was compelled to back them some. If it was under saddle, the rider had to turn his horse round when he broke. These rules must have been detrimental to the making of fast time, though as fair for one as another of the parties engaged in the match. Our American rule on this subject favors speed; and some think, indeed, that, as often administered, it favors breaking and running, to the disadvantage of the steady, honest horse that keeps to his gait, and wins, if he wins at all, by trotting.

Our law on this point is good enough, however, provided it is lawfully administered; and it does not operate as a check to the driver in obtaining the best speed of which his horse is capable. I do not myself admire those horses which are more relied upon to win for aptness in breaking and running a little when in a tight place, than for downright speed and bottom at a fair trot; but, as I have said to gentlemen who have complained that such was the case, the remedy is sufficient, if the judges will fearlessly apply it. If the judges did this, we should soon hear no more about drivers "learning horses to break." I think that the pride of our art in training and driving is to teach them to maintain their trot, and not to break. If the horse may break and run, I can easily see how it may be beneficial to teach him to break; but if, when he breaks, he is to be immediately pulled to a trot, or pulled up, I think it will be better to teach him not to break.

My remarks in this chapter are merely prefatory, as will be seen. Indeed, we must jog along gently with this matter until we have got through certain preliminary work, and put the fast trotter into regular training. I purpose, then, to take a firm hold of the reins, and increase the speed until the parties interested in the performance think that we are going along fast enough, and can stay the distance, even though it be three-mile heats. It must, however, never be lost sight of by the reader, in the course of this work, that I am a practical man, one mainly governed by the teachings of experience, and therefore not inclined to the laying-down of mere theories in regard to the training and general treatment of horses. If I had had less to do with them for nearly forty years, I might be more positive in my assertions than I now intend to be. Between the outward forms of such trotters as Dutchman, and Peerless, or Flora Temple, there is a vast difference; and between these types, more or less nearly approaching the one or the other, the variety of form is immense. I have been led to believe that the constitutional differences, including temper, disposition, and that intangible but very potent quality called pluck, are as numerous as the varieties of form. Now, in the management and training of the horse, the general rules which are applicable in nearly all cases must be relaxed, or stringently followed, according to the constitution, disposition, and capacity of the individual horse in hand. It would be easy enough for me to say, "Give the horse in training plenty of work, but not too much." The advice would be good, though general. The trouble would be in finding out how much was plenty and not too much. Here the judgment and experience of the man in charge would have to be carefully exercised; and if, by perusing this work as it progresses, the reader can master some of my experience, and make it his own, I shall be satisfied.

II.

Handling of the Colt. — The Trot a Natural Gait. — Great Speed the Result of Long Handling. — Method for the Colt. — Moderation best in Feeding. — Early Maturity followed by Early Decay. — The Trotter should live Many Years. — Feeding of Weanlings. — No Physic unless the Colt is Sick. — Feeding of the Yearling. — The Starving System worse than High Feeding.

THE training of the trotting-horse is really to be commenced from the time he is handled when a colt; for it is not simply the putting of him in such bodily condition as may enable him to exert all his powers, but also the careful and continued cultivation of his gifts as a trotter. Whatever encourages his tendency to make the trot his best way of going, is a part of his training; and therefore the natural disposition to trot must be improved from the very first. I have heard it said by some that there is no natural disposition in a horse to trot, or rather was none until men had handled him, and induced him to use that mode of action. It is a very common notion that the horse has but two natural paces,— the walk and the gallop,— and that trotting is wholly artificial. I have seen this set down in some books, but I venture to deny it. My conviction is, that the trot is natural to the horse; and I feel bound to give some reasons for my belief. In the first place, then, I ask whether a colt can now be found any where that does not trot sometimes, and that when he is by the side of his dam, before ever the hand of a man has been laid upon him? If it is said that this results from the long domestication of his ancestors, my reply will be, that it happens among the produce of horses whose ancestors for more than a century — ay, for more than two — have never been used for trotting purposes, and never were taught to trot at all, if it is true that the Arabs of the Desert only use their horses at the two so-called natural paces, — the walk and the gallop. Besides, although I have never been in foreign parts myself, I have been informed by gentlemen of observation and credit, whose means of noticing this point have been wider if not greater than my own, that wild horses trot when moving about at ease, or at play, or coming towards an object. It is true, that, if they are at all alarmed, they immediately strike into a gallop; but this only shows that the gallop is the best natural pace for speed, and not that the trot is no natural pace. I am also informed that other wild animals of desert places, such as wild asses, zebras, quaggas, and the like, sometimes trot; and, if I had not been told so, I should have inferred it from the fact that almost every animal that goes on four legs, whether domesticated among us or wild in our country, trots at times. Deer trot in the woods: I have seen them do it. The largest and noblest of our native animals is the elk, and he is a trotter.

If any of my readers, when riding in the Central Park, will take occasion to observe the elk that was sent to Mr. Wilkes from St. Louis for that institution, I will bet a trifle that they will see her trot, and go a pretty good trot, too, if she is put up to her best pace. Away, then, with the notion that the trot is wholly an artificial gait. If it were, I think the attempt to breed trotters would have been a failure; whereas, everybody knows that it has been successful. There is, however, a mixture of truth in the assertion that the trot is an artificial gait. It is not the readiest way for the horse to go at speed. A very poor running-horse — I mean a turf-horse — could distance the best trotter that ever was started; and the best trotters never reach their best speed until they have undergone a good deal of handling and cultivation. This handling, from the very first day that the colt begins to eat, should be very different, in my judgment, from the method I have seen the best breeders and trainers of thoroughbred runners adopt with their stock.

Now, to begin with the colt. Just as soon as the mare is quiet while you are doing so, you may handle the colt. Do it in such a manner as to make him tractable and kind. Speak softly to him, encourage him to come up and smell of your hand; and, when you touch him, do so gently and soothingly. From the first week of the horse's life until the last, you will find that he will be inclined to do what you require of him, provided you can make him understand what it is. Some men that have hold of horses apparently don't know themselves, and therefore it is not to be wondered at that the horse don't. Just as soon as you get familiar with the colt, which will be very soon if you commence while he is very young, rub his head occasionally, pat him, and sometimes pick up one of his legs. Do it gently; and by so doing you will teach him to let it be done quietly when the time comes at which it must be done somehow. It is understood, of course, that the mare and colt have shelter at night, and run out during the day, — on fine days, at any rate. Now, if the young one is never touched until you want to take hold of him for some needful purpose, you will find that he has become wild, and will try to break things before you can manage him.

The breeders of race-horses understand this very well, and they commonly take great pains with their colts. But as to early feeding, their method is one which I advise the breeders of trotters not to follow. It is, that as soon as the colt will eat bruised oats, which will be at less than two months old, he is to have all that he can consume. Nay, I find that one gentleman, and one of a great deal of ability, too, in that line, advises to begin with giving him oatmeal in gruel before he can eat the bruised oats. This is to be followed up with four quarts or more of oats a day, when he is weaned, besides the pasturage. I say to the reader of this, do no such thing with the colt that is to be a trotter,—or, rather, do it with great moderation. Never mind oatmeal gruel; never mind bruised oats while he is with his dam. The milk of the mare, she being kept in good heart, and the grass, will afford her colt all the nourishment he needs, and ought to have. This is Nature's plan: the other is the "forcing system," and ever so much more artificial than the trotting-gait. I do not undertake to disparage the method pursued by the race-horse men, so far as it only concerns their own purposes. That purpose I take to be early maturity; and I am convinced that very early maturity will not be advisable in the case of the fast trotter. Early maturity means early decay, in nineteen cases out of every twenty.

Now, in order that a horse may become a first-rate trotter, it is necessary that he should last a good while. He won't jump up to his greatest excellence at three years old, or at six either, if his excellence is going to be very great; but will probably be improving most when the thoroughbred horse of the same year has been long gone from the turf. I don't know of a single thing in nature that comes to maturity early and lasts long. This system, then, is not calculated for the trotter; because to be great it is absolutely necessary that he should last long. The case is different as regards the running-horse; for his career may be brief, and yet very brilliant. It is to be considered, too, that the constitution of the colts is different. The thoroughbred horse is naturally inclined to mature at an earlier period than any other, I think; and it is certain, that, being of a leaner and more wiry build, he may stand high feeding at an earlier period than the half-bred trotter.

And besides all this, I have other reasons against giving young colts much grain. The physiologists all agree, that, in order to thrive, the horse, young or old, must not only have his stomach supplied with a sufficient quantity of nutritious food, but also with enough matter not so highly nutritious to distend it. A horse or a colt fed only on the substances which go to make up his substance would starve, though you gave them to him in the greatest abundance. Why this is they do not know, and I am sure I don't; but it seems to me that it is a reason for not cloying the young animal with all the highly-nutritious food he will eat. If his appetite is satisfied with oats, he will not be likely to eat the grass and hay that nature requires. There is another thing on this point which has occurred to me, but I only throw it out as a suggestion. While the animal is young, a good distension of the stomach is calculated to produce that roundness of rib which we see in so many of our best horses. Now, this capacity of the carcass, if it proceeds in part from proper distension of the stomach,— and by that I do not mean the paunch,— is not going to be obtained by the feeding of food in the concentrated shape. Bulk is required; and the pulp and essence need not be given in large quantity until the organization is formed, and extraordinary exertion is required of the horse.

When the colt is weaned, I should give him from three pints to two quarts of grain a day. The quantity may be varied according to his size; for, if he gives indications of a large frame and loose habit, he will require more than a compact colt, who keeps in good order, and fills out with substance as he grows up. The pasturage is still the main thing; and, if that is good, two quarts of grain will be much better than more of the latter, and little or nothing to be picked up on the bare herbage. With proper care and attention, a good bite of grass may be secured for the colts until very late in the fall; and they should have all the hay they will eat when it begins to fail. The grain should be oats of good quality. I do not like to let colts have corn at all when young; and even to old horses I think it should be fed very sparingly. In the winter of the first year, the colt must have a good place to run in, and be well housed at night, and regularly fed and watered. It must be understood, from what I have said above, that he is never to be turned out to take his chance among a lot of promiscuous stock, old horses, cows, calves, heifers, and what-not. If he is, you may look for a wretched young thing, standing shivering on the hillside, and hardly able to put one leg before the other, instead of the gay and frisky colt that you had when he nibbled the growing grass by the side of his dam. All along, from the time of his weaning, it will do good, and can do no harm, to give him a nice, warm mash, with a few oats mixed through it, now and then. It does the whole system of the alimentary canal good, improves the digestion, and increases the nutrition. There need be no fear of its scouring the colt; and, in cases of scouring, I have very often found that it cured it. Give the colt no physic unless you are sure that there is something the matter with him. Physic is to cure sickness. Its prevention belongs to diet, careful observation, and general treatment.

When the colt is a yearling, his allowance of oats may be increased to four quarts a day. His other food must be good and abundant; and that is to be the main-stay. My principle is to give oats sparingly until the time comes to put the horse to some work; and I think it will commonly result in this: that the horse will have all the size that in the order of nature he should have had, and be of a much hardier, healthier, and more enduring constitution than he would have been if he had been forced along rapidly by means of all the highly-stimulating food that he could be got to consume. It will take longer to mature him by feeding only moderately of grain at this early period, but he is meant to last longer; and I repeat that early maturity is not favorable to long endurance. By the other method, you may show me a colt at two years old that looks more like a horse than mine will at three; and at three more like a grand horse than mine will at five. But now I shall begin to overtake you. When yours is five or six, he is at his very best, perhaps past his best. Put them together at eight, and I have got by far the best and most useful horse. At ten, you have probably got no horse at all worth mentioning: while mine is now "all horse," and in his true prime.

If anybody thinks to follow the old starving, corn-stalk fodder, fed-in-the-snow system, under cover of what I have said on this subject, he must go to the devil his own road. My system is one of generous feeding, but not of stuffing a young colt with all the highly-stimulating food he can possibly be got to swallow. Above all, avoid Indian corn in all shapes for young colts, and take care that they have plenty of pure water. If there is not a running-stream in the pasture where they are kept, be sure that they are watered at least three times a day, and that they have all they want.

We shall next come to the regular breaking, harnessing, and driving of the young colt in his two-year-old stage, which is of very great importance to his after character.

III.

Feeding of the Two-Year-Old.— Mouthing and Bitting. — Lounging. — Temper. — Leading on the Road. — Much Walking to be avoided. — When harnessed, a Wagon better than a Sulky. — Amount of Work to depend on Constitution and Condition. — Remedy for Broken Gait. — Pulling to be avoided. — Increase of Feed.

IN the two-year-old, in spring, the grain is to be increased to five, or even six quarts, of good oats a day; and now the colt is to be mouthed and bitted. He should have a good loose box, with an outside lot attached. It is unnecessary to describe the processes of mouthing, bitting, and lounging. The latter must not be continued long at a time. Half an hour will be enough; but, if he takes it well and steps off gayly, you may keep him moving a little longer. He must be lounged round both ways, changing the direction from time to time; for so giddiness will be prevented, and the bit brought alternately to both sides of the mouth. Great care must be taken not to overdo the thing at this time; for, when the colt gets fatigued and worried, his temper begins to suffer as well as his condition. It would be easy to repair the latter, but the mischief done to the former in early life can seldom be repaired. I am convinced that nine out of ten of the horses we find mischievously disposed, or even positively vicious and treacherous, are so by reason of having been improperly handled when young. There was Dutchman — he was not a sulky horse nor vicious by nature. You could get him to do his best whenever you called for it on the course or the road, but in the stable, look out! He wanted a great deal of watching. If a man attempted to put his harness on or take it off, without tying him up, he was lucky to get away with the loss of most of his clothes. Dutchman would take hold like a bull-terrier, and shake till his hold came away. He was also a kicker. In ordinary cases, I would not give much for a horse of this temper for the performance of any thing very great upon the course; but like Flying Childers and English Eclipse, both of whom, I am told, were ill-tempered, and ill-formed in some points, Dutchman was "a horse above ordinances."

In handling the two-year-old trotter, then, the utmost care, as well as gentleness and firmness, should be exercised. In former times, it was not customary to handle colts until they were five years old; but experience has since shown that they can very well be broken at two years old, and can be got to trot at three. The matter depends not upon the doing, but upon the manner of its doing. If the breaker or owner finds that the young thing can trot a little, and is always hankering to see him "do it again," or do a little better, he will soon have one that can't and won't do any thing worth his or anybody else's seeing. Progress, to be good and safe, must be gradual, but it should be continual. There is no sense at all in working a colt along so that he can trot well at three or four years old, and then turning him out until he is five or six. He should be kept at it gently, so as to hold fast all he knows at least; and this he is sure to do if not forced off his legs.

When the colt has been mouthed, bitted, and lounged in the lot, he will be led out upon the roads, and thus accustomed to meet and pass vehicles, horsemen, cattle, and the like. He is then to be broken to the saddle; during which process he should be ridden about the country roads, and not kept out so long at a time as to become leg-weary. The weight upon his back must be remembered; and the rider should often ease him by dismounting, and leading him. A great deal less walking is now given to horses of all ages than was formerly the case. When I was a boy, and riding for my uncle, an immense deal of walking exercise was thought to be beneficial. I used to ride horses as much as twenty miles a day, at a walk; and it was deemed needful to do this all along during their preparation. I have long seen the fallacy of that, and discontinued it. The old notion was, that it improved the horse's bottom; but I am satisfied that the usual effect was to make him leg-weary, to dog the heart out of him with this monotonous, tread-mill sort of work, and so take away his speed. He might go a distance then, in the race, because he went comparatively slow. It must always be remembered that a slow horse can keep at his best pace longer than a fast horse can at his, though in condition, bottom, and game they be equal. In training horses now, I usually walk them but once a day, and then only for a comparatively short distance.

When the colt is broken to the saddle, his work in harness is to be commenced. It should be to a skeleton wagon, not to a sulky; for the reason that, with the four wheels to the former vehicle, the weight will be kept off his back. Many use the sulky, but I am satisfied that the wagon is best. There will be no difficulty in getting the colt to draw if he has been handled rightly up to this time. Our system in this is radically different from that of the English, as I am informed. Instead of putting the colt into the shafts of a single vehicle, and coaxing him to go off nicely with it, by which means, when he starts, he feels that he is doing something, and soon becomes satisfied and likes it, the English begin his harness-work by putting him into a double-break wagon, which weighs about half a ton, by the side of an old horse. When the colt is at home between the shafts, begin to drive him moderately. Take him sometimes on the track, and at other times on the road. Don't keep him dogging along at the same rate, but give him lively spurts now and then. By this means he will extend himself without hurting himself, and will improve in speed. As long as he does this, you are doing right, and he is doing well. As soon as he seems to get tired of it, and appears to be either restive or sluggish, let him up a little. You must watch for these symptoms carefully; for this is a critical time. If you overdo him much now, it will be a long while before he is himself again.

The work must be according to his constitution, to the rate of his growth, and to his heartiness of feeding. This jogging will probably be about five or six miles a day, and the spurts not above a quarter of a mile. He must be carefully watched to ascertain whether he improves or not. If not, he is to be let up a bit; for his improvement at this age ought to go on all the time, and will if he is all right. Rapid improvement, however, must not be expected: ever so little will do, but it ought not to stop altogether. At this time, you will often see him break his gait; and this is an indication that he has had too much work for his age, and has got sore on it. But it may not arise altogether from overwork; therefore, put the rollers on, and work him gently, changing them from leg to leg as required. The colt now finds something on his legs, besides the boots, which was not there before; and it will alter his way of going. He must be nicely handled now. You must use all your observations and best judgment, with a light but firm hold of the reins. In all probability, he will trot square again with the rollers on; and, as soon as he does so, let him up for a little while. When the broken gait shows, he must not on any account be kept on without a change; for, if he is, it may become confirmed. On the other hand, I never like to let them up until I have got them to trot square again; for, if they are so let up, they may not trot square again when their work is resumed. In all his work, the colt is to be taught to go along without being pulled hard. His mouth may be easily spoiled for life by teaching him to tug at the bit now; and he is not at all likely to make a fast trotter, if to trot he must always have his weight upon the driver's arms. There have been some fast trotters and stayers that were hard pullers; but they would have been better horses but for that fact. Still, it is to be remembered, that, when going fast, the colt or horse will often want to get his head down, and feel the bit sensibly. He will not, in nine cases out of ten (or cannot, which comes to the same thing), do his best without it. The object of the driver should then be to support him with as little pull as possible, but still to support him. The horse with a good mouth will always feel the driver's hand; and, when the latter is as skilful as he ought to be for the handling of the first-rate, fast trotter, he may play upon the rein with a touch like that of a harper upon the strings, and the horse will answer every touch with the music of the feet and wheels.

On the other hand, if, when the colt takes hold of the bit, the driver does nothing but hold on like grim death to a dead darkey, it soon becomes a pulling-match between them; and, before the colt is of age to trot fast and stay a distance, his pulling has become a vice of the most troublesome and mischievous description, his mouth has become so callous that he pulls a wagon and driver along by the reins instead of the traces, and, by the dead drag between him and the man behind him, he loses a great deal of the power that will be wanted to sustain him when the pinch comes. It is not to be forgotten, however, that many trotting-horses *must* be pulled considerably to get them to trot fast, and keep trotting. When this is the case, it is utterly useless to expect to get rid of the pull and preserve the trot by means of substituting a severe bit for the plain snaffle. It will not do at all; because it is not a certain amount of severity on the mouth that the horse wants, but a sort of stay, upon which he can fling himself in the flying trot, and without which he is either unable or unwilling to put out his best efforts.

There was a notable instance of this in the trotting-horse Alexander, which was taken to England many years ago, and could not be got to trot a bit by those who had purchased him, expecting great things. Afterwards Bill Whelan went over with Rattler; and the gentlemen who had Alexander no sooner saw him ride the former against the Birmingham mare than they got him to go and look at Alexander. Whelan found the horse in his stable, well taken care of, and in fair condition; so that, at first, he was at a loss to know why he would not trot. However, he told them to throw a saddle on him, and let him take a little jog with him. Forthwith, the groom came out of the harness-room with a bridle and bridoon-bit; whereupon says Whelan, "What are you going to do with that?"

"Put it on Alexander."

"No, you don't!" says Whelan, and went into the room to look out a bridle and bit for himself. There was, he says, a tremendous array of all sorts of bits, and instruments of torture, that had been got together "to hold Alexander." He managed, however, to find a plain snaffle, and put that on him. Everybody there looked at him as if he was a lunatic; but Bill jumped into the saddle, and jogged away with Alexander. He coaxed him, and clucked to him; and by and by Alexander, as he lengthened his stride and quickened his action, began to pull upon the plain snaffle. But Whelan was something of a puller himself; and, instead of his pull being the main haul of strength and stupidity, the hand of a master was upon the bridle. He warmed Alexander up in a good stretch, and then brought him back by the starting-place at such a rate as amazed the Englishmen present.

"That's the way we ride our trotters in America," said Whelan. "Alexander is as good as ever he was. You may match him against any thing in this country but Rattler; and I'll engage he won't lose it, if I ride him."

A match was soon made; and the American horse Alexander, ridden by Whelan, won it with ridiculous ease. I have mentioned this for the purpose of impressing upon the reader the immense importance of a light, firm, sensational hold upon the reins. Mere dragging is of the utmost mischief. There is a kind of magnetic touch which the horse no sooner feels than he seems inspirited and animated with new life; and this is especially the case when he is a little tired. The right kind of touch and movement of the reins and bit is worth more in an emergency than all the whip-cord and whalebone in the world.

As the training, or rather breaking, of the two-year-old goes on, and his growth advances with the season, his feed may be increased. He may have six quarts of oats, or even eight, if he is large and a good worker, with as much good hay as he will eat up clean. This, however, is to be reduced when there is occasion to stop his work and exercise; for instance, when he has been let up after having been going with a broken gait. He ought to be allowed to nibble a little fresh grass night and morning, and should sometimes have two or three carrots sliced up with his feed. Some will say, "When he has been let up, there is a fine chance to physic him:" but my maxim is, that, if the colt is in good bodily health, and the operations of the internal organs are going on right, he does not need physic; and there is no use in a violent interference with the course of nature. In the morning, before the colt is hitched up to go to work, give a slight feed, — say a quart and a pint of oats, — and let him drink about two quarts of water. On days that his work is not to be done early, his feed in the morning may be increased; but its quantity should be regulated by the hour at which he will be driven. At night, he is always to have all the water he wants. His temper and disposition are to be carefully watched, and so are those of the lad who takes care of him. The boy ought to have a pride in, and an affection for, a colt in his charge; and, if he has not, he shall not be long about a colt of mine. A lad who does not show an active liking for the horse he looks after almost always neglects him; and, wherever I detect the absence of this feeling in one about my stables, I change his occupation, or send him away altogether. But, as a general rule, the boys are very fond of their horses, especially of colts that show promise; and, in these cases, it is more likely that they will do harm by over-feeding than by neglect. This is to be looked after; for, though the amount of feed be measured out to each lad, I have known many that will be always watching slants to get an extra quart of oats for their colts, or will even carry ears of corn about in their pockets to shell into the manger. See that the colt is fed as you wish him to be, rather than as the boy who looks after him wants to feed him.

IV.

Effects of Early Development. — Colts often overworked. — Fast Three-Year Olds and Four-Year Olds. — Risk of hurting Stamina. — Earlier Maturity of Running-Horses. — Evils of over-training Colts.

THE question as to whether the early development of trotting-horses will have a tendency to impair their endurance in point of time is one of great interest and importance. Theoretically, some years ago, it was generally held that it would do so; but there is some reason to believe that this was a mistake. Still, I am satisfied that unless the work is given in a limited and judicious manner, there will be very great danger of its having a pernicious effect on the young colt. At present, we have hardly seen enough of the young trotters trained at three and four years old to determine, absolutely, whether the practice is altogether prudent or otherwise. A great deal depends upon the constitution and development of the colt himself; and still more, perhaps, upon the sagacity and care of the man who has him in charge. In many cases which have come under my observation, young things have been overworked; and, when it was found that they began to hitch and hobble, a good let-up would do more to restore the stroke than any thing else. It is quite certain to my mind that there is some risk in the training of colts to such a mark as shall fit them to trot mile heats at three years old; and some that have displayed uncommon fast time in public at their three and four year old stages, would probably have been much better off to-day, if they had never been put through the strong preparation necessary to the accomplishment of those feats.

It does not follow, however, that a subsequent failure of a horse to carry out his early promise resulted from the fact that he was trained at an early age. These colts are liable to the vicissitudes which attend other horses; and, therefore, they may go amiss in a manner which in nowise depends on their early work. Still, there is a presumption where a fast colt gives out at a time of life when he ought to improve, that he had too much work for his stamina at three or four years old; and, with one of much promise at three, I should decline to match him, unless I was convinced that I had a tolerably easy thing. It is not the fast trotting that will do the mischief, but the amount of work needful to put the youngster in fix for a repeating race. Yet it is well known that some colts and fillies who did great things in public at three and four years old have since turned out good horses.

It will have been gathered from what I have said heretofore, that my system contemplates the development of much speed without much work. Some may say that this is impossible; but my experience is that it is quite practicable, and a great deal more likely to be followed by the result desired, than keeping the colt continually hammering at all he knows. The system which I have laid down heretofore for the management of the two-year-old is still to be followed in its general principles when he is three, with such modifications as his increase of age justifies. It will be much better to err on the side of a little indulgence, than to run the risk of knocking him off his legs and so overboard, by too much work. The first race that I remember between three-year-old trotters was some thirty-four years ago. It took place on the Hunting-Park Course, Philadelphia, and there were three engaged. Peter Whelan had Gipsy, George Woodruff had a gray filly that I looked after, and there was another one. Gipsy won it in two heats, and the time was somewhere about three minutes and seven seconds. We thought it good at that period, and so it was. In considering the fast time made by our best trotters of late years, we ought not to forget that the tracks and all the appliances have been improved, as well as the horses. Go upon the Fashion and Union courses in the trotting-season, and you will find them so ordered as to be as smooth as a bowling-alley. It is scarcely necessary to say that the courses thirty years ago were very different.

The next very prominent trot between young horses was that in which Ethan Allen defeated Rose of Washington when they were four years old. It was the first time that a young stallion had appeared in public at that age; but Holkam and Roe had great confidence. Ethan was indeed a superior colt, and has since turned out a superior horse. He had a good one to beat, too, in Rose of Washington; and she has also turned out well. It cannot be said that their training and race hurt either of them; but it must not be forgotten that both were in the hands of wary and experienced men. Their time (2m. 36s.) was the best then, but it has since been very much reduced in Kentucky. Lady Emma affords another instance of speed and handling when young, with subsequent improvement into a first-rate, fast, and lasting trotter. At three years old she went half a mile in public in one minute nineteen and a half seconds, and a mile in two minutes fifty-two seconds, or thereabouts. The training and racing she had as a three-year-old did not at all impair her bottom, as her more recent performances have abundantly shown. In this regard, I look upon Lady Emma as a strong case in point. She steadily increased her speed every year of her training, and in bottom she was second to none.

A friend of mine, who is a noted admirer of running-horses, has always insisted that this mare was thrown back to some ancestor in the pedigree of Old Messenger — very likely Flying Childers himself, he says. It is true that she looked like a thoroughbred four-miler; but I would not take it upon me to affirm that the likeness came from such a remote ancestor. Shepherd Knapp and Jessie were another pair that were trained early, and with no ill-effect, even though their race was one of uncommon severity. They were four years old, and trotted five heats, the best of which was two minutes and forty seconds. It was the second heat, and was won by the filly after she had previously won the first. Upon seeing the time of this heat, I concluded that the colt could beat her; and he won the three subsequent heats, the best of them being in two minutes forty-one seconds. But though, in view of his recent doings in France, it cannot be said that this severe race did the colt any permanent injury, it would be too much to affirm that it did him any good. Next year, while in training for his match with Harry Clay, he continually hit himself in the elbows, by reason of excessive knee-action as it appeared; and this prevented the bringing of him up to the mark. This horse recently trotted two miles and a half in France, in six minutes and fourteen seconds; which is a trifle better than the rate of two-thirty to the mile.

The mare Cora was another very fast trotter at an early age. She went in two minutes and thirty-seven and a half seconds, at three years old, in Kentucky; and her improvement since has been very marked. She was sent to me by her then owner in 1866, but did not remain long enough to be put in condition. Within a week or ten days, she was sold for a very large sum to a gentleman of great experience and knowledge in respect to trotting-horses. Like Lady Emma, this mare is noted for bottom as well as speed, — a proof, I think, that her early training never hurt her stamina. But I do not say that she would not have been just as good without quite so much of it as she had at three years old; and, unless there is some great object in view, I should not subject a good three-year-old to a strong preparation. If, however, a man can sell a colt at three or four years old, for eight, nine, ten, or eleven thousand dollars, by being able to show great speed and ability to repeat, it is an object worth some risk and trouble. It is by no means certain that the colt will ever attain to the rank of a *first-rate* trotter, even though he be very fast at three or four years old, and the training by which his precocious speed was developed has not hurt his stamina, his temper, or his legs. I think that the first class of trotting-horses will still be very select; though, other things being equal, a fast four-year-old is more likely to reach it than one not so fast.

The instances we have had, however, of wonderful trotters that never exhibited any extraordinary speed until they were from six to ten years old, cannot be disregarded. I shall have occasion to particularize them hereafter, when we come to speak of the training of the matured trotter. Meantime, I need only mention Flora Temple, Mr. Bonner's mares Peerless and Lady Palmer, and the late little horse Prince. But as long as customers are to be found for fast three and four year olds at very high rates, they will certainly be trained; and my object is to induce the owners and handlers to guard against the forcing severity and the heart-breaking dogging with which the process is too often accompanied. There is another reason likely to be sufficient to induce gentlemen to train three-year olds; which is, that it is often desirable to show the produce of stallions at as early a period as possible. This has no doubt operated quite as strongly with the Kentucky breeders as the desire of getting high prices for the colts they trotted. All the fast colts that they have shown there have not, however, been equally fortunate with Cora. Ericsson, who made the best four-year-old time, and another that went with him, have not improved upon their colt form. The gray colts raised by Mr. Alexander, and recently sold at high figures to gentlemen in this vicinity, may have better luck.

Another gray that showed much speed and cleverness at

a very early age was Mr. Hall's colt, Young America, by Hoagland's Gray Messenger. He trotted two races at two years old, on this Island, and won them both. In the first trot he beat a colt by Ethan Allen, and in the next defeated Rocky Hill. The time of this last was about three minutes and six seconds. The produce of this gray horse of Hoagland's inherit the trotting gift very strongly from him, together with the hearty constitution and cast-iron legs that have commonly been found united in the descendants of Old Messenger. Another thing was, that he got most of them gray and in his own likeness. The premature death of this horse was much to be regretted; for his cover seems to have been almost, or quite, as sure to bring a trotter as that of Hambletonian. His colt out of the Flatbush Maid, and another one of the same age out of Lady Moscow, have had the benefit of a good sound tuition without any forcing and they are a very good example of what may be done with four-year-olds without hurting them in the smallest degree. Blonde is another of the same strain and stamp, and there is a suspicion out that she is very fast.

The colt Bruno, by Hambletonian, out of a mare said to be of French origin, is another very remarkable instance of great trotting speed early developed. There is no question in my mind about his ability to have beaten any thing that has yet appeared upon the trotting-turf at four years old; and as there is no reason to believe that he has been at all injured by his training up to this time, the presumption is that he will be in the first class of trotters. Taken altogether, I look upon Bruno's three-year-old race as more remarkable than that of Cora in Kentucky, though her three-year-old time was about a second better than he made. The long-scoring, the repeating of the heat, and the shutting-up of an enormous gap during the last, contributed to enhance the marvel of the performance.

It may be doubted whether the taxing of a three-year-old's speed and endurance with such severity ought not to be avoided. My own opinion is against it; and therefore I should not make a match in which a colt of that age was likely to be called upon to exert all his powers, unless the circumstances were extraordinary. A great deal, however, depends upon the constitution and forwardness of the colt. A handy, vigorous, clean-actioned little fellow like Bruno, may be more fit to trot a race at three years old than a gangling, loose horse would be at five. The trainer and owner, with all the circumstances before them, must judge for themselves: but, as a *general rule,* do not treat your colts worse than you do your criminals; if the matter is doubtful, give the colt the benefit of the doubt,— refuse to conclude the match if it is not made, and pay forfeit if it is. When I say doubtful, I do not mean the winning of the money, because that is always doubtful, but the inflicting of an injury upon the colt, either to his legs, temper, or stamina, by too much exertion in preparing or in trotting.

If, after all, a man makes up his mind to risk young things in tight places, where the violent and continued exertion of all their powers will probably be called for, it may be well enough for him to approach in his system of raising and feeding his colts, the forcing method of the running-horsemen. In order that the colt may be able to stand up under the treatment calculated for an older horse, he must be made *old* as soon as possible; and strong feeds of oats from the first time he can be got to eat them is the way to do this. Thereby the time of maturity may be anticipated; but at the expense of the thoroughness of the maturity, I think, and certainly at the great risk of its endurance. As I before had occasion to state, rapid arrival at maturity is almost always followed by premature decay, and this is especially the case with things forced by high feeding when very young. It is also to be kept in mind that the running-colt, during his training and his race, has some compensation for his youth in the way of weight, which the young trotter cannot have. A two-year-old colt running in this country will only carry a very light boy, and the three-year-old weight is but ninety pounds for colts and eighty-seven for fillies; whereas the young trotter will have to pull as much as George Wilkes, Lady Emma, or General Butler, in a race in harness. Moreover, the running-race for two-year-olds is commonly but a short dash; while the three-year-old trotter is called upon to go races of heats, and the four-year-old mile heats, three in five.

But if, after all is said, the owner of the promising three-year-old determines to match and train him, he had better be sure that the preparation is not too severe. It will be better to rely upon the speed and goodness of the colt, and the ability and management of the driver to win, than to screw the young thing up to the pitch of condition at the risk of upsetting him. If the colt is overtrained now, he is not only damaged for the time being, but the injury to his legs, temper, or constitution, will very likely be permanent. There are colts, just as there are some old horses, that will stand almost any thing, and no amount of ignorance and recklessness seems sufficient to spoil them; but these are the exceptional cases, to be avoided, not imitated. With all the care that we can take, and all the caution that we can exercise, we shall find enough of our promising youngsters disappoint us in the expectations we have formed, without running the risk of ruining them by tasks too severe for the immature condition of their bones and sinews, and for that lack of seasoning which accompanies their early years. I admit, that, when a man has a fast colt, the temptation is strong to earn honor and profit by the public display of his powers: but in almost every instance it ought to be resisted; for its premature indulgence is too often like the conduct of the improvident savages, who cut down trees to get at the fruit.

V.

Actual Training of the Three-year-old. — No Physic and no Sweat at first. — Danger of "Overmarking." — Strong Feed of Oats and Hay. — Bran-Mashes. — Rubbing the Legs. — Full supply of Water. — Management before and in the Race. — Strains likely to stand Early Training. — The Abdallahs.

HAVING given my views as to the prudence of training a three-year-old colt for a race, I shall now make some remarks upon the course advisable to be followed where the match has been made and the race is to come off. The colt may have been kept in the stable all the winter, or he may have had the run of a lot on fine days, with a loose box at night. In either case, his work in the spring is to be exactly like that which he was called on to do in the fall of his two-year-old stage, beginning very gently, and taking care never to keep him so long at it as to fret and discourage him. No physic is required, nor is any sweat demanded to begin with. It is to be remembered that the growing animal does not make internal fat like an old horse, and that the system has not attained the firmness and hardness which will bear scraping and squeezing to be drawn fine. If a colt is stripped of his fat and reduced in flesh as old horses are, his growth is stopped, and the muscular development that is now in process is interfered with to the lasting disadvantage of the animal. Therefore, the utmost caution is required in dealing with them; and the effect of the work is to be carefully watched from day to day by the person having them in charge. Before the work is begun at all, it must be apparent that the colt is full of health, and possessed of that buoyancy and elasticity of spirit which a young thing ought to have anyhow, and which are absolutely necessary to bear him up under the treatment to which he is now to be subjected. If he is bold and familiar, and a little given to mischief, so much the better; that is a very different thing from vice, and much to be preferred to flightiness and nervousness.

Begin with a little walking exercise every day, and from that proceed to moderate work in harness. See that every thing is done to make the colt enter into his work with good pluck, and take care that the jogging is not carried so far as to make it monotonous and disgusting to him. It should not be confined to the course, but he may be driven about the country-roads when they are good; and the spurts of speed in which he is indulged should be lively but short. By this means he will always leave off with a desire to go a little farther, and will dash out with alacrity when he is called upon to go again. The speed will be increased, in nine cases out of ten, by this treatment; and the gait will be maintained square and open. Speed can neither be created nor preserved by forcing when young. If the colt goes frisking and playing along, he feels well at his jogging, and you may send him a trifle farther in his spurts. But if, on the other hand, he looks dull and jaded, and requires to be urged, save him. It will do harm instead of good to keep him at it: for he is in danger of being "overmarked;" and, if that once takes place in the course of this his first preparation, you had better pay forfeit, and give him a long let-up. So, also, if he begins to hitch and hobble in his gait, you must let him up in his work. It is of no use to keep on in *hopes* that he will go square again. The more you keep on, the worse the mischief will be. Study the disposition of the colt. If you cannot understand him, it is not at all likely that he will understand you.

I have seen many very promising three-year-old colts broken in their gaits, and got to paddling, solely by the obstinacy of the man in charge, who had determined to "*make* trotters out of them." It was this foolish attempt at "making" that prevented their being trotters in good time. The three-year-old colt, of the two, is more difficult to deal with than the two-year-old. The former is shedding his colt's teeth, his mouth is broken, his gums sore, and his system more or less fevered. His food is not thoroughly masticated, and sometimes he will not consume his usual quantity. There is a vastly greater difference between him and an old horse, than between him and a two-year-old, in solidity of bone, in duration of sinew, and development of muscle. The difference between the two and three year old, in reference to their ability to stand work, is one of degree only, and not of kind. When the two-year-old is well formed, hardy and lusty for his age, he is more fit to take work than a three-year-old with a broken mouth and fevered system. It being discovered, however, that the colt in training is doing well, the system I have indicated is to be pursued in such degree as his constitution and disposition call for.

The feed is now to be according to his size, appetite, and work. Eight, nine, ten, or, in some extraordinary cases, even twelve quarts of oats a day may be given. Once in a while he may have a very little corn; but there is no real occasion for it, except in case of a poor feeder. There is no doubt at all about the fact that oats are the best food for a horse. They supply the greatest quantity of the constituents of the muscular fibre which the horse is always expending, while corn supplies the fatty matter in greatest quantity. Therefore, keep the corn for the bullocks and hogs, and give oats to the horses. Some say that corn may be fed to colts, because its silicious particles go to make up bone; but enough of these earthy matters will be found in the hay, in the husks of the oats, and in the water. In this training the colt is to have all the hay that he will eat up clean. His general health and the condition of his bowels are to be watched, and a bran-mash is to be given when it is thought that it will be beneficial. It may usually be ventured on at least once a week, unless there is a tendency to looseness. Its effects are comforting and soothing, and it promotes the secretions as well as empties the bowels. He is to be fed and to have a little water before going to work, in the same way as I have laid down in regard to the colt at two years old.

The legs of the colt may be hand-rubbed a little during his course of training; but they do not want it like those of a battered-up old horse: and my motto is that what is not wanted ought not to be attempted. Water is to be kept away from the legs of the colt as much as possible: they are to be kept clean by means of the brush and cloth. As his work goes on, his brushes may be extended to a quarter of a mile; but he is always to be kept well within himself. It is to be borne in mind that there are no great things to be done with him this year, except to develop his speed, and see to it that he is kept in good health. More will have to be done in conditioning by and by; but it will be a year or two, perhaps three, before he is fit to stand the "grand preparation," as our friends the race-horse men call the thorough-training process. Meantime, it is to be thought, that if he has had his health, has stood his work well, and has shown an increase of speed, you will be wanting to see what he can do towards the race. But you must withstand the temptation to do any thing like what he will be called on to do in public; for, if he does it for you now, it is likely enough that he will not be able to do it on the day in question. Eight or ten days prior to the race, having ascertained that he feels in good health and strong heart, brush him half a mile. You can tell by the way he finishes, and by how he feels afterwards, whether he will be likely to stand the mile-heat out and to repeat it. Unless the trainer can form a judgment in this matter, there is very little chance for the colt in the race, except the other man is equally incapable of forming an estimate of his colt's stamina without repeating him. During the whole course of the work, the colt is to have a full supply of water every day; but he is to have it at different times, and not to be allowed to distend himself with a great quantity of water at one time. The night before the race, the muzzle is to be put on, if he is a gross feeder, and is likely to eat the straw of his bedding. Before this, the usual quantity of oats and about a pound and a half of hay may be given. If the colt has been in the habit of drinking a large allowance of water, he may have two-thirds of a pailful before he is muzzled for the night; but, if he has usually only consumed a small quantity, do not give him quite so much. This water will all have been absorbed and thrown out of the system again before he is called upon to act. Next morning early, before he goes out to walk, let him have two quarts of oats, and about the same quantity of water. Usually, he need only take walking exercise on this morning; but if he happens to be a strong, hearty fellow, and given to be riotous in disposition, he ought to be jogged four or five miles. At about eleven o'clock feed him from a quart to three pints of oats, and from half a pound to a pound and a half of hay. Less than half a pound is not sufficient to stay the stomach; more than a pound and a half is likely to be mischievous, and to interfere with the wind.

Between those quantities, the trainer must judge according to the disposition and constitution of the colt. He is not to be drawn fine and reduced like an old horse; but, at the same time, he must not be called upon to perform the unusual feat before him with any thing like a full stomach. If he is distressed after the heat, and seems weak, give him a little gruel, or a small quantity of wine and water; or you may even administer a little good brandy. It is astonishing what a dose of brandy will sometimes do for a horse when he is badly off, and it looks as if he was going to be beaten. It will not do, however, to be giving brandy unless it is clearly required; and here, again, the trainer must use his own judgment, and have firmness enough to follow its dictates. There are always enough outsiders, who, having nothing at stake and no responsibility, will give advice *gratis;* but it is commonly to be disregarded.

In deciding upon what a colt may be safely called upon to do at an early age, his breed, as well as his form, disposition, and constitution, must be taken into account. Those strains which are related more or less closely to the blood-horse may be trained at an earlier period, and will stand more work, than the colder-blooded sorts. This is well understood by those who prepare the steeple-chasers of England and Canada. Some of these horses are quite thoroughbred, some nearly thoroughbred, and some not above half-bred. Now, it has been found by experience, that of two horses apparently alike in stoutness and excellence of constitution, but one nearly thoroughbred and the other only half-bred, the amount of work which will improve the wind and speed, and harden the condition, of the former, will almost certainly overmark and ruin the chance of the other. Then the muscles shrink, and become soft and unstrung, instead of increasing in volume and consistency; then the eye is dull, and the feed is no longer consumed with relish in sufficient quantity. The breed is therefore to be considered as well as the natural constitution of the individual horse in hand.

The stock of the famous horse Abdallah, who was by Mambrino, a thoroughbred son of imported Messenger, would almost all stand training at an early age; and what is, perhaps, more important, it did not appear to impair their future durability. It is now thirty years ago since I rode two famous trotting-horses of his get. One of them, Ajax, was foaled in 1834; the other, Hector, the next year, 1835. At five years old, they were both capital trotters; and by and by, when we come to speak of the trotting-horses with which I have had to do in the course of my career, I shall have more to say about them. Fourth of July, a gray horse by Abdallah, was another good trotter at five years old. Medoc was another of his get that was justly noted; and there was Brooklyn Maid, a very fast mare, and a noted sticker. In 1840, when she was only five years old, this mare trotted a fifth heat in two minutes and thirty-six seconds. Considering that this was twenty-five years ago, it must be regarded as a capital performance. The Abdallahs came on early, and lasted long. They were commonly full of spirits, wild and playful as kittens, with first-rate stamina, and always ready to trot. Through this grandson of his, the strain of old Messenger was diffused east and west in this country; and at this day it seems to have parted with none of its blood-like, speedy, and enduring qualities. His son Hambletonian also gets produce which stand work early, and promise to be in nowise deficient in endurance. During the time he was in Kentucky, Abdallah did a great deal for the trotting-horse out there; and they have wisely re-enforced the infusion by further importations of the Messenger blood.

When it is considered that their trotting-stallions have been very often well-bred, and then put to thoroughbred mares, it must go far to account for the extraordinary feats performed there by colts that were only four years old. I see no absolute reason to deny the statement made, that Mr. Alexander's colt Bay Chief, by Mambrino Chief, out of a thoroughbred mare, trotted half a mile, at four years old, in one minute and eight seconds. It is to be regretted that the wounds he got in the battle with the guerillas have ruined him. Ericsson's mile — the fourth heat — in two minutes thirty and a half seconds was an astonishing thing for a four-year-old, especially when it is added that it was done to a wagon. It does not appear upon the record that this was the case, for the way of going is not set down; but I learn from a gentleman of unquestionable veracity, who had to do with the colt at the time, that he trotted to a wagon.

Kentucky Chief, who won the first heat, and afterwards went to California, where he died, was another good one. He went in harness. Idol was another very fast one when young; and Brignoli was thought to be about as good as they are made. Royal George was another very fast one; and quite recently there have been Mr. Alexander's gray geldings Dudley and Bull Run, and his bay stallion Bay Chief. The information as to Morgan Chief, or Ericsson, as he is now called, having trotted that mile in two thirty and a half, to wagon, came from a gentleman who had an interest in him at the time, and brought a trotter from Kentucky to me to be trained last fall. He said, too, that he was a great, overgrown colt, standing about sixteen and a half hands high, and could trot faster to a wagon than he could to a sulky. That was the same meeting where Cora made her two minutes thirty-seven and three-quarters, and Medoc, since called John Morgan, won at two and three mile heats.

VI.

Characteristics of the Stars. — Of the Bashaws. — The Clays. — The Trustees. — Natural Trotters in England. — Of Trotters that paced. — To make Pacers trot.

THE produce of American Star are hardly as safe to train early as those of Messenger through Abdallah, Mambrino Chief, &c., by reason of their being more fragile about the legs. When, however, the two lines are combined, this is rectified; and the cross seems to make a very fine, fast trotting-horse, as near perfection as may be. Such is Mr. Bonner's gray mare Peerless, who was by Star out of a gray mare full of the Messenger blood. She is the fastest that I (or, indeed, anybody else) have ever driven to a wagon. Dexter is another capital instance of the value of this cross. Some of the Stars have given out in the legs; but their pluck is so good that they stand up to the last, when little better than mere cripples. It is no wonder that they have great game and courage; for Star's grandsire was the thorough-bred four-miler Henry, who ran for the South, on the Island here, against Eclipse, in 1823. I went to see the race, and got a licking for it when I came home. The Messenger cross gives the Stars size, strength, and bone, and counteracts their hereditary tendency to contraction of the feet. It would not do to breed the Stars in-and-in, as has answered so well with the descendants of Messenger. Widow Machree, a daughter of Star, was a very fast, game mare, and an all-day trotter. The little horse Bolly Lewis was another good one by him, and Goshen Maid still another. She went the fourth heat to a wagon in 2.32½.

The Bashaws were not commonly trained early; and they were not natural trotters in the same degree as the horses of the Messenger line. The Bashaws originated from Grand Bashaw, a horse imported from Barbary; and they have been principally represented through his son, Young Bashaw, and his sons, Black Bashaw, Andrew Jackson, and Saladin. Black Bashaw did not trot in public; neither did Abdallah, Messenger's grandson. The latter never was in harness in his life; but you could jump on him bare-backed, and he would go right away a fifty-clip. In those days, entire horses were not trained. It was thought that they would be ruined for service if they were "put through the mill" for racing purposes; and so, when they showed a good gait, they were reserved for the stud. The notion also prevailed, that it would ruin a trotter to train him before he was five or six years old. The only Bashaw that I know of that trotted at three years old was the gray filly before mentioned, beaten by Gypsy in 1830. My uncle, George Woodruff, had a very high opinion of the Bashaws. He handled more of them, including Lantern and George Washington, than any other man, I think. He had old Topgallant, a son of imported Messenger, and a noted old-time trotter. More will have to be said about that class of horses hereafter.

Young Bashaw became much noted through his son Andrew Jackson, who was one of the first stallions that ever trotted in public. His best performance was at Centreville some thirty years ago — it was 1835: he went two miles in 5.18. He got Long-Island Black Hawk, who was the first horse that trotted a mile in 2.40 to a 250lb. wagon. It was against Jenny Lind, who went to a skeleton wagon, and won the second heat in 2.38. The stallion beat her the race, which was the first he ever went. Black Hawk won the stallion stake on Union Course in 1849. He beat Cassius M. Clay; and St. Lawrence paid forfeit. This Long-Island Black Hawk was a capital horse. He could pull any weight, and was good for a long distance, as the race of three-mile heats in which he beat Americus showed. The wagons and drivers weighed 350 lbs. He is not to be confounded with the tribe of Black Hawks that left the trotting-place up in Vermont, and flew all over the Western country, some years ago. This was a horse of another stamp altogether. I have said that I did not think the Bashaws quite equal to the Messenger line for natural trotting. It is, however, hard to separate them, as the dam of Young Bashaw's dam was a Messenger mare; and the lines have been otherwise closely mingled. George Woodruff is of opinion that Black Bashaw, who was the sire of Awful, Lantern, &c., would have got as many fast trotters as any horse that ever lived if he had had good mares. He stood at ten dollars, and hardly ever received a good mare. Afterwards, his fee was raised to twenty dollars; but he still had common mares. The Monmouth-Eclipse mare, that was the dam of Lightning, was an exception. Awful was a capital trotter — perhaps the best of the Black Bashaws. George Woodruff drove him in 2m. 25s. over Point-Breeze Park, in a trial, before he brought him on here.

It is said that Henry Clay, a son of Andrew Jackson, is still living in this State. He got Cassius M. Clay, who was the sire of George M. Patchen. The dam of this last famous trotter was said to have been got by a son of imported Trustee. Trustee got but few trotters. The chestnut horse, so-called, who went twenty miles in harness, was by far the best of the few he got; and I believe that his dam, Fanny Pullen, put the trotting action into him. There was another got by imported Trustee, called Trustee, Jr., who trotted ten miles well. There have been other Clays who got a few very good trotting-horses about here; but, as their produce was not trained early, it is unnecessary to mention them in this connection. And there have been some whose reputed pedigrees were too uncertain to be relied on. Prince, the Buffalo horse, burnt last fall in Massachusetts, was one that nobody can tell any thing about. The other Prince, the chestnut horse that beat Hero the pacer ten miles, was a thoroughbred, according to the accounts I have had. I had supposed that Lady Palmer was the only thoroughbred trotter in this country; but they say that Prince was got by Woodpecker out of a thoroughbred mare by Langford, and was first trained to run.

Little attention as there has been paid to the cultivation of the trotting tendency in England, I find that there have been some thoroughbred trotters there, and some that were very nearly thoroughbred. A gentleman who is well informed in the matter tells me that a large number of the horses got by Lord Grosvenor's Mambrino, the sire of Messenger, had the natural trotting gift; that Infidel, by Turk, was a natural trotter, and, after he was put out of training as a race-horse, trotted fifteen miles an hour on the road between Newcastle and Carlisle; Scott, by Blank, was another; and Pretender, by Hue and Cry, out of a thoroughbred Pretender mare, another. And further, that he saw Von Tromp, half-brother to Flying Dutchman, whipped and spurred above an eighth of a mile before he could be got out of a fast trot into a gallop. This horse is now in Russia; and it is a reasonable opinion, that, if he were here, he would get good trotters out of trotting-mares, and put the staying stuff into them. Having been got by Lanercost, out of Barbelle, his blood is very stout. I think there can be but little doubt of the fact, that the only infusion of thoroughbred blood into the trotting-horse to be relied on to improve the latter as a whole ought to come from families, who, as thoroughbreds, have shown a disposition to bend the knee, and trot. Those having a strong dash of the Messenger blood would be apt to succeed; and it has succeeded in some notable instances. John Morgan was out of a Medoc mare; and Medoc was by American Eclipse, who was out of Messenger's daughter, Miller's Damsel. I know of a thoroughbred colt now in training as a runner, that shows right smart trotting action. It is believed that he can go a four-minute clip, and that without the least education. I attribute it solely to the Messenger blood there is in him, Eclipse having been his grandsire.

It is a circumstance not to be passed over without notice, that a number of our fast trotters were pacers first, and were trained as such before they struck a trot. After some time they changed their gait, and not only went fast, but were square and steady as well. Pelham was a notable instance of this. He came off the ice from Maine, where he had been a very fast pacer; and, in 1846, I got him in Boston. From the time he struck a trot he improved right along, and soon became an uncommon good one. Horace Jones had him afterwards, and then Whelan. He made the best time on record, in harness, in a race against Lady Suffolk and Jack Rossiter, — 2.28. The mare won it, but Pelham got two heats. He was a square-gaited horse as a trotter. Pilot was another pacer that quitted it for a better gait, and went like a humming-bird as a trotter. When he first struck a trot it surprised his owner; but he improved so rapidly, that, before very long, he trotted in 2.28½ at Providence.

Another very remarkable instance was that of Cayuga Chief. This horse was not only a pacer, but single-footed when at a moderate rate, like the old Narraganset pacers. He belonged to a livery-stable keeper at Worcester, Mass., and was let out as a hack. His easy gait and fine appearance — he was brown, with a blaze in the face, and very handsome — made him a great favorite with the ladies; and, whenever there was a riding-party, he was spoken for beforehand by some of the belles. He paced fast when called upon; but, carrying a lady, he always went ambling off single-footed, in the easiest and most gentle style. He was at this until nearly the fall of 1839, and then the ladies of Worcester had to say good-by to their favorite as a saddle-horse. One day he struck a trot, and went very fast.

His improvement was as rapid as that of Pelham and Pilot, perhaps more so; for in 1840 he trotted his first race at Centreville, and did two miles in five minutes and fifteen seconds.

Tip was another fast pacer that saw the error of his way of going, and took to trotting. He belonged to Rochester, and was afterwards sold to a gentleman in Jersey. As a pacer he was very fast. After he had begun to trot, Spicer got him, and he trotted in public low down in the thirties. As a general rule, those horses that have been pacers have been very steady, and, when trotting fast, have seemed afraid to break. But some of them have caused a good deal of disappointment and some profanity by taking to pacing again all of a sudden, in the middle of a race, or even in the middle of a heat. There was a roan horse called Dart, that had been a pacer, but had struck a trot, and he was in my charge. He could go like a bullet; for I have driven him a quarter of a mile to a wagon in thirty-four seconds, with my watch in my hand. Finally he was matched, and we thought we had a good thing of it; and so we should if the brute hadn't kicked over the milk-pail. He won the first heat easily; but in the next, when quite within himself, he suddenly struck a pace, just as if he was determined to show the company that he could go both ways. All my efforts to get him down to a trot were fruitless. Dart wouldn't trot; and so, when we came to the gate, I just made him dart out of the course, without going near the judges. Still, I should not be afraid of this in a pacer that had taken up a trot and gone that gait a reasonable time with steadiness. A trotting-horse is so much more valuable than a pacer, that, if I had one of the latter that could go in 2.20, I should watch carefully for the chance to make a trotter out of him.

Any pacing-horse can be made to trot by putting rails down, and making him move over them. His fore-feet will get over clean; but he cannot shuffle his hind-feet over at a pace without hitting, and he must trot very soon or fall down. This method is sometimes adopted; but it is much better when the horse strikes a trot himself without these impediments. This he is most likely to do after having been driven a good distance and got tired. The reason that should prevent us from driving a trotter when tired, for fear of making him break his gait, will rather be for driving the pacer when a little tired; for his gait is not one that we wish to preserve, and this is a means towards the changing of it. It is more laborious than any other way of going. The trotting-horse, moving the near fore-leg and the off hind-leg together, and then the off fore-leg and near hind-leg together, keeps upright, and is like a ship sailing steady on an even keel. The pacer, moving both near legs together and both off legs together, has a rocking motion, like that of a ship in a rolling sea. The pacer, though knowing no other gait but a gallop or a walk besides his pace, is likely to change it for the first time when he has been driven so far with that movement as to become tired. If he then strikes a trot it eases him; and it then becomes the business of the driver to encourage him in his new gait by every means. The best way to proceed with a pacer that has struck a trot in this manner is put the rollers on him the next time he goes out. The effect is the same on him as on the young trotter whose gait has been broken. They must be changed from leg to leg as occasion may require; and when a pacer is got to a square trot, he is to be kept at it by the nicest kind of handling. Other fast pacers beside those I have mentioned have made trotters. Among them there was American Doe. Sim Hoagland handled her; and drove her trotting in 2m. 39s., he weighing more than two hundred pounds.

VII.

Horses that pace and trot too. — Not to be trusted on the Course. — Trotters that amble off in a Pace when first out of the Stable. — Speed, and its Relation to Stoutness. — The Gray Mare Peerless. — Styles of Going. — Gait of Flora Temple and Ethan Allen. — Bush Messenger's Get. — Vermont Hambletonian's Get. — Influence of Messenger. — Hobbling in Jogging.

I LAST spoke of the natural and fast pacers which had afterwards taken to trotting, and made fine horses for the course at that gait. It must be added, that much care and patience are necessary in the treatment and handling of them while they are in the time of transition between the pace and trot and not thorough at either. Some remain all their lives capable of pacing and trotting: and these are useless for the course, by reason of the fact, that, if matched to pace, they may strike a trot, and so lose; and, if matched to trot, they may fall into a pace, and lose that way. But they are often fine, lasting road-horses, able to go a distance, and to make such fast brushes by pacing that no road-trotter can get by them. It was one of this sort that beat the dam of Flatbush Maid on the road; and it was only by changing the gait that it was done. That mare, the dam of the Maid, was a good one. The horse who got the little bay out of her was a pacer, — a chestnut. I recollect his winning a race here years ago. He had good blood in him, and could trot as well as pace. The mare was one of the Messenger tribe, — a gray, flea-bitten about the head and neck.

Besides those who pace and afterwards make reliable trotters, and those who pace sometimes and trot sometimes, there is a class that begin from a walk in an ambling pace, and go from that into the finest kind of a fast and steady trot. Some of our very best trotters of old times, and modern days as well, have had this habit of going off in a little pacing amble before they squared away in the flying trot. I like this kind. They begin with this kind of dainty amble, and some might think that they couldn't trct much; but it is only like the play of the tiger before he makes his spring. It is interesting to note the difference in trotting-horses as they begin, before they get into the stride. Old Topgallant was one of those that go ambling off, though it was not invariable with him: it was with Tacony and with Lady Moscow. Duchess, who beat Lady Suffolk, was another that began with this sort of amble. Sontag was another; and, more than that, she was a natural pacer before they made a trotter of her. It may be judged that she was a good trotter; for when Whelan had her she beat Flora Temple, who was in Warren Peabody's hands. But Flora did not stay beat long. The very next week I took her, and beat Whelan and Sontag without much trouble. Three of the best mares in the country now may be noticed as going off with the kind of dainty amble that I have mentioned as a characteristic of Topgallant, Tacony, Lady Moscow, and Sontag. Mr. Bonner's gray mare Peerless always does it, and so does the famous chestnut Lady Palmer The other I now call to mind is the young gray mare that Dan Pfifer has, — Mr. Lorillard's Blonde. She goes off in just such a way. This young mare is going to be very remarkable if she has luck. She was by Hoagland's Gray Messenger, and her dam by Old Abdallah. The old mare was a vicious jade, and of no use whatever except for the blood that was in her. She could kick higher than a man's head, and frightened one or two in this neighborhood, who tried to drive her, into fits. But the union between her and Hoagland's horse just hit the bull's-eye. The produce, Blonde, has been in Pfifer's hands ever since she was broken, and she is now "as fast as a ghost." She is only five years old, and has trotted a quarter of a mile in thirty-two seconds and a half. If she gets steady, as there is reason to believe she will with further handling, experience, and age, she is going to be one of our very best trotters.

Some people say, "What's the use of a horse going a quarter fast?" Now, they must go a quarter fast before they can go a mile fast; and, when I have one that can go a quarter at that rate at five years old, I shall take very good care that she don't go that lick any farther just then. I drove Mr. Bonner's gray mare Peerless a quarter of a mile in thirty seconds, and it was to a wagon. I mentioned before that she was the fastest I ever drove to a wagon, or that anybody else ever did. It was on the Union Course. Capt. Moore timed her, unknown to me, or to any one else but himself. He had his race-horses there then, and almost slept with one eye open. Afterwards he came up to my house, and began to question Crepe Collins, and some of the others, about the gray mare "that Hiram had been driving." The opinion of many then was, that, though fast, she could only go a quarter of a mile; and I wanted them to think so. Crepe knew it, and made some misunderstandable sort of an answer. The others assured the captain that she was of "no account." But he was certain that he had timed her right; and, to make sure that there was no mistake in the distance, he went and got his chain and boy and measured the ground. This mare, that people thought then could only go a quarter, carried me afterwards two miles to a wagon, Hoagland's weight some three hundred and eleven pounds, and finished well up with Lady Palmer, who is the best-bottomed mare to weight in the world, and one of the fastest.

Gray Eddy was another of the kind that always amble off; and a capital horse he was. Flora does not amble to begin; but, in jogging off slow, she goes rolling and tumbling along, as if she had no gait at all, and was capable of none. But when she squares away, and begins to deliver the real stroke, she has as fine and even a trot as any horse in the world. Her gait, in the rushes of lightning-speed when she darts up the stretch, is as square as ever was seen. It would be impossible for her to go as fast as she does if there was any hitch about her then. Ethan Allen goes right out of his tracks in a square trot from the beginning, and very few can head him for half a mile. Ned Forrest and Daniel D. Tompkins, the two that trotted at Philadelphia for $5,000 a side, went square from the walk like Ethan. That match was three-mile heats, to go as they pleased, on the Hunting-park Course, at Philadelphia, in 1838. General Cadwallader owned Ned Forrest, a black horse of unknown pedigree. Mr. Walton owned Daniel D. Tompkins, and George Youngs rode him. He came from Massachusetts, and was of the Maine, or Bush-Messenger, blood. That Bush Messenger was one of the last colts that old Messenger got, if not the very last. James Hammil rode the black horse; but Daniel D. won the first heat in such style that General Cadwallader sold out his chance in the race for five hundred dollars. Anderson & Spicer, of New York, bought it, and put Forrest in harness. Spicer got in and drove him, but the other won it without any trouble. Daniel D. Tompkins was brought from Massachusetts to New York in 1834. I handled him then. He was a good little horse, a chestnut, under fifteen hands, with pluck enough for the biggest that ever trotted.

This Bush, or Maine-Messenger, line was another very good ramification of the Messenger blood, and of great value to Maine and Massachusetts. The horse got a large number of fine trotters and some first-rate ones. The latter were nearly all chestnuts. I mentioned this fact to the friend who sometimes comes here to "talk horse" with me; and says he, "Now here's a glorious confirmation of the old maxim, 'Like produces like, *or the likeness of some ancestor!'* The Gray Messengers take after Mambrino, old Messenger's sire; these chestnut-Bush Messengers take after Blaze and Flying Childers, the sire and grandsire of Sampson, who got Engineer, Mambrino's sire. Now, here you see, Hiram, is a proof."

"Stop!" says I. "What you say is all very fine; but I think it just as likely that the Bush Messenger's dam was a chestnut, as that his colts were thrown back to Flying Childers."

The Bush Messenger, besides Daniel D. Tompkins, got Gen. Taylor, a very famous trotter and sticker: he was also a chestnut. Henry was another of the tribe, and the same. Independence another, and a chestnut. And Fanny Pullen another of the same color. She had Trustee, the twenty-miler, by imported Trustee; and he was also a chestnut horse. Considering the good blood he inherited on both sides, it is no great wonder that he was a horse of such bottom and endurance. The Eaton horse, in Maine, is a near descendant of the Bush Messenger; and he has kept up that line of trotters. Shepherd F. Knapp is one of his colts. While Maine had the Bush Messenger, Vermont got the blood of the old imported horse through Hambletonian, who was really a grandson of his. This horse got as good trotters as the Bush Messenger. He was the sire of True John, Green-Mountain Maid, Gray Vermont, and Sontag, — all first-rate horses. So it is clear, that besides the lines through Mambrino and Abdallah, and through Mambrino, Mambrino Paymaster, and Mambrino Chief, which diffused the blood of Messenger over Long Island, through New-York State at large, and in the blue-grass regions of Kentucky, there are to be taken into account those of the Bush Messenger and Hambletonian, who carried the strain into the Eastern States.

It is curious to estimate the influence of one horse, especially if he lives to a great age, gets stallions that become noted, and stock distinguished for fine constitution and longevity. Messenger covered some twenty seasons in this country; and as he had plenty of mares, and was a sure foal-getter, he must have been the sire of about a thousand horses. Then comes the fact that his sons were as long-lived and as thoroughly employed in the work of increase as himself, and that his grandsons continued to possess the fine qualities and peculiar gifts which he owned and conferred. In this way, and taking into account the singular faculty these horses have had of stamping the living image of their line upon their produce, and of infusing into their sons and daughters the less tangible but not less real attributes of pluck, resolution, and endurance, we shall be enabled to make some estimate of the incalculable influence Messenger has had upon the trotting-stock of this country.

It has been found that the blood of this famous horse "hits" with almost any other strain; perhaps it would be more correct to say, that the constitution of the Messengers is so good, and their individuality so strongly marked, that, in the produce of their crosses with other families, their blood always predominates. With the Stars it is of the greatest value. The noted horse Brown Dick, whose trotting education was received during the three or four years he was in the hands of Dan Pfifer, was the first of this cross that attracted my notice. His history is this: A man named Dubois, who lived up in Orange or Duchess County, had a colt by Star, that was wicked, and not thought much of. Dubois, being in New York, bought an old gray mare of the Messenger blood, out of a cart, and, taking her home, had her covered by the Star colt before he was made a gelding. The produce was Brown Dick. His dam was a pacer; but the colt soon became a fast and reliable trotter under Pfifer's management. He first trotted at six years old. His best race was against Patchen; and he won it in 2.28, 2.25¼, 2.28. He and Patchen and Miller's Damsel trotted another famous race on the Union Course. There were five heats; and the time was 2.26¼, 2.26½, 2.29, 2.28¾, 2.29. Five heats all inside of 2.30 was no common performance. The stallion finally won it, which was a proof of his staying powers.

To conclude with the different ways trotting-horses have of beginning, it will be as well to mention, that I have known some who hobbled off at first as if they were lame. I could name some who would have been pronounced lame, when led out with a halter or driven at a slow jog, by almost any horseman, but were, nevertheless, perfectly sound, and only required to be suffered to go along at a good gait to establish the fact. I have known one or two very famous trotters that went as if they were lame all round when jogging slow. I have heard of running-horses of whom the same was said. The Queen of Trumps, a famous English mare by Velocipede out of Princess Royal, had this peculiarity. I am told, that, when she was saddled for the Oaks, any man who did not know of it would have made oath that she was lame on all-fours. But she won the race with ease, and afterwards carried off the St. Leger "in a walk," as our friends over the water say. A. J. Minor, the able and clever gentleman who trained for Mr. Ten Broeck in England, and now has charge of Kentucky and Mr. Hunter's horses, tells a good story about that saying. A horse called Tom something,—I forgot what,—ran a race for a cup at a country meeting, and, with a very large allowance of steel and whalebone at the finish, got the award in his favor by half a head. Minor says he had about a hundred stripes in the last fifty strides. As he was being led off to the stable, some of the trainer's friends, who had not seen the race, met them, and cried out, "How about t' race for t' coop?"—"Oh, the cup!" says the trainer, swinging his hat in the air, "why, old Tom *won in a walk.*"

I have found some horses that were not lame, but went

as if they were, by reason of one leg being a little shorter than the other. Sometimes there's a difference in the fore-legs; at others it is in the hind ones. Careful observation by a man of experience will detect this, and the remedy is easy. The horse must be levelled by a thicker shoe on the short side.

VIII.

Treatment the Winter before Training. — Frozen and Slippery Roads Bad. — Fattening up, an Evil. — The Feed in Winter. — Treatment in complete Let-up. — Clothing. — The Feet. — "Freezing out" Mischievous. — Horses that need Blistering. — Food and Treatment. — Stabling all Winter. — Treatment and Exercise. — Constitution to be kept in View. — Shedding-Time. — Walking Exercise. — Jogging. — No Fast Work at First. — No Physic commonly required.

BEFORE entering upon the training of the trotter, it will be necessary to say something in regard to his treatment during the preceding winter; for upon that a good deal depends as to the method and time which will be required to get him into condition. If he has been trained and trotted in the previous summer and fall, his system at the beginning of the cold weather is sure to be somewhat in an inflammatory state from high feeding; and it is probable that his legs will be a little stale from the amount of work they have undergone, and the severity with which he has, perhaps, banged them about. Various methods and degrees of treatment may be adopted, and the choice of them should depend altogether upon the state and constitution of the horse. If he is of a hardy habit, is in robust health, and his legs are all right, he may as well be driven moderately during the winter, and kept as road-horses are. Care is to be taken, of course, that he is not suffered to extend himself upon rough, hard roads; and I think those who have him in charge should be wary of sleighing, and of driving when the roads are frozen and slippery. The horse may be shod how you please; but ingenuity cannot prevent his slipping and sliding to some extent, when before a sleigh or a wagon, upon a frozen road. He is therefore liable at such times to wrench and strain the muscles and ligaments; and, though no mischief may be apparent, the wear and tear is by no means as moderate as it is supposed to be, even though he is driven slow.

Care must also be taken that he is not fattened up. Some horses make flesh very fast when their work is small and irregular, and load the intestines and heart to such a degree, that the trainer has no end of trouble and anxiety to get it off. It is not only useless, but positively mischievous; and hence the grain is to be reduced in winter to a little more than half the quantity he was accustomed to consume when in training. With this he may have a few carrots now and then, and a bran-mash occasionally. The hay he has should be good, clean, and sweet. Sufficient attention to this matter will well repay the little extra expense and trouble which may be called for to secure it.

Should it be found, at the end of the season, that the trotter is stale, that his constitutional health and vigor are somewhat impaired, and his legs the worse for wear, it will not be wise to drive him during the winter. Instead of that, he may have a complete let-up, with a loose box, and a small outside lot to run in. The good rest is Nature's great restorative, when the constitutional powers have been heavily taxed by a long course of training, and severe work upon the course in the engagements the trotter may have been called upon to fulfil. To prepare him for his wintering, you should begin by gradually removing the clothes in which he has been accustomed to stand in the stable; for during the time he runs out he is to have no artificial protection against the weather but that which the shelter of his box will afford when he seeks it. His own coat is to be his only clothing. His shoes should be pulled off; and his feet may be pared down, so as to remove the bruised and broken edges of the crust and prepare for the even growth which will follow. A pair of short tips may then be put upon the fore-feet, which will prevent the hoof from being broken, and let the horse down upon his heels so as to make them *expand*, and prevent any tendency towards contraction. During the period that he thus runs out, all grooming and dressing of the coat may be dispensed with; and the grain fed to him is only to be about half of that which he has had when training, and was kept up to the trotting-mark. In this way the horse may be expected to winter well, and to renew, in a measure, the freshness and elasticity of youth. In my opinion, this system is much to be preferred to that often adopted of turning the horse out into a field, to endure the bitter blasts and intensely cold nights of a severe winter, with nothing but a hovel for shelter, and sometimes not that. Because training or the performance of difficult feats requires high feed, sweats, and some degree of artificial warmth, I can see no reason why the horse should be subjected to another violent extreme when let up.

A horse turned loose to undergo this "freezing out," as it is called, is apt to be neglected as to feed as well; and, though he may escape any violent active disorder, he is liable to come up in the spring reduced in flesh, general health and vitality, much and permanently impaired in the wind, and worse off in every way than he would have been if treated according to the other system. Besides this, horses turned loose upon the frozen turf are apt to do more hurt to their legs than the treatment is at all likely to cure; and I can see no advantage to be gained by the "freezing-out" plan, in any point of view.

Another class of horses whose case must be considered embraces those whose legs are in such a state that blistering or firing has to be resorted to. These should be kept in the stable altogether during the active part of the treatment; and their food should be of a light, cooling description, consisting of mashes and carrots to a considerable extent, and without oats while the feverish, inflammatory symptoms prevail. Physic is not required, as a general rule; but cases will arise in which a fevered and an inflammatory condition may demand the use of a ball, or other light dose of medicine. When the immediate effects of the active treatment by the blister or firing are over, the horse may have a loose box and a lot outside the same, as is recommended for those not fired or blistered. Care must be taken while the blister is on that the horse is securely tied; for, if not, he may rub and even gnaw the part so as to injure the sinews under treatment. His food should be altogether soft, unless he has engagements in the spring. In that case, he must be given from four to six quarts of oats a day, according to his constitution and the existing state of his system. On the one hand, he must not be suffered to get flabby and washy by too much soft food when engaged; and, on the other, care must be taken that he does not put on flesh and make much internal fat during this time of rest. If the former error is fallen into, he will be unable to stand the work of an early preparation, and will come to the post weakened and with poor wind. If the latter mistake is made, and he is found loaded with too much flesh when taken in hand in the spring, he may be overdone in the getting of it off, and come up to trot in bad heart, sore all over, and deficient in speed. The feed of moderate quantities of oats, with mashes, hay, and some carrots, will commonly answer best. The horse will make flesh then, if he is in health and his stomach has recovered its tone; but the superfluity resulting from this diet will be more easily got off than that produced by a higher allowance of strong food. There is plenty of room for the exercise of sound judgment in this matter; and the discretion therein should not be left, as it too often is, to some well-meaning but inexperienced person, whose only plan is to give the horse all he will eat of all sorts of feed.

It is my conviction that flesh can only be got off in the

spring by slow degrees with safety. The physicking and sweating sometimes recommended, and often resorted to, are mischievous, in my opinion; and I know that any thing like rapid work and hurry at the beginning, with a horse overfed during the winter, and very likely infirm in his legs, will be apt to knock him off before he has got the use of them, or the muscles and sinews have recovered much of their tone. There is another way of wintering trotting-horses, which, having engagements in the spring, are to be prepared at an early period to fulfil them. When such a horse is found to be clean and strong upon his legs at the close of the season, and the trainer knows that he was then all right and in fine health and freshness, as well as in hard condition, an intermediate way of wintering may be wisely adopted. Instead of being driven on the road as was first mentioned, or turned into the loose box with run of the lot as was next described, the horse may be kept in the stable all the winter, which is to say in a loose box. His clothing is to be reduced to a thin sheet; and the food, according to his constitution and heartiness, will be regulated pretty much like that of the one that runs in the box and lot. He may have soft food enough to cool him out, such as a few carrots every other day, and a bran-mash now and then. Large quantities of carrots are not to be given; and care is to be taken that he has stout feed enough to keep his flesh firm and elastic. Exercise, every day that the weather will admit of, under saddle or by leading, is to be given; and his coat may receive a nice little dressing once or twice a day.

This horse being directly under the trainer's eye all the time, and treated with a view to his early preparation and trotting, will be kept much nearer the mark of condition than those before mentioned, and will be apt to take his work in the spring of the coming year with better pluck and less risk than any of them. It remains to be added here, that horses turned out into the field should have a good feed of oats twice a day. Their exposure to the severity of the weather demands food calculated to keep up their animal heat, and compensate for the rapid waste which must be going on through the efforts of nature to supply adequate warmth. Yet it is too often the case that the horse gets no grain at all, and that the hay fed to him is of poor quality. Reduced vitality, and loss of strength, are sure to follow a course of modified starvation, and very frequently worms and the heaves are among the consequences which it entails. For these reasons, in addition to those before mentioned, the turning-out of horses used to good stabling, high feed, and warm clothing into the field, to rough it during the winter season, is to be avoided.

With reference to the feeding of those either driven on the road, kept in the stable and exercised, or run in the box and lot, I repeat that the loading up with flesh and internal fat is to be guarded against. The constitution of the horse himself is to be the main guide of whoever may have him in charge, as to the amount of grain to be fed. If he is naturally washy and soft, and given to sweat easily and profusely, he should be kept on stronger feed and have fewer mashes and carrots than one of the opposite tendency. In all cases, however, the diet may be cool, and the bowels kept easy during this period of rest. The system of each horse must be studied and understood in order to profitable and proper treatment in this regard; for the conclusion of every man of sense and experience touching it is, that there are hardly any two alike.

As I have before remarked, the horse who is turned loose to run in a lot, with a box to go into when he is inclined to do so, will be altogether without clothes. The one that has been under treatment by blister or actual cautery will be better for a light blanket without a hood. And that kept in a loose box, and exercised upon the road or an exercise-ground, under saddle or in leading-reins, will require nothing but a thin sheet.

In the spring, the shedding of the coat is rather a critical time with the horse; and it is a bad practice to attempt to hurry this operation of nature. Many people are over-anxious to see their horses shed early; and it is true, that to be backward in shedding is not a sign of a high state of health. But it does not follow that means shall be taken to loosen and remove the old coat before the constitution is quite ready to renew it, and has, in fact, begun to do so. The hair should be suffered to come off naturally; and as the lads in care of good horses are anxious to get rid of it early, so that they may present a fine appearance the sooner, it will be proper to see that they do not rub it off. Some people give boiled flaxseed or linseed-meal and the like to make their horses shed early; but I am opposed to the practice, being convinced that it is dangerous and mischievous. This sort of poulticing inside opens the pores, starts the coat, and sets the horse to sweating before the season is sufficiently advanced to warrant it; and the risk of coughs, and inflammation of the lungs, is thereby needlessly increased. The bran-mashes, by which the horse's bowels have been kept in regular order, may be adhered to, but the flaxseed and linseed should not be given. The tendency of them is to relax the system suddenly, and to cause the old hair to come away before the new coat is well started to take its place.

As the weather gets bright and favorable, the horse's exercise may be increased under saddle, or in leading-reins, from two to four miles. The mettled, high-strung horse must have more of this walking than the others; but they should all have enough to moderate their exuberant spirits at coming out, and to stop their dancing, capering, and setting their backs up at every thing they meet. This is not to be regarded as a part of the training proper; but still it is necessary that it should be attended to, for in these walks the muscles are gradually getting their tone, and the horse is being thus prepared for the jogging with which his training really begins. We have all of us experienced how soon we get tired with walking, and how even standing up for a considerable time pains the muscles of the legs at first, after a season of repose and inactivity. This should convince us, that, after the rest the horse has had during the winter, the change to work should be gradual and slow at first. As soon as the horse has been thus prepared, and the roads and weather have become sufficiently favorable, he may be put in harness or to a wagon, and his jogging may begin. Whether he shall go in a sulky or to a wagon should depend upon his disposition, in a great measure; but it will be also necessary to consider the nature of the engagements he is under in the early part of the coming season. The distance he is to be jogged must be according to his constitution and ability to perform without fatigue; and of this the trainer must judge from what he knows of him, in reference to former experience, and what he observes as the horse goes from day to day. A good deal of caution is necessary at first; for, until hardened a little by custom, the horse will be easily overdone, and a great deal of time will be lost solely by reason of having been in too great a hurry. No rule can be laid down for the amount of jogging the horse should have: it is a matter for the judgment of the trainer, in view of the nature of the animal being trained, and of the effect that it is observed to have on him as it is carried on.

For the first week or ten days, there is to be no fast work at all; but, at the expiration of that time, the muscles and tendons ought to be seasoned enough to justify the trainer in indulging the horse with slight spurts. In these he may be permitted to move along lively without over-taxing his powers or his wind. No rule can be given as to their length. The only thing to be said is, that they ought not to be very frequent and never long. The judgment of the trainer should enable him to determine how frequent they may be, and to what distance he may venture to send him without danger of overdoing the thing. It must be remembered, that, at this early stage of his preparation, the horse can bear very little compared with that which he will endure with ease, and which may be undertaken with impunity, when his condition has become forward. It is a rule with some to administer physic before the work of the horse is commenced, but I have never been able to perceive the wisdom of such a course. It is to be supposed, that, if the horse has been wintered well, the secretions will be moderately active, and the bowels regular when the time to commence work comes. In such a case, what necessity can there be for physicking? It may be apparent that some medicine is required to abate internal heat and humor, or it may happen that the horse is gross and fleshy from having been overfed while standing still. In such cases a mild dose of medicine may be given with advantage; but, instead of administering it before the work is begun, I commonly prefer to jog for a few days, then let up, and give the medicine. The work, of course, is not to be resumed until the effects of the mild course have passed off; and then it is to be carried on with quite as much care as in those cases where there was no necessity for physic perceived.

IX.

Feed while Jogging. — Brushing in the Work. — Length of the Brush. — Advance of Condition to be noted. — The Feed. — The first Trial. — Of the Sweats. — Feed and Clothing Afterwards. — Tight Bandaging bad.

WHILE the jogging, the first part of the trotting-horse's preparation, is in progress, the strength of the feed may be increased, though not up to the extent that will be requisite when the work is made longer and sharper. He may have, during this first part of the preparation, from eight to ten quarts of oats a day, according to his capacity as a feeder, and the demands made by nature for supply of strong food under work. As the oats are increased, the horse will want less hay, but may still have all that he will eat up clean. After taking his feed of oats, he will not consume as much hay in general. But some horses are such gluttons that it is necessary to limit them as to hay, almost from the first. There are even some who will eat the straw of their bedding when they have had all the grain and hay that ought to be fed to them; and, with these, it sometimes becomes necessary to put on the muzzle long before the time for the trial or the race. No carrots are now to be given, and I believe corn to be unnecessary and often mischievous. It is heating, and does not contain as much of the stuff that goes to make up hard flesh and elastic muscle as oats. There may be instances, however, in which a light feeder can be got to eat up his oats and a handful of corn as well, when the latter is mixed with them. In such a case it is well to give it; but in no case should corn be used as a *substitute* for the allowance of oats the horse in training ought to have.

While the jogging and after-preparation are going on, a bran-mash now and then will be proper. Probably about once a week will be often enough, and not too often; but this will be indicated by the condition of the horse's bowels and by his constitutional tendencies and requirements. If his bowels are relaxed, the use of the bran-mash is not apparent; and if he is of the light, washy order, never having much substance, and easily melting away when put into sharp training-work, mashes are to be given more sparingly than with one of the opposite character. The trainer is never to relax his vigilance of observation, or let his judgment go to sleep and trust to arbitrary rules.

After the week or ten days of moderate jogging, which has been directed to begin with, the muscles, tendons, and joints will have got some tone, and the wind have improved sufficiently to allow of the horse being sent along at half speed; and he may be started up and moved at three-quarter speed for about half a mile. This brush of half a mile at three-quarter speed may be increased if the horse feels fine, wants to do all he knows, and improves under his work. The next step will be, as soon as you perceive that he stands up well to his work, comes out cheerfully, and takes it with a relish, to brush him along at speed for a quarter of a mile, or even for half a mile, according as the distance is indicated in the individual case. This brush will open his pipes, and, by making him blow, set the machinery in motion which is to give him wind and throw out the blood from the internal organs when he is called upon to make his extraordinary efforts in the race. He is not, as a matter of course, to be forced in pace up to the extreme that he may be capable of in a close brush with another horse, when the stakes are up and the heat hangs in the balance. Care is also to be taken that his natural ardor and willingness are not suffered to lead into difficulties.

High-strung, generous horses are apt to want t) do more work and to do it faster than is good for them; and this frequently misleads inexperienced persons, who seeing them all on fire to go, and never satisfied unless suffered to cut loose, imagine that it can do no harm to indulge them when they feel so fine. These are just the horses that require to be watched narrowly, and taken in hand; for their exuberant spirits and eagerness to perform are not often accompanied with the power to keep on and stand up under a severe preparation at such a rate. On the other hand, there are others lazily inclined, but requiring a great amount of work to make them fit. These are commonly able to bear as much as it is deemed necessary to give them and they must be wakened up from time to time, so as to make them get out of their sluggish habit and square away.

As the training goes on, the improvement in the condition of each horse is to be carefully watched and noted, so that the time when it will be safe and useful to give the first trial may be observed. Those that were in stable condition at the commencement of the preparation will be ready for this test before the ones that were turned out; but no rule can be laid down as to the amount of work the horse ought to have before the trial may be ventured on. His condition as he appears while at work, and during and after his speedy brushes, is to be the guide by which the trainer's judgment in this matter must be directed. During the fast work, preparatory to the coming trial, the horse will have been put upon his largest allowance of strong food. Some will not eat more than eight or ten quarts of oats a day; and it is necessary to be very vigilant and careful that these light feeders are not over-marked in work. Twelve or thirteen quarts is about what a good feeder ought to have. Some will eat sixteen quarts of oats a day, but my belief is that three quarts of it does more harm than good. With such an extraordinary consumption of strong food, there must needs be an extraordinary amount of strong work done to keep the flesh down and get rid of these superfluities, inside and outside, which experience has shown must be eliminated before the horse is capable of his best achievements. Now, if it were a mere question of bodily health and vigor, we might say, the more oats the horse eats the more work he can do with impunity, and the better his condition will be on the day of the race. But it is not a mere question of bodily health and vigor; for the extra amount of work made necessary to get off the effects of the extravagant quantity of food consumed, and keep the horse only in proper flesh at the same time, imposes a terrible task upon the legs, which are commonly the first part of the machine to give out in horses whose work is fast and severe. This is a consideration which has made me averse to giving any horse in training more than thirteen quarts of good oats a day, unless there is something peculiar in the animal and the circumstances of the case.

During the preparation which precedes the first trial, it will be necessary to give the horse one or two sweats. Whether it ought to be one or two must be indicated by the condition and nature of the animal, the races in which he is engaged, and resolved by the judgment of the trainer. The amount of clothes in which he shall be sweated must be determined by the same considerations. Some may require a blanket and hood, and a wrapper round the neck to start the perspiration out of them; while there are others that will sweat freely with but little clothes, and scrape well when more have been thrown on at the end of the jog. One thing may certainly be said, that a sweat obtained without the use of heavy clothing is more satisfactory and better than one with it, provided the latter method does not include a good deal more work to get the sweat. Only a moderate quantity of clothing and little work while the horse is going, are the best for a sweat, if a good scrape can thus be obtained. When the horse comes from the drive, and is taken out of the wagon, he will soon be ready to scrape. That done, he must be blanketed up again, and walked about out of the draft. A favorable day for the sweat ought to be taken advantage of, as a matter of course. Another light scrape may probably be had after some little time spent in walking in the blankets; but, if the perspiration does not continue so as to give this second scrape, it is not to be forced by more work in the clothes. To be of use in itself, and as a satisfactory indication that the condition of the horse is advanced, it must come of itself. During the time this sweating and scraping process is in course of operation, the trainer having the conduct of it should not be in a hurry. The same things that are said to cure a man's cold — patience and a little water-gruel — will often do wonders in procuring a good sweat. Commonly, however, it is easy enough to get the sweat and scrape, but more difficult to cool the horse out properly. In order to do this well, he is to be clothed again, and led very gently about for a considerable period, so that he may become cool gradually, and the perspiration may dry away by degrees. This walking is to be out of all draft as much as possible; and it will not do to hurry it over, and go to the stable, until the horse has cooled off well and gradually. When the proper state has been reached, the horse is to be taken into the stable, and his body is to be well dressed. This done, he is to be re-clothed, and again led into the air.

A few sups of gruel, made of Indian meal or fine shorts, from half a pint to a pint of the meal stirred into a bucket of water, may now be given to the horse, or water with the chill taken off it may be used as a substitute for the gruel. When taken into the stable again, which will be after a little more walking about in the air, the legs are to be put in tubs of warm water, the body clothing being kept on. The legs are then to be well washed with the water and castile soap, and when dried off to be bandaged. These bandages should be of light flannel, and it is immaterial whether it is red or white. They are not to be put on tight. The legs of a horse ought never to be bandaged tight, for such a course impedes the circulation into the feet, where there is a great necessity for it; but, losing sight of this, the bandages are sometimes pulled so that it looks as if they were intended to serve as a tourniquet, and stop the circulation of the blood altogether. Neither can it serve any useful purpose, that I can see, to bind the suspensory ligament up to the bone of the leg. Nature intended that in the horse it should stand out from it, as we see in the fine flat legs of the best runners and trotters. Whatever support is required may be obtained with only a moderate degree of tightness; and I have sometimes thought that an elastic stocking, such as our best surgeons use in cases of bad strain to the nerves and muscles of the human foot and ankle, would be a very useful article in a training-stable.

The difference between tight bandaging and elastic support was brought very prominently to my notice not long ago. A lady seriously injured her foot and ankle by falling down stairs, when coming in a hurry to receive a friend. She was unable to walk for months, and finally could not bear the injured foot upon the floor ever so lightly. Treatment by various lotions and liniments was adopted, and tight bandaging was prescribed by the surgeons of the city where this accident happened. But the foot got no better; and, fearing that permanent lameness might be the result, the lady came to New York, and was treated by Dr. Carnochan. He abolished the tight bandaging, substituted an elastic stocking made by a very clever mechanic, and insisted that the foot should be put down, and used a little every day without crutches. The result was a perfect cure, in an astonishingly short time. Had the numbing process by means of the tightened bandages been persevered with much longer, the use of the member would have been permanently lost, and the lady a cripple for life. This was a suggestive case to me. Tight bandaging of the legs of a horse is a very bad practice, and therefore you should see that they are properly put on and not drawn tight.

When all is done, and the horse nicely cooled off, he may have a good scald mash, and less hay than on other occasions for the night. On the morning of the day after the sweat the horse ought to feel limber, elastic, and buoyant in spirits. In his jogging, which must be of two or three miles, as you judge him to need, he may have a couple of brushes of a quarter of a mile each, at nearly or quite full speed, to open his pipes, and enable him to stretch himself. When horses have been well sweated, and have got well cooled out of it, they are full of alacrity and ardor, and feel like going fast with ease and pleasure to themselves. Therefore, the time is proper to put in these short and sweet brushes, during which the horse may be expected to go a little faster, without urging, than he has at any other time during his preparation.

X.

Work after the Sweat. — Trial after the Sweat. — Preparation for the Trial. — Amount of Work. — No arbitrary Rule possible. — The Mile-Trial. — Of Condition, Game, and Bottom. — Work after the First Race. — Preparation for Three-mile Heats. — Much slow Work reduces Speed. — Time of Three-mile Preparation. — Of the Trials. — Work after the Final Trial.

AFTER the horse has had the sweat, as before directed, the regular work is to be resumed and carried on as before, and the feed is to be the same as it was before the sweat. It will be well to bear in mind the object of the sweats, which is to loosen the flesh, and to remove the fat and other superfluities which add nothing to the horse's strength, impede his wind, and make so much more weight for him to carry in his training and in his races. On the other hand, the regular work is not to take away the substance, but to increase the volume of muscle, harden its consistency, and increase its elasticity and strength. Thus the sweats merely reduce, while the regular work reduces the soft parts to some extent of itself, but builds up and develops the moving powers. It follows, that, when the horse in hand is of a weak and soft habit, great care must be taken that he is not sweated too much in clothes; for, if he is, he will shrink in the course of work, and become thin and dry after one or two races. If the time of training could be extended, and there was no danger to the legs and constitution in making the work severe, the sweats might be dispensed with almost or quite altogether. But this is not the case; and therefore the sweat in clothes is resorted to in order to get rid of the superfluities more rapidly and with less risk to the legs than the regular work would do.

Where the horse is of good constitution, but positively infirm in his legs, there must be more sweating in clothes and less work without them than in other cases. In five or six days after the sweat, the horse should be ready to stand a half-mile trial. Unless something has gone wrong, he ought to be fit to go that distance under the watch, and thus afford a certain indication as to his speed and advance toward racing condition. It will not be necessary to muzzle him over night for this short trial, unless he is a rank feeder. His oats are not to be reduced in quantity; and he may have his usual allowance of hay, unless he has been accustomed to eat a great deal. His morning feed before the trial may be a little less than usual, and the water reduced to correspond. The half-mile trial being found satisfactory, the work will be carried on as before. Let him jog till he has emptied himself, then move him at three-quarter speed, with sharp and lively brushes to make him square away and get up to his best rate. The amount of work must be gauged by the judgment and skill of the trainer, in view of how the horse goes on and improves, and of his known breed and character. It is quite certain that the thoroughbred horse will improve under an amount of work that will overmark and utterly destroy the chance of almost any horse coarsely bred. Therefore, it is to be expected that a well-bred trotter will take more work with advantage, provided his legs stand, than one of a poorer grade in blood. But, beyond this, it is found by experience that there is a great disparity in the capacity of horses of the same grade to stand work and improve in condition. No rule can be laid down beforehand by which it can be useful and safe to regulate the amount of work it will be proper to give. Until the horse has been trained, it is impossible to say what he may bear, and what is required to bring him quite fit on the day that he is to trot for money.

Therefore, the trainer must be vigilant as the work goes on from day to day; and, if the slightest symptoms appear to indicate that the limit has been reached, the horse must be eased. Experience, judgment, and skill are imperatively demanded at this juncture; and, where they do not exist in fair degree, it will be the best course to keep on the safe side, and be sure that the horse is well within himself. It is true that he may not be up to the keen edge of which he is susceptible; but there is no remedy for this except at the risk of overdoing him altogether, which risk is great in such circumstances in any hands but those of a skilful and watchful trainer. It will not do to carry on until the horse is off his feed, dull in the eye, and his coat begins to stare, because the game is up when this is the case. The point at which his work ought to have been eased is passed, and it will take some time of nice handling and gentle work to get behind it once more.

In five or six days, or a week after the first trial, the horse will be fit to be tried a mile, if he has been doing well. It being found that he is "all there," this will commonly be sufficient for a mile race. Even if the race is two miles and repeat, it will sometimes be best to avoid further trial. It depends upon the condition and character of the horse and the state of his legs and feet. If he is known to be a stout one, and his legs are all right, another trial may be had prior to the two-mile race; and in this the horse may be repeated. But if the speed is there, and the trainer is satisfied with the condition, it will be safest to take a good deal on trust rather than insist on its exhibition before the race. If the trainer knows his horse, he will have a safe rule to go by; if he does not know him, he must rely, to a considerable extent, upon his own judgment; for, when the horse is not *known* to be stout, there is all the more danger of giving him too much in the trials. The horse that is fit to trot mile-heats, three in five, in which the heats may be broken, is able to trot a two-mile race, so far as condition is concerned. Natural stoutness and game are demanded for long races. Now, without condition the horse cannot have "bottom," which is simply capacity to endure. Without game, which is the pluck to try till the last chance is out, the bottom may exist to very little purpose. Therefore, though the horse cannot have the bottom without condition, he may have the condition without the bottom and its necessary concomitant — game. It follows, that the saying often heard, "condition makes bottom," is only true to a limited extent. It enables the game and naturally stout horse to make avail of all his bottom, and put forth his powers to the uttermost degree. Again, it is said speed makes bottom; but this is next kin to nonsense. As long as there is nothing like equal speed against it, it enables the fast horse's driver to keep him well within himself, and thus to dispense with the bottom which, against another of nearly equal speed, would be necessary to save the heat. And speed is of very great importance in another point of view. It enables its possessor to go ahead, take which part of the course he pleases, and fret and worry the other horse. Very few horses have the courage and temper to go on behind at their best pace, and persevere to the end without breaking. Therefore, the horse of known bottom may act bad when he finds himself out-trotted from the score in a long race, and is urged all the way; and if the driver pulls him together, the other may steal away and open such a gap that the closing of it at the end of the heat will be a terrible up-hill task, unless the other "comes back." Speed, then, may be an available substitute for bottom; but it cannot be bottom itself in any sense. The slow horse in condition can keep at his best rate longer than the speedy horse can at his. Hence the old saying, "He can't go fast enough to tire himself."

When the horse has appeared in his first race, showed the speed you might reasonably look for, and given evidence of satisfactory condition, he is not to be treated exactly as before in getting ready for the next. It is proper now to reduce his work; for if he is kept at it, just as he was before his first engagement, he is almost certain to lose speed. The condition is about there, and what it lacks may be looked for to follow the means taken to increase the speed after the first race. The work is to be less in quantity, but with numerous short brushes and merry rallies, leaving the horse in good heart and high spirits, thinking well of himself, and on good terms with his daily training-ground, the course.

Should the race for which the horse is in preparation be three-mile heats, the work must be longer and not so sharp as for mile heats, three in five, and two-mile-heats. The lasting qualities are to be developed by more jogging, and not so many spurts of speed in comparison. Still, the work is not to be so slow and monotonous and extended as to take speed away. Many a race is won by a good brush on the stretch, which would have been lost if the speed had been dogged out with a great deal of walking and slow jogging. I have found it so often the case that a large amount of slow work has knocked off the speed, that I deem one of them incompatible with the other, and look upon this as an established principle. Therefore, there are to be lively spurts from time to time, when the preparation is for three-mile heats, and the jogging is not to be carried on so as to take out the heart and inclination of the horse for these spurts. To produce the horse full of staying condition, and with all his speed, is the proper aim of the training art. To have him capable of going on for a long while, but deficient of his known rate of speed, is not art; and to have him speedy for a little way, but unable to stay the distance which he is known to be able to endure, is not art either.

For the three-mile race a longer time will be taken in training than for one of mile-heats, three in five, unless a shorter engagement has intervened; and, when the horse is brought to the post for the long race, he ought to be as near the pitch of condition as art can get him. About three weeks before the race is to come off, he may have his first trial, which will be a mile. Half-mile trials are to be dispensed with here; for the object was to get the three-mile distance "into the horse," and a performance of half a mile would afford no useful indication. It would only tell that he had certain speed.

The mile trial having been satisfactory, the work is to go on; and in ten days more, or thereabout, the horse will be fit for his final trial. In getting ready for this, his hay and water over night may be somewhat reduced, and the muzzle is to be put on. The full allowance of oats is to be given. At the actual trial, commence with a mile at good speed. At the end of it, blanket up and scrape, and walk about for thirty-five minutes. Then repeat two miles out. If in this the horse does well, shows speed and freshness, and finishes with *go* in him, you may be pretty well satisfied that he is in good condition and capable of making his race. A further trial is unnecessary, and would be likely to result in mischief.

The trials are never to be as long as the race for which the horse is being trained. In the three-mile preparation there will be walking exercise, probably five or six miles a day, and three or four of driving, with spurts of speed therein; but, as I said before, no rule can be laid down for the actual amount of work; that must depend upon the horse. I mention the above as a probable amount, because it is not likely that a horse unable to stand up under something like it will be matched three-mile heats. If he is, his owner may look to lose, unless the other is inferior in speed and of the same kidney. From the time of the final trial to the race, the work should be the same as it was before, unless the wisdom of a change was indicated by what took place *in* the trial. If in that performance the horse showed plenty of speed, but pulled up distressed at the end of the two miles of repeat, it would be an evidence that he is not up to the mark in condition, and the work should be increased. In any case, it will be of great importance to have the wind clear for the race, and four or five days prior to that event the horse should have a light sweat. A jog with hood and wrapper, so as to get a nice scrape, is all that will be required, the cooling-out to be as before directed. All through the preparation, if the race is to be in harness, it will be advisable to change the sulky for a skeleton wagon occasionally, so as to get the weight off the back. If the race is to be to a wagon, the horse is not to be worked in a sulky at all.

XI.

Stout Horses stand a strong Preparation. — State of the Legs to be watched. — Idlewild and Lady Palmer. — No Device a Substitute for Work. — Ten-mile Preparation. — A steady rating Capacity wanted. — The Preparation to be Long. — The Feed to be Strong. — Effects of the Work to be watched. — The Trials. — Management of the Race. — The Races of Kentucky Prince and Hero the Pacer.

IT will have been gathered from what I have said, that, even when good condition has been attained, there will still be a great difference in the performance of horses as soon as the distance they are required to go is long; and that, in getting a whole stable of horses into fix to trot races, there will seldom be two whose treatment during their preparation ought to be the same. The natural game and stout horse will stand a stronger preparation, and may be relied on for a greater performance than another will ever be capable of, with all the aid that the trainer can give him, provided the legs of the former stand. There is a small class of trotting-horses, and of thoroughbred running-horses, too, who require an immense amount of work to get them fit to do their best, and who cannot be relied on to do any thing like their best without it. The training of these, seeing that they can hardly have too much work, judiciously given, for their constitution, would be much simplified, if it were not for the danger that their legs and feet may give out, while their appetite and general health remain good. In preparing them the state of the legs must be particularly watched; and if any weak or inflammatory symptoms manifest themselves under the severe work which is necessary to bring them to the wiry condition in which they will do their best, the sweats must be more relied on to reduce their superfluities than the strong work they would otherwise demand and might have with entire safety.

If the legs of these horses stand, so that with the ordinary amount of sweats and the extraordinary amount of work they can be brought to their best condition, they may be relied on to last: they will trot all day and the next day too. But when the danger to the legs has been such that it was necessary to give many and heavy sweats, and only an ordinary amount of work, there is always some chance that they may cut up soft, *for them.* There is still the condition, so far as the absence of internal and external fat and other gross superfluities is concerned; but the muscular system has not had the great amount of work to give it tone and power to endure, which their particular hardy and high-strung organizations, and the extraordinary tasks they are called on to perform, above all others, require. There have been two notable instances of this about here,— one of them a thoroughbred runner; the other thoroughbred also, but a trotter; and both mares. The first-mentioned, Idlewild, required a vast amount of hard drilling to make her fit; and it was not safe to bring her to the post against a good horse without it, although her speed was something wonderful. The other is Lady Palmer, Mr. Bonner's chestnut mare by Glencoe, and therefore a sort of aunt to Idlewild, whose dam was by Glencoe. In spite of excellent bodily condition, apparently, it would not do to rely upon this mare to make one of the extraordinary performances of which she is known to be capable, unless she had had a great amount of severe work in the attaining of it. The wind in her and Idlewild might be good enough — though it would be more likely not to be good without the hard drilling; for what is called "good wind" depends largely upon the muscular action of the heart — and still, for want of sufficient work to build up and give lasting tone to the wiry, harp-string powers, there might be a failure to come up to expectation in a really great task.

Hence we see where the sweating in clothes would fail to make these horses fit, though they might be in "bodily condition;" and thus the futility of substituting the Turkish bath, or any thing of that kind, for natural work in the training of horses, may easily be perceived. As a rule, the best horses take the most work, for two reasons. One is, that they do not part with their hard flesh half as easily as those do who are naturally soft and more vascular. The other is, that the great performances for which these horses are likely to be called upon can never be expected until the moving powers have been well-seasoned, and have come to possess their lasting tone. I am assured, that, when the flat-race trainers first began to fit horses for steeple-chase running in England, they were amazed to find that they gave out suddenly, dead beat, when they would have sworn that their condition was good. They soon found that the failure was a consequence of want of work for the *jumping powers.* They had only been worked over the flat; and, though their bodily condition was as fine as could be, there was a want of power in the muscles which send the horse up and forward in taking leaps. That power they soon learned could only be gained by leaping-practice in the training. Thus it will be perceived that *custom,* as long as the constitutional health and the legs remain sound, is the great agent in fitting all sorts of animals for the performance of extraordinary feats. It is said that Milo of Crete could carry an ox, but it was one that he had carried every day after it was a calf. All that time he had been "in training;" and as training without any let-up for a long period must exhaust the sources of vitality, and impair the constitution prematurely, it is very likely that Milo died before the ox did.

In the preparation for a ten-mile race, there must be an increase of work even over that indicated for the three-mile heat engagement. A great burst of speed is not to be looked for anywhere in a race of ten miles; but victory is to be expected more from a steady rating-trot, which can be taken up at the beginning and maintained to the end. In nineteen cases out of twenty, this will cut down the opposing horse in a race of this length, even when his speed is greatly superior, unless he has been taught to keep this even rate in his preparation. If this tuition has not been given, he will either make bursts above the distance-rate every now and then, or he will pull and fight at his driver in his efforts to do so. In either case, the rating-horse has got him, provided his driver keeps up the rate, and does not let the other have a chance to recuperate when he begins to tire.

Of course, no horse who is not naturally stout and well on his legs ought to be matched and trained for a race of ten miles. This being found to be the case, the work must be given like that for the three-mile heats, but larger in amount. Thus, on two days in a week, make it a fourth longer, and on other days an eighth longer. At the same time that care is to be taken not to dog and worry the speed out, there is no occasion for the ripping spurts which intervene in the other training: the horse is only to have enough of them to keep him cheerful and lively, and to vary the partial monotony of the steady work. This preparation will be greater in length than any of the others, for a horse is not to be got up to the ten-mile mark at a good rate in a few weeks. While he is undergoing it, he may have all the grain he will eat, even if it is fourteen or fifteen quarts; but you must see that he eats all up and keeps the manger clean. Long and strong work demands strong feed and plenty of it. A horse may do a long day's work now and then in stable-condition, but this is as nothing to being called upon to do a large amount pretty rapidly every day. The strong feed and strong work, as I said in a former part of this work, are dangerous to infirm legs; but a horse to go ten miles should be one of well-tried strength in this particular. Therefore the strong work and all the oats he will eat may be ventured on in his preparation for this distance.

In the course of it, before his first trial, it will probably have been deemed necessary to give him a couple of sweats; and, after he is well over them, his work may often be increased with advantage. But vigilance is to be exercised all along to see that the point at which the work begins to be too severe is not reached. The trainer's judgment as to the effect the increased work has upon the constitutional health and legs is all in all here. He will still have a guide, — the horse's known habit and breed; but it will not do to trust to these alone. That would be like steering by the stars at sea, to the neglect of the compass. Now, the stars, as seen by the helmsman, will give a general indication of the course, but not the exact course by compass. And so the habit and breed will furnish general probabilities, but not the particular niceties to be arrived at by carefully observing the effect of the increased work from day to day. The horse will not feel any the worse, in all probability, after the first day or the second; but, as it goes on, the likelihood of overmarking him is increased. Five weeks before the race the ten-mile horse may have his first trial, which will be two miles, at two-thirds speed. A scrape may be taken; and the horse will be cooled out in conformity with the directions before given, by slow walking in clothes in the air, but out of a draught of wind.

In ten or twelve days after the first trial, he ought to be ready to go two miles and repeat. Let him go the first two miles at two-thirds speed. Then blanket and scrape, and walk about for twenty-five minutes. In the second two miles he may go his best; that is, his best rate *for two miles.* Then clothe him well and get another nice scrape. Supposing the horse to have done well all along, he will now be near fine staying condition. Let the work be carried on according to your best judgment, from what you observed in the last two miles of the repeat, how he finished it and behaved afterwards. Ten days before his race he will be ready for his final trial, five miles out. From his performance of that, and its effect on him, the trainer ought to be able to form a definite judgment as to his condition; and here condition is as absolute a necessity as stoutness. The most skilful and experienced man may be deceived as to the stoutness of a horse in a ten-mile race, when he has not proved it by going one; but the trainer ought not to be mistaken in his condition.

Upon the judgment to be formed now, the tactics to be adopted in the race will mainly depend. If the horse is known to be a stout one, and his condition is as good as can be, the policy will be to go along at a good rate, not caring if the other goes faster at first, but to keep up at that rate, or thereabouts, and force the other to keep at it too, when he would rather slacken up a little. By this means any extra speed your opponent may have had at the start will have disappeared long before the finish. You will have got him down to your speed, and have your extra stoutness to win with. It is to be remembered that the speed of a speedy horse diminishes very rapidly when he begins to tire; and that keeping him going at a steady rate for a great distance, even though it is much slower than his best rate, tries his stoutness. If there is a soft place in him, this plan is much more likely to find it out than any other. If he could go part of the way fast, and another part a moderate jog only, he would be apt to recuperate, and recover speed for the finish; but when the rating-horse follows steadily, mile after mile, as sure to come to time as a clock, the other is not able to make his own pace, except it be a moderately fast pace all the way, and this is sure to cut down his speed. Speed can only be made an available substitute for bottom in races of moderate length. Ten miles is toc far for it.

In the year 1853, the horse Kentucky Prince was matched in two ten-mile races against Hero the pacer, in harness, and placed in my hands by Mr. R. Ten Broeck to be prepared. Prince was a chestnut with one white heel, and very nearly thoroughbred if not quite. He was by Woodpecker out of a mare by imp. Sarpedon; which horse also got Alice Carneal, the dam of Lexington and the mare that was the dam of Lady Palmer. Prince showed his breeding in every point but his lop ears, in which he was like the Melbournes in England. He took his work well, and a great amount of it. The first race came off on the Centreville Course on the 1st of November. It was for $5,000 a side, in harness, drivers to weigh 165 pounds. Mr. Joseph Hall matched Hero, and Spicer drove him. Prior to the start, Mr. Ten Broeck, who was then and still is a very good judge in such matters, advised me to trail, and let Hero make his own pace until the end of the seventh mile, believing that the last three miles would do to cut down Hero's speed. But I replied, that his speed was very great, he having gone a mile in 2.18½, and that it would be better to take the starch out of him to a considerable extent earlier in the race. I did not then suppose that he would make the pace quite as good as he did from the start; but I was convinced, that, if he did so, it would be my best policy to keep it good. Mr. Ten Broeck, however, adhered to his opinion; and, at starting, I set out to conform to it. The pacer took the lead, and made the first mile in 2.44. The next was still better, 2.36; and the third, 2.33½. This was pretty hot for the distance we had to go, and I lay well behind. In the last quarter of the third mile, I saw indications that the pacer was going to slacken his speed; and I felt like pulling out and making him keep it up, or thereabouts, for fear that I should slip by and take the track. If I merely lay in his wake for four miles, he could go as slow as he pleased, and have three miles of fast work in for the end. Half way up the stretch stood Mr. McMann, a great friend of Mr. Ten Broeck's. He had a deal of money bet, and so had I. As I got abreast of him I said, "I shan't win if I stay here." "Then go on," he replied; and, pulling out, I went on as though going to try for the lead. This compelled Hero to keep the pace good. The fourth mile was done in 2.39, and the fifth in 2.37. Five miles in 13.09½. The sixth mile was 2.46; and now it became clear enough to me that Hero was tiring, and the race safe.

It will be remembered, that, in the early part of this work, I remarked that the pace was a much more laborious gait than a trot, for a long distance. It results, that, when a pacer begins to tire in the legs, he gives out, and goes altogether unless he gets rested. Hero had had no ease, and in the early part of the seventh mile he was beaten. The rating for six miles, though nothing like his highest speed for one mile, had "cooked his bacon," to use a common expression. I took the lead, and jogged round this mile in 5.08 1-2, the next in 6.16, and the ninth in 6.19. The last mile I drove in 2.39. Hero had been stopped in the seventh mile. Mr. Ten Broeck had money laid that Prince would trot the tenth mile in three minutes; and, when I started the horse up to win it, he felt so well that he went much faster than I supposed him to be going. If the pacer had been suffered to slack up when he began to get a little tired, he might not have got so completely tired as to go all to pieces. Ten days afterwards we went a race of the same kind on the Union Course, for $5,000 a side. This was play or pay, and had been made before the other race took place. I took the lead in this, Hero making it a waiting race from the start. The first mile was 3.01, the second 2.52, the third 2.49, the fourth 2.45 1-2, the fifth 2.41, the sixth 2.46 1-2, the seventh 2.38 1-2, the eighth 2.42 1-2, the ninth 2.40, the tenth 3.12 1-2. Hero quit in this mile. The total time of this was 28 m. 08 1-2s., and Prince won it easy. Hero made a good race too; for the nine miles in less than twenty-five minutes showed good rating, and great power of lasting at the pacing-gait.

XII.

Early Reminiscences. — My first Race. — My Second. — Lady Kate against Time. — Paul Pry against Time. — The Riders of Thirty Years Ago. — Requisites of a Good Rider. — Drilling Horses. — Lady Sefton.

BEFORE we proceed much farther, I purpose, in answer to letters which I have received, to say a little about the commencement of my career among horses, and some of those events in which I then participated. The writers have been good enough to say that they think some of my personal reminiscences and recollections of the horses of old times will be of great interest and some use. The first race for money in which I was engaged took place thirty-four years ago, and I was then fourteen years old. It was at Philadelphia in 1831; I being then with my uncle, the trainer, George Woodruff, at the Hunting-park Course. We had Topgallant, Columbus, and a number of other trotters in the stable. The course used to be a favorite resort of such gentlemen as Gen. Cadwallader; Mr. William Fetterall, who owned Daniel D. Tompkins; Mr. Jeffries, who afterwards owned Dutchman; and the like. These gentlemen were always anxious to see a little sport; and one day they got up a small purse, to be trotted for under saddle by any horses that we boys could pick up. I started off from where they were all assembled, and took a horse out of the plough in a neighboring field. It was Shaking Quaker, who had belonged on Long Island prior to that time, and could go a little. Opposed to me, there were Peter Whelan and James Hamill, both of whom had got horses taken promiscuously out of some of the vehicles on the course. We started; and I won it with ease in two heats, the best being 2.57.

I very soon had another mount, and this was of more importance. Mr. Frank Duffy had at that time a little mare called Lady Kate, that was a good goer. He had gone from Philadelphia to Baltimore, and matched her against time to trot fifteen miles within the hour. This Lady Kate was a handsome little thing, about Flora Temple's size, and a good deal like her in appearance. She was good under saddle; and the notion prevailed that Mr. Duffy was going to ride her himself. But this was a slight mistake on the part of the backers of Time. The match had been made catch-weight, and Mr. Duffy came on for me and another to ride her. He was very much afraid that one of us would not be able to ride the distance out, and do justice to little Lady Kate. It was on the Central Course, Baltimore; and Mr. Duffy, with the mare's bridle thrown over his arm and a big saddle on her, was a sight to see, as he led her up and down, and took all the bets that were offered on *time.* But the backers of the "old devourer" saw another sight prior to the start; for, just when they had expected Mr. Duffy to mount, I stepped "out of the woods," with a little saddle all ready, and changed it for the heavy one that was on her.

There was a terrible time among those who had laid against Lady Kate; but they could not deny the fairness of the strategy that had been practised to get bets, and so I mounted without objection. The little mare and I got the word, and away we went as well as could be. On the back-stretch in the eighth mile, Mr. Duffy asked me if I could ride it out without tiring; to which my reply was, that I could ride the little mare the fifteen miles within the hour, and a little more to boot. I was just as easy as I had been from the start, and she was going along in the prettiest winning manner. The other boy's friends, however, were very anxious that he should have a share of the riding; and so, at the request of his father, who had come on from Philadelphia with him, I got off at the end of eight and three-quarter miles. At the end of the twelfth mile, money was laid that the mare would do sixteen miles within the hour, and she accomplished it with great ease. The sixteenth mile was made in 3m. 10s., and she had three minutes and nineteen seconds to spare out of the hour. She could have gone eighteen miles in the hour just as well as not. The race took place about four weeks after the one in which I rode Shaking Quaker from the plough; and, if I had not ridden that, I do not think I should have been selected to ride Lady Kate. I shall now describe a big time-race; which is all the more interesting because it was done by a grandson of the imp. horse Messenger, who was gray like himself, and had most of the prominent characteristics of that celebrated breed. I think it of the more importance because of the theory now started by some, that a cross to the thoroughbred stallion is not the way to breed trotters. It has not *been* the way up to this time, except in the case of those got by this thoroughbred horse Messenger in this country, and by his sire, Lord Grosvenor's gray horse Mambrino, in England. I do not mean to commit myself, just here, to any theory of breeding; but will point out the indisputable facts, that here was a thoroughbred stallion that got trotters of true action and bottom to stay all day, and that his sire had got plenty of them before him, they both being trained and successful *running*-horses.

Now let us pass to the race and its preliminary history. It was in 1833, when my father kept the Harlem-park Course, at its first opening, that a Scotch gentleman named McLeod owned a gray gelding called Paul Pry. This horse was about twelve years old, sixteen hands high, coarse, and raw-boned, but with a blood-like head and neck, and all the points good, though very plain. He was a flea-bitten gray, and was thought to have been got by imp. Messenger himself. But this was not possible, as Messenger died in 1808; and the truth no doubt was, that Paul Pry was either by one of Messenger's sons or out of one of his daughters. This gray gelding belonging to Mr. McLeod was matched about this time for $250 a side to trot sixteen miles within the hour, and then $250 more a side for every quarter of a mile from sixteen up to seventeen miles and three-quarters. Thus the whole amount at stake was $2,000 a side. Paul Pry was trained for this performance on the Harlem-park Course, under the management of Mr. William Niblo. I gave him his work under saddle. He had it all that way of going, for he pulled so hard in harness as to make any work that way unadvisable. The training lasted from seven weeks to two months; and, after having got him into shape, we felt confident that he would win all the money up. His even rate and staying qualities were what we depended upon; for Paul Pry was at no time a horse of brushing speed, and for this match he had been trained to get the distance into him, rather than develop his speed. He could not go better than 2.45 or 2.46 to a mile; but, what he could do, he could keep on doing for a long time when up to the mark in condition.

The trot came off on the Union Course on the 8th of November. I rode the horse, and rode him all the way. He won it easily. At the end of the seventeen miles and three-quarters I jogged him another quarter, making eighteen miles; and he had a minute and some five or six seconds to spare out of his hour. I am persuaded that I could have ridden twenty miles within the hour if it had been needed. At the end of his fourteenth mile, up to which the horse had been going very easily and evenly, and not pulling at all, a gentleman struck in to keep me company. But Paul Pry was immediately on his mettle; and I was compelled to beckon the gentleman to keep back when he was at least one hundred and fifty yards behind me. Seeing that he finished his eighteen miles fresh, and that at the end of the fourteenth he would not let another come within a hundred and fifty yards of him, I have reason to think that he could have trotted twenty miles within the hour. But Paul Pry was better in a race against time than in one with another horse; for, when he had company, he would pull desperately, and fight with his rider or driver.

There are not many riders nowadays that a man would like to rely upon to ride eighteen or twenty miles in an hour, the horse to trot. At the time I speak of we had a number that could ride trotters sixteen, seventeen, eighteen, nineteen, and even twenty miles within the hour. We had some that would have been backed to do much better than that. George Spicer offered a bet that he would ride one hundred miles on trotting-horses in five hours' time and, Jack Harrison offered to back me to do the like. Nearly all the trotting at that time was done under saddle. Consequently, we had fine saddle-horses, and a great number of good hardy riders, who could maintain their clip with the knees and thighs, and give their horses all the support they needed with their hands. The number of men among us that can now ride a fast trotter twenty miles an hour is not large. It is to be regretted, I think, that the saddle-work and use of trotters in that way fell so nearly altogether into disuse. It is very fine to see a lot of good trotters go away under saddle in the hands of competent riders, and make a fast race. The young men and lads now have but little chance to learn the art of riding the trotting-horse strong and well, for they have next to no practice. As those who were brought up in the old school got too heavy for the business, there were no others coming up to supply their place; so that it would be difficult, at this day, to get three or four competent riders of trotting-horses together. It requires a combination of qualities. The rider must have good judgment; he *must* be very strong and lasting, or else there will be danger of his giving out, and, when he does so, the best horse in the world would be likely to follow suit.

When Capt. Moore offered to put Idlewild into a stake against George Wilkes, Lady Emma, Gen. Butler, or any other trotters that might choose to enter, the old mare to go four miles while the trotters or any one of them went three, he relied upon the notion that riders of the right weight could not be found to ride the trotters. In England they formerly had an idea that weight made but little difference to a trotter, and that a light-weight was not calculated for the trotting action. Thus it will be found, that, in many of the old English trotting-matches, the horses carried as much as 168 pounds, even when they were made catch-weight. This was never our opinion in America, as the doings at Baltimore with Lady Kate showed; but there was this truth about the notion — it was better to carry the weight with a good rider that could last all the way, than to put up a light boy who could do nothing after the first two or three miles but just sit on the horse.

The trotting-horse, to do his work well under saddle, has got to be extended so as to go with ease to himself and without danger of breaks. A very considerable pull is often required; and some of those which are not "pullers," in the language of horsemen, would be thought by an amateur to have a great deal of weight on the bit by the time they had gone two miles. They are seldom to be found without a disposition to pull somewhere in the race; and, with a very light boy on the back of them, it would probably be all over then. I find, in looking back at an old English book with which I sometimes amuse myself, that, when Robson's mare trotted seventeen miles in fifty-three minutes, she was ridden by a boy out of the racing-stables, who could ride a trotter, and only weighed about seventy pounds. Now, this mare could not have been a puller, and in that particular, with ability to go a distance, it would be hard to find one like her. Still I venture to say that it would be easier to find such a mare than such a boy. I was light when I rode Lady Kate and Paul Pry, but not so light as that by a great deal. I have said that Paul Pry did not pull in the eighteen-mile race except when the gentleman struck in to keep us company and excited him. That means, that he did not pull so as to distress himself or tire me. He always went up to the bit. In harness, he would pull a man out of the sulky, whether there was company by him or not. Two years before I rode him the time-race, he went against Lady Seyton, three-mile heats in harness. The Lady was the queen of the trotters of that day. She was a chestnut, about fifteen hands two inches high, and blood-like in appearance. My father had her in charge, and I took care of her. Joel Conkling drove, and Matt Clintock drove Paul Pry. The race was over the Centreville. When they started, the gray settled down upon Matt's arms, and pulled about a ton. Lady Seyton went on, and distanced him the first heat in 8m. 11s. That was the first time it was ever made in harness, and the mare was the best of her day.

XIII.

Messenger's Son, Topgallant.—His wonderful Endurance.—My Uncle, George Woodruff.—Topgallant's Race when Twenty-two Years Old.—His Race when Twenty-four Years Old.—Three-mile Heats.—His Race of Three-mile Heats the next Week.

I SHALL now proceed to say something about one of the most remarkable trotting horses that this country ever produced. He was in fact, in some respects, the most extraordinary trotter that ever came under my observation. In the capital points of longevity and endurance, I never knew quite his equal, all things taken into account. When I say longevity, I mean length of days while serviceable as a trotter, and able to meet and beat, very often, the best of his time. I do not mean vegetating about, half dead at the root and rotten at the trunk, as many of the horses spoken of for their longevity have been. It will be remembered that in the early part of this work, while speaking of the best method to be adopted in the raising of colts and the treatment of young horses, I declared my conviction, that, to a certain extent, early maturity and early hard work in training and racing were nearly always followed by premature decay. I have also spoken of the iron constitutions and uncommon durability in point of time, as well as endurance in going a distance by reason of natural stoutness, which were inherited in a remarkable degree by most of those closely descended from the famous horse imported Messenger. That horse I never saw, for he died about seven years before I was born; but, with one of his best sons I had no little acquaintance.

I speak of old Topgallant, one of the best and stoutest that ever looked through a bridle. It will soon be forty years since I first rode the horse at his exercise; and, after he began his racing-career and went into my uncle's hands, we had many a long day together. As I have said, Topgallant was a son of imp. Messenger. He was a dark bay horse, fifteen hands three inches high, plain and raw-boned, but with rather a fine head and neck, and an eye expressive of much courage. He was spavined in both hind-legs, and his tail was slim at the root. His spirit was very high; and yet he was so reliable that he would hardly ever break, and his bottom was of the finest and toughest quality. He was live-oak as well as hickory, for the best of his races were made after he was twenty years old. Topgallant was raised on Long Island. He was more than fourteen years of age before he was known at all as a trotter, except that he could go a distance — the whole length of the New-York road — as well as any horse that had ever been extended on it. Topgallant then belonged to a gentleman named Green; and Mr. M. D. Green, who now resides in the city and is well known, must be acquainted with many particulars about the horse. After a time, when he was well stricken in years, Topgallant was taken to Philadelphia, where he was engaged in many races. It was prior to this when I used first to ride him for exercise.

In the year 1829, when in his twenty-second year, Topgallant trotted four-mile heats against Whalebone, over the Hunting-park Course, Philadelphia; and there were four heats before it was decided. Like Topgallant, Whalebone was a New-York horse. Prior to that time he had been owned by Capt. Dunn, one of the partners of the firm of Brown & Dunn, livery-stable keepers. Whalebone was a remarkably handsome horse, — a fine blood bay, sixteen hands three inches high, and he had but one eye. He ought to have been called Waxy, instead of Whalebone; for in all these particulars he resembled the famous

English thoroughbred of that name, who was the son of Pot-8-os, and the sire of Whalebone, Whisker, Woful, Web, Wire, etc. Of his pedigree nothing was known. He looked like a thoroughbred horse, and was one of the most splendid geldings I ever saw. At the time of the race, Whalebone belonged to Mr. Coddle of Philadelphia, and George Spicer rode him.

Topgallant was trained and ridden by my uncle, George Woodruff, who was then a young man. He was then five feet ten inches high, and one hundred and forty-seven pounds in weight. A finer rider of a trotting-horse was never seen. He was straight, spare, and sinewy, very strong and lasting. He is still the same upright, spare, sinewy man, and as spry as ever with a horse, though more than sixty years of age. Topgallant won the race after a desperate struggle. Whalebone got one heat, and there was a dead one. The time of the heats in this famous race was as follows: 11m. 16s., 11m. 06s., 11m. 17s., and 12m. 15s. Forty-five minutes and forty-four seconds for the sixteen miles, which is just 2m. 52 1-8s. to the mile! Now, was there a horse before, or has there been one since, that in his twenty-second year could beat it? I might go further, and ask whether there will ever be one that can do it again.

The rate of this race was better than twenty miles an hour; and it may well be thought that the old horse of twenty-two years old, who could trot four four-mile heats at a gait that would have made twenty miles in less than fifty-eight minutes, could have gone the twenty in an hour. He could have gone along at an even rate, had it been twenty miles against time, and would not have been pushed along so as to make four miles in 11. 06s., which was at the rate of 2m. 46½s. to the mile. In long performances against time, it is the level, even rate that wins. If Capt. McGowan had been made to go his fifth, sixth, seventh, and eighth miles in 11m. 06s. instead of 11m.

34½s. in which he trotted them, it might have a vast difference at the end of his twenty miles.

But we have not done with this gallant veteran yet. True, he was then in his twenty-second year, and spavined in both legs; but he was a young one compared to some of the poor decrepit animals we sometimes see staggering about, overkneed, and twisted up and knuckled behind, and utterly ruined in constitution, as well as in their legs, before they are ten years old. We must follow the evergreen, live-oak, old Topgallant into his twenty-fourth year, and see what he did when his days were nigh unto those of a quarter of a century. It was in 1831, two years after the race above mentioned, and when the old horse was in his twenty-fourth year, that he and Whalebone and six others met on the Hunting-park Course at Philadelphia, and trotted a race of three-mile heats. Thus there were eight trotters in the race: Dread, ridden by George Spicer; Topgallant, ridden by Matt Clintock in the first three heats, and by Uncle George Woodruff in the fourth; Collector, ridden by Peter Whelan; Chancellor, ridden by Frank Duffy; Whalebone, ridden by Frank Tolbert in the first two heats, but in the third by George Woodruff; Lady Jackson, ridden by John Vanderbilt; Moonshine, by James Hammil; and Columbus, by George Woodruff, until he broke down in the second heat. Dread was a handsome bay gelding, about fifteen hands and an inch, a beautiful goer, and a horse of capital bottom. Columbus was a bright bay horse, sixteen hands high. In the first part of his career he was called the Acker Colt, and at that time George Spicer took care of him. He afterwards went to Philadelphia, and passed into my uncle's care. He was the first horse that ever beat eight minutes in a three-mile heat. Peter Whelan rode him in 7m. 58s.; James Black of Philadelphia owned him at that time. Chancellor was a handsome dapple gray, with a long tail. At that time most of our horses were docked. He was about fifteen hands two inches, and had a deal of style. A little after this race, in the same year and on the same course, he trotted thirty-two miles in two hours; and in that Harvey Richards rode him. Lady Jackson was a red gray mare, fifteen hands and half an inch high. She was quite handsome. Moonshine was a dark gray gelding, fifteen hands and a half high with a long tail. He was a fine, stylish horse.

The odds at the start for the first heat was on Columbus, a hundred to seventy against the field. It was one of the finest sights I ever saw when these eight splendid bays and grays, all in the finest order, and their jockeys in the richest and most varied colors and beautiful costumes, came thundering along for the word, in a group, at the flying trot. Eight such horses and such riders had never met before, and it is doubtful when they will again. Never, certainly, until the good old customs of using trotting-horses under saddle, and requiring the jockeys to ride in dress, are revived.

At the period I speak of, and prior to that, the riders of the trotters had always to be dressed in jockey costume for the race; and there was a great deal of expense and taste laid out in the rich velvets and silks of vivid hue of which the jackets and caps were made up. The word being given, away they went for the first heat of three miles; and Collector had the speed of the party. Columbus did not go as well as usual. At this distance of time, and referring to nothing but my own memory, I do not venture to place all the horses. If it be required, with some further consideration and a look at a document or two calculated to freshen my recollection, I may hereafter do that. I know that Collector won the heat with great ease in 8.16; and that Peter Whelan said afterwards that he could have distanced the whole of the others, in his opinion, if his party had let him go along. The next heat was won by old Topgallant; and in this Columbus broke down. Thereupon, George Woodruff mounted Whalebone for the third heat.

The excitement was very great, and away they went again. This time Dread won; and Whalebone, not having won a heat in three, was ruled out. Now, then, George Woodruff mounted old Topgallant for the last struggle. At that time there was no rule against having more than one horse entered and started in a race of heats from the same stable. In this race we had three, — Topgallant, Whalebone, and Columbus; and such were the vicissitudes and fortunes of the day, that, before it was over, my uncle had ridden them all three. The only horses that had won a heat were Collector, Topgallant, and Dread; and, of course, these alone came to the post for the fourth heat, the great riders, Peter Whelan, George Woodruff, and George Spicer, being on them respectively. The veteran of twenty-four years, old Topgallant, went away under full sail, and led them for two miles and some two or three hundred yards; but Dread then came along and passed him, and won the deciding heat easily.

These horses, it will be perceived, trotted twelve miles; and here was old Topgallant, beaten in the race, it is true, but winner of a heat, and second in the last heat, thus getting second place in the race. The following week, after this great race at Philadelphia, we went to Baltimore, where they gave a purse of three hundred dollars, three-mile heats. Topgallant and Whalebone contended for it; George Woodruff riding Topgallant, and George Spicer, Whalebone. Topgallant won it. This shows the tremendous endurance and recuperative energy of that wonderful horse's constitution. One week a very hard race of four three-mile heats, against all the best horses of the day: the next week another race of three-mile heats against Whalebone; and this Topgallant won easily, being, as I have before said, but which cannot too often be repeated, in his twenty-fourth year.

It is here worthy of remark that Whalebone himself was

driven by my uncle, George Woodruff, thirty-two miles in two hours, over the Hunting-park Course, Philadelphia. In the course of this race against time, the first sulky used broke down on the backstretch of the course, and another had to be sent for and taken to the spot. This caused a delay of four minutes; but nevertheless, when hitched up again, Whalebone went on, and won the race easily. For my part, I admired Whalebone greatly, but I was much attached to old Topgallant. I took care of him at the time of the great race between the eight at the Hunting-park Course, and the one the following week at Baltimore; and I have always been proud, that, so early in my experience of trotting-horses, I knew this almost everlasting son of the renowned Messenger. I have said that this famous trotter was spavined in both hind-legs, and so he was; but the spavins never made him lame, and were really no detriment to him. As a rule, no horse, ever had better legs than the Messengers.

So far as I am informed, there is not another instance in the annals of either the running or the trotting turf, of a horse which has raced and won, especially three and four mile heats, when upwards of twenty years of age. The oldest I can find on the running-turf was Buckhunter, a gelding by the Bald Galloway, who ran in England when upwards of sixteen years old, and might have run on some time longer if he had not broken a leg. The Messengers were always a lasting and long-lived breed of horses. Topgallant was twenty-eight when he died. His sire, Mambrino, was upwards of twenty when last advertised to cover in England, and was eleven when he ran his last race. His sire, Engineer, ran till he was ten, and died at the age of twenty-seven. In this country a daughter of the tribe, Lady Blanche, the first filly that Abdallah got, went a trotting-race when she was about twenty. These things must be borne in mind.

XIV.

The Indian Horse Lylee. — Runjeet Singh's Passion for Horses. — The Battles fought for Lylee. — Description of him. — Lady Blanche. — Awful. — His Race with Screwdriver. — Blanche, Snowdrop, and Beppo. — Death of Blanche. — Ajax and Oneida Chief. — Their Road-Race to Sleighs. — Brown Rattler.

ALTHOUGH Topgallant was the most remarkable instance of extraordinary trotting power and endurance, when at a great age, that ever came under my notice, he was not the only one. Most of those which have been celebrated for this capital excellence were of the Messenger blood; and it will be remembered that I noticed this point in that strain of horses when mentioning them in the prior chapters of this work. Singularly enough, it happens that I took up an old book of travels a day or two ago, which made mention of a very celebrated horse, one who is indeed historical, that had all the external points of that family. I do not, of course, pretend to say that he was of the blood, for the horse in question was in the East Indies; but, as he was undoubtedly produced by a union of the Arab or other Eastern breed with some horse either English or of English origin, he may have been more nearly related to Messenger, Mambrino, and Engineer, than one would at the first suppose, when I say that he lived and died on the banks of the Indus. I allude to the old horse Lylee, the prime favorite of the Maharajah, Runjeet Singh, the old "Lion of the Punjaub" as the British called him. This great warrior prince had, in common with many other remarkable men, an extraordinary passion for horses. It was so strong, that it passed into a proverb in the East, and some said amounted to a species of insanity. His name was great among all the teeming myriads of that ancient land; and whenever it was mentioned, either by Brahmin, Mussulman, or European, it was almost always coupled with that of his favorite steed, the gray horse Lylee.

Old Runjeet spent untold millions upon his stud; and his horses were caparisoned in so sumptuous a manner that it would have raised the envy of a Broadway belle. Bridles and saddles inlaid with gold and studded with precious stones; necklaces of costly gems, fastened underneath with onyx (believed to possess talismanic virtue); and hangings of the richest stuff which goes to make the famous shawls of Cashmere, — were the trappings of the celebrated stallions. But though more richly adorned than the steed of Caligula, the horses of Runjeet Singh were kept for use as much as show. The old monarch was a desperate rider, as well as one of the greatest warriors that India has ever seen. He computed, that, from first to last, Lylee had cost him no less than three millions of dollars and the lives of twelve thousand men. The horse, when he first became celebrated, was the property of Yan Mohammed Khan, who ruled a great tract of country, and had his capital at Peshawur. The fame of Lylee soon spread through all the vast regions watered by the Indus and its tributaries; and Runjeet Singh, unable to obtain him by negotiation, went to war for him. After a long contest, the arms of the Maharajah prevailed; and he made it a preliminary condition of peace that Lylee should be delivered to him.

Mohammed Khan had failed to defend the possession of Lylee by the sword, and now sought to evade his delivery by chicane. He at first pretended that the horse was dead, and, when Runjeet was not to be put off by that subterfuge, sought to impose another horse on him instead of the real Lylee. Before Runjeet Singh had obtained possession of the horse, Yan Mohammed died, and his brother, Sooltan

Mohammed, succeeded to the throne at Peshawur. He continued to interpose prevarication and procrastination to the demands of the Maharajah; but the matter was finally brought to an issue by one Ventura, an Italian soldier of fortune, and a general in Runjeet's service. Having made another formal demand for Lylee, he was met, as all the other negotiators had been, with quibbles from Sooltan Khan; whereupon, calling up a lot of soldiers whom he had instructed to straggle after him into the courtyard of the palace, he declared Sooltan his prisoner. Thereupon Lylee was delivered up; but, to maintain possession of him, the Maharajah was obliged to fight another war.

In 1839, this horse was seen by some English officers. He was then *very old*—they could not say how old—and feeble; a flee-bitten gray, standing over sixteen hands high, and with all the plain strength of a coarse, thoroughbred horse. So much for Lylee, whose description would answer well for one of the Messengers.

We will pass from him to one that was unquestionably of the Messenger blood,—the gray mare Lady Blanche, by Abdallah. This mare was raised by Mr. John Treadwell, who also raised her sire Abdallah, on the island here. She was certainly one of the first foals, if not the very first, that Abdallah got. According to Mr. Treadwell, and the unbroken tradition of his men, she was the first got by that grandson of imported Messenger. Lady Blanche was a handsome gray mare, fifteen hands two and a half inches high, with a long tail. She was foaled in 1829, and, when rising six years old, was matched against Awful to trot under saddle for two thousand dollars a side, half forfeit, over the Centreville Course. At that time, Awful was owned by Mr. S. Neal of New York. He cut his quarter, and was compelled to pay forfeit. He was a bay, fifteen hands two inches high, and a lofty goer.

After this match, he was sold to the Messrs. Anderson of New York, and matched against Screwdriver, a sorrel pony, the property of Washington Costar of New York. The race was three-mile heats, in harness, over the Centreville Course, for one thousand dollars a side; and Awful won it easily in two heats. I afterwards beat him several times with Dutchman, but shall reserve reciting the facts until we come down to the career of that horse. On the day set down for the race between Lady Blanche and Awful, the mare was led on to the course by Mr. Treadwell, his farmer John being already in the saddle to ride her. Much to the disappointment of many, forfeit was declared on the part of Awful. After that Mr. Treadwell used to drive Lady Blanche on the road, in an old stick sulky that he had got, and he put her through some sharp work. At a later period, Tom Hyer had her, and banged her up and down the roads and all about New York for a long time. He always thought a vast deal of this gray mare; and, if she had not inherited the cast-steel qualities of the Messenger tribe, I doubt whether she would ever have recovered from the effects of his system of driving.

The mare was getting on in years, all battered up, and apparently worn out; so Tom Hyer sold her in the ring at Tattersall's for less than one hundred dollars. Mr. George Hopkins bought her, and sent her to the West, — to Wisconsin, I believe. She was there until she was more than twenty years old, when he got her back, and sold her to Mr. S. D. Hoagland. Her capacity as a trotter at such an age was very remarkable. She was either twenty-three or twenty-four years old, — probably the latter, — when she went against Snowdrop and Beppo on the Union Course. Snowdrop was a white gelding, fifteen hands high, — a handsome horse: I drove him. Beppo, a chestnut, scant fifteen hands, and a stylish stepper, was driven by Dan Pfifer. The old mare, driven by Sim Hoagland, won it in four heats, the best of which was 2.43, or thereabouts. The next week, Lady Blanche and Beppo went to wagons, the same drivers. Hoagland's weight at that time was from two hundred and five pounds to two hundred and ten pounds; but old Blanche was well put up to pull it. Blanche won the second race. Prior to those, she won one on the road, ridden by Harry Jones; but I did not see it.

In 1855, this famous old mare literally "died in harness." Mr. Hoagland had been working her with the intention to take her to Baltimore to trot against Sorrel Fanny, who had challenged the world, for her age. She was twenty-two; Blanche was twenty-five, and would certainly have warmed her if she had lived a little longer. Mr. Hoagland had been at the track that morning with Blanche, and she never went better. She looked as fine as silk, too, considering her great age and what she had gone through. He put her under the shed at John I. Snediker's, and all at once saw a spasm go through her. As soon as the mare could be got out of the shafts, she laid herself gently down, and died of enlargement of the heart. You may see her picture at Hoagland's, at East New York. It represents her doing all she knows; and Sim is well painted, with a look of satisfaction beaming on his face, driving her.

Another instance of great staying power at an advanced age was Ajax, who was also by Abdallah. He was out of a good little road-mare, and was a handsome, stout, brown horse, fourteen hands three inches high, with a long tail and slim at the root like his sire. This little horse had immense power. He was built a good deal like his nephew Dexter, by Hambletonian, but was even thicker through behind. When Ajax was sixteen years of age, he was matched to trot against Mr. Charlick's bay mare twenty miles under saddle, for one thousand dollars a side. Stephen Weart owned Ajax; Isaac Woodruff rode him. C. S. Bartine, who afterwards drove Trustee the twenty miles within an hour, rode Mr. Charlick's mare. Ajax beat her very handily. The mare was pulled out before the finish; and the little horse went on, and completed the distance.

Ajax was foaled at Bath, Long Island, in 1832. In

1836, when he was four years old, I drove him a mile on the Centreville Course in three minutes and thirty seconds. At that time he belonged to Mr. Edwards of Philadelphia. Being disposed of, he fell into the hands of Mr. Samuel Coope of Brooklyn, and was used by him on the road for some years. In the winter of 1842, I drove him a noted match to sleighs against the celebrated pacer Oneida Chief, who was afterwards taken to England. The Chief was the best pacer we had had at that time; but, nevertheless, Ajax was matched to go the length of the road against him, from Bradshaw's, near Harlem Bridge, to the pavements at Twenty-eighth Street. Oneida Chief was a handsome chestnut, with three white legs and a blaze. He stood about fifteen hands and half an inch. The match was made one afternoon to go the next day. Mr. Harry Jones drove the pacer. It was a very cold day, and the snow somewhat drifted. At that time there were but few houses along the road, except for public accommodation. Where the Central Park now is was a rough, desolate tract.

At the start from Bradshaw's, I went away at a good rate, for I knew the bottom of the gallant little Ajax, and relied upon it to cut down his opponent in the length of the road. It was lined on both sides, from Bradshaw's to the city; and I question whether there were ever as many out at one time since that day. There they were in the snow, buttoned and muffled up, and their noses blue with cold, or red from the effects of the hot apple-jack they ran into the houses every now and then to take. At last we came, squaring away, and going through them pretty fast. The snow flew where it had drifted; and the runners of the sleighs made it shriek again, as they slid over it to the music of the bells. I kept ahead, making the pace hot; and, when we had gone two miles and a quarter to Yorkville, Jones gave it up, and stopped the pacer. After that, many others turned in to brush with me as I went along; but none of them could live far with Ajax. As we neared the city, the crowds grew greater; there was more noise and cheering, and more furious jangling of the sleigh-bells as the gentlemen drove their horses about, up and down the sides of the road. The more the noise and confusion, the greater the speed of Ajax. He got upon his mettle; and towards the last of it, we went so fast, that the people could recognize neither him nor me, and remained in doubt what it was that had gone by like a flash, through the crowd, and won it. There was not a horse in America capable of beating Ajax from Bradshaw's to the pavement on that day. That was sleighing!

In the following year, Ajax, being then eleven years old, was matched against Brown Rattler of Baltimore, three-mile heats, under saddle, on the Beacon Course, New Jersey. I rode Ajax; James Whelply rode Brown Rattler. The day was rainy, and the course very heavy. Ajax carried fifteen pounds over weight; for, with the saddle, I was a hundred and sixty pounds. We distanced the Baltimore horse the first heat; the time of the miles being 2.44, 2.42, 2.37,—total three miles, 8.03. Ajax was a wonderful little horse to carry weight and stay. Indeed, he was only little in height, being a big horse on short legs. Ajax went another race with a horse that was afterwards taken to England, besides the one with the pacer Oneida Chief. It was Sir William, a chestnut gelding, fifteen hands and an inch high, and with one white foot behind. He was a fine-looking horse, and a great strider. Whether they put him to good use in England, I have never learned. The race between him and Ajax was three-mile heats, under saddle, on the Beacon Course. Sir William was handled by George Spicer, and ridden by John Spicer. Ajax got one heat, but lost the other two and the race.

XV.

The Trotter Dutchman. — Description of him. — Pedigree doubtful. — Dutchman and Locomotive. — Dutchman and Yankee Doodle. — Dutchman, Fanny Pullen, and Confidence. — Dutchman and Lady Slipper. — Dutchman, Lady Warrenton, Teamboat, and Norman Leslie. — Dutchman and Greenwich Maid. — Dutchman and Washington. — Dutchman, Lady Suffolk, and Rattler. — Description of Lady Suffolk and Rattler.

I SHALL now give a sketch of one of the most famous trotters that ever was known. I speak of Dutchman, who, for the combined excellences of speed, bottom, and constitutional vigor, equal to the carrying on of a long campaign and improving on it, has had few if any equals, and certainly no superior. His time for three miles still stands the best on the record. Flora Temple and General Butler, both horses of great speed and bottom, tried to beat it, but failed; and yet it was not up to the highest mark that Dutchman could have made that day. But of this feat I shall speak as it comes along in the order of his performances, before entering on which it will be proper to give some idea of his appearance. Dutchman was a bay gelding, fifteen hands three inches high, very powerfully made, with every part clean cut, and the very best of legs and feet.

He was raised in New Jersey; but I never knew his pedigree, nor ever met any one who did. This is to be regretted; for he was a horse of such great stamp and high courage, that it would be interesting to know at least a little of the sources from which he sprang. This, however, we never can know. I have seen letters which purported to give his pedigree, but have never met with an account which at all satisfied me, or corresponded with that which was said about the horse when I first knew him. It has been said that he was got by a thoroughbred imported horse, and I have no doubt that his ancestry was well bred. His form, temper, and general characteristics denoted a horse of very considerable breeding; but the definite accounts that I have heard and seen in regard to it rest upon insufficient authority to satisfy me. He was not the coarse, ungainly horse that many suppose him to have been. His points were good, though some of them were rather plain, and every thing about him indicated a horse of uncommon resolution and bottom, with a strong dash of temper.

When I first saw Dutchman he was five years old, and belonged to Mr. Jeffers of Philadelphia. He worked in a string-team in a brick-cart, and did his full share of the hauling. It was found that the bay horse was a good stepper, and they began to drive him on the road to a wagon. He could then go a little better than a mile in three minutes. Mr. Jeffers soon sold him to Mr. Peter Barker of New York, and he had him pricked and docked. The operation was performed by George Hazard, and before Dutchman had entirely recovered from its effects he was engaged for his first trot. The match was mile and repeat, in harness, with a horse called Locomotive, to go on the Harlem track. It was made in a hurry one afternoon, and Dutchman was taken out of the pulleys the next day to trot. Harry Jones drove him, and Albert Conklin was behind the other horse. Dutchman won this in two heats.

The same year, later in the fall, he trotted a match for $1,000 a side, from Cato's to Harlem, along Third Avenue. The distance was about four miles, and they went to road-wagons. Mr. Barker drove Dutchman. The other, a brown gelding called Yankee Doodle, was driven by Mr. Daniel Costar of New York. Dutchman won easily. His speed and bottom were now so well thought of, that in 1836 he was entered in a sweepstakes with Fanny Pullen and Confidence. Fanny Pullen was afterwards the dam of the chestnut gelding Trustee, by imported Trustee, who first trotted twenty miles within an hour in harness. She was herself a chestnut, standing fifteen hands high, and was raised in the State of Maine. Confidence was a handsome bay gelding, fifteen hands high. Of his pedigree nothing definite was known. He was afterwards purchased for Mr. Osbaldeston, the "Old Squire" of English sporting history, and taken over to that country. Mr. Osbaldeston drove Confidence there many years, and trotted him some races. That gentleman had some of the best racers, hunters, and steeple-chasers in England; but, when he wanted first-class trotters, he took good care to send to America for them.

The sweepstakes race was $1,000 each, two-mile heats, in harness, over the Centreville Course. Joel Conkling drove Dutchman; Harry Jones, Fanny Pullen; James M. Hammill of Philadelphia, Confidence. The latter was a Philadelphia horse then, being owned by Daniel Daniels of that city. Daniels was called "Deaf Dan" at that time; and he is the man to whom Dr. Weldon alluded in his famous letter vindicating the probity of turfmen, and insisting upon the veracity of trainers. The betting ran very high on the race. The Eastern men backed Fanny Pullen with great spirit. The Philadelphians put up strongly on Confidence. The New-Yorkers stuck to Dutchman, and a very large amount of money changed hands. Dutchman won it in two heats, and Fanny was second, the time being 5.17½ and 5.18½. The first heat was the fastest two miles that had been made in harness. Dutchman was in for business now. Only a little time elapsed before he was matched to go four-mile heats under saddle against Lady Slipper.

It was over the Centreville Course; and the day was that for the great match between the North and the South, in which John Bascomb ran against Postboy, four-mile heats, over the Union Course. The two races attracted immense numbers of people, for the courses were so near together that both events could be witnessed without any trouble. The running-race came off first; and, after it was over, the road to the Centreville was as full of carriages and wagons as it could be. There were many thousands of people present when the horses were brought out on the course. Dutchman was the favorite. He was ridden by William Whelan, and won it in two heats. Lady Slipper was a white mare, about fourteen hands three inches high. George Spicer rode her that day. She was afterwards taken to England, but I do not know what was made of her there.

The same year, in the fall, Dutchman was entered in a sweepstakes with Lady Warrenton, Teamboat, and Norman Leslie, three-mile heats, under saddle. It came off at Trenton, N. J., and was five hundred dollars each. Lady Warrenton was a white mare from Baltimore, standing about fifteen hands high; and she was a good one. Teamboat was a chestnut gelding, sixteen hands high, and so called because he had been employed in one of the teams that pull the barges along the levels. Norman Leslie was a black gelding, fifteen hands and an inch high. Lady Warrenton won this race; and it was the first time that Dutchman met with a defeat. In the following week, he was matched with the Lady, three-mile heats, under saddle, over the Hunting-park Course, Philadelphia. In this race, George Spicer rode Dutchman, and beat the mare in two heats. It was a rainy day, and the course was heavy. This made little difference to Dutchman, who was a strong horse, able to go in heavy ground, and keep going with the weights up. He was also a grand horse for all sorts of weather; and, when once in fine condition, would stand as much wear and tear, and keep going on, as long as any horse I ever knew, and this when the races were all of long heats. Soon after this race, Dutchman fell lame behind, and was turned out. He ran out for sixteen or eighteen months. When he was taken up to be put in work again, he came to me; and this was the beginning of

10

a long and eventful connection between us. At the first of it we did not meet with success; but I knew, that, if he kept on, it would be sure to come. He was then ten years old; and his first trot in my hands was against Greenwich Maid, a bay mare, fifteen hands high.

The race was two-mile heats, in harness, over the Beacon Course, New Jersey; and the mare won it in two heats, the best of which was 5m. 16s. Shortly afterwards, Dutchman trotted two-mile heats against Washington over the same course. Washington was a gray gelding, sixteen hands high, very speedy, but having the peculiarity that he would go all to pieces if not checked up close. He also beat Dutchman in two heats; and the best of them was 5m. 16s., as Greenwich Maid's had been.

The same year Dutchman went for a purse over the Beacon Course against Lady Suffolk and Rattler, two-mile heats, under saddle. Rattler was a bay gelding, fifteen hands high, a fast and stout horse, though light-waisted, and delicate in appetite and constitution. At that time he would sometimes only eat six quarts of oats a day; and the trainer was doing uncommonly well when he got nine quarts into him. He was afterwards taken to England, and, take him for all in all, was the best American trotter that ever went there. William Whelan went over with him, but not before we had some desperate struggles between him and Dutchman.

Lady Suffolk was a gray mare about fifteen hands and an inch. She was got by Engineer, son of imported Messenger, and was certainly a tremendous mare, well worthy of her illustrious descent. She was bred on Long Island, in Suffolk County, and thus got the name of Lady Suffolk. When she was three years old, David Bryan bought her of the farmer who raised her, for ninety dollars. In the race of which I am now writing, Bryan rode Lady Suffolk, Bill Whelan rode Rattler, and I rode Dutchman. We won it in two heats, of 5.11–5.13.

Shortly after this, a match was made between Dutchman and Rattler to go three-mile heats under saddle, for two thousand dollars, on the Beacon Course. Dutchman was the favorite, but Rattler was in fine condition that day; and a desperate struggle ensued between the horses and their riders, William Whelan and myself. In the first heat, we went away together; and at any time in the course a sheet would have covered both horses. It was very close at the finish; but Rattler won by half a length. Dutchman made a break in the heat, the only one he made in the race; and that enabled Rattler to win it in 7m. 45½s. The second heat was like the first. We went away together; and it was hard to say which had the advantage for two miles and a half. Sometimes one would be a head in front, and then the other would come up and get the lead by a neck. But they were never clear of each other; and, at the drawgate in the third mile, it was head-and-head. But Rattler now broke (this was the only break he made in the race), and Dutchman won the heat in 7.50.

I have not since seen such a heat as that which ensued. Over the whole distance of ground, three miles, it was literally a neck-and-neck struggle. Nothing could have been finer to the spectators than the desperate and long-sustained efforts of these capital horses, aided by the exertions and judgment of the riders. Neither horse was clear of the other at any time; and, when we had both used our utmost endeavors to land a winner, if only by half a head, the judges declared that it was a dead heat in 8.02. In the fourth heat, the struggle was again as close as could be for upwards of two miles; but then the unrivalled bottom of Dutchman obtained the superiority. At the end of the eleventh mile, the pace and distance began to tell on Rattler; and Dutchman won it handily in 8.24.

Just such a race as this it has never been my fortune to see since, and nobody had seen such a one before. For eleven miles the horses were never clear of each other;

and, when Dutchman left Rattler in the twelfth, it was by inches only. Moreover, there were but two breaks in this race, and each horse made but one in his twelve miles. That was trotting; and, though both the horses afterwards acquired more speed, they never exhibited more obstinate game or more thorough bottom than in this race. Rattler was an honest, fast horse, with a great deal of bottom in his light, waspy, wiry make. He was a very long strider; and, when going his best, it sometimes seemed as though his thin waist would part in the middle. That was the last time of his trotting before he went with Whelan to England. In that country he beat the Birmingham mare and Glasgow mare, and challenged the world.

I was within an ace at one time of going over with Dutchman to take up the challenge, but did not do so Whelan says he could have beaten me in England; for Rattler had taken to hearty feeding and gained strength, and much improved in speed. But the truth is, that Dutchman had shown increased speed, too; and I had no doubt then, nor have I had any since, about his ability to beat Rattler, if he had gone to England and done well. I think, too, that the strong probability of this will appear to the reader, when we come to review the performances, since unequalled in spite of all our improvement and latter-day advantages, which Dutchman afterwards made in my hands. As I have said above, his three-mile time yet stands at the head of the record; and, though it is often said that it would be very easy to beat it, I think we may reasonably conclude, in view of the failure of Flora Temple and General Butler to do so, that it is not quite so easy as it seems. Besides, I always remark, when this allegation is made, that it would have been easy for Dutchman to do the three miles faster than he did; and this I shall prove when we come to speak of the time-race. It would, however, be easy for Butler to beat it under saddle.

XVI.

Dutchman and Lady Suffolk. — Dutchman, Lady Suffolk, Mount Holly, and Harry Bluff. — Dutchman and Awful. — Dutchman against Time, Three Miles. — The Race and Incidents.

IN resuming the history of Dutchman, we begin again at the close of the great race of four three-mile heats; in which he won a hard and very stoutly-contested struggle with Rattler, just prior to that horse's voyage to England, where, as I have before remarked, he greatly distinguished himself under the care and superintendence of Wm. Whelan. It was not only found that he was vastly superior to any English-bred trotter, but also to those which had been imported into England from this country. Several of these had been horses of fine speed and bottom. It was, however, no more than might have been expected, that Rattler should excel them all; for he was very near indeed to Dutchman when he left this country. It was a very close thing between them; and I have learned, that, after he arrived in the island, the air and strong feed so agreed with him, that he displayed more vigor and bottom than he had done while he was in this country.

It was now the spring of 1839, and Dutchman had been in my hands a year. We commenced the operations of that memorable season with a trot between Dutchman and Lady Suffolk, over the Beacon Course, New Jersey, two-mile heats, under saddle. As a matter of course, I rode the old bay horse, and David Bryan rode the gray Lady of Suffolk. Dutchman won it handily in two heats of 5m. 9s., 5m. 11s. That was the beginning of the season, and early for a beginning at that. In the month of May we went to Baltimore, to trot three-mile heats, under saddle, with three other horses. There was Lady Suffolk, who was now developed into a regular campaigner, and was a wonderful mare; Mount Holly, a white gelding, fifteen hands high—how related to the Messenger horse of that name, who is among the forefathers of the Black gelding General Butler, I am unable to say; and Harry Bluff, a bay gelding, fifteen hands three inches high. Dutchman won the race in two heats of 7m. 56s., 7m. 53s.

On our return home from Baltimore, we had a meeting with Awful, the bay gelding before spoken of as having been matched with Lady Blanche, the daughter of Abdallah, when six years old, and paid forfeit to her in consequence of lameness; and, as having afterwards defeated Screwdriver, three-mile heats, in harness, over the Centreville Course. The race between Dutchman and Awful was on the 4th of July, and was three-mile heats, in harness. Dutchman won it, distancing Awful in the first heat, in the then amazing time of 7m. 41s. At the start for this race, the odds were 100 to 25 on Awful; and the result, with the time in which it was achieved, caused a large amount of wonder and discussion. This three miles in harness was then the greatest performance that had ever been made; and it will be found, upon investigation, that it has very seldom been surpassed since that date, almost twenty-six years ago. Flora Temple was the first that ever beat it; and, if I am not mistaken, the only others that have done so are General Butler—when he went in harness against Dutchman's saddle-time—and Stonewall Jackson of Hartford, in his three-mile race in 1866 on the Fashion Course against Shark.

It will be remembered, in estimating the merit and value of this performance, that since it was made, above a quarter of a century has passed away, of an age renowned above all preceding ones in history for progress; that all the efforts of breeders, breakers, trainers, and drivers have been directed to improve the speed of our trotting-horse to the highest rate attainable, consistent with the faculty of endurance; that neither pains nor perseverance have been spared to perfect our modern courses; and that all the skill and ingenuity of an intelligent class of our mechanics have been successfully applied to the production of the best and lightest vehicles for trotting purposes. The sulky in which Dutchman trotted on that day weighed 82lbs. I have now two that weigh less than 60lbs. each. My weight in driving was from 148lbs. to 150lbs. Dutchman took the lead at starting, and kept it all the way. The time of the first mile was 2m. 34s.; the second was trotted in 2m. 33s.; and, in the third, we returned to the rate of the first, 2m. 34s. By considering this, we shall perceive the even rate and great durability of this renowned horse. He put the miles closer together than any horse had ever done prior to that race, and finished the three miles in less aggregate time, taking the whip nearly all the way and never making a break. I ventured to keep him going from the score, and to put the whip on from time to time; and for this I had warrant in three things: I knew he was honest, and would answer every call to the last gasp; I knew that he was as stout as oak and as tough as whalebone, and needed no saving; and I knew that he was in good condition. Whenever the reader has got hold of a horse in whom these good qualities are united, and who is to trot a long race against another, supposed to be his superior in point of speed, he need not be afraid to burst him off and keep going. But he had better be quite sure that they are all there; because, if it should turn out that any of them is lacking, it would probably endanger the race.

It is a matter of course that 7m. 41s. in harness would not be a great performance at this time; and it is very likely that a horse or two could be found able to trot three miles in harness in 7m. 31s., when thoroughly fit and properly driven. But it must not be forgotten that the conditions then existing were very different from those we find in operation now. All these improvements and alterations to which I have alluded above have been in favor of the horses of the present day; and therefore the champions of old times are entitled to much allowance in forming an estimate of the comparative greatness of their performances.

A match was now made between Dutchman and Awful, to trot over the Beacon Course for $1,000 a side, mile-heats, three in five, in harness. It took place on the 18th of July. Dutchman was the favorite for this, and won it handily in three heats, of 2m. 35s., 2m. 32s., 2m. 35s. That same evening the match against time was made which has, ever since its performance, been one of the most famous events in the annals of our turf. Mr. John Harrison backed Dutchman to trot three miles under saddle over the Beacon Course, on the 1st of August, for $1,000 a side. Mr. Isaac Anderson backed time. The horse was to have two trials, if necessary, and was to be allowed an hour between them. The time set was 7m. 39s. If Dutchman made the three miles in that, or in less time, he won the match. He had gone in 7m. 41s. in harness, as I have before remarked, and therefore it was a good match for the backers of the horse. It seemed to me that the only question was whether Dutchman would be fit and well on the day. If he was he could not lose it. At the time it was made, the horse, as I have said in speaking of his Fourth-of-July trot, was in condition. He was well seasoned; and, between the making of the match on the 18th of July and the 1st of August when it was trotted, he had just his usual work. Prior to this time, Dutchman had been purchased of Minturn, Conklin, Vooris, & Co., for $3,000, by James Hammil of Philadelphia. He was bought by Hammil for Gen. Cadwallader, heretofore spoken of as one of the most liberal turfmen of that day.

The 1st of August came; the ardent summer sun rising bright and clear, and assuming his reign over a very warm day. We let him sink towards his haven in the golden west before we prepared for the race. The course was fine, a large concourse of people were in attendance, and the odds were two to one on Dutchman when we brought him out and stripped him. At six o'clock in the evening, he was saddled; and I mounted, feeling fully confident that the feat set would be done with much ease. We were allowed a running-horse to keep company; and I had a nice blood-like mare, she being under my brother Isaac.

We went off at a moderate jog, gradually increasing the pace, but conversing part of the way at our ease. Isaac asked me how fast I thought I could go the mile; to which I replied, "About two minutes, thirty-five." It was accomplished in 2m. 34½s., and Dutchman never was really extended. Now occurred a circumstance which must be related, because it was curious in itself, and had its effect on the time. Mr. Harrison, the backer of Dutchman, had lent his watch to a friend, and was not keeping time of the horses himself as they went round. As we came by the stand, some bystander, who had made a mistake in timing, told him that the time of the mile was 2.38, which was a losing average. He therefore called out to me as I passed him, to go along; and go along I did. Dutchman struck a great pace on the back-stretch, and had established such a fine stroke that the running-mare was no longer able to live with him. My brother Isaac got alarmed, and sung out to me that I was going too fast. I replied that I had been told to go along. It was not my conviction that the horse was going too fast even then; for if ever there was one that I could feel of, and that felt all over strong and capable of maintaining the rate, Dutchman did then. Nevertheless, I took a pull for Isaac, and allowed him to come up and keep company for the balance of the mile. It was performed in 2.28 very handily.

The third mile we kept the same relative positions; Dutchman being under a good pull all the way, and able to have left the running-mare had he been called upon so to do. The rate was now very even; and it was maintained until we were within about two hundred yards of the stand, when I was notified to check up, and come home at a more moderate gait. I therefore crossed the score at a jog-trot, and Dutchman was at a walk within fifteen yards of it. The last mile was 2.30, the whole being 7.32½. Great as this performance was thought at the time, long as it has since stood unequalled, and great and deserved as has been, and is, the fame of those who have endeavored to surpass it, I declare that it was not by any means all that Dutchman could have done that day. I am positive, that, if he had been called upon to do so, he could have trotted the three miles in 7.27, *or better*. This is no light opinion of mine, taken up years afterwards on inadequate grounds, and when those who might be opposed to it had gone from among us: it was the judgment of those who saw him in the feat, observed him all through, and noticed how he finished. He as much surpassed any thing that the public had expected of him as could well be conceived; and yet the three-mile heat in harness in which he distanced Awful was warrant to look out for something great. It has always been my conviction, and will remain so to my dying day, that Dutchman could have done the last mile handily in *two minutes and twenty-six seconds;* and I even hold to the opinion that he could have done it in 2.25. The people who witnessed the race thought so too.

As for the second mile, which he made in 2.28, it was one of the easiest I ever rode in my life. In the great burst of speed he made when Harrison called to me to go along, and Dutchman went away from the running-mare, the horse was strong, collected, and his long, quick stroke very even. At all other times in the race he seemed to be going well within himself; and, in setting down his mark that day at *seven minutes twenty-seven seconds,* I am confident that I allow him quite time enough. The truth is, that he was a most extraordinary horse. There have been many trotters that could go as fast for a little way; but the beauty of Dutchman was, that he could go fast and go all day. To beat the time he actually made would be easy enough to a fast horse of good bottom; but to beat the mark I have set as that of which he was capable, and I know I am inside the truth, would not be so easy. It is, however, never to be lost sight of, that the tendency of things ever since Dutchman's day has been towards increased speed. There has been a general set of the current in that direction; and horses that are comparatively at a stand-still as regards other horses of their own day have, nevertheless, advanced in regard to time and the dead.

XVII.

Dutchman and Washington. — Dutchman, Washington, and the Ice Pony. — Washington's best Mark. — Dutchman and Rifle. — Dutchman, Americus, and Lady Suffolk. — A Great Race in a Great Storm. — Dutchman, Oneida Chief, and Lady Suffolk. — Dutchman's Last Race. — His Death.

SHORTLY after Dutchman's great time race, he left my stable, and was taken to Philadelphia by James Hammil, who, as before mentioned, had purchased him for Gen. Cadwallader. In the spring of 1840 he returned to New York in charge of Hammil, and was matched against Lady Suffolk to trot over the Centreville Course, two-mile heats under saddle. Hammil rode Dutchman, and Bryant the Lady of Suffolk. She beat Dutchman the first heat in 4m. 59s., and I then mounted for the second. She beat him again, the time being 5m. 3s. I could not quite satisfactorily account for his being beaten in that time, after what I knew he could do when all right. Whether he was short of work, I cannot precisely determine, as he was not in my hands, and I had not seen him in the course of his training that year; but he did not appear to be as stout and as willing as I had found him the previous season, and afterwards found him again.

That same summer he trotted with Washington over the Centreville Course, two-mile heats in harness. Washington was then in my stable; and with him I beat Dutchman in two straight heats, the best being 5m. 16s. From thence we went to Philadelphia, and trotted over the Hunting-park

Course for a purse, two-mile heats in harness. Washington beat Dutchman again in two heats, the best of which was again 5m. 16s. In the first heat, Hammil drove him; in the second, George Spicer got in. Our next meeting was on the Herring-run Course at Baltimore, where I trotted Washington against Dutchman and Ice Pony two-mile heats in harness. The Pony was a brown gelding, fourteen hands three inches high, and a fine, gallant-going little horse. He had not what I consider great staying qualities; but he had the gift of speed in a high degree. He got the name he bore from having trotted on the ice in Maine, from whence he came. Col. C. Bartine drove the Pony, Hammil drove Dutchman, and I drove Washington. The latter won it in two straight heats, and the best of them this time was 5m. 16½s. The pony led for a mile and a half; but I judged that he would be sure to "come back" to us before he had got twice round, and so kept my weather-eye on Dutchman. I must mention here, that, prior to this trip South, I trotted Washington against Dutchman two-mile heats in harness over the Beacon Course, and won in two heats, the best of them being 5m. 16s.

It is rather a curious circumstance, that, when Washington was all right he could trot two miles in harness in just five minutes and sixteen seconds; and, if called upon for better time, he could not make it. That was his best mark; but, if in condition, he could be relied upon to do it with certainty. After our return from Baltimore, we trotted two-mile heats in harness over the Beacon Course, New Jersey, and Dutchman won it in three heats. Washington got the first in 5m. 16s. again. Dutchman got the second and third. Dutchman now returned to Philadelphia, and met Rifle in two races on the Hunting-park Course, mile-heats, three in five, one in harness, the other under saddle. Rifle was a handsome little bay horse, fifteen hands high. He and Lady Suffolk performed the first great feat in double harness, distancing Mr. Frank Duffy's bay-team, Apology and Hardware, in 5m. 19s. The first mile was 2m. 42s., the second 2m. 37s.

At that time this was considered a very great performance, and it was so. We had not then the number of opulent gentlemen trying to get fast horses for double harness that we have now. Mr. Bonner's mares, Flatbush Maid and Lady Palmer, have gone the distance over the Fashion Course, driven by himself to his light road-wagon, in 5.01¼, — an astonishing thing. But it is to be remembered that Suffolk and Rifle made their performance more than twenty years ago, and that time, in all ways of going, has been greatly reduced since then.

The Lady and Rifle were driven by James Whelpley. The first race between Dutchman and Rifle was in harness. I drove Dutchman, and Whelpley Rifle; and I won in three heats. In the saddle-race, he beat me the first heat in 2.34. James Hammil then got on Dutchman, won the second heat in 2.38, and got the third and fourth handily.

In 1843 Dutchman was brought to New York again, and placed in my charge. Our first race that season, and it was the last season that the old horse trotted on the turf, was against Americus and Lady Suffolk, two-mile heats in harness, over the Beacon Course. Bryant drove the Lady, Spicer Americus, and I Dutchman. Dutchman won the first heat, Americus the second, and Dutchman the third. Lady Suffolk was third in all the heats. In a week or ten days thereafter, we went three-mile heats in harness, over the Beacon Course, and it was a tremendous race of four heats. The first was won by Dutchman. The second was stoutly contested, but Americus won it. The third heat was very hotly contested, and resulted in a dead heat between the old horse and Americus. Lady Suffolk was now ruled out for not winning a heat in three, and the betting was heavy, Dutchman having the call.

The long summer day had drawn rapidly to a close. At the same time the heavens were overcast; and with fading gleams of dim, yellow light, the sun sank into great banks of clouds. They mounted higher and higher, and seemed to lie like a load upon the weary earth. The heat was intense; and not a breath of air was stirring to break the ominous repose. With the last flicker of day, the swift scud began to fly overhead, and the solid-seeming clouds to tower up and come on like moving mountains. It was dark when we got into our sulkies; and, soon after the start, the storm burst upon us with a fury that I have never since seen equalled. The wind blew a hurricane, and the pelting rain fell in torrents, as though the sluices of the skies had opened all at once. Nothing could have overpowered the mighty rush of the wind and the furious splash of the rain but the dread, tremendous rattle of the thunder. It seemed to be discharged right over our heads, and only a few yards above us. Nothing could have penetrated the thick, profound gloom of that darkness but the painful blue blaze of the forked lightning. I could not see, in the short intervals between the flashes, the faintest trace of the horse before me; and then, in the twinkling of an eye, as though the darkness was torn away like a veil by the hand of the Almighty, the whole course, the surrounding country, to the minutest and most distant thing, would be revealed. The spires of the churches and houses of Newark, eight miles off, we could see more plainly than in broad daylight; and we noticed, that, as the horses faced the howling elements, their ears lay back flat upon their necks. Between these flashes of piercing, all-pervading light and the succeeding claps of thunder, the suspense and strain upon the mind was terrible. We knew that it was coming so as to shake the very pillars of the earth we rode on; and, until it had rattled over our heads, we were silent. Then, in the blank darkness, as we went on side by side, we would exchange cautions. Neither could see the other, nor hear the wheels nor the stride of the horses, by reason of the wind and rain.

"Look out, Hiram," Spicer would say, "or we shall be into each other."

A few strides farther on, and I would sing out, "Take care, George: you must be close to me."

Now, the noise of the wheels and the tramp of the horses could not be heard in the roar of the wind and the patter of the rain, and yet our voices could be and were. For a mile and a half, in the very centre, as it were, of this Titanic war of the skyey elements, we went side by side. Then Dutchman lost ground. The track was clayey, and he, having on flat shoes, began to slip and slide at every stride. Americus gradually drew away from him; and, when I reached the stand at the end of the second mile, I stopped. I have seen a great many summer storms in my time, and have been out in not a few of them; but, of all that I remember, none quite equalled, in terrific fury and awful grandeur, that which burst over the Beacon Course just as we began that heat. Spicer says the same.

After this great race upon the Beacon Course, I took the old horse to Baltimore, and trotted him three-mile heats over the Kendall Course, against the pacer Oneida Chief and Lady Suffolk. To the best of my knowledge, that was the last appearance of Dutchman upon a race-course, and he was then fifteen years old. The pacer beat us handily that day, and Lady Suffolk was second. Dutchman was then sold to Mr. George Janeway of New York, who afterwards purchased Rifle, and drove them together in double harness as his private team.

In 1846, after Mr. Janeway had owned him and used him on the road about three years, Dutchman had another trot in public, going with Rifle in double harness against a team from Brooklyn. It was the length of the road from the New-York pavement at Twenty-eighth Street, to Bradshaw's at Harlem, to carry two men in each wagon. I drove the old stavers, Dutchman and Rifle; and we won it easily, beating them some three hundred yards. So these two veterans of the turf and old opponents made their last race upon the road, and in firm alliance; and, vanquishing their opponents easily, the golden rays of victory lighted up the sunset of their declining day.

In the following year, Dutchman died in Mr. Janeway's stable. I was sent for the night before he expired, and, on my arrival, found him down, and paralyzed in his hind-quarters from an injury to his spine caused by his struggles when cast in his stall. It was a touching and deplorable sight to see the fine old horse, game to the last, struggling with his fore-legs and raising his head, unconquered still, but totally helpless in his hind-quarters. At times, he would bend his neck and look round at his haunches, as though to discover why there was no longer power in the hips, thighs, and stifles that had sent him along so many years and never tired. I saw that all feeling in the parts was gone, and that hope of his recovery had gone with it. There was talk about cramp; but I knew that it was cramp of the "silver cord," and that Dutchman would never rise upon his legs again. He died the next morning; and then departed one of the best trotters, take him for all in all, that I have known.

It is rather to be regretted that something definite could not have been ascertained in regard to the pedigree of Dutchman. He was so fast, so stout, so sound, and so determined, that a knowledge of the sources from which he sprang would have been valuable as well as interesting. Since I commenced this work, I have been shown a letter from a young man whose father knew where Dutchman was bred, and remembered him as a colt. According to this authority, which is vague and uncertain, Dutchman was got by an imported thoroughbred horse out of a common country mare. The imported horse had been landed in Virginia, and had found his way into the south-west part of Pennsylvania. This was what the father of the writer of the letter always heard and believed, and told to his son.

It is, as I have said above, too vague and unsubstantial to build upon; but from Dutchman's form, character, and peculiarities, this was the sort of parentage that many would have been inclined to ascribe to him. He was not a coarse horse, though bony and strong; and there was the appearance of a deal of breeding in his head and neck and his carriage, especially when going at a good rate. His temper and endurance also indicated that he had good blood in him; and I have no doubt whatever of that fact. But there is no means that I know of tracing the source of it at this time; and, though the account in the letter alluded to may be true, it does not appear to be entitled to be regarded as more than probable.

XVIII.

Other Performances of Dutchman. — Application of facts to Principles. — Dutchman's steady Improvement. — Endurance of Trotters and Running-Horses compared.

I FIND, on referring to some old documents, that I have omitted three races in the career of Dutchman; and these I now propose to add to his history. It would not much matter if I let it go as it was; for I am not pretending to write a complete register of the races in which the horses I refer to were engaged, but merely give my recollections of the events prominent in my memory, and, for that reason, most likely to be interesting and useful to the general reader. But the memory once aroused, the chain becomes more complete, link by link; and, as I peruse the result of my labors on the printed page, it often occurs to me, that something has escaped me which I can supply. Thus it came into my head, that, besides the races between Dutchman and Rattler of which I have spoken, there was another; and going over the piles of papers and odd matters in my possession, respecting the events of many bygone years, I find that Dutchman and Rattler trotted three-mile heats under saddle on the Beacon Course, New Jersey, in October, 1838. It was for a purse of $300, free for all. Rattler was distanced in the first heat in 8m. 01s. Dutchman was the favorite at the start at 2 to 1, his condition being superior to that of Rattler. Besides that, the course was heavy, which suited Dutchman better than it did Rattler. Before the trot came off, Dutchman was put up at auction with his traps — a sulky, blankets, harness, etc. He was knocked down to me at $1,500. I bought him in under instructions from his owners, Minturn & Co., not to let him go for less than a price they named in confidence.

In July of the following year Dutchman was matched against Awful, three-mile heats in harness, on the Beacon Course. We staked $5,000 for Dutchman against $2,500 on the part of Awful. There was a very large attendance, many people having come on from Philadelphia, Baltimore, Boston, and Providence. Dutchman was the favorite at 100 to 40. The strangers took the odds largely: otherwise there would have been but little betting, for the New-York public had a very high opinion of Dutchman. At the start in the first heat, Awful took the lead, and kept a length ahead for half a mile. At the end of the first mile, which was done in 2.34, he was leading half a length. The second mile was 2.35, and Dutchman had established a good lead at the end of it. I pulled him all the way in the third mile; and he won the heat as he pleased, making that mile in 3.09, the heat in 8.18. The second was a better heat. The first mile 2.47, and the others 2.36 each, making the heat in 7.59. Still, it was quite an easy thing for Dutchman. On the 7th of May, 1840, Dutchman walked over for a purse of $200, two-mile heats in harness, at the Hunting-park Course, Philadelphia. This was while he was in the hands of Mr. Hammil, and before he brought him back to New York.

I now propose to examine how far the career of Dutchman on the turf goes to support the principles I ventured to lay down in the early part of this work, when speaking of the treatment and usage I deemed most proper for trotting-colts and young trotting-horses. It should be the aim of the breeder and trainer to produce just such horses, except in one particular, which is that of temper. Dutchman was a little too rough in the stable, and, if not closely watched, was apt to take the jacket off a man's back at a mouthful. Otherwise, he was all that any one could wish for. He was very fast; he was one of the stoutest horses that ever was called upon to go long heats, and repeat them until the day was done; he had one of the best constitutions that ever came under my observation; and he kept on improving until he was ten or eleven years old, in spite of the many hard races at long distances in which he was engaged. He still remains the champion three-miler; though I am confident I should have beaten his time with Dexter in his late race against Stonewall Jackson of Hartford, if we had had a fair day and good track. In fact, although Dutchman's time has stood so long at the head of the column, and is pretty hard to beat even in these fast days, it will not do to let it become a superstition with us. We should take a lesson from what occurred in respect to Fashion's running four-mile time on the Island; which was long deemed invincible by gentlemen of the old school hereabout, until one fine day, not very long ago, Capt. Moore's mare Idlewild and John M. Clay's colt Jerome Edgar met in a four-mile race on the Centreville Course, and both of them beat Fashion's time all to pieces.

As I have said before, Dutchman did not do his best when he made his 7m. 32s. He never was fully extended but once in the race, and almost walked in; I having pulled him to a mere jog-trot two hundred yards from the stand. I put down his mark that day at 7m. 27s., *or better;* and therefore I certainly think that a good horse in these times, and carrying only a hundred and, forty-five pounds, ought to do it in 7m. 32s. My weight, without the saddle, was about a hundred and fifty pounds. Of course it will take a horse that can stay the distance to beat Dutchman's time; for one that is going to come back before the three miles are accomplished can never do it, no matter how fast he may be. The fact that it has stood so long unequalled should admonish us, I think, that we have of late rather neglected to cultivate lasting qualities in our trotters, and that we have almost entirely allowed saddle-races and long heats to pass out of practice. I am induced to say here of the two horses that started in harness against Dutchman's time, they both lost rather by ill-luck and inadvertence than by reason of lack of ability. Flora Temple would, in fact, have accomplished the feat, had she been allowed the distance that the Centreville Course is more than a mile, three times over. But this could not be; for, when gentlemen have taken a course for a mile at the beginning of a race, they will have to take it for just that distance, and no more, at the end thereof.

General Butler lost by reason of his bad breaks in the third mile. Now, in my judgment, he did not break because he was tired, but because of the injudicious striking-in of one of his managers to go with him with another horse at that juncture. Had it been left to Butler and young Ben Mace's running-horse that went with him from the first to finish it alone, I have no doubt he would have kept on and won it. I had money laid the other way, and considered it as good as lost. This General Butler is a very remarkable horse. He is one that you do not feel confidence in betting on, and are afraid to bet against. On the day that he made his great two-mile time to wagon against George M. Patchen, he was a wonder. I am rather inclined to the belief that he could have equalled Dutchman's three-mile time that day, and have done it to a wagon.

In regard to colts, I have previously observed that the forcing system in the raising of trotters was not advisable. I am satisfied that it is not only expense laid out to no use, but for a purpose which is likely to be mischievous. Very early maturity is only to be attained accompanied with the liability, the almost certainty, of corresponding early decay; and, to achieve such excellence as that to which Dutchman attained, the trotting-horse must have all his powers long after the period at which most running-horses have left the turf. The reason is obvious. The trotter has to be educated up to his best and strongest rate, and the education takes many years. Dutchman improved until he was ten or eleven years old, and it may be questioned whether his very best capabilities were ever brought out; for the change into new hands just when he had come to the highest pitch that we know of was not altogether favorable to continued advance. Therefore, when a trotting-horse has attained the age of seven, and is aged, or arrived at natural maturity, he has only just reached that stage when we may begin to expect the development of his finest powers; and that development, according to my experience, is likely to be gradual, and to continue for a long time. No doubt many horses never improve after they are seven; and in some cases the speed comes to them all at once, as the saying is. In the former, the constitution, breeding, or form is probably defective.

A century of work would not improve some horses. They get to their best early, and only because their best is very bad. In the other instance, it will commonly be found that those who have jumped up all at once have been horses who have changed their gait, and got to going square, or have *changed hands*, and in different treatment have done first what they could have nearly done before with the same handling. Hence, while there is but little reason for being in a hurry with a young trotting-colt, and none at all for the expectation that he may arrive at his best early, except when his best will be but bad, there is every reason for giving Nature full time to perfect the hardy, enduring frame in her own cunning way without forcing.

It is altogether likely that Dutchman might have been made a bigger horse, though he was big enough in my judgment, and an earlier horse, by means of strong feeding when very young; but I am of the opinion that neither his stoutness in a race of heats, nor his constitutional ability to resist the wear and tear of the race of life, would have been improved thereby. On the contrary, reason and experience, to my mind, lead to the conclusion that they would have been damaged. Our trotting-horses, as a rule, endure much longer than our running-horses. If it be said that the conditions of training and racing are not the same, I reply, that in old times the running-horse endured and was kept upon the turf more than twice as long as he is at present, and ran much harder races.

The distance and weights in England used to be three and four mile heats, and the weights from about 140 pounds to 168 pounds; yet the horses used to run until they were not merely "aged," but old. Whereas, at the present time, they commonly retire before they are seven; and take away two geldings, Throgsneck and Red Oak, there is not a prominent race-horse in this country, England, or Ireland, to-day, that is eight. Now, that arises in a great measure from the forcing system adopted to make colts at three years old as forward as they used to be at five; and, with regard to the trotter, it ought to be avoided. He *must* last many years to make a first-rate one; whereas the running-horse is commonly as good at four or five years as he ever would be, if he could run on until he was twenty. There is nothing in the thoroughbred horse that entails earlier decay than other strains are liable to. If of good sound family, such as Messenger belonged to, and not subjected to severer treatment and greater strain than horses of other breeds are called upon to endure, I am satisfied that the thoroughbred is the hardiest as well as the speediest and stoutest animal that the art of man has been able to perfect.

Another point against which I warned the owners and handlers of young trotting-horses was the practice, beginning to obtain to a mischievous extent, of taxing their powers severely while they are in the sap and green of youth. We find that Dutchman never trotted a race until he was six years old, and that he had no training to undergo until he was seven. Does anybody think that he would have been a sound, fast, strong horse at eighteen, if he had been put through the mill of hard training, high trials, and severe races at three or four? It is the "grand preparation" and the screwing-up in the high trial that take away the steel and life of the young horses. Very often the race itself is an easy one for the winner; but the mischief has been done before the race was come to, and the young horse is seriously damaged, if not ruined for life. A horse like Dutchman does twenty times more hard work as a trotter, than twenty of the early, hard-trained, tried, and raced ones can ever do; and it don't hurt him one bit.

Some will say the comparison is not fair: Dutchman was a very extraordinary horse. I answer so he was; but, if you want one approaching his excellence in all points, don't you go to stuffing your colts with bruised oats and oatmeal before they are weaned, and ramming them up to the full extent of their powers, in training, trials, and the like, at three years old. I know that the man who has got a three-year-old flyer or two to sell at a high price will call these sad, old-fogy notions, say that I am behind the age, and that the early system is the thing. So it is *for him*, because he is going to *sell* the colt that has been hurried along to an unnatural and fleeting precocity; and when he has been sold, and the nine days' wonder of the big price has passed away, that is probably the last we shall ever hear of the colt, and the seller will have one more of the same sort, or may be as fast and younger, to dispose of next year. But you want to produce, if possible, one that in the course of time — time, that tries all — shall earn a solid and enduring reputation as a good trotter; therefore follow the old racing maxim, "Wait and win."

You will have to be at the expense of some money and more patience in the extra year or two that must elapse before your colt can be put to *strong* work, and you must wait for the reward. The opposite doctrine to that which I have laid down is exactly in point with the resolution of the fool in the fable: "I'll not wait for the slow operation of this goose in laying one golden egg a day: I'll kill her, and get them all at once!"

XIX.

The Story of Ripton. — Description of him. — Ripton and Mount Holly. — Ripton and Kate Kearney. — Peter Whelan and George Youngs. — Ripton and Don Juan. — Necessity of Work and Practice. — Ripton, Dutchman, Confidence, and Spangle. — Ripton, Duchess, and Quaker. — Ripton and Revenge. — Ripton and Lady Suffolk. — A Fast, Close Race.

BEFORE my experience was completed with Dutchman, another horse came into my hands, who was second only to that famous trotter, in my estimation, for speed and bottom, and ability to stand wear-and-tear, when he had had good practice and had come to a ripe maturity. I speak of Ripton, who became very celebrated just before Dutchman left the turf; for the road had passed into the possession of Mr. Janeway. Ripton was a very handsome bay horse, with four white legs and a blaze in the face. In that particular he was like Dexter, who is now a greatly esteemed favorite of mine, and brown. Like him, too, he was a little horse in inches, but good and substantial in make and girth. He did not stand above fifteen hands high; but he had fine power, and was a horse of uncommon fire, spirit, and determination. His style of going was very fine, — as near perfection as any thing I have ever seen; but, from the fact that one foreleg was whited higher up towards the knee than the other, casual observers often fancied, when he was going fast, that he lifted that foot the highest, and slapped it down with extraordinary vim. That was a mistake, — a mere optical illusion. He went as level as the flow of a smooth stream that is swift and deep. I cannot say what his pedigree was.

I have heard something of his having been got by a certain horse; but it is only hearsay, and of no value or authority. In 1835 he was brought to New York from the Eastern States, and offered for sale, being then five years old. Mr. Peter Barker, who owned Dutchman at the time, agreed to buy him if he suited in a trial. They tried him on the Centreville Course in harness; and he made his mile, driven by Joel Conklin, in 2m. 46s., in great style. He was afterwards sold to Mr. George Weaver of Philadelphia, and went into the hands of James Hammil. Ripton's first race was for a sweepstakes, in which Mount Holly and another were also engaged; but the third did not start, and Ripton beat Mount Holly handily in two straight heats. Ripton then passed into the hands of George Youngs, who had very great celebrity as a rider and driver of trotting-horses, and deserved it all. He was one of the best horsemen that I have ever known. Ripton was brought back to New York, and trotted over the Beacon Course, mile-heats, three in five, in harness, against Kate Kearney. Kate was a bay mare, about fifteen hands and an inch high. She belonged to Mr. Stacey Pitcher. Ripton won the first heat; and then, after a good deal of consultation between the parties, they agreed to draw the race. The fact was, that Ripton was very high strung, and had run away with his driver a day or two before. He had given some indications of an intention to bolt again, and they were shy of him.

His next change was into the hands of Peter Whelan, the elder brother of my friend William. Peter, like George Youngs, was a capital rider and driver. I am told his brother thinks that he and I excelled Peter and George soon after, if not at that time; but I have my doubts whether anybody ever excelled either of them much, especially in the saddle. Peter Whelan died in Philadelphia in 1840, and Ripton was then sent to me. He was then ten years old, with all the requisites to make a very fine trotter, such as he afterwards became, but was not altogether then. I had had him some two months, and it was in summer time when I trotted him over the Beacon Course, two-mile heats, under saddle, against Mr. James McMann's Don Juan. The Don was a handsome chestnut gelding, fifteen hands two inches high, a stylish and fine-going horse. We got the start for the first heat. Ripton took the lead, was never headed, and won it with great ease in 5m. 19s. It seemed so certain, that the spectators thought he could not lose it, and odds of 100 to 5 were currently offered and laid. I remember the circumstances well, not only from the fact that it was the first time I had ever seen as much odds laid between two horses, but from the unexpected termination of the race. In the second heat I took the lead again, and it seemed all my own for a mile and a half. I then felt Ripton going to nothing between my knees. McMann and Don Juan passed us, and the latter won it handily in 5m. 33s. Ripton was much distressed; and, believing that he had no chance to win, I drew him.

Now, this was a case showing the absolute necessity for a good deal of work and practice as a trotter to enable a horse to endure through two two-mile heats. Ripton was a horse past the age of constitutional maturity; he was well in health, apparently in good bodily condition, and he was a game and stout horse; but he had never been trotted much, and lacked the practice and seasoning which braces and hardens the muscles, and enables the animal to endure. He was just like a horse trained over the flat for a steeple-chase, which always tires, no matter how good his bodily condition may be, from the fact that the muscles which have to be violently exerted when he rises in his leaps have had no practice of that sort. It was a case which made a marked impression upon me at the time, and I afterwards found that the conclusions I had come to in regard to it were correct. Ripton was noted afterwards for his game and bottom, and also for requiring a great deal of work to bring him out fit for one of his best performances.

In 1841 I took Ripton to Philadelphia, and trotted him over the Hunting-park Course, two-mile heats, in harness, against Dutchman, Confidence, and Spangle. Confidence was a very fine horse, — a handsome long-tailed bay, fifteen hands and an inch and a half high. He belonged to Mr. James Berry, of whose death recently in Cincinnati I was sorry to hear. Spangle was a horse fifteen hands and an inch high, and was so called because he was spotted. In this race, William Whelan drove Confidence, Hammil Dutchman, George Woodruff Spangle, and I Ripton. Ripton won the first heat in 5m. 19s., Dutchman took the second, and the third was a dead-heat between him and Confidence. Spangle was now ruled out for not winning a heat in three; and I drew Ripton, leaving Dutchman and Confidence to contend. The former won it.

That summer I went to Saratoga with a stable of horses belonging to a well-known gentleman named Beach. On my return to New York in the fall, I borrowed Ripton of his owner, Mr. Thomas Moore of Philadelphia, and entered him in two sweep-stakes, two-mile heats in harness, with the brown mare Duchess and the roan gelding Quaker. The latter was a one-eyed horse, fifteen hands and an inch high. Duchess was a plain little mare, scant fifteen hands. The first of these stakes was to come off over the Hunting-park Course, Philadelphia, and the other in two weeks' time over the Beacon, New Jersey. At Philadelphia, Ripton won in two straight heats handily. At the Beacon he was the favorite against the field at small odds, and won again in two heats with ease.

His next trot was at Philadelphia, in the winter of that year. It was in the month of December, over the Hunting-park Course, four-mile heats under saddle, against a gray horse called Revenge. William Woodruff rode Ripton. The course was very heavy, as was to be expected. Ripton won it in two heats. He wintered that season in Philadelphia, and came back to me in the spring.

His first trot in 1842 was in May (just when the much talked-of match between Boston and Fashion was pending), and it was over the Beacon Course, two-mile heats in harness, against Confidence and Lady Suffolk. Whelan drove Confidence, Bryan Lady Suffolk, and I Ripton. Confidence was the favorite; but Ripton won in two heats, in 5m. 10½s. and 5m. 12½s. He won these heats very easily, and thus added much to his reputation.

The following week the great four-mile race between Boston and Fashion came off over the Union Course. It was a regular carnival all over this part of the Island, and immense numbers of people attended. The sportsmen had come from all parts of the country to see this great race between the famous old horse and the Jersey mare. After it was over, and the mare had won, almost all the people proceeded to the Centreville Course, to see Lady Suffolk and Ripton trot two-mile heats in harness. At the start, he was the favorite at two to one, but the mare beat him. She won the first heat in 5m. 10s., and the second in 5m. 15s., in good style.

Ripton did not act as well as I could have wished and expected; and I was anxious to give the gray Lady of Suffolk another meeting, that same distance and way of going. In about six weeks or two months, I was afforded the opportunity. It was at the Hunting-park Course, Philadelphia, two-mile heats in harness, and Ripton and Lady Suffolk were the only ones in it. Ripton went away at score, and took the lead. He kept it throughout the two miles, and did the heat in the then unparalleled time of 5m. 7s. The accomplishment of this feat in harness caused a vast amount of interest and excitement among trotting-men. It was like that which sprung up when Flora Temple outdid herself, and morally distanced all that had gone before by making a mile in harness below 2m. 20s. When we started for the second heat, the odds were large on Ripton; but he met with a mishap, and it was all that I could do to save his distance. The check-piece of the bit got into his mouth, and he couldn't trot. At one time he was a full distance behind the Lady; but with a sudden jerk I drew the bit square in his mouth again, and got him to going time enough to save another start. The odds were now two to one on the Lady.

The third heat was one of the closest and finest things, from end to end, that I have ever seen. That between Dutchman and Rattler, in their great race of four three-mile heats under saddle, was no nearer thing. At the start we went away together, and kept on almost neck and neck for the first mile. The second was just the same, — a ceaseless fight all the way, every inch being contested, and neither having a shade the best of it to all appearance. A hundred yards from home they were head and head, and apparently doing all they knew. The struggle was tremendous, and they trotted as if their lives depended upon it. Bryan used the whip freely; and now, close at home, I rallied Ripton with the bit, and called upon him for one final dash. The little horse answered the call very gallantly, and, amidst the most intense excitement of the spectators, beat her home just two feet. The gray mare fought for every inch, and stretched her neck like a wild goose on the wing; but the nose of the little bay horse was first past the post, and he got the heat and race. I do not think that I have ever seen a better race than this, which I have briefly described above. The time of the first heat has since been beaten by Flora Temple as much as sixteen seconds and a half; but in those days this performance by Ripton was considered very great, and was great.

The observations I have made heretofore in regard to improved tracks, light vehicles, better training, higher breeding, and general advance in speed and speedy methods, will all have to be considered in this case. If Ripton had not got the check-piece of the bit into his mouth in the second heat, I believe he would have won this race easily.

As it was, I had a deal of trouble to get him inside the distance. The third heat was a close struggle, and anybody's race every inch of the way. Suffolk tried her utmost, and hung on to the last stride, like a dog to a root. It is not certain to my mind but that she might have won it, if Bryan had let his whip alone, and helped her out with the bit. I am of the persuasion, that, unless a horse is a real slug, the whip does more harm than good in a head-and-head struggle. Natural emulation then incites the horse to do all he knows in such circumstances; and the business of the rider or driver is to aid his efforts and assist him, not to keep leathering away at him with the whip; which is no aid at all, and is more likely to make him swerve, or give up in disgust. In a tight squeeze, with a generous horse, the bit is the thing to win with.

XX.

Ripton, Brandywine, and Don Juan. — Ripton and Quaker. — Ripton and Spangle. — Ripton, Lady Suffolk, and Washington. — Ripton and Confidence. — Ripton and Americus. — Ripton's Performances in 1842 recapitulated. — Conclusion enforced. — Time wanted for Maturity. — Ripton required much Work.

AT the close of the last chapter, I recounted the incidents of the race between Ripton and Lady Suffolk at Philadelphia, in which 5m. 07s. was made by him in the first heat, which was the first time that mark had been made in harness. The time of the other heats was 5m. 15s., 5m. 17s. Before proceeding further with the history of the famous little trotter Ripton, I shall make mention of several races which have since come to my recollection that occurred prior to the period at which he made the 5m. 07s. The first of these was a race against Lady Suffolk in the spring of 1841, mile-heats under saddle, over the Beacon Course. Ripton was defeated in the race, and I attributed it to his carrying extra weight. I rode him myself, and, with the saddle, weighed a hundred and sixty-seven pounds. This was a trifle too much for the little white-legged horse; and, after a tight race, the Lady beat us. Another race I had forgotten was one at two-mile heats under saddle, over the Beacon Course, against Brandywine and Don Juan. Brandywine was a black gelding, about fifteen and a half hands high. Isaac Woodruff rode him. William Whelan rode Don Juan, and William Woodruff Ripton. The latter won it in two heats. In this race Ripton trotted half a mile in 1m. 11½s., which was then thought an amazing thing. It does not appear upon the record, as a matter of course; but the time was taken and immediately announced by so many careful and accurate gentlemen that there is no doubt about the fact; and it is proper that it should be mentioned here.

Two more races in 1841 have to be noticed. They both took place in Philadelphia, over the Hunting-park Course. The first of them was two-mile heats under saddle, for a purse of two hundred dollars, against the bay horse Quaker. The latter was a great bay gelding, seventeen hands high, Hammil rode him, and William Woodruff rode Ripton. The little horse defeated the big one in two straight heats. Late in December of that year, and when there was at least three inches of snow on the track, Ripton trotted two-mile heats in harness, against Spangle. George Youngs drove the latter; and I drove Ripton, who won in two heats. I do not remember the time; but I know it was slow, which was to be expected in that weather and on such a course.

We are now in a position to resume our account of the doings in which the little horse was a chief actor in 1842, after the 5m. 07s. time in harness, which concluded the last chapter. The next succeeding race that year was in the latter part of June, over the Eagle Course, Trenton, New Jersey. It was two-mile heats in harness, Lady Suffolk and Washington being in with Ripton. In the first heat nothing particularly deserving mention occurred. I won it handily with the little horse in 5m. 16s., Lady Suffolk second. The odds had been large on Ripton after the first heat; and most of those who had taken them were very vociferous, and in ecstacies of delight; but this did not last long.

In the first mile of the second heat Ripton acted badly. The mare was a long way ahead at the end of it; and, as Bryant passed the stand, he sung out at the top of his voice, "Can I distance him?" There was such a shout of "Yes! go on!" in reply, that it seemed as if the whole multitude had answered. Very soon after we rounded the turn in the second mile, Ripton got levelled, and began to trot in his fine, commanding style. He gained fast on the mare, kept on going to her, and, about a hundred yards after they passed the half-mile pole gave her the go-by, and won the heat handily in 5m. 18s. The excitement, as the little horse shut up the great gap, was intense; and, at the end of the heat and race, Bryant was much disappointed. He declared that he would not trot Lady Suffolk against Ripton any more, unless it was under saddle. Early that fall, Ripton met Confidence, two-mile heats in harness, over the Centreville Course. We won it in two heats; the time of them being 5m. 13½s., and 5m. 14½s.

The following week, they went over the same course again, two-mile heats to wagons, each weighing a hundred and eighty-one pounds. Ripton won the first heat in 5m. 15s., and that was the fastest; but Confidence got the second and third heats. The weight was a trifle too much for the little horse, but we soon had our revenge. The next trot in which Ripton was engaged was a sweepstakes and purse to the amount of $1,150, on the Beacon Course; and Confidence was also in it, together with Lady Suffolk. It was three-mile heats in harness. Ripton won the first heat handily, in 7m. 56½s. The second heat he also took, and the time of that was 7m. 59s. It was, however, a closer thing for two miles between the three; and the finish for second money, between Confidence and Lady Suffolk, was a very fine and near race. I recollect that I got home handily enough to turn round in the sulky and see the struggle, as they came out, for the second money. William Whelan was driving Confidence, and a very little way from home Lady Suffolk appeared to have the best of it; but Whelan shook his horse up, and came with such a rush that he beat her on the post by a neck.

The next race we went with Ripton was over the same course It was against Americus, two-mile heats to wagons. George Spicer drove Americus, who won it in two heats, the fastest of which was 5m. 14s. I believe that was the fastest two-mile time to wagons that had then been made. We went one more race that season with Ripton, and it was also over the Beacon Course. It was a match against Americus, three-mile heats, in harness, for $1,000 a side. The interest felt in the match was large, and people generally thought Americus would win it. The attendance on the course was very great. Americus was the favorite at the start at 100 to 60. In the first heat, Ripton went away, and, taking the lead, maintained it for two miles very handily; but, in passing the stand to go into the third mile, he unfortunately struck his ankle. This caused him to fly up as if he had been shot; and he acted so badly in the third mile that he was nearly distanced. I managed, however, to avoid that, and saved the right to start. Most people thought it was of no use, and the odds current on Americus was 100 to 5. Even at that rate the layers far outnumbered the takers. The latter were few and shy.

Nevertheless, when I felt of Ripton in the second heat, and "put the question to him," as much as to say, "Can you do it now?" he said "Yes!" So, coming up the stretch on the first mile, I took the lead with him: he was never afterwards headed in the heat, and won it handily. There was much excitement and some tribulation among those who had laid the long odds. Americus still had the call, the majority depending on his reputation as a horse of good bottom. I concluded that it would be best to make a waiting race of it, and so, at the word for the third heat, pulled behind and trailed. Here I kept for two miles. On passing the stand the second time, Ripton began to pull very hard; and the purchase of my foot against the iron of the sulky was so powerful that it parted, and the end going forward, struck Ripton on the thigh. He gave a wild bound, and I came very near going overboard. I managed to save myself, however; and, putting my foot under the iron, I bent it back, so that it did not touch the horse. I got him down to his work, and still continued to trail to the half-mile pole. I was satisfied then, from the way Ripton was going, that the race was safe; and, pulling out, I challenged Americus to come along and trot for it. He was not quite willing. As I came up to his head he broke; and, passing him, I won the heat with ease, and so got the race. The layers and losers of the great odds were sorely tried by this result, which was a very good ending to the performances of the little horse in that year. Ripton then left my charge, and was taken back to Philadelphia; prior to which, however, three matches had been made for him to trot in the following spring. They were against Americus, for $1,000 a side each, three mile heats, two-mile heats, and mile-heats, three in five.

But, before we take leave of Ripton's performances in 1842, it will be interesting and useful to recapitulate them, so that their quality and amount may be taken in at a glance and appreciated. He trotted then, in that year, as follows: two-mile heats in harness, which he won in two heats, beating Confidence and Lady Suffolk; two-mile heats in harness, which he won in three heats, beating Lady Suffolk; two-mile heats in harness, which he won in two heats, beating Lady Suffolk and Washington; two-mile heats in harness, which he won in two heats, beating Confidence; two-mile heats to wagons of 181lbs., which Confidence won in three heats; three-mile heats in harness, which Ripton won in two heats, beating Confidence and Lady Suffolk; two-mile heats to wagons, which Americus won in two heats; three-mile heats in harness, which Ripton won in three heats, beating Americus. Here were six races of two-mile heats, and two of three-mile heats. Four of those at two-mile heats Ripton won, and both of those at three-mile heats he won. The two he lost were to wagons. He trotted fourteen two-mile heats and five three-mile heats in that season, and of these he won thirteen.

I have recapitulated these facts for the purpose of using them to enforce the theory I have laid down, to the effect that the trotter, if he is going to be a superior one, needs a long time to mature. It will be recollected, that, when I first trotted Ripton two-mile heats under saddle against Don Juan, he died away to nothing in my hands in the last mile of the second heat, when the race seemed to be all his own. But, with three years more of work and practice, he had acquired stamina to make such a season as I have related, and to put a fitting climax to it by beating Americus in a race of three three-mile heats, winning the second and third heats after the odds of twenty to one had been current against him. He had been all the time "a-coming," as we horsemen say; and it was only now that he could be said to have reached maturity as a trotting-horse. Yet he was fast when young and green; for, as I have said, when he was brought here at five years old, never having been on a track in all probability, he trotted a mile in harness in a trial driven by Joel Conkling, in 2m. 46s. That does not sound so fast now; but this was just thirty years ago, and it was a very great performance for the young horse, under all the circumstances. It was seven years from that time before he made the season of 1842, the trotting of which I have related. He was then twelve years old, and had only then come to his best and greatest stoutness as a trotter. In fact, it was this continual increase of staying power that made him so formidable, and enabled him to win three-mile heats against such a bottom horse as Americus, when it was deemed by the great majority that he had no chance, and a hundred to five was the current odds against him.

Ripton also affords a fine example of another thing I have endeavored to impress upon the mind of the reader, viz., the great difference there is in the amount of work and general treatment required by different horses. Any man who pretends to lay down fixed rules for work and feed in training is either a fool or an impostor, and very likely both. The most that can be done is to furnish general principles, the application of which to particular cases is to be left to the judgment of the individual. Ripton, of all the horses that I have ever had, was one of those that required the most work. He was so resolute and game, and his spirits were so high, that, if not kept down by a good deal of steady work, he was almost certain to run away as soon as he was suffered to go fast. With the work most horses require, he would have been almost or quite unmanageable. It was so when George Youngs had him in his youth; and it was so still in his old age, when he was broken down and had been withdrawn from the turf. There was no vice about the little horse; but the exuberance of his spirits was such, when he was at all indulged, that he would run away out of mere fun.

XXI.

Ripton's Three Matches with Americus. — Ripton in Mud. — Ripton in Snow, — Sleighing on the Harlem Road. — Ripton and Confidence. — Owner's instructions. — An Old Horse to be kept Warm between Heats. — Match with Bay Boston.

AFTER Ripton's arduous and successful season, at the close of 1842, ending with his victory over Americus in the great race of three-mile heats, he went into winter quarters at his owner's, Mr. Moore of Philadelphia; and when the time came to prepare him for his three matches with Americus, three-mile, two-mile, and mile heats, in harness, he went into the hands of George Youngs. The first of these races was the one at three-mile heats, which came off early in May, on a Monday. The others followed after intervals of a week. They were all trotted on the Beacon Course. The three-mile heat race was won in two heats by Ripton; the fastest of the two being 7m. 53½s. Next week, at the two-mile heats, it was the same. Ripton won handily in two heats, having taken the lead at the start in each, and never being headed in either of them. The next week came the mile and repeat race. The track was very heavy, and the odds large on Ripton. They went sloshing along through the mud; and the little white-legged horse won with ease in two heats, the best of which was 2m. 38s.

I may here observe that Ripton was one of the best mud-horses I have ever seen. From his general characteristics, one would scarcely have supposed that he would go dashing along through the mud when his stroke was throwing it all over him, and the spats were hitting him under the belly almost in shovelfuls. But so it was. In snow, too, he was capital, — without any exception, the very best sleigh-horse that I ever pulled a rein over, and I have driven many of uncommon excellence. Next to Ripton, Gray Eagle was the best horse for snow that I have ever known. It made but little difference to the former whether the sleighing was good or indifferent, for he would go through icy water and slush as if he liked it; but it made a great difference to the driver.

Our principal sleighing-place was from the pavement to Harlem Bridge, along the road; and many a time I have driven Ripton the length of it at wonderful speed. Great fun, sleigh-riding, when the air is keen and frosty, the sky clear, the snow deep and crisp, and you can dash along at a rate down in the thirties with confidence that your trotter will hold out to the end. Ripton was one of these, — the best of them, the King of the Sleighers! What a peal his bells would ring as he dashed down Yorkville Hill, pounding away with those white legs of his as if he would strike down to the ground, no matter how well packed and deep the snow might lie. Here would be a group at this house, and another at that, taking their hot toddy to keep the cold out; and as they heard the swift shaking of the bells, and the fast stroke of Ripton's feet like a charge beat upon the drum, they would run to the door and windows, and crowd the stoop, and cry "Hallo! here comes Hiram and the white-legged pony!" It's more than twenty years ago since those times; and there is no jingling of the sleigh-bells there now, no matter how good and deep the snow may be. The street railroads have done for all that.

After these three races of which I have spoken, Ripton went into William Whelan's hands, and was entered in a purse to be trotted for on the Beacon Course. But, prior to the day of action, something became the matter with one of the little horse's hind-legs, and he had to pay forfeit. At first it was feared that he would break down if put in strong work again; but the leg got better, and he came back to me. After some little time, but still that same season, we matched him against Confidence; Ripton to pull a wagon, and the former to go in harness, mile heats, three in five, for $1,000 a side, on the Beacon Course. It will be remembered that Mr. Berry declared that some time before, at the close of a race in which we beat Confidence and Lady Suffolk with Ripton, that Confidence should not trot with the little horse in harness again. So we agreed to pull a wagon.

The match came off on a fine fall day in September, and there was a very large attendance. Everybody was pleased to see the old and well-tried favorite, Ripton, on the course again, and able to contend for the specie. He was not in the best of fix, though; for he still had a game leg, which made it a dangerous race for him, to say nothing of his going to wagon while Confidence was in harness. But, for all that, the people laid odds on him; and Jack Harrison, who had made the match, backed him for a large amount. Prior to the start, he and Mr. Moore gave me instructions how to drive the race. My own opinion differed from theirs; but finding them very confident, and obstinate in their notions, I started out to do as they said. It was upon the old principle and maxim of the sailor, "Obey orders, if it breaks owners!" The result was not favorable. Confidence won the first heat in 2m. 35½s., and the next in 2m. 37s. Everybody now thought it was as good as over; and the long odds of one hundred to five on Confidence were freely offered, and no takers. At the close of the second heat, I remarked to Mr. Moore and Jack Harrison that their method did not seem to answer. "Well," said they, "you've no chance to win it now, so do as you please."

But there was a chance, and I knew it. The first thing I did was to change the wagon. The one I had been driving was a very nice one, which had been built by Mr. Joseph Godwin, and only weighed 74lbs. It had got doubled up, principally from Ripton's hard pulling in the first and second heats. In order to change it, I borrowed a wagon of Fred. Johnson, and that only weighed four pounds more than the other. These two were the earliest of the very light wagons: there was not another like them at that time. Instead of letting Ripton cool out, I just took him out of one wagon and put him into the other, and jogged him up and down the backstretch until it was time for the next heat. When a horse is old and a little crippled, it does not answer to let him get cool and stiff between the heats. I like to keep such an one warm and limber. The previous exertion, by starting the circulation and setting up violent action all through the system has counteracted, for the time being, the stiffness, soreness, and lameness which are in a measure chronic; and, this being so, it seems to me advisable to keep steam up a little during the interval between heats. Having kept Ripton jogging until we were called up for the third heat, I gave him a sharp brush of half a mile preparatory to it. In the course of that enlivening brush, I cut him with the whip twice pretty hard; and he went away from it like a bullet. This was the first and last time that I ever whipped the little horse, except in the finish of a heat. He was the last horse in the world to want it, save in the nip and tuck of a long and desperate race. His style of going was very free and determined, head up and tail right on end over his quarters, and cutting through the air with a sharp swish as he worked it from side to side, just as a fighting-dog does his when he has got a punishing-hold.

Ripton was now boiling hot and well settled. At the first coming up, we got the word; and, shooting him out, I took the pole from Spicer before we had gone seventy-five yards. Of course Ripton had now a good lead; and, trotting in his old style, he was never headed, and won the heat easily in 2m. 38s. Such a shout as there was when the little horse came slashing in ahead was never hardly heard on any other occasion at the Beacon. Jack Harrison hugged me, and tossed his hat up in the air. The odds swung right over. It had been a hundred to five, and no takers, on Confidence; and now a hundred men shouted all together, "A hundred to fifty on Ripton!"

Again I kept the little horse jogging until it was time to start. He won the fourth heat, taking the lead at the start, and not being headed in it. The time of it was 2m. 39s. The fifth heat was a mere repetition of the fourth. Ripton won it easily in 2.41. This was the second race that he had won against odds of one hundred to five; and, at this distance of time, I say, with all confidence and without egotism, that he would not have won it but for the decided "persuasion" he got between the second and third heats. The horse was old and partly crippled, and it don't answer to go to coddling with such a one when the race is in hand. He had to have something to wake him up, and let him know that real business was to be transacted, and he must "do or die," as the saying is.

A word here may not be out of place in reference to instructions from owners or backers of horses to drivers. If the horse is strange to the driver, the latter is in need of all the instructions the other parties, who are supposed to know something, can give. But it commonly happens that the driver knows the horse quite as well, and a little better, than they do; and, furthermore, he generally knows something of the opposing horses in the race, which is a very material consideration in determining the method which ought to be pursued. In this case of Ripton's, and in that in which I drove Prince the chestnut horse against Hero the pacer ten miles, the horses could not have won if the instructions I received had been carried out to the end. Yet the gentlemen who gave them had experience in such matters, and were rather remarkable for sagacity, than the reverse. It ought to be considered that the instructing of a driver in a trotting-race is a very different matter to the giving of orders to a boy in a running-race. The driver is always a man, with the experience that a man may possess in that profession. He has also commonly trained the horse, and therefore knows his peculiarities and disposition; that is, he ought to know them. It follows that, in most cases, instructions to the driver are unnecessary if not mischievous. As to whether the driver ought to follow them when he *thinks* them wrong, is a difficult question. But, if I am *convinced* that they are wrong, I either disregard the instructions when the pinch comes, or refuse to drive the horse. My business as a driver is to win races; and if I know, as well as I can know any thing beforehand, that a certain method pointed out is not the way to win, but to lose, I just follow the instructions as long as it answers and until I can see a chance to do better. This trot with Confidence was the last Ripton was engaged in that year, 1843. He started only four times that season, and won all the races.

In the following year he remained at Philadelphia with his owner, Mr. Moore, and did not trot in public at all. In 1845 he was brought to New York in the spring, but fell lame, and was sent back to Philadelphia again. He soon got right, and was trotted against Americus, mile heats, three in five, in harness, over the Hunting-park Course, Philadelphia. The race came off in the first week of June, and was a very good one of five heats. Of these, Ripton won the first, second, and fifth; Americus winning the third and fourth. So Ripton got the race, and purse of $200. The time was 2.40, 2.38, 2.39, 2.41, 2.45. In the September of that year I was living at Boston, and made a match for $500, half forfeit, for Ripton to trot two-mile heats, in harness, against Bay Boston, a horse fifteen hands three inches high, over the Cambridge Course. Having made this match, I sent to Philadelphia for the horse, and they started with him. On the way they stopped at New York, and trotted him for a purse of $300, two-mile heats in harness, on the Union Course. His opponents were Duchess driven by William Whelan, and Americus by George Spicer. A. Ten Eyck, formerly and better known as Brommy, drove Ripton. The mare won the first heat, Americus took the second, and Duchess was distanced for foul driving. Several spokes were knocked out of Ripton's wheel. Americus won the third heat and race. Immediately after this race, Ripton was sent on to me; but I found, the first time I drove him, that he was lame in the hind-leg again, and not likely to stand the work and race. I therefore compromised the match by paying something, and sent the little horse home to Philadelphia.

XXII.

Ripton and Lady Sutton. — Lady Sutton and Lady Moscow. — Death of Lady Moscow. — Her Burial-place. — Her Produce. — Horses she trotted against. — Ripton and Lady Suffolk. — Ripton, Sorrel Ned, and Snake. — Ripton and Jersey. — Ripton's Last Race.

AFTER I sent Ripton back from Boston with this secondary lameness in the hind-leg, it was a good while before he was fit to trot again. A long rest, however, did a great deal for him; and in 1847 we deemed him well enough to trot a race of two-mile heats in harness, on the Centreville Course, for $1,000 a side, against Lady Sutton. The Lady was a little brown mare, about fourteen hands and three inches high, stoutly made, and with much speed and good bottom. She is the only one of Ripton's old opponents that is yet alive; and she may be seen here any day, as gay as a lark for an old one, as I shall presently show. In the race which took place in November, James Whelpley drove the mare, and I drove Ripton. The Lady took the first heat after a stout struggle, and then they laid two to one on her. But I was satisfied that little white legs had yet plenty of trot in him, and resolved to do my utmost to get it out. The second heat was desperately contested. For the last half mile the horses were neck-and-neck, doing all they knew under the whip. It was a very close thing, and a dozen strides from home seemed to be anybody's heat; but the old horse lasted the longest, and, lifting him with the bit in the last stride or two, I landed him before her by three feet.

There was very little to choose between them now, and

we prepared for the deciding heat. The mare was young and fresh, the horse old and stiff, and she had the call in the betting. At the word, she made a rush for the lead, took the pole, and went on ahead for a mile and three-quarters. At the last turn, on swinging into the stretch, she took the centre of the track, leaving the privilege of the inside to Ripton. I took it, and, giving him a sound cut or two with the whip, challenged her for the heat and race. Another desperate struggle ensued. Both were whipped at nearly every stride they took, and both answered the call with the utmost gallantry. The mare had a little the best of it till we were close at home, but Ripton's perseverance at last prevailed. He got to her head, and finally succeeded in beating her two feet in one of the finest finishes ever witnessed on that course. The time of this race was 5m. 15s., 5m. 15s., 5m. 18s.

As I observed just now, Lady Sutton may be seen here any day. She returned to the Island last spring, after a long absence, to be put to New-York Ledger, by whom, I believe, she is now in foal. Here, in John I. Snedicor's pasture, she had a fond companion, until within these few hours, in her old opponent, Lady Moscow, another very famous mare of her own age, or it may be a year older. When these two old competitors met in the pasture after never having seen each other for many years, it seemed as if a mutual recognition took place. Go by when you would, you would see the two little old mares close together, grazing aloof from the other horses in the pasturage. They both throve amazingly, and got young again to all appearance, in their companionship. When anybody went near them, they would throw up their heads together, and stride a trot, like a spark of the fire of other days. Each had done a vast amount of hard work, and their years put together made almost or quite half a century. Lady Moscow looked the younger of the two, but she has gone first. She was taken with a sort of paralysis on Wednesday night, and died Saturday, Sept. 9, in the afternoon. The seat of the disease was the base of the brain, and all the veterinary art in the world would have been insufficient to save her. She was buried on the Union Course, in the spot where Young Dutchman, George M. Patchen, and other famous trotters, lie. She belonged to my old friend Sim. Hoagland, and died within a stone's throw of the spots where he saw the last of Lady Blanche, the first foal that Abdallah got, and of his stallion Gray Messenger, whose produce has turned out so well. So we shall add to the relics we possess of Abdallah, Messenger, etc., some mementoes of this good old mare. Dr. Pilgrim is to have her near fore-leg. I am glad to say that Lady Moscow leaves a very promising representative in her son, the young gray stallion Privateer, who divides Sim's love and admiration with his half-brother, New-York Ledger.

As we stood there on the green hillside, looking at the mare that lay dead before us, it was really touching to see poor old Sutton, wandering round her dead companion, as if unable to make out what had befallen. Two other mares were near at hand; but Sutton did not seem to notice them at all, her gaze being fixed from time to time on her whose sinews were relaxed and whose hoofs at last are still. In her time she trotted successfully with Lady Sutton, Lady Suffolk, Jack Rossiter, Moscow, Americus, Pelham, Mac, Trustee, Confidence, Vermont, Zachary Taylor, and many others. She has been reported dead once or twice, but four days ago she was alive and well. A year or two since, somebody pretended to have her at St. Louis; but she was all the time in this State, owned by Sim. Hoagland. The man who pretended that he had her West was an impostor.

To return to Ripton, after these few words about the old mares who were on the turf with him. Very late that year, Dec. 28, the little horse trotted a race of two-mile heats in harness on the Union Course, against Lady Suffolk. The Lady won in two heats,—5m. 18 1-2s., and 5m. 25 1-2s. This concluded 1847. In 1848 and 1849, Ripton did not trot, but remained at Philadelphia, and was driven on the road by his owner. In the fall of 1850, it was deemed proper to bring him out again; and he was entered in a purse at the Hunting-park Course, Philadelphia, with Sorrel Ned and the brown gelding Smoke. It was mile-heats, three in five, in harness. George Youngs drove Sorrel Ned; O. Dimmick, Smoke; and William King, Ripton. It was on the 11th of October, and a trot of five heats took place for the money. Ripton won the first heat in 2m. 40s., and was second to Sorrel Ned in 2m. 39s. for the second. Smoke got the third, in 2m. 38s.; and Sorrel Ned won the fourth and fifth, in 2m. 43s. and 2m. 47s.

Ripton was not in good condition for this race, having had but little work. He was now nineteen years old, and had accumulated fat inside. As he had always required a great deal of work to make him fit, the brief preparation for this race was not enough. But, believing that about three weeks more would bring him to tune, they matched him against Sorrel Ned for $1.000, to trot over the same course, mile-heats, three and five, in harness, on the 4th of November. George Youngs drove Ned, and William King handled Ripton. At the start, the old horse was the favorite at slight odds. He won the first heat by a length in 2m. 42s., and his friends began to sport their money with confidence. But, as Sorrel Ned had only been beaten a length, his friends were not much disheartened; and they took the odds offered by the Ripton party quite freely.

The second heat was well contested by Ripton; but Ned won it under the whip, in 2m. 42s. again. The betting was now even, and both sides a little anxious. The old horse was stiff and a trifle lame; but his backers relied upon his fine pluck and sound bottom to pull him out victorious from among the pieces of the broken heats. The third heat Ripton won; and, singularly enough, the time was 2m. 42s. again. The old horse was now a strong favorite at two to one, but still the takers were rather abundant. They started for the fourth heat, and there was much breaking and running on both sides. At the outcome they were both trotting, and crossed the score neck-and-neck, making a dead heat of it in 2m. 44s. The drivers now charged each other with foul driving, and a good deal of crimination and recrimination ensued. The judges ordered them to get ready, and trot the race out. The fifth heat was won by Sorrel Ned in 2m. 46s., and it was nearly dark when they finished it.

By the time they were called up for the sixth heat, it was so dark that the judges could hardly see a man across the course. Sorrel Ned's friends declared that Ripton was the best *runner* of the two, and asked for the appointment of patrol judges. Thereupon, the judges sent out ten men, with instructions to post themselves at various points around the course, and take notice whether the horses were trotting or running when they passed them. This was the best that could be done under the circumstances; but it was pretty clear that there would be a variance and dispute in the reports of these patrol judges, and how their differences were to be reconciled might well bother everybody. From the start the horses went away together, and soon disappeared from the eyes of the judges, who saw no more of them until they came home. At the outcome, Ripton was a length ahead on a trot, and Sorrel Ned ran over the score. The time of the heat was 2m. 47s., and both drivers complained of foul driving on the part of the opposer.

The patrol judges came, and made their reports: some declared that Ripton had passed them on a run, while Ned was trotting. Others gave in the reverse as the fact when the horses went by where they were stationed. The one at the third quarter had been knocked down, run over, and considerably injured by Ripton; and I should say with the English jury, when the judge told them that the assault was proved, and the plaintiff was a great sufferer by the battery, "sarved him right." What business had he on the track, in the way of the horses. The judges heard all sides, and deliberated, and finally concluded that the evidence was too conflicting to warrant a decision either way: all bets must be declared off, and the main stakes drawn.

This was not Ripton's last regular race on the course. He belonged at the time to a gentleman named William McCray of Philadelphia. Although he was nearly twenty years old, I still had a great fondness for Ripton, and went on and bought him. I gave $250 and another horse. In the following winter he was put up at a raffle for $1,000. The tickets were disposed of, and the raffle came off at the Union Hotel, Broadway. Mr. Samuel Isaacs won, and so Ripton became his property. He did not keep the old horse long, but sold him to John Ryerson of Patterson, N. J. Here he was worked on the road.

In the following year, they matched Ripton to go two races under saddle against a horse called Jersey. They were half-mile heats, and were trotted in the lane at Patterson. I believe the old horse lost one, and won one. In the July of 1852, Mr. Ryerson brought him to the Island, and entered him in a purse of mile-heats, three in five, on the Centreville Course. George Rayner's chestnut gelding Selim and my mare Boston Girl were also in it. Ripton was hardly in condition for the company. His day was almost done; and he was distanced in the first heat, which Selim won in 2m. 35s.; and this ended his public career. He was afterwards taken to the western part of the State, I believe; and there was a report current, some years after that, that he broke a leg and had to be shot. By that time the country swarmed with Riptons. You might find them trotting on the Island, at Albany, and as far west as St. Louis; and there were besides a number of Young Riptons and Riptons, jun. But there were none like the old horse, the gay-heart of the course, when he used to come tramping on with his tail right on end, and dashing down his white legs in the style that showed they meant real business.

XXIII.

Ability to pull Weight considered. — Form best calculated for it. — Mere Bulk useless. — Long Striders seldom Weight-pullers. — Kemble Jackson. — Description of him. — Kemble Jackson and Washington. — Kemble Jackson and the Nelson Colt. — Kemble Jackson and Black Harry. — Kemble Jackson, O'Blenis, Lady Brooks, and Pelham. — Kemble Jackson, Mountain Maid, and Flash. — The Kemble-Jackson Check. — Kemble Jackson, O'Blenis, Pet, Iola, Boston Girl, and Honest John.

AS the development and improvement of the fast trotter has exerted, and must continue to exert, a vast influence upon the general horse-stock of the country, used for road-purposes, it is necessary to consider another qualification besides those of speed and bottom. A horse may be fast on the course before a light sulky, just as a running-horse may be very speedy for a mile with about a hundred pounds on his back, but not calculated for general use on the road, or to improve the common road-stock as a stallion. The ability to pull weight is a quality of exceeding value; and, when it is found in connection with speed and stoutness, we may safely say that the three prime characteristics of the harness-horse are obtained. It is to be remembered that the ability of which I speak is that which can pull at a great rate; so that putting on extra weight, up to a reasonable point, shall make no very great difference in the performance of the trotter. Almost any horse can pull a moderate weight at a slow pace, on a good road; but those that can take along about four hundred pounds, and keep the pace good for two or three miles, are, and always have been, rather scarce.

There is a great difference in the ability of fast trotters in this respect; and the common notion that a great bulky horse is best calculated to do so is a fallacious one. For a draught-horse, great size and bulk, to throw an immense steady strain into the collar, may be valuable; but, when the weight is to be taken along at a great rate, other things are of more importance than mere size. In the first place, then, as to height, I do not think that a tall horse has any advantage in this regard over one of about fifteen hands and an inch, or fifteen hands two inches high. The tall horse is apt to be leggy; and his height often comes from extra length in the canon bones, which multiplies no power. Length in the arms, shoulders, thighs, and haunches is a different matter. It follows that the extra height of the horse may be rather a disadvantage than the reverse, in regard to pulling weight at a fast rate.

Mere bulk is also useless. Everybody must have seen horses big enough to pull a ton, to look at, and able to trot very fast in a sulky, or to a skeleton wagon, but unable to act to advantage to three or four hundred pounds. The weight-pullers, as a general rule, are of medium size, with a fine, quick stroke, not over long, and they bend the knee well. They need to be spirited goers, keeping well up to their work all the time; and, unless their temper and pluck are both good, they will sulk, or give up from faint-heartedness, when they feel the weight, and the speed begins to tell. But though mere bulk is useless for the purpose, a fair amount of substance is required; and it will be found in nearly every case, that, though the weight-puller may not have a large frame, he possesses a large muscular development. Long striders are seldom good at weight. Being greatly extended, with a load behind to be pulled along, they are unable to recover, and shove their haunches in quick, without extra exertion, under which they soon tire. Here they more than lose in time of stroke what they gain in space, and loiter, as it were, in their action.

There are, however, some few exceptions to this; and one or two of the most notable I shall mention farther on. The same thing happens, but I think in a smaller degree, to a long-striding running-horse going in mud. Between twelve and thirteen years ago, there was a race of three-mile heats on the Union Course, in which six of the best fast weight-pulling trotters that ever were seen were engaged. It was a sweepstakes with a purse added, and amounted in all to $4,000. The winner of that race, Kemble Jackson, was the best weight-puller and long-distance horse combined that I ever trained and drove; and as I believe that quite as much is to be gained by reciting the lessons of experience as laying down theory, I shall recount his brief performances on the trotting-turf, and give some account of this his last and greatest race. Besides, his case is of great importance in another point of view; for, although a trotter of remarkably fine speed and power, he was such a bad breaker, and had such a singular knack of sticking his head down between his knees when he did break, that at first he was beaten by horses much inferior to himself in speed and bottom.

Kemble Jackson was a chestnut stallion, with a white hind-foot. He was by Andrew Jackson, a grandson of the imported Barbary horse Grand Bashaw. Kemble's dam was a good trotting-mare, whose pedigree is not known. He was fifteen hands three inches high, a compact horse, of good substance, but not great weight, and he had a plump, muscular development. He belonged to Mr. Reynolds of New York; and his first appearance in public was at the Centreville Course, Long Island, on the 12th of December, 1850, when he was matched three-mile heats, to 250lb. wagon, against Washington. This was a severe race at that season of the year, and the track was very heavy. Whelpley drove Kemble Jackson; and Joel Conkling, Washington. The latter won it in two heats of 9m. 12s., 9m. 10s.

The next season, in April, Kemble Jackson was matched against the Nelson colt, three-mile heats in harness, for $500 a side. It was the first trot that spring on the Union Course, and the track was very heavy. Kemble Jackson won it in two heats, 9m. 06s., 8m. 49s. On the 20th of October following, he fulfilled another match. It was three-mile heats to 250lb. wagons, against Black Harry, for $1000 a side, and was trotted on the Union Course. James Whelpley drove the stallion; and George Nelson, Black Harry. The latter won it in 8m. 38s., 8m. 41s. In 1852, Kemble trotted but one race. This came off on the 28th of October, on the Union Course. It was three-mile heats in harness, for a purse of $500, $100 to the second horse. O'Blenis, Kemble Jackson, Lady Brooks, and Pelham were in it; and they ended in the order named. O'Blenis won in two heats, and Pelham was distanced. Kemble Jackson secured second money. The time was 8m. 52s., 8m. 53s. In the spring of 1853, Kemble was in the hands of Charles Brooks, and made his first trot on the Centreville Course, April 21, for a purse of $150, mile heats.

In 1853, in April, Kemble Jackson came out again, and trotted mile-heats, best three in five, to wagons, against J. Nodine's chestnut mare Mountain Maid, and a bay gelding called Flash. Mountain Maid won the first heat in 2m. 47s., and the second in 2m. 50s. The stallion was second in these heats, driven by Charles Brooks; and I was then asked by Mr. Reynolds to get in and drive him. I did so, and won the third heat in 2m. 34s. The fourth heat was dead between Kemble and Mountain Maid, in 2m. 36s., and the fifth she won.

The stallion was then sent to me to be handled; and, in order to prevent him from throwing down his head between his knees when he broke, the well-known Kemble-Jackson check, since in use all over this country, and introduced in England also, was invented. It answered well in this case, and must always be of great use in similar ones; but I think it is often applied in cases where it is not only unnecessary, but does harm instead of good. The stallion was yet wild and uncertain, though capable of fine speed and up to great weight. A stake was opened for a race of three-mile heats, to wagons of two hundred and fifty pounds, which, with the weight of the drivers, a hundred and forty-five, would make at least three hundred and ninety-five pounds to pull. It was to be trotted on the Union Course on the 1st of June, 1853, to be $500 each, and the course to add $1,000. Six entered; the five competitors we had to look to meet being O'Blenis, Boston Girl, Pet, Iola, and Honest John. This was goodly company.

O'Blenis was a bay gelding by Abdallah, got when that famous old horse was in Kentucky. He was sixteen hands high, and an uncommon good, game horse. He was a long strider; but for all that was up to weight, could pull it at a great rate, go a long distance, and stay heats. This character, and he deserved it all, made him the favorite against the field for the stake. George Abrahams trained and drove him. Boston Girl was a bay mare, fifteen hands two inches. I do not know her pedigree. Fish & Raymond owned her. She was a strong mare, with fine, bold action, and a desperate hard puller. John Nelson trained and drove her. Pet was a bay gelding, about fifteen hands and an inch. He was a finely-turned horse, well made, and a very handsome, square trotter. Henry Jones had him. Iola was a brown mare, sixteen hands high. She was rangy and blooklike in appearance, with fine trotting action. Charles Brooks drove her. Honest John was a bay gelding, with fine white legs and a narrow stripe on the face. He was sixteen hands high, and a fine, rangy-going horse. George Spicer had him, and drove him in the race. It closed about five weeks before the day of trotting; and long before that time I had got Kemble steadier, and he had gradually come so that he would stand forcing without breaking. This was not all done by coaxing. Although he was a very high-spirited horse, he got one or two severe lessons in the course of his training. A little whalebone and whipcord is sometimes very beneficial, but it takes care and judgment to find out when to apply it.

XXIV.

O'Blenis against the Field. — Immense Attendance at the Race. —Expectations that Kemble would break. — His Great Victory. — His Early Death. — Weight-pulling Mares. — Lady Palmer. — Peerless. — California Damsel. — English Theory about Trotting-Weight.

THE race before alluded to, in which Kemble Jackson, O'Blenis, Boston Girl, Pet, Iola, and Honest John were engaged, had been made about five weeks before the day came for action. As I have before mentioned, the stallion had been prevented from throwing down his head in his breaks by means of the "Kemble-Jackson" check; and, though he was wild and uncertain when he first came into my hands, he had gradually become so steady, and could go so fast and easy with great weight behind him, that we looked forward to the trot for the three-mile-heat race with considerable confidence. But the other parties had also been at work; and the horses had all done so well, and given such evidence of speed and stoutness in their trials, that, to our surprise and to the astonishment of most other people, every one of the six came upon the course in good order to contend for the money. The owners and trainers all thought so well of their horses that they backed their own.

The general public, however, had a strong favorite, as usual, and the famous son of Abdallah was the horse. He was backed at even against the field, and a vast amount of money was laid. It was no great wonder that people in general should have such faith in him, for he was a capital horse; and it was to be remembered, that here was the neighborhood in which his famous sire Abdallah had stood so many years, and in which the great speed and invincible bottom of his immediate descendants had been most often and most completely exhibited. But there were some men whose foolhardy confidence and over-anxiety to back him against such a strong field I was a little surprised to see. The argument of some who ought to have known better was, "He can beat five as easily as he can beat one!" Now, a very superior horse *can* beat five middling ones as easily as he can one, even in a race of heats, if there is no accident befalls; but how is it if one of the five does not turn out middling on the day, and, taking a heat from the favorite, breaks the race up into nobody knows how many fragments? Here, the field being strong in numbers, as well as good in quality, there was great reason to believe it would be too much for any named horse. Still, O'Blenis was the favorite with the multitude, and much money was laid.

The attendance of people was so large, that the like had never been witnessed at a trotting-race. No such assemblage had come together on the Union Course since the famous four-mile race between Fashion and Peytona. I should think there were 15,000 people present, and the whole inside circle of the course seemed to be filled with vehicles. There was great excitement; and it was not without a little trouble and a good deal of patience that we got the stretch clear, when we had hitched up our horses and began to jog them up and down. At length we were called up, and at the first or second time of scoring got the word to a handsome start. I had the pole with Kemble Jackson, and soon took the lead. The first mile was trotted in 2m. 41s., and he had a good lead at the end of it, and O'Blenis second. I found him going so well, and getting away with the weight so easily, that I was quite willing to have O'Blenis force the pace, which he now did. The second mile was done in 2m. 39½s.; and, during the whole of it, everybody was on the lookout to see Kemble Jackson break. But so far he gave no indications of a break to me, and led by the stand at the end of this mile as handsomely as before. The third mile was done in 2m. 42½s., making the total of the heat 8m. 03s.; and Kemble was first at the outcome. He had not been headed in the heat, and won with lengths to spare. O'Blenis was second, Pet third, Iola fourth, Boston Girl fifth, and Honest John sixth.

The excitement was now redoubled. The great body of the spectators were much pleased with the fine style in which all the horses had trotted, and with which the stallion had won. The friends and backers of O'Blenis and of the other losers of the heat were not at all cast down; but those who had put their faith in Kemble Jackson were much elated. More money was laid. The backers of O'Blenis would not hedge, thinking he was about sure to win the next heat; and those who stood upon the other horses thought so too. "The heats," said they, "will be broken, and we shall all have a good chance to come out best: it's anybody's race!" The truth was, that they all looked for Kemble Jackson to get up, and were much surprised that he had not done so "the first time of asking;" that is, in the heat he had won. Everybody knew that this trick of his had lost him his races prior to my getting him, and they concluded that he had not altogether forgotten to practise it in so short a time.

So now we came up for the second heat, and got the word for the start. Iola and Pet had the best of it; and Brooks and Harry Jones bulged them off in the lead at such a rate that I was forced to let them take the pole on the turn, for fear that the stallion, not being settled, might get up in a great rush at that moment. But, when we got in the straight work of the backstretch, I found that he was well down to his work, and felt that I might safely send him along. Doing so, I passed first one and then the other, and came on the home-stretch with a clear lead. The first mile was done in 2m. 41s., and Kemble Jackson in the lead. O'Blenis now came at me; and, not being in the mind to resign the pole again, I called upon Kemble, and trotted the second mile in 2m. 39s. The third mile was an easy one for the stallion. He did it in 2m. $44\frac{3}{4}$s., and so won the heat with ease in 8m. $04\frac{3}{4}$s. Kemble never was headed but once in the race, and that was by Iola and Pet when they got the best of the last start. He made no break throughout; and he was such a capital horse that day, that I know I could have beat eight minutes with him in both heats, if it had been necessary for me to do so. I never touched him with the whip, nor spoke to him; and he trotted away as lively with the great weight as if he had been going only in a sulky. Everybody was satisfied, and everybody but the heavy losers pleased. Even the latter professed no regret for the result; and yet more money had changed hands than was ever laid on any other trot. Kemble Jackson had done his work so well, and had won it in such grand, commanding style, that those who laid and lost against him, in common with the great body of the people, loudly proclaimed their delight at having been present to see such a performance. The owners and trainers of the other horses were also well satisfied; for, though beaten, O'Blenis, Boston Girl, Pet, Iola, and Honest John had done well. They came in at the end of the second heat in the order named; and though neither of them won, they all beat their trials. The fact was, that Kemble Jackson had come out in such an extraordinary manner as to upset all outside calculations, and set at defiance all speculations drawn from his previous performances. He proved himself a stallion that day entirely worthy of his sire, the renowned Andrew Jackson; and I think it was a misfortune that he lived but a very short time after the race. A few days subsequent to the trot, he left my stable for the Red House, Harlem, where he stood to cover; and in the course of two or three weeks he died there of rupture.

One of the best weight-pullers that I have ever known is Mr. Bonner's chestnut mare Lady Palmer; and his gray mare Peerless is just about as good. In a public trial, there being about two hundred people present, Sim. Hoagland and I drove them two miles, wagons and drivers 311lbs. Palmer won it in the amazing time of 4m. 59s., but I was close to her at the finish with Peerless. Palmer is one of the exceptions to the rule, that long-striding horses are not good to pull great weights. She is a very long strider; and no one would take her to be the weight-puller she is, until he had experience of her wonderful power in that regard. In everything except her stride, however, she fills my notion of what a fast weight-puller should be. She is medium in size, about fifteen two inches; in nothing bulky, but with good substance, and when in condition seems made of wire and whalebone. But her long stroke is unfavorable to the pulling of great weight fast; and nothing overcomes the disadvantage of it, but the energy with which she shoves her haunches in, her very strong loin, and the terrible resolution with which she all the while goes up to the bit. Blood tells here.

Her old antagonist Columbia, afterwards called California Damsel, was another famous weight-puller. It was a great treat to see these capital chestnut mares trot their races on the Union Course; Palmer driven by Hoagland, and Columbia by the late Horace Jones. The first match between them was in November, 1860, mile heats, three in five, wagons and drivers 330lbs. Palmer won it in four heats, of which Columbia got the second. The time was 2m. 33s., 2m. 34½s., 2m. 35s., 2m. 38s. Three days afterwards they went again, two-mile heats, same weight. Columbia won in three heats, Palmer getting the second of them. The time, 5m. 08¾s., 5m. 07s., 5m. 08½s. The mares Palmer, Peerless, and Columbia were as good weight-pullers as have been known since Kemble Jackson's time. But in comparing what he did in the three-mile race against O'Blenis, Boston Girl, Pet, Iola, and Honest John, with their speedier and more modern performances, it must be remembered that he took along more weight by 65lbs. than Palmer and Columbia did in their matches, and more by 84lbs. than Palmer and Peerless did in their best trial. An addition like either of those to weight already high makes a vast difference. The English had a theory once, that weight was of no moment in trotting; and some of the best horses they ever had, such as Archer and Ogden's mare, carried about 168lbs. in their performances, although the matches were made catch-weight. It is curious that they should have cherished such a delusion; for in reference to running-horses they appreciated the effect of weight closely enough. About the close of the last century, however, some of the more reflective began to doubt this maxim; and when Robson's mare Phenomena came out, she being a very easy-going-trotter and no puller, they got a boy out of the racing-stables at Newmarket, and practised him in the riding of her. They soon found out the difference between 168lbs. and the comparative trifle that the boy rode. The mare won her two matches, doing seventeen miles in fifty-six minutes in the first, and seventeen miles in fifty-three minutes in the second. Her owner then offered to match her to trot *nineteen miles and a half* in an hour; but the backers of time declared they had had quite enough of Phenomena and her boy from Newmarket.

XXV.

The Gray Mare Lady Suffolk. — Her Pedigree. — Place of Breeding. — Sale to David Bryan. — Description of Lady Suffolk. — Her Performances. — More than Fifteen Years on the Course. — Trotted 138 Races, and won 88 Times. — Suffolk and Sam Patch. — Suffolk and Black Hawk. — Suffolk and the Virginia Mare. — Suffolk and Rattler. — Suffolk, Dutchman, and Rattler. — Suffolk and Awful. — Suffolk, Napoleon, Cato, and Ion. — Suffolk, Dutchman, and Rattler again. — Suffolk and Dutchman.

ALMOST everybody in this country has heard more or less of Lady Suffolk, the famous old gray mare, whose name stood once at the head of the record, as having made the fastest time. It will be twenty-eight years next month since I rode her in the first race she ever trotted. And as I know it will be interesting to the gentlemen who knew her to recall some of her exploits, and useful to those of a later date to be somewhat acquainted with the history of such a celebrated trotter, I shall proceed to relate about all I know respecting her. Lady Suffolk was bred in Suffolk County on this island, and hence her name. Her dam was by Plato, a son of imported Messenger; and her sire, Engineer, was also by Messenger: so she was closely inbred to the horse from whom the best strains of trotting-blood originally proceeded. The dam of Lady Suffolk was bred by Gen. Floyd, of Smithtown, Long Island. His son sold her to Mr. Charles Little, who parted with her to Mr. Blaydenburgh. While she was owned by the latter gentleman she was put to Engineer, a good running-horse by imported Messenger, but without a clear pedigree on his dam's side.

The filly foal produced by the Plato mare and Engineer was dropped in 1833; and when two years old she was sold to David Bryant, a man who knew but little about the management of trotting-horses at that time, and was always a hard, reckless master for the wonder he had got hold of. When young, Lady Suffolk was an iron-gray, rather dark than light; but in her old age she became almost white. She was, in my judgment, but little, if any, above fifteen hands and an inch high. It has been stated in print, and I have often heard it said, that she was fifteen two; but I never called her more than fifteen one, or fifteen one and a half at the outside. She was well made, — long in the body; back a little roached; powerful long quarters; hocks let down low; short cannon bones, and long fetlocks. For many years her ankles were straight, pastern-joints fine; but, prior to the close of her long and very extraordinary career, she was a little knuckled. She had good shoulders, a light and slim but yet muscular neck, a large, long, bony head, and big ears. To look at her, the worst point about her was her feet. They were small and crimpy, — what is called mulish; but they were sound and tough in texture. In trotting, she went with her head low, and nose thrust out. Her neck was very straight. I have seen it stated that it was finely arched, but it is all a mistake: if there was any deviation from the straight, it inclined more to the ewe-neck than to an arch.

In February, 1838, being then five years old in reckoning, but not quite so much actually, Lady Suffolk made her first public trot. She continued on the turf until the latter end of October, 1853, a period of more than fifteen years; during which time she met almost all the celebrated horses of the day, and trotted no less than one hundred and thirty-eight races, besides receiving three forfeits. As they were all races of heats, and many of them four or five heats, I estimate that she took the word from the judges above four hundred times, perhaps nearer five hundred. She won eighty-eight times, besides three forfeits; and the amount she earned in stakes and purses was no less than $35,011.

When it is remembered, in addition to all this, that the heats in her races were as often two and three mile as one, and sometimes four-mile heats, it will be plain to everybody that the mare had inherited in great perfection the hardy constitution, unflinching game, and enormous stamina with which her grandsire, Messenger, was so eminently gifted. It was all but marvellous, that, until she was more than twenty years old, the gallant gray mare stood up under the system, or rather want of system, pursued by her owner, and, in season and out of season, always answered when he called.

The Lady began in a modest way. She was not one of the high-priced and precious youngsters whose fame is sounded far and loud before they have had saddle or harness on; but being at a trot we had up at Babylon, on a terribly cold day in February, 1838, Bryant put her in to trot mile heats, under saddle, for a subscription purse, which amounted to the munificent sum of eleven dollars. I was there, and he came to me to ride her, to which I readily consented; for I liked the looks of the wiry little gray mare, and knew that she could trot a little. The horse opposed to us was a bay gelding called Sam Patch, so named after his owner, who rode him. We started, and the Lady won the first heat in 3m. 01s.; Sam got the second in 3m. 03s.: but the Lady let out another link in the third heat, and beat him handsomely in 3m. 00s. It has been stated that the best time in this race was 3m. 01s; but I know that the third heat was no more than 3m.

As the spring came on, Bryant put her in training; that is, he fed her, and gave her plenty of work; which, in fact, was about all she wanted to get into fair condition at any time. On the 20th of June, he trotted her for a purse on the Beacon Course, New Jersey, two-mile heats in harness. The other was a black gelding called Black Hawk, that Wm. Whelan had. Bryant drove the mare the first heat, but was beat in 5m. 42s., and then came for me to drive. I consented, but had no confidence that she could win it. I was not mistaken; though she made another good game heat, the time of which was 5m. 42s. again. For a five-year-old mare, and one that had been raised rather on the pinching than the forcing system, this was a fair race; and most people would have given her a short holiday after it.

But Dave Bryant had no notion of letting her stand still when there was the ghost of a chance to make a few dollars; and two days afterwards he had her at it again, two-mile heats, under saddle. This time, too, it was against a mare that had come on from Philadelphia with a great reputation and a host of backers. She was a handsome chestnut, and called then the Virginia Mare. Afterwards they changed her name to Lady Victory, and then to Kate Horn. George Woodruff had brought her on from Philadelphia, having tried her two miles before he came, over the Hunting-park Course, in 5m. 09s. Many gentlemen from Philadelphia had come to the Beacon to back the Virginia Mare; and she was the favorite at one hundred to twenty-five. There were two others in the race besides the chestnut and Suffolk; and the chance of the latter was thought so ill of, that Bryant could get no one to ride her. In this emergency he swore he would ride her himself, and mounted. George Woodruff was to give the Philadelphians a signal when he had the race safe; but the gray mare was all on edge that day: the saddle-work suited her. She went ahead, and won the first heat in 5m. 15s.; and George Woodruff made no sign. Still the confidence of the friends of the Virginia Mare did not leave her. But the Lady of Suffolk won again, in 5m. 17s.; and Uncle George Woodruff never made that signal. It was a heavy blow to the Philadelphia party, and a wonderful hoist to Bryant and the young gray mare. This was on the 22d of June.

On the 4th of July he had her out again, at the same Beacon Course, to trot two-mile heats under saddle, against no less a horse than Rattler, who was then in charge of

Peter Whelan. It resulted in a race of three heats. The lady won the first in 5m. 29s. The second heat was a very severe one. The last mile they were head-and-head nearly all the way; and, after a desperate struggle home, Rattler just won by eight inches. Nothing but the fine riding of Peter Whelan, who was a splendid horseman, enabled Rattler to snatch this heat from Lady Suffolk. Bryant now came to me, and asked me to ride. I told him, that, in my opinion, the mare could not win; and that if I found it was the case I should not punish her. The truth was, that she had had a little too much of it for a five-year-old; and, with all her wonderful toughness and elasticity of constitution, she had gone off since she won in 5.15, 5.17. In the third heat with Rattler I found she could not win, and took her in hand on the second mile. He won it in 5.40, and she was distanced. We had another race that day, in which I drove Dutchman; but that is nothing to the purpose here, except to say that Lady Suffolk's next race was with him and Rattler. It was at the Beacon, on the 1st of October, two-mile heats, under saddle. The Lady was distanced the first heat in 5.17.

On the 8th, Bryant had her out again to trot two-mile heats in harness, against Awful, also at the Beacon. Awful beat her in 5.28, 5.21½. On the 15th, at the same place, the Lady again trotted two-mile heats in harness, this time against Napoleon, a big bay gelding, Cato, a brown gelding, and Ion. Napoleon won in three heats,— 5.42½, 5.38, 5.39. Cato won the second heat. Bryant drove Lady Suffolk in the first and second heats; and then, according to his usual practice when there was no chance left, he came and invited me to drive. The track was heavy in this race. This was on the 15th. Two days afterwards, Bryant had her in Philadelphia, and then and there trotted her two-mile heats under saddle, on the Hunting-park Course, against Polly Smallfry and Madame Royal. The gray mare won it in two heats, in 5.18, 5.26. The next day, the 18th, Lady Suffolk was trotted again; this time three-mile heats under saddle, and against Rattler, Lady Victory (formerly the Virginia Mare), and Ben Franklin. Rattler won in 8.11, 8.17. The track was heavy.

On the 22d, Bryant had Lady Suffolk back at the Beacon again, where he trotted her two-mile heats under saddle, against Dutchman and Rattler. As I was sick, Peter Whelan rode Dutchman, and William Whelan at this time had Rattler. Bryant rode the Lady. Dutchman won in 5.38, 5.52. The track was heavy. Lady Suffolk's owner was not yet content with her season's work. On the 24th, he trotted her mile-heats, three in five, in harness, against Dutchman. The mare was unsteady, and no wonder. She broke up several times; and I distanced her the first heat in 2m. 49s.

Thus late in season, within a month and a day of Christmas, the work of the young gray mare for her first season of fifteen on the turf had come to a close. She had trotted eleven races, — two of mile heats, eight of two-mile heats, and one of three-mile heats. For a five-year old mare, this was an immense amount of fast work; and it is to be remembered that her opponents were not middling horses, but some of the best that ever appeared on the trotting-turf. Dutchman, Rattler, Awful, &c., were the competitors of this young mare in her first season. But although Lady Suffolk received no apparent injury from the number of her arduous exploits, the example set by Bryant in trotting her so much is not one to be followed. Indeed, I recommend that it shall be carefully avoided; for the mare's escape from evils which might reasonably have been expected to follow was purely exceptional. Such an amount of trotting with elder horses of first-rate powers would ruin an ordinary five-year-old; and it was only because Lady Suffolk was "a horse above ordinances," like English Eclipse, that she was enabled to stand it with apparent impunity. Therefore, while remembering her astonishing endurance and success, let us avoid the great risk which Bryant needlessly incurred of prematurely using up one of the best animals that ever took hold of a trotting-bit. And here, too, it is also to be borne in mind, that the breeding of the mare must have been such as to produce an enormous amount of stamina, and capability to resist wear and tear in every sense. What, then, was that breeding? The answer is simply, that she was at least three-fourths thoroughbred, and was also bred in-and-in, her sire and the sire of her dam having both been got by imported Messenger. Let not these things be lost sight of as I continue her history.

XXVI.

Regarding Early Maturity. — Lady Suffolk and Apollo. — Lady Suffolk and Dutchman. — Suffolk and Cato. — Suffolk, Lady Victory, and Lafayette. — Suffolk, Henry, Celeste, and Cato. — Suffolk and Don Juan. — Suffolk and Ellen Jewett. — Suffolk and Independence. — Suffolk and Dutchman. — Suffolk, Celeste, and Napoleon. — Suffolk against Time. — Suffolk against Bonaparte. — Suffolk and Aaron Burr.

THE commencement of Lady Suffolk's history interested those who remembered her performances five-and-twenty years before, and revived the discussion about the forcing-system and early maturity. It was admitted that David Bryant trotted the mare too much in her first season; but some still held that early maturity was a good thing, and predicted that it will be hereafter one of the chief aims of the breeders. I am somewhat afraid that it will; and being convinced that it will be mischievous, and end in the premature decay of many good horses, I have protested against it. The argument is this: if a colt can be made as good at three years old as another will be at five or six, there is a great saving of time and expense. Now, this is not the proper way to state the question; for a colt may be as fast at three as another is at five or six, and still be an inferior horse; and it is my opinion that the method adopted to make him at three equal to what the other will be at six is almost certain to render him an inferior animal as regards duration.

As I before stated, when treating of this matter, early maturity is almost always followed by early decay. If it could be had without that result, it would of course be a good thing to strive for; but the forcing with strong feed when young, and the hard work of training and trotting at an early age, so overdraws upon the constitution, and makes such inroads upon the legs while they are supple and growing, that the horse is often practically ruined before he is a horse at all. For those who raise colts to sell, it is a profitable system; it being for their interest to get them taken off at three, rather than at five or six years old: but next to nobody wants a trotting-colt merely because he can go very fast at three years old. If there is not a good chance for future improvement, and promise of reasonable duration upon the turf or road, the colt is really worth but little. I am satisfied that this improvement and duration are not half as likely to follow in the case of one who has been forced by high feed and trained early, as in that of one who has been treated more according to the order of nature.

Expedition in such matter is commonly compensated for at the expense of the purchaser. I can remember when it took three times as long to tan a hide of sole-leather as it does now. The increased rapidity of the process is no doubt a gain to the tanner, and also to the manufacturing shoemaker; but how is it with the people who wear out the boots? One pair of the old sort of soles would wear out four of those tanned by the new process.

In this work, I have mentioned many famous trotters who improved in speed and bottom until they were eight or ten years old, and lasted until they were fifteen, — some of them until they were twenty. None of these horses were forced by high feeding when sucklings and yearlings, and none of them were trained at two and three years of age. If they had been, it is my belief that their careers upon the turf and road would have been ended just about where they began under the system which then prevailed. What has been the result of the forcing and early training of the thorough-bred running horse? Simply this: he is faster than he ever was at any former period, but his decay is very early and very rapid. In old times, when they never started until they were four or five years old, the great racers often ran on until they were ten or twelve. They now reach a pitch of astonishing speed and power at three and four years old, and few remain in active service on the turf after they are six The racing-trainers do not deny that the early maturity and training of the colts impair the durability of the race-horses; and this being so, I deny that the system ought to be adopted with our trotters. To follow a method for obtaining certain results at three years old at the expense of half or three-fourths the value of the horse when he becomes seven or eight, is just like the conduct of the directors of joint-stock companies when they pay dividends out of the capital stock.

Lady Suffolk's second year upon the turf (1839) was as arduous as her first. She trotted twelve races, — one of mile heats, two of mile heats three in five, eight of two-mile heats, and one of four-mile heats. Her season began on the 26th of April, when she trotted two-mile heats under saddle against Apollo, at the Beacon Course, New Jersey. Apollo was a blind horse, a chestnut gelding. The mare won the first heat in 5m. 21s.; and, finding the blind one had no chance, I drew him. On the 27th of the same month, and at the same course, Dutchman and Lady Suffolk went two-mile heats under saddle. I beat her the first heat in 5m. 16s., and in the second led all the way, and won as I pleased in 5m. 9s. At the first turn of the second mile in this heat, and when the Lady was close to me, I just touched Dutchman with the spur; and he shot away from it, twenty-five yards ahead of her, like an arrow from a bow. The Lady lay by all May and June, but came out on the 3d of July, feeling very fine, to trot Cato at the Beacon, two-mile heats under saddles. She won the first heat in 5m. 39s., and he was then drawn.

Bryant then took her to Philadelphia, and on the 24th of that month trotted her against George Woodruff's Lady Victory and Mr. Duffy's Lafayette. The latter was a brown gelding, about fifteen handst hree inches high; and he was a good horse. It was two-mile heats in harness, and a very fine race ensued. They all got a heat, but Lady Victory won. She took the first, Lafayette the second, Suffolk the third; and in the fourth "Uncle George" came again with Lady Victory, and won. The time was 5.28, 5.31, 5.32, 5.42. A match between the two mares grew out of this race; and the next day they trotted it over again. It was a near thing, but Suffolk's great recuperative powers enabled her to stay the longest. She won the first heat in 5m. 38s.; Lady Victory got the second in 5m. 35s.; but Suffolk secured the third in 5m. 40s. Here were seven two-mile heats by these mares trotted in two days, and still Bryant thought the Long-Island mare had not had enough. He went off and matched her to trot mile heats against Lafayette the next day, — he to carry two in a buggy, and she to go in harness. The buggy weighed 112lbs.; Mr. Duffy, the driver, 150lbs.; and his friend 111lbs. This was 373lbs. Lafayette beat the Lady in 2m. 52s. and 2m. 50s.; she being stiff and sore and utterly unfit to trot.

She had a rest through the month of September, and on the 3d of October came out on the Beacon to trot two-mile heats in harness, against Henry, Celeste, and Cato. Henry was a handsome chestnut gelding in the stable of Harry Jones. Celeste was a flea-bitten gray mare in mine. Henry won the first heat in 5m. 28s; Lady Suffolk took the next in the same time, and the third in 5.26; thus winning the race. The next week the same horses, together with Don Juan, trotted two-mile heats in harness, on the Centreville. Harry won this in 5m. 20s., 5m. 28s. I was second with Celeste, and Lady Suffolk was distanced in the second heat; but this was caused by my having run into her, and upset her sulky.

On the 23d of October she went two-mile heats under saddle against Don Juan on the Beacon, and beat him handily in 5m. 14s., 5m. 24s. Bryant now took her to Boston; and at the Cambridge Course, on the 15th of

November, trotted her four-mile heats under saddle, against Ellen Jewett, a little bay mare. The gray mare took the lead in each heat, and was never headed. She won in 11m. 22s., 11m. 34s. That very same day, Bryant actually trotted her mile heats, three in five, in harness, against Independence. The latter was a chestnut gelding and a good horse. He had not great speed then; but he afterwards came here, and got to be very fast. He beat the Lady in 2m. 45½s., 2m. 45s., 2m. 47s. Even this was not enough for Bryant. He trotted her the same race against Independence the next day, and got her beat again as he deserved. But she won two heats — the second and third — in this second race. The time of the five was 2m. 52s., 2m. 53s., 2m. 49s., 2m. 47s., 2m. 50s. That ended her racing for the year, and there is no need to recapitulate her performances.

She had again proved herself as hard as steel and as tough as whalebone; and Bryant had given another notable specimen or two of his reckless and foolhardy way of carrying on a campaign. At Philadelphia he trotted her three days in succession. On the first of them, four two-mile heats; on the second, three two-mile heats; on the third, mile heats, — all in harness. Then at Boston he trots her four-mile heats, and mile heats, three in five, in harness, on the same day; and mile heats, three in five, in harness, on the following day; and in this last there were five heats.

Lady Suffolk had now been two years on the turf. She commenced in 1840 on the 6th of May, by trotting two-mile heats under saddle, at the Hunting-park Course, Philadelphia, against Dutchman. The bay horse beat her in two good heats, — 5m. 5s., 5m. 6s. Two days afterwards, they trotted three-mile heats under saddle, over the same course; and Dutchman was again victorious, making the heats in 7m. 51s. each. It was rather a singular circumstance that they should have been just alike in time. In less than a week after these two hard losing races, Bryant trotted Lady Suffolk on the Centreville Course, Long Island, against

Celeste and Napoleon, two-mile heats in harness. Celeste was the gray mare heretofore mentioned as in my stable. A race of three heats resulted; in which Napoleon won the first, and Lady Suffolk the second and third. But Napoleon was distanced in the third heat; so my mare was second in the race. The time was 5m. 26s., 5m. 33s., 5m. 32s.

On the 11th of June, Lady Suffolk trotted a mile against time, on the Stevens Running Course, Hoboken. The match grew out of a remark made by a gentleman in conversation, that Bonaparte was the only horse capable of trotting a mile over that course in less that 2m. 40s. So Lady Suffolk was backed to beat that time. The track was sandy and very deep, but it was not at all holding; and the gray mare went away at a slashing gait, and did the mile in 2m. 32s. Much amazement was caused; but I cannot see that there had been any good reason for the belief that the course was so very slow for a trotter going under saddle. If she had had wheels behind her, or if the ground had been heavy and holding as well as deep, it would have been different. The Lady now enjoyed her ease until the 30th of June, when she trotted four-mile heats under saddle, against Bonaparte, on the Centreville Course. This Bonaparte was a chestnut gelding, sixteen hands high, and well bred. He had been worked on Mr. Stevens's running-track at Hoboken, and was thought to be very fast, as well as stout. His time over that course was such that they thought no other horse could equal it, until Lady Suffolk knocked it all to pieces. On the trotting-course, Lady Suffolk beat him easily enough, — four-mile heats. In the first of them I rode him, and the time was 11m. 15s. In the second heat, William Whelan rode him; and he was again beaten handily in 11m. 58s.

Lady Suffolk was not engaged again until the 21st September, when she trotted with Aaron Burr, two-mile heats, on the Beacon Course. Aaron Burr was a small but handsome and well-bred blood bay horse. He was in my stable. In this race he won the first heat; but the Lady took the second and third after a close contest. The time was 5m. 22s., 5m. 21s., 5m. 35s. He had trotted up to her so well in this race that I was still of opinion that he could beat her; and in consequence they were matched for $2,000. But the little horse went amiss, and paid forfeit. Still the Lady was kept busy. On the 24th of September, she was trotted two-mile heats under saddle, against Dutchman, on the Beacon Course, and beat him in 4m. 59s., 5m. 3½s. A match was forthwith made for one thousand dollars a side, half-forfeit, that she could beat any horse that could be produced the next day, mile heats under saddle. The Lady was on hand on the morrow, but the other side paid forfeit. The time soon came when she had to pay.

On the 29th of that month, being engaged to trot with Dutchman and Washington on the Beacon Course, she was found to be unable to start. It was announced that she was lame; but certain suspicious people would not believe it, and got up a clamor. In order to satisfy them, the mare was led out; and lame, indeed, she was. She could hardly put one of her fore-feet to the ground, and was literally on three legs. Very few believed that she would ever come right; and I no more expected to see her trot again that year than I expected to see the grass grown again in the winter. Nevertheless, after a rest of a couple of months, she appeared as sound as a new dollar, to trot on the Beacon, a match of two-mile heats under saddle, against Don Juan. The race was set for the last day of November, and he paid her a forfeit of $500. The work she did that year was not as great as she had done in 1838 and 1839, but it was still a great deal; and luckily she went into winter quarters, giving every promise of another fine campaign next season.

XXVII.

Suffolk, Confidence, and Washington. — Suffolk, Confidence, and Aaron Burr. — Suffolk, Awful, and Aaron Burr. — Suffolk and Ripton. — Suffolk and Oneida Chief the Pacer. — Suffolk and Americus, Five-mile Heats. — Suffolk, Ripton, and Confidence. — Suffolk and Rifle *vs.* Hardware and Apology. — Longtails and Docking. — Suffolk and Ripton. — Suffolk, Beppo, and Independence. — Suffolk, Beppo, and Oneida Chief. — Suffolk, Americus, Ripton, Washington, and Pizarro. — Suffolk, J. C. Calhoun, and Fairy Queen.

IN 1841, Lady Suffolk commenced her campaign at the Centreville Course on the 4th of May, in a trot of two-mile heats in harness, against Confidence and Washington. The gray mare was successful, winning in two heats of 5m. 13½s. and 5m. 41s. Washington was distanced. In her next trot on the Centreville, she went against Confidence and Aaron Burr, mile heats, three in five. Aaron Burr was in my stable. He was a bay gelding, about fifteen hands two inches high, a good stepper and long stayer. This race was won by Confidence. I must now mention the trots at the Hunting-park Course against Dutchman, and the trots in which Lady Suffolk contended with Ripton; for, though they have been mentioned in the sketches given heretofore of those horses, it is desirable that they should be recapitulated here, in order that, having Lady Suffolk's performances before him altogether, the reader may be better enabled to comprehend the immense stamina and marvellous bottom of the gray mare. In the two-mile-heat race at the Hunting-park Course, Lady Suffolk beat Dutchman in three heats,—5m. 12½s., 5m. 19½s., 5m. 21s.

This was in harness. The second, of three-mile heats under saddle, she also won in 7m. 40½s., 7m. 56s.

It is perfectly clear to my mind that Dutchman was a little off in this race; but it is also clear that the gray mare was then very good. On the 13th of June, at the Beacon Course, we had a very tough race of three-mile heats in harness, between Lady Suffolk, Awful, and my horse Aaron Burr. The odds was on the Lady at the start; and she won the first heat in 8m. 2½s. Aaron Burr was second, and close to her. The next heat was dead between the Lady and Aaron, in 8m. 3s. The betting was very lively now, she being the favorite at odds. But the third heat I won with Aaron in 8m. 8s., and was satisfied that I had my Lady beat. She was second, and Awful ruled out for not winning a heat in three. The fourth heat was won by Aaron Burr in 8m. 16s.; and there was much lamentation among those who had laid odds on Lady Suffolk. They attributed her defeat to David Bryant, who persisted in driving himself, when they wanted to put another man in his place.

On the 5th of July, at the Beacon, the Lady beat Ripton, under saddle, mile heats, in 2m. 35s., 2m. 37½s. Ripton carried a hundred and sixty-nine pounds instead of a hundred and forty-five pounds; for I was then twenty-four pounds over weight. On the 22d of the same month, and at the same course, Lady Suffolk beat Awful two-mile heats in harness, in three heats. He won the first in 5m. 26½s., and it was thought he had got her; but the Lady went away, and won the second heat in 5m. 28s., and then the third in 5m. 24s.

Five days after that, at the same course, the gray mare met Oneida Chief the pacer. This horse was in my stable: and, when he went in harness, I drove him; but, when it was under saddle, I did not ride him. He was a light chestnut, with a white mane and tail, and was a stayer as well as fast. In this race on the Beacon, which was two-mile heats under saddle, the odds were a hundred to sixty on the Chief at the start. But the mare went away, and distanced him in 5m. 5s.; winning the race with very great ease. Suffolk had now done a good deal of work, and had been on the whole very successful. Early in the fall, the great match of the year came off on the Centreville Course. It was five-mile heats to wagons, for $5,500. Bryant drove his mare, and George Spicer did the like for Americus. The betting at the start was a hundred to seventy on Americus. It was the greatest betting-race we had had for some time; and the gelding fully justified the good opinion of those who laid odds on him. He won the first heat with ease in 13m. 54s.; the fastest mile being the fifth, in 2m. 40½s. It was now "a horse to a hen" on the gelding. In the second heat he again beat her easily in 13m. 58½s.; the best mile being the fifth, 2m. 44s. This closed the performances of 1841: in which year she had trotted two races of mile heats, six heats; four races of two-mile heats, ten heats; two races of three-mile heats, six heats; and one race of five-mile heats, two heats.

In 1842 the mare began at the Beacon, on the 7th of May, two-mile heats in harness, against Ripton and Confidence. The white-legged gelding won it in 5m. 10½s., 5m. 12½s. Three days afterwards at the Centreville, it being the day that Boston and Fashion ran, Suffolk turned the tables on Ripton. It was the "ladies' day" all round at both courses, and the mares won. Suffolk beat Ripton in 5m. 10s., 5m. 15s. I have always had a notion that Ripton was defeated that day, not because the mare was too good for him, but by reason of something I afterwards learned, not necessary to be mentioned here. I drove the little horse myself. At the Hunting-park Course, on the last day of that month, they met again, two-mile heats in harness; and he beat her in three heats, she winning the second. In the first, as I have related in giving his history, Ripton made the best two-mile time in harness then on record, — 5m.

7s. It had, however, been surpassed under saddle by Suffolk herself. Two days afterwards, Suffolk and Rifle performed a feat which long stood on the books as the best of its kind. They went in double harness against Hardware and Apology, two-mile heats. Hardware was a big, tall, bay horse, with a short switch tail. Apology, when he came to me in 1835, was one of the handsomest horses I ever saw.

In those days it was the fashion to have horses pricked and docked; and so he was deprived of the long tail that then adorned him. It was a foolish fashion. The long tails of the present day not only make the horses look stylish, but are of great service in the heats of summer when flies abound, and, do what you will, cannot be kept off the sides and flanks of our animals, except by the switching and lashing of their own tails. Still, I am not in favor of having them trail the ground, like the trains of ladies in their full dresses; for then they are an inconvenience and unnecessary bother to the trotter and his driver. There is a moderation in the matter which should be followed. Some people now-a-days seem only to look for a tail, — a long, big, luxuriant tail. If they find that, they seem altogether careless as to what sort of a horse is before it. Now, I advise buyers and breeders to look the horse over first, and, if they find him suitable, take him, no matter about the tail. Old Abdallah, rough, raw-boned and uncouth to look at, but a king among horses, had nothing but a rat-tail.

Now, to come back to the double-harness trot at Hunting-park Course, from which I have been thus led away: Suffolk and Rifle distanced Hardware and Apology the first heat in 5m. 19s. It was justly considered a very great performance; and, though we have seen Mr. Bonner drive Palmer and the Flatbush Maid two miles in his road-wagon in 5m. 1½s., we must remember that twenty-four years ago, when Lady Suffolk and Rifle did their feat, driving in double harness was not much followed, and they had next to no practice with each other. This is a consideration that must not be lost sight of; for, though it is possible and probable that the *Ledger* mares might have beaten Suffolk and Rifle, it is just about as certain to my mind as any thing can be, that hardly any other team, of those that have been since prominent, could have done so.

At the Eagle Course, Trenton, Lady Suffolk was beaten, two-mile heats, by Ripton, in 5m. 6s., 5m. 22s.; and, on the 1st of August, he beat her and Confidence, three-mile heats in harness, in 8m., 7m. 56½s. The backers of Suffolk growled lustily, and said, that, if Byrant had let George Spicer drive, she could not have lost it. The reason given was that she had made better time some other day; but this was fallacious reasoning. There never was a horse yet, and there never will be, in my opinion, who, being capable of a really great thing, can be relied upon to do it all the time. Therefore it is the height of foolishness to expect that a trotter will always go up to the best mark he has made, unless he is a young and constantly improving horse. In order to the accomplishment of the great feat, there was probably a combination of favorable circumstances. Weather, track, driver or rider, and ability of opponents, were all happily in a concatenation for speed; and, in addition to and above all this, the horse was right in tune, keyed up to the finest pitch. Now, these things may all fall in and combine again; but it is perfect nonsense to expect that they are going to do so every day the horse trots in public. Yet a great many do so expect; and, when the race is over, these are the ones who fall to cursing the driver or owner, and blaming and underrating the horse, when there is in truth nothing blamable but their own extravagant expectations. It is true that Bryant would drive, and that Spicer could drive better; but I do not admit, that, had Spicer been behind the mare, she could have beaten Ripton and myself. Lady Suffolk after that beat Independence, two-mile heats in harness. He was a long-tailed, chestnut horse, about fifteen hands two inches high. In this trot he was out of condition, and was distanced the first heat in 5m. 37s.

In 1843, Lady Suffolk, Beppo, and Independence went mile heats, three in five, under saddle, on the Beacon Course. This race was on the 4th of July. It is to be remembered that it was catch-weight, and that she carried 143lbs., which was two pounds less than required by the rule. The Lady was ridden by Albert Conkling. Beppo was a little chestnut gelding, with a high head, short switch tail, and very gay and gallant style of trotting. He belonged to Mr. James Valentine, and was very fast. As early as 1836, this little horse, in a trial at the Eagle Course, Trenton, two days before he went a race, trotted half a mile in one minute and nine seconds. George Youngs rode him on this trial, and also in the race with Suffolk and Independence. There were five heats of it. The Lady won the first in 2m. 28½s. The second was dead between her and Beppo in 2m. 28s. The third, Independence won in the same time; and the Lady took the fourth and fifth in 2m. 29s. and 2m. 32s. Independence was ridden in this race by Lewis Rogers, formerly of the Red House, New York. On the 12th of the same month, and at the same course, there was a race between trotters under saddle, catch-weight, and Oneida Chief pacer, in harness. Suffolk carried 143lbs. as before, and Beppo 135lbs. It was here that the Lady made the time which stood at the head of the record for ten years (when Tacony beat it); and here also it is to be noted that the weight she carried was two pounds under the rule. She won in three straight heats in 2m. 26½s., 2m. 27s., and 2m. 27s. It has often been said that in this race she was just off grass; but this is a mistake. She had gone a race eight days before, as I have shown, and was well enough seasoned for mile heats under saddle when she made the fast time.

On the 19th of July, she met Beppo again under saddle, and beat him in 2m. 30½s., 2m. 42½s., 2m. 28s. On the 15th of August, she went three-mile heats under saddle against the pacer Oneida Chief, who beat her in 7m. 44s. and 7m. 52s. The mare was a little off, and Bryant was badly blamed again; but I am unable to see the justice of it. In September they went again mile heats, three in five; she under saddle, and the Chief in harness. As usual, I drove the horse. The mare won that day in three straight heats; and it is a singular circumstance that the pacer pulled a shoe off in each heat. The time was 2m. 29s., 2m. 30s., 2m. 28½s. Suffolk then beat Confidence in harness in 2m. 38s., 2m. 39s., and 2m. 41s. At the Kendall Course, Baltimore, Oneida Chief beat her three miles under saddle, in 7m. 48s.; and he beat her and Dutchman, three mile heats in harness, in three heats. The pacer won the first in 7m. 59s., Lady Suffolk got the second in 8m. 15s., and the Chief the third in 8m. 1s. It will be seen by the foregoing, that the mare was not successful at long distances that year; and, if we should look no further, we might be led to conclude, that, though she had gained in speed, she had weakened in bottom. In 1844, Lady Suffolk began with long heats, and was successful.

On the 20th of May, at the Beacon Course, she beat Americus, Ripton, Washington, and Pizarro, two-mile heats in harness, in three heats, 5m. 17s., 5m. 19s., 5m. 18s. At Centreville, on the 6th of June, she won again at three-mile heats in harness, beating Columbus in 7m. 51s. and 8m. 2s. Then she went three-mile heats on the Beacon against Americus and Columbus. Americus won in 8m. 53¼s., 8m. 1s.; and Columbus was distanced. The mare beat Duchess and Washington, over the Beacon Course, in the mud, in four heats. Washington won the first in 2m. 38s. Lady Suffolk won the other three in 2m. 33½s., 2m. 34s., 2m. 37s. In October, Lady Suffolk went mile heats, three in five, against J. C. Calhoun and Fairy Queen, two pacers. They had five heats of it. Calhoun won the first and second in 2m. 29s., 2m. 31s. The trotting-mare took the other three in 2m. 28s., 2m. 29s., 2m. 30s. That concluded her performances in 1844. We shall find, that, next year, she and Americus went at it in downright earnest, and trotted some desperate races of long heats. They trotted five times, and Lady Suffolk won three of the five races; but particular mention of these I must postpone until the next chapter. Americus and Lady Suffolk were very close together as trotters. Both were fast, and both were stout enough to go long heats and repeat them often.

XXVIII.

Suffolk, Brown Columbus, and Americus. — More Races with Americus. — Suffolk and Duchess. — Suffolk and Moscow. — Suffolk, Moscow, and Americus. — Suffolk and James K. Polk the pacer. — Suffolk and Hector. — Suffolk at Saratoga. — Suffolk and Roanoke the pacer. — Suffolk and Lady Sutton. — Suffolk and Ripton, between Christmas Day and New Year's. — Suffolk, Lady Sutton, and Lady Moscow. — Moscow's son, Privateer. — Suffolk, Sutton, and Americus. — Suffolk and James K. Polk. — Suffolk lamed at Saratoga.

I HAVE now brought the public performances of Lady Suffolk down to the year 1845, of which I am about to speak. Her trotting began that season on the Union Course on the 28th of April, when she went two-mile heats in harness, against Brown Columbus and Americus. Brown Columbus was brought here by Mr. Underhill, who sometimes drove him. In this race with Suffolk and Americus, I drove him myself. He was a horse about fifteen hands three inches, a little scant, perhaps, and used to hit his knees, so that we had to trot him in boots. I am very often asked what is the remedy when a horse hits himself in action. The true answer is, that, if it is habitual, there is no remedy but to put boots on. Lady Suffolk won the race in two heats; in both of which Columbus was second and Americus third. The time of it was 5m. 20s., 5m. 29s. A week afterwards Lady Suffolk went two-mile heats in harness, over the Centreville Course, against Americus. The race was a good one of three heats; of which the Lady won the first and third, and Americus took the second. The time was 5m. 9s., 5m. 16s., 5m. 12s.

On the 19th of May, Americus, Lady Suffolk, and Brown

Columbus went three-mile heats in harness, on the Union Course. Americus won in two heats; Suffolk was second in both, and Columbus distanced in the last of them. The time was 8m., 8m. 5½s. The Lady was kept hard at it, as usual; and, on the 3d of June, trotted three-mile heats in harness, over the Hunting-park Course, Philadelphia, with Americus. She won in three heats, of which Americus got the first. The time was 8m. 2s., 8m. 7¼s., 8m. 17s.

On the 8th of October, Lady Suffolk trotted mile heats, three in five in harness, over the Beacon Course, with Duchess. The latter was a brown mare about fifteen hands high. She had a habit of switching her tail as she went; and, like Flora Temple and Lady Clifton, she was capital at coming in on the home-stretch. If she was on good terms with an opponent when she swung into the straight side, it was very difficult to beat her out. William Whelan drove her in this race. They had four heats of it, and Duchess won; Suffolk only getting the third. The time was 2m. 37s., 2m. 35½s., 2m. 35¼s., 2m. 39s. Five days afterwards, Lady Suffolk went against Moscow, mile heats, three in five, in harness, on the same course. Moscow was a bay gelding, with white legs and a bald face. He belonged to Gen. Dunham, and was a big horse, sixteen hands high, raw-boned and up-headed. He was a hard puller. In this race, Hunt drove him. The Lady won in five heats, the third and fourth of which were won by Moscow. The time was 2m. 34s., 2m. 29½s., 2m. 30s., 2m. 34s., 2m. 36s. On the third day afterwards, and still on the Beacon, they went the same race again; and now Moscow beat her in four heats, of which she got the second. The time of these was 2m. 33½s., 2m. 31½s., 2m. 40s., 2m. 35s.

The last trot of Lady Suffolk in that year was at the Hunting-park Course, Philadelphia, where, on the 29th of October, she went three-mile heats in harness against Americus, and was defeated in two straight heats. The time was 8m. 5s., 7m. 59s. She had been successful this year, on the whole, having trotted two races of two-mile heats, both of which she won; three of three-mile heats, one of which she won; and three of mile heats, three in five, one of which she won. She had not a saddle on her back in that season in any public performance, nor did she go to wagon.

In 1846, Suffolk did not trot a great number of races. She began late in the year, and put them close together, all on the Union Course. Her first race was in September, the 27th, when she went mile heats, three in five, in harness, against Moscow and Americus, and won in three straight heats. Americus was second in the first heat, but Moscow beat him in the second and third. The time was 2m. 37½s., 2m. 37s., 2m. 35s. Ten days afterwards, the same horses went two-mile heats in harness; and Americus won it in two straight heats, Lady Suffolk being second in both of them. The time was 5m. 13s., 5m. 11s. The next week they went mile heats, three in five, in harness; and Suffolk won in five heats. Americus got the first in 2m. 34s.; Suffolk took the second in 2m. 34½s., and the third in precisely the same time. The fourth was a dead heat between Americus and Moscow in 2m. 35s.; and the Lady came along in the fifth, and won in 2m. 38½s.

In just a week from that day, that is, on the 22d of October, the Lady met James K. Polk the pacer, at three-mile heats. He was to go in harness, with a driver to weigh 140lbs., which was five pounds under weight; while she went under saddle, with the weight of 145lbs., according to rule. This pacer was a hard horse to beat in such a race. He was a chestnut gelding, fifteen hands three inches high, handsome, and a blood-like horse, with a long, sweeping tail. He was also a very hard puller. Albert Conklin drove him, and won in two straight heats. The time was good, — 7m. 46s., 7m. 46½s. Time-bets were made upon the Lady; and her time taken in the first heat was 7m. 49s. She went a faster mile in the race than he did; for her middle mile was 2m. 30s., while his was 2m. 31½s. This mile was the fastest in the race. On the 18th of November, they met again at two-mile heats; Lady Suffolk in harness, the pacer to a wagon. He beat her again in two heats of 5m. 8½s., 5m. 16s. The heats were both close, for her time was but half a second more in each. That finished her trotting in the year. It was a light one for her, but, next season, Bryant made her do enough to more than make up.

In 1847, Lady Suffolk's first trot was on the 7th of June, when she went against Hector, the little brown horse by Abdallah, of whom I have heretofore made mention. It was upon the Union Course, and the race three-mile heats under saddle; the Lady staking $500, to $300 on the part of the horse. She won it in two straight heats, — 7m. 56s., 8m. 6½s. Two days afterwards, they went two-mile heats under saddle, each to carry 184lbs. She won again in two heats; the time being 5m. 16½s., 5m. 24s. This was great weight to carry on a horse's back, exceeding the heaviest welter weights in the English steeple-chases, which seldom go above 168lbs. On the 14th of July, at the Centreville Course, the Lady under saddle went against James K. Polk the pacer to wagon, two-mile heats. She distanced him the first heat in 5m. 3s. Back again at the Union, on the 28th of the same month, she beat Moscow, mile heats, three in five, to wagons of 100lbs. The mare won it in three heats, — 2m. 37½s., 2m. 43½s., 2m. 39½s. Aug. 5, at the same course, she went mile heats, three in five, to wagon, against Moscow in harness, and won again in three straight heats, — 2m. 42½s., 2m. 33½s., 2m. 36s.

Suffolk now took a trip to Saratoga with the other fashionables, who gladly welcomed at the Springs the coming of the Lady in White. On the 14th of August, she trotted mile heats, three in five, to wagon of one hundred and one pounds, against Moscow in harness, and beat him in three straight heats, — 2m. 52s., 2m. 54s., 2m. 44s. From Saratoga, Lady Suffolk returned to Centreville, to go three-mile heats against the chestnut pacer James K. Polk. It was on the 13th of September. She went under saddle, he in harness. He beat her in two heats of 7m. 44s., 7m. 53s.

On the 1st of October, at the same course, she went against Roanoke the pacer, two-mile heats in harness. This horse was a roan, about fifteen and a half hands high, compactly made, with a long tail. He was known from one end of the country to the other almost. At that time Isaac Woodruff had him. In the race with Suffolk, he won the first heat in 5m. 13s., but was distanced in the next in 5m. 12½s. On the 15th of that month, at the Union Course, the Lady went two-mile heats under saddle, against James K. Polk the pacer to wagon. The chestnut beat her in two heats of 5m. 4½s., 5m. 9s. On the 28th, the Lady of Suffolk went two-mile heats in harness, at the same course, against Lady Sutton. This mare was a brown, low but sturdy, strong and game, — a mare of very fine stamina and endurance. At the time of this trot, James Whelpley had her. Suffolk won the race in two heats, — 5m. 10s., 5m. 12s. The Lady continued her doings very late that year; for the last race she went was on the 28th of December, on the Union Course. It was two-mile heats in harness, against Ripton. The Lady won in two heats, — 5m. 18½s., 5m. 25½s., — extraordinary time, it must be admitted, to make after Christmas, and before New-Year's Day. It will have been seen that the Lady was very successful this year: for she won nine races out of eleven; and, in the two wherein she was beaten, it was by James K. Polk the pacer, and not by any trotter.

In the following year, 1848, she did not do as much trotting, by reason of having met with an accident in the middle of the season. At the time when this befel her, she had been winning races hoof over hoof, and, but for the hurt she got, would very likely have made as successful a season of it as any she had seen. Lady Suffolk began operations that year at the Centreville Course on the 19th of May. She went mile heats, three in five, in harness, with Lady Sutton and Lady Moscow. The latter was a handsome bay mare, and of great speed and bottom. At that time she was owned by John Cutler of Albany; but afterwards became the property of my neighbor and friend, Sim Hoagland of East New York.

In 1865 we saw the last of her, as I mentioned at the time. But Sim has one of her colts; and, unless I am mistaken, he is a real good one. It is the solid, little gray horse Privateer, by Gray Messenger. I have had my eye on the little fellow out of the window, as he has gone by my door, on many a morning; and I predict that he will not disgrace his distinguished parentage. The race made by these three ladies was a remarkable one of six heats. They were all three stayers. Lady Sutton won the first heat; Suffolk second in 2m. 33s.; and the second heat was an exact repetition as to positions and time. The third heat was won by Suffolk, Lady Moscow being second, in 2m. 35s. Suffolk also won the fourth heat, and Lady Moscow was again second. Time, 2m. 37s. The fifth heat was won by Lady Moscow in 2m. 38s., and Suffolk was second; and the sixth heat Sutton won in 2m. 36s., Suffolk second. John Case drove Lady Moscow in that race.

On the 7th of June, at the same course, Lady Suffolk, Lady Sutton, and Americus went two-mile heats to wagons; and another exceedingly good and obstinately contested race was the result. Lady Suffolk won the first heat in 5m. 21s., Lady Sutton second. The second heat was dead between the mares in 5m. 13s. The third heat was also dead between the mares; and Americus was ruled out for not having won a heat in three, or made a dead heat. The time of the second dead heat was 5m. 17s. The ladies went off again; and, after a capital race, Lady Suffolk won it in 5m. 22s.

The Lady of Suffolk now had a let-up until the 4th of July, when she met her old and vigorous opponent, James K. Polk, two-mile heats; but, while she was under saddle, he went to a wagon of two hundred pounds. It was at the

Centreville. The Lady won in two heats, — 5m. 12s., 5m. 14s. On the 17th, at the same course, Lady Suffolk and Lady Sutton went mile heats, three in five, in harness. Lady Suffolk won in three heats, — 2m. 31s., 2m. 32s., 2m. 32. On the 22d, she went two-mile heats against James K. Polk, — she in harness, the pacer to a wagon weighing 220lbs. A close, desperate race of four heats followed. The Lady won the first heat in 5m. 22s. Then the pacer took a heat in 5m. 16s. The third heat was dead in 5m. 17s.; and the fourth heat the Lady won in 5m. 16s. With the weight behind him, the pacer, although defeated, must be held to have been an uncommonly good horse that day.

Having, perhaps, acquired a taste for the fragrant waters and other pleasant follies of the mountain springs last year, Lady Suffolk again left the briny shores of her native island to visit Saratoga in the height of summer-time. It was not with as good results as before; for here the accident befel which compelled Bryant to let her up for the balance of the year. The trot was mile heats in harness, between Lady Suffolk, Lady Moscow, and the gelding Moscow. Lady Suffolk won the first heat, but pulled up lame from having sprained her ankle. Nevertheless, Bryant started her for the second heat; but, before she had gone far, the mare was so lame that her driver was compelled to bring her to a stand-still, and the others went on and finished the race. It was won by the bay mare in four heats. Lady Suffolk trotted no more that year; and some thought, as she was led limping away on three legs, that the trotting-turf had seen the last of her. But this was a great mistake. The injury was not permanent; and the rest gave her wonderfully strong and elastic constitution a chance to restore the tone of her system. She recovered to such a purpose, that, the next year, she trotted no fewer than twenty races, as we shall presently see.

XXIX.

Suffolk and Lady Moscow. — Suffolk, Mac, Gray Eagle, and Gray Trouble. — Suffolk and Pelham. — Suffolk, Pelham, and Jack Rossiter. — Lady Suffolk, Lady Sutton, and Pelham. — Suffolk, Trustee, and Pelham. — Breeding of Trustee. — Description of Trustee — Suffolk and Long-Island Black Hawk. — Description of Black Hawk. — Death of Trustee.

WE now come to 1849, in which year, as I remarked in the last chapter, the gray mare came out fresh and fine after her let-up by reason of the accident at Saratoga, and trotted twenty races. This arduous season began at the Union Course on the 21st of May. Lady Suffolk and Lady Moscow went mile heats, three in five, in harness; and the bay mare won in four heats. Suffolk took the first, but lost the other three. The time was exactly the same in three of these heats, 2m. 34s. The second heat was 2m. 30s. The Lady now went down East, and trotted three races in Providence, R. I. The first was on the 5th of June, mile heats, three in five, under saddle. She went against Mac, Gray Eagle, and Gray Trouble, all under saddle. Mac was a very famous horse, and very fast. He was a brown gelding, fifteen and a half hands high. When he first came to my notice, he was owned by Mr. Robert Walton of Boston. He sold him to Harry Jones of New York, who in turn disposed of him to Mr. John McArdle of Albany. Gray Eagle was a gray gelding, fifteen hands high, and one of the most beautiful little horses ever seen. He was well broken, and a splendid driver, looking magnificent when going. Gray Trouble was a handsome gray gelding, fifteen hands three inches high, of elevated style, and a long strider. Gray Eagle belonged to me. William Woodruff rode him in this race. Bryant rode Lady Suffolk, and was 156lbs. with the saddle; so that she carried eleven pounds over weight. Mac won in three heats; and Trouble got into trouble in the first, for he was distanced in 2m. 29½s. The time of second and third heats was 2m. 32s., 2m. 31s. Suffolk was second in all the heats.

On the next day, Lady Suffolk, Gray Eagle, and Mac went mile heats, three in five, in harness. The Lady won in three heats, and Gray Eagle was second in them. Mac was distanced in the second heat. The time was 2m. 35½s., 2m. 34s., 2m. 38½s. Next day, Lady Suffolk and Mac went two-mile heats in harness. The horse acted badly, and was distanced the first heat in 5m. 20. On the 14th of June, the horses that had been at Rhode Island were at Boston; and there, on the Cambridge Course, Lady Suffolk made the fastest heat she ever trotted. She went mile heats, three in five, under saddle, against Mac and Gray Eagle. The first heat was Mac's in 2m. 31s., and the Lady second. Gray Eagle was then drawn. The Lady won the second heat in 2m. 26., and Mac took the other two in 2m. 27s., 2m. 29s. On the 25th of June, Suffolk was back at the Union Course, and there went against Pelham, mile heats, three in five, in harness. Pelham was a bay gelding, owned in Boston by Mr. Robert Walton. The horse came originally from Maine. He was sold by Mr. Walton to Mr. Dennis McReady, and afterwards came into the hands of Mr. Jacob Sommerindyke. He was a fast and stylish little horse, standing an inch under fifteen hands high. In this race he was distanced in the second heat. The time was 2m. 29½s., 2m. 33½s.

On the 2d of July, at the Centreville Course, Lady Suffolk had a close race of mile heats, three in five, in harness, with Pelham and Jack Rossiter. The latter was a handsome bay gelding, called little, but really about fifteen hands and an inch and a half high. He was in the hands of Otis

Dimmock, who lived when a boy with Mr. Stevens of New Jersey, and used to ride the race-horse Henry at exercise, after he bought him. He used to exercise him on the sandy roads, and, I am informed, says he believes Henry could then trot a mile in three minutes. This was good for the horse that beat Eclipse a four-mile heat; and it is interesting and important from the fact that Henry got the dam of American Star, whose stock all trot and can almost all stay. It shows that the trotting faculty was inherent in the blood of Henry. I should have been less surprised to hear that Eclipse could trot a mile in three minutes; for he was a grandson of Messenger, being out of his daughter, Miller's Damsel.

In this race at the Centreville, there were five heats. The Lady won the first and second in 2m. 32s., 2m. 32½s.; Jack Rossiter second in the first heat, and last in the second. The third and fourth heats, Pelham won in 2m. 38s., 2m. 29½s. The fifth heat was won by the Lady in 2m. 34½s., Pelham second. Back now to the Union, where, on the 9th, Lady Suffolk went against Mac, mile heats, three in five, under the saddle, and was beaten in four heats. She won the first and fastest in 2m. 28s. The time of the others was 2m. 30s., 2m. 31s., 3m. 30s. On the 10th of July, the Lady went two-mile heats under saddle, against Mac and Jack Rossiter. Mac won in two heats; the Lady being last in the first, and then drawn. The time was 5m. 9s., 5m. 18s. On the 3d of August, at the Centreville Course, the Lady and Lady Sutton had one of the best, longest, and most obstinate struggles that there is on record. Pelham was in with them. It was mile heats, three in five, in harness. Isaac Woodruff drove Lady Sutton, and Harry Jones Pelham. Bryant drove Lady Suffolk. The contest may be said to have been altogether between the mares; for Pelham was last in the first and second heats, and distanced in the third. The first and second heats were won by the gray mare in 2m. 29½s., 2m. 31s. The third and fourth were secured by the brown mare, in 2m. 30s., 2m. 31½s. The fifth and sixth were dead heats, 2m. 32., 2m. 31s.

When they came home in the sixth heat, they both preferred charges of foul driving. As proof that Bryant had fouled him, Isaac pointed to one of his wheels, in which one spoke was broken out and five or six more damaged. Bryant, however, maintained that Isaac was in fault, and showed a bruised face. The judges were unable to decide the point between them; and so, sending out patrol judges, they started them for another heat. This was won by the gray mare in 2m. 38s. On the 28th of September, the mares went again in the same way, at the same course, and Suffolk won in four heats. Lady Sutton won the first. The time was 2m. 32½s., 2m. 33½s., 2m. 34s., 2m. 36s. On the 8th of October, still at the Centreville, Lady Suffolk went two-mile heats in harness, against Lady Sutton and Pelham. They had three heats of it, and the brown mare won. Pelham got the first heat, Sutton second, in 5m. 16s. Lady Sutton won the second, and Pelham was second, in 5m. 17s. In the third, Pelham was distanced, and Lady Suffolk was second, in 5m. 20s.

The next race was one of three-mile heats in harness, on the 17th of October, between Lady Suffolk, Trustee, and Pelham; and, before giving it, I am induced to say a little about that famous horse, the first twenty-miler. He was got, as most of my readers have heard, by the thoroughbred horse imported Trustee, out of the trotting-mare Fanny Pullen. This mare was bred in Maine; and it was long supposed that she was a descendant of the Maine Messenger; but, from a letter which was published in "The Spirit," from one who speaks by authority, it now appears that she had no known Messenger-blood in her, but had the blood closely of a thoroughbred imported horse, who is not otherwise known much about. But I think, that, for the game and lasting qualities of Trustee, we must look in a great measure to his sire, the imported horse, who was of very renowned blood. He was got by Catton, a game, strong horse, and a four-mile runner at high weights, who was bred from the Mercury line of Eclipse; and is said to have done as much for Yorkshire, in England, as any stallion they ever had there, getting alike race-horses, hunters, and trotters for the stage-coaches.

Trustee's dam was one of the most famous blood-mares, in the estimation of the English, that they ever rejoiced in. He was out of Emma, by Whisker, who was own brother to Whalebone, Web, and Wire. So Trustee was related to Glencoe; for Web was his grandam. This Emma was also the dam of West Australian's dam, and of Mundig and Cotherstone, both of whom won the Derby. Mundig, as well as Trustee, was by Catton. The trotter Trustee was a chestnut horse, about fifteen hands two inches high. He was a strong horse, with a very high rump. It looked to be higher than his withers; and this was especially the case when he was going. He was a low-headed horse, and a stout puller. It will be remembered, that, earlier in this work, I stated that hard pulling was a habit to be carefully discouraged in dealing with trotters; but that, at the same time, there were many horses that could not or would not do their best without pulling. Therefore, when a horse pulls, I do not think it at all expedient to get rid of the pull by means of punishing-bits, bridoons, or such-like devices. When a horse gets his head down in breaking, as Kemble Jackson did, it is a different matter; but the trotter that goes at his best rate while pulling hard had best be borne with. If you get rid of the pull by means of the appliances I have alluded to, you will soon get rid of some of the trot.

It is often said that a horse cannot pull hard and last; and this is contrary to the facts I am about to mention. Trustee lasted; and he was a hard puller. Captain McGowan lasted; and he is the hardest-pulling horse in America, I suppose. Dexter pulls a pound or two, I can assure you; and he has shown his capacity to go on. The truth is, that the pulling-horses last well enough, but the drivers do not last so long.

It is just so with the runners. Look at English Eclipse, who "pulled a ton," as the saying has it, when he distanced his fields. Look at Norfolk, a desperate hard puller, but, nevertheless, a thorough stayer. I mention these instances in order that you may not be led away by a theory that is groundless. To say that a horse can't stay *because* he pulls, is not true. To say that he might stay as well if he did not pull so hard, and that he would be much more pleasant to ride or drive, is the correct thing.

To return to Lady Suffolk. In the three-mile race between her and Trustee and Pelham, there were three heats. Trustee won the first of them in 7m. 45½s., and the mare was second. Pelham was third, and then drawn. The mare won the second and third heats in 7m. 52s., 7m. 57s. Lady Suffolk's next trot was with Long-Island Black Hawk. This latter famous horse was by Andrew Jackson, out of Sallie Miller, a mare owned at Philadelphia. She was a good one. In 1834 she made Ed. Forrest go in about 2m. 31s., over the Centreville. Afterward, in 1836, at the same course, I held her by the bridle while Andrew Jackson had the amorous intercourse with her from which Long-Island Black Hawk sprang. The latter, as his name indicates, was black. He had four white legs and a star, — a horse of the finest symmetry, standing fifteen hands two inches and a half high, and a splendid goer. He was a great weight-puller, and the first that went in 2m. 40s. to a wagon and driver of three hundred and ninety pounds weight. It was in his match with Jenny Lind, who belonged to Mr. Joseph Goodwin. This race between Suffolk and Black Hawk was at the Union Course, on the 24th of October. It was to wagon and driver of 350lbs.; and the mare won in three heats. The time was 2m. 45s., 2m. 40s., 2m. 43s.

On the 7th of November, the Lady went three-mile heats in harness, against Trustee, on the Union, and beat him in two heats of 8m. 13s., 8m. 15s. On the 12th, at the Centreville, she went two-mile heats against the pacer Dan Miller.

The mare was under saddle, the pacer in harness. They had three heats; of which he won the first, and she the second and third. The time was 5m. 3½s., 5. 12s., 5m. 19s. The old mare was taken from the Island to Boston to wind up that season. There, on the 22d of November, she went with Trustee two-mile heats, — she to a wagon of a hundred and fifteen pounds, and he to a fifty-pound sulky. She beat him in two heats of 5m. 57s., 5m. 34½s. On the 29th, she went mile heats, three in five, in harness, against Gray Eagle; and he beat her in three straight heats of 2m. 37s., 2m. 40s., 2m. 38s. The Lady's last race that season was on the 12th of December. She went two-mile heats against Gray Trouble, he in harness and she to wagon. She beat him in two heats of 5m. 38s., 5m. 36s. This brought her to the end of 1849; in which year she trotted sixty heats, many of them being two and three mile heats.

That two-mile heat race at Boston, in November, was the last that Trustee ever trotted with Suffolk. He was entered in one with her and Moscow the next year, but did not trot it. The year following that, he came to his death at Cincinnati. It was in the Queen-city Course, where, as appears from his letter in "The Spirit," Mr. Larkin (name not on the bills) went a buffalo-hunting with some Indian braves and a great medicine-man called Crisp. On the 13th of July, 1851, Trustee, Gray Eagle, Shavetail, and Bluffer went a race of three-mile heats in harness, on the course named. The day was extremely hot. Trustee won the first heat in 8m. 38s.; but, being in poor condition, succumbed to the heat soon after starting for the second three miles, and literally died in harness. Gray Eagle came near dying, too, and was only saved by prompt blood-letting. The others went three heats and the Bluffer was drawn.

XXX.

Lady Suffolk in 1850, 1851, 1852, 1853. — Her Retirement and Death. — The Story of Flora Temple. — Opening Chapter of her History, by George Wilkes.

I DO not propose to follow the career of Lady Suffolk in all its further details. Sufficient has been said to show what a wonderful mare she was; and, before she left the turf, the shadow of another, and a greater than she, began to appear upon the dial. In 1850, Lady Suffolk trotted sixteen times, mostly with success; in 1851, fourteen times; in 1852, fifteen times; in 1853, twice, and in both of these races she was defeated. That was about the last of the famous gray mare. She became the property of Mr. Ezra White, and died in honorable retirement. She never had a foal. The greater than she, to whom I have alluded, was Flora Temple; and her first appearance in history is so finely and graphically told in the first chapter of her life by George Wilkes, that I mean to make it a part of this book, as follows: —

CHAPTER I.

The sun shone beautifully in the summer of 1850. It shone with peculiar brightness all along the Hudson River at that time, and especially in Duchess County; but nowhere in the wide world, in the summer of 1850, did its beams fall with a more sweet and mellow radiance than in the little village of Washington Hollow, about four miles back of the town of Poughkeepsie. It seemed, indeed, to come into the village with peculiar gladness; and, from the way its glitter played among the leaves of the trees, and its broad, warm flood spread itself fondly upon the field and mixed wantonly with the very earth of the road, it appeared as if it never desired to withdraw. And every thing in Washington Hollow seemed to respond in peaceful happiness to these visits of the sun; and day in and day out, whenever the sun shone, which it did in Washington Hollow nearly the whole of its allotted term, the village looked precisely as cheerful as it did the day before.

On one of the finest of these kind of mornings in Washington Hollow, in the month of June, of the year of grace aforesaid, Jonathan A. Vielee stood listlessly at his stable-door, looking out into the road, thinking, doubtless, as was common with the inhabitants of that village, that he had never seen the sun shine so bright before, when his attention was attracted by the faint clank of a bell; and, turning that way, he saw a stout drover coming down the road with fifty or sixty head of cattle, one of which bore the bell that had struck his ear. The cattle filed before the practised and admiring eyes of Mr. Vielee; and after them came the drover's wagon, drawn by two stout mares, driven by a sleepy-looking negro; and on the other side of the road, but near enough to exchange a nod with Mr. Jonathan A. Vielee, rode the drover on a graceful gray stallion, keeping his charge in line. Mr. Jonathan A. Vielee looked approvingly upon many of the cattle: he thought the brown mares that drew the wagon a very serviceable pair of "horses-of-all-work;" and he admired the tall stallion on which the drover rode, as a fine piece of flesh, that showed a good many signs of "blood;" but, in all this scrutiny, Mr. Vielee saw nothing to excite him from the delightful state of tranquillity which the soft and quiet beauty of the morning had put him in. Just, however, as he was about turning his head again to the advanced part of the line, something riveted his attention.

This something, which riveted the attention of Mr.

Jonathan Vielee, was a little, rough-coated bay mare, not over fourteen hands two inches high (4 feet 10), tied at the tail of the wagon by a rope-halter some three or four feet long. There certainly was nothing in the conduct of the little bay mare to deserve this attention from the practised eye of Mr. Vielee. She was going quietly along, not tugging at her halter, but yielding to it, and apparently enjoying the bright sun of Washington Hollow, as it laved her sides and back, and bathed the landscape far and near, as if she had belonged to Washington Hollow itself. To judge by her manner, as she ruminated over a sweet quid, which was occasionally replenished by a sturdy little boy of six years of age, who held handfuls of succulent fresh hay to her over the tail-board, she was in much the same tranquil, shiny-morning mood as Mr. Vielee himself. Nay, it is not impossible (if a certain theory of animal intelligence be true), that, as she dropped her large, intelligent eye reflectively upon Mr. Jonathan Vielee, she thought, just at the moment when Mr. Vielee mentally exclaimed, "That's a mighty game-looking little mare!" — we say it is not impossible, that, at that very moment, she might quietly have thought, "There's a man who knows something about a horse!"

And Mr. Jonathan Vielee would not have been misrepresented by the little mare, had she even given utterance to this idea. He had a sharp eye for the points of a horse; he had dealt a great deal in that way; and, as he gazed at the little mare's blood-like head, traced her fine, well-set neck, firm shoulders, strong, straight back, long barrel well ribbed up, powerful forearms, fine pasterns, short cannon bones, and general display of muscle, he thought he would like to inquire into her mouth, and take a peep or two at her feet. Mr. Jonathan Vielee hailed the drowsy-looking nigger who drove the wagon, and brought the drover to a stand-still with a more respectful but not less meaning signal. Then those civilities which are due between all people in bright mornings, as well in Washington Hollow as everywhere else, passed between the drover and our good friend of Washington Hollow; and presently Mr. Vielee had the little bay mare by the nose, and was studying every mark upon her teeth. He then took hold of her feet; and the little mare lifted them successively in his hand with a quiet, downward glance, that seemed to say, "You'll find every thing right there, Mr. Vielee, and as fair and as firm as if you wished me to trot for a man's life!" And so Mr. Vielee did; and, as he dropped the last foot, he liked the promise of the little mare amazingly; and it struck him, that, if he could get her for any sum short of $250, she would be a mighty good bargain.

"She is about five years old?" said Mr. Vielee, inquiringly.

"You have seen for yourself," replied the drover.

"I should judge she was all right?" again suggested Mr. Vielee, partly walking round the mare, and again looking at her up and down.

"Sound as a dollar, and kind as a kitten," responded the drover, as firmly as if prepared to give a written guarantee.

"Not always so *kind*, neither," said Mr. Vielee, looking again steadily at the mare's face; "or I don't understand that deviltry in her eye. But that's neither here nor there: you say the mare is for sale. Now, let's know what you'll take for her."

This inquiry of Mr. Vielee's was the opening of a highly scientific display of diplomacy between him and the rider of the gray stallion; which, after lasting some three-quarters of an hour, during which the little bay mare was put through all her paces in one of Mr. Vielee's wagons, resulted in her passing permanently from the halter at the tail of the wagon into the possession of Mr. Jonathan Vielee, for the sum of $175.

"And a pretty good price at that," said the drover to himself, on pocketing the cash, "for an animal that only cost me 'eighty,' and who is so foolish and flighty that she will never be able to make a square trot in her life."

The drover could give no satisfactory answer to Mr. Vielee's inquiries about the origin, or, to speak more professionally, about the *pedigree*, of the little bay mare. All that he could say was, that he had bought her in Utica of a young man who had for some time been endeavoring to dispose of her in connection with another little mare, which he had vainly endeavored to drive with her in double harness. The fault of the team laid against the crazy disposition of the little creature whom we have now under consideration; so, when they were offered for sale together, in a place where both of them were known, our intractable little beauty was invariably rejected, and finally the owner was obliged to dispose singly of her mate.

This was all the drover could tell about the matter; but, had he been thoroughly instructed in the antecedents of the little bay mare, he might have told him that she was foaled in Oneida County, near Utica, out of a mare the very picture of herself, who had been most happily united with a fine stallion, named One-Eyed Hunter, who was by Kentucky Hunter, well known among the thoroughbreds of the Western and Southern States. She was docked with a jack-knife before she was an hour old, and stood on her feet at that time, having the same gray hairs at the roots of her tail that she brought into Washington Hollow, and carries to this day. Her owner, Mr. Tracy, kept her till she was four years old, when, finding her wilful and unserviceable, he disposed of her to Mr. William H. Congdon of Smyrna, Chenango County, for the sum of *thirteen dollars*. Mr. Congdon, after keeping her a while, disposed of her to Kelly & Richardson for sixty-eight dollars; and, after changing hands once or twice more, she found herself at last standing as we have described her, on a bright Sunday morning, in the centre of Washington Hollow, listening attentively to the conversation that was passing between the drover and Mr. Jonathan Vielee.

Now, if the little bay mare could have foreseen and comprehended the brilliant influence which this bargain between the drover and Mr. Vielee was to have upon her destiny, she could not have evinced more joy than she did on this bright, soft, sunshiny summer morning, in the year of grace 1850, when she was taken from the tail of the drover's wagon, and led into Mr. Vielee's comfortable, well-aired stable. She danced around him, as he led her across the road, to the full stretch of her halter; she tossed her head gayly up and down; she ran forward, and put her nose playfully over his shoulder; and, when she got into her clean, cozy, well-strewn stall, she whinnied long and slowly and repeatedly, with profound delight.

But, if this pleasure on the part of the little bay mare proceeded from any notion that she had found an established home, her calculations were very much astray. Mr. Vielee was a practical man of business; and his main idea in the way of business was to turn a rapid penny, and invest the profits of one good transaction immediately into another. He knew that he had a most promising piece of horseflesh, — one that united all the outside conceivable marks of merit; and, with a correct judgment, he concluded that the city of New York — the great arena where the best trotting-blood of the country is collected and pitted in continual contest — was the place where the new-found jewel would command the highest mark. "There's no telling what she may not be able to do in time," thought Mr. Vielee in connection with this resolution; "for if, with that fine make and immense muscle, she only settles into a handy style of going, — a style that don't waste any of her power in false action, — she may yet be able to beat 'em all."

With such thoughts as this in his head, Mr. Vielee kept the mare in his stable barely two weeks; and, at the end of that time, he took her to New York. As he took her there to sell, it is not necessary to this history that we should trace his steps, further than to say, that, finding an opportunity to double his money, he sold the rough-coated, unknown little bay mare to Mr. George E. Perrin of this metropolis, for the sum of $350.

In the hands of Mr. Perrin, the little bay mare, who had proved so intractable, so flighty, so harem-scarem, and, to come down to the true term, so *worthless*, to her original owners, was favored with more advantages than ever she had enjoyed before. She was not only introduced to the very best society of fast-goers on the Bloomingdale and Long-Island Roads, but she was taught, when "flinging herself out" with exuberant and superabundant spirit all over the road, as it were, to play her limbs in a true line, and give her extraordinary qualities a chance to show their actual worth. If ever she made a skip, a quick admonition and a steady check brought her to her senses; and when, in her frenzy of excitement at being challenged by some tip-top goer, she would, to use a sportsman's phrase, "travel over herself," and go "up" into the air, she was steadied and settled down by a firm rein into solid trotting and good behavior in an instant. The crazy, flighty, half-racking and half-trotting little bay mare became a true stepper, and very luckily passed out of her confused "rip-i-ty clip-i-ty" sort of going, into a clean, even, long, low, locomotive-trotting stroke. Many a man who came up to a road-tavern, after having been unexpectedly beaten by her, would say to her owner, as they took a drink at the bar, "That's a mighty nice little mare of yours; and, if she was only big enough to stand hard work, you might expect a good deal from her."

There was at that time, as there has been for the last twenty years, many horses of great repute upon the roads in the vicinity of New York; and, among the horses which now and then came in disdainful contact with the little bay mare, was one of considerable speed and fame, called "The Waite Pony."

If his oats had sprouted into salt hay under his touch, the proud and supercilious Waite Pony could not have been more surprised, one fine afternoon in that same summer of 1850 so often already noticed, when, in a mile contest in that stretch of road which lies between Burnham's and Elm Park, the little bay mare beat him to what is called "a stand-still," and deposited her owner in advance of his at Stryker's Bay. This caused the little bay mare to be looked at very closely by everybody on the stoop of the house at Stryker's Bay; and, while the idlers and horse-sharps were descanting on her points, the owners of the respective horses made a match that they should go against each other on the Red-House Track on the following afternoon. It was a mere road-match, this match between the Waite Pony and the little bay mare, — a match of fancy, not of profit; but, though of this nature, the reputation of the little mare had been growing so rapidly of late that a large number of the *habitués* of the road were present at the contest.

The track was a half-mile track, the same that is still attached to the above-named house; and the race was for a single mile in harness. At starting, the odds were all against the mare: but they changed as soon as she got off; and she won with the greatest ease, and with the power, as was plain to every looker-on, to have reduced the time of the performance by several seconds. As, however, the time was considerably over three minutes, it did not increase the reputation of the mare as much as it discounted her competitor. A match was, therefore, soon after made between her and a fine horse known as Vanderburg's gray stallion, for $500 a side, mile heats, the stallion to go to a 250lb. wagon, and the mare to go in harness. This match came off on the Union Course, Long Island, and was easily won in three heats by the mare in very handsome time.

The next exploit of the little bay mare was the winning of a stake, on Sept. 9 of that same year of grace, on the same course, for which she was entered after arriving on the ground. She was not in racing-trim. On the previous day, she had been driven very hard; and, on coming home that night, was treated with a "warm mash," and virtually put to bed. On the next morning, however, she looked so fine that her owner concluded to go and see the race; and on the road she behaved so well, and beat so many going down, that he determined, "just for a flyer," to let her try her mettle for the purse. The race was a race of mile heats in harness; and the horses entered were Whitehall, Delaware Maid, Napoleon, and Hiram. The first-named horse, a fine brown stallion entered by James Whelpley, was the contestant of the greatest promise: but all the others were well thought of; and their owners, being among the most popular patrons of the trotting-turf, had given to the race considerable interest.

It was a bold exploit to enter that comparatively unknown little runt of a mare, under such circumstances, against such horses; and when her owner, unable to obtain a trotting "skeleton," determined to put her through in a common road-sulky, his conduct was looked upon as audacious in the extreme.

At length the start was given, and away they went. The five horses and sulkies were all well together for a few seconds, when Whitehall, with a fine, bold stroke, drew out of the clump, and took a commanding lead: the little bay mare, however, in the battered road-sulky, kept making her long, low, sweeping stride directly in his wake, with the regularity of machinery, and threatening to travel past him the first moment he should lose his foot. At the first-quarter pole, there was but one length distance between the stallion and the mare; at the half-mile, but barely two: while the others, with the exception of Delaware Maid, who was tolerably well up, were being tailed off in most disastrous manner. In this order, the heat was won by Whelpley's stallion; the little bay mare, with the heavy road-sulky, whom nobody thought would have the least chance in the world, being second; Delaware Maid, third; while Napoleon and Hiram were "distanced." The two latter being now out of the race, the little bay mare secured a trotting-sulky for herself: and the record gives her the three succeeding heats in the improving time of 2.55, 2.52, and 2.49; Delaware Maid being third on each occasion. The greatest excitement attended the conclusion of the third and fourth heats; and, when the race was done, the spectators advanced and felt the little heroine all over, as if they could not comprehend how such a *petite*, indifferent-looking creature could stand the weight and fatigue, and yet maintain the speed she did.

The latter was the first exploit that introduced the little bay mare to the pages of the "Racing Calendar." She was recorded under the modest name of "Flora;" and it was little thought by those who placed after her name on this occasion the mystical figures "2 1 1 1," that she was destined in future to render those tables so illustrious."

After this trot, the little bay mare, or Flora Temple as we are now at liberty to call her, passed into the hands of John C., the brother of George E. Perrin, for the sum of $575, — a very handsome increase over the price paid by Mr. Jonathan Vielee to the drover, and more than seven times as much as the sum for which she had been gladly parted with by her Utica owner some three or four months before.

Soon after obtaining possession of her, the new owner of Flora Temple, with unbounded confidence in her speed and lasting qualities, matched her that winter against the bay horse of Mr. Edward White, for *three*-mile heats in harness, to trot in the following spring (1851), for $2,000, half forfeit. About six weeks before this match was due, however, the mare met with an accident in her exercise which would have rendered her unfit to go; but, this accident being unknown to Mr. White, and his own horse being "out of trim," he paid forfeit, and the match was "off."

Nothing was done with the little bay mare in the spring, summer, and winter of 1851. The fright which she had taken, from the shafts of her sulky knocking against her heels in the accident referred to, rendered her apprehensive, wild, and flighty; and it was found necessary to take her out of training, and put her on the road. In that position she remained till the following summer (1852), when her owner, finding that she had regained her confidence and steadiness again by beating with great ease the bay mare Philadelphia Sal round the Red-House Track for a stake of $200, made a match against Young Dutchman, for $250 a side, mile heats, best three in five, in harness, to come off on the Union Course, on Nov. 10. Though this match excited considerable interest, there was nothing about it to particularize. The mare won in three heats, placing herself indisputably "well up" among the first-class horses by recording the time at 2.40, 2.39, and 2.36. She was then taken out of training, and put in winter quarters at Jamaica, L.I.; and, as we have given her an opportunity to express herself in thought once or twice before, we may be allowed to imagine, that, when she left the course at the close of the last contest, she might have meant to say, in her low neigh of triumph, "Little as I am, I am now mistress of the trotting-course, and let no one henceforth value me at less than $2,000!"

XXXI.

Capacity of Small Horses to pull Weight. — Flora Temple and Centreville. — Flora and Black Douglas. — Flora and Young Dutchman. — Flora and Lady Brooks. — Flora and Highland Maid. — Breeding of Highland Maid. — Description of her. — Her Races with Flora.

IT will be remembered that I have spoken of three prime qualities in the trotting-horse; viz., speed, bottom, and the power to pull weight. I was already confident that little Flora possessed the last, as well as the other two. People are apt to think that great size is demanded for a weight-puller, but there are plenty of notable instances to show that this is a mistake. Still, though there need not be great size, and though some big horses are the very worst of weight-pullers, coming right back as soon as they are required to take along a wagon and a heavy man, strength is certainly demanded. This strength in small horses is the result of a nice adaptation of parts, together with particular power in the loin and hind-quarters. If a little horse of that sort be particularly examined, it will commonly be found, that, though they are low, they are long in all the moving parts; and their quarters are generally as big, and sometimes a deal bigger, than those of many much larger horses.

Having in my mind the conviction that Flora was a weight-puller, as well as fast and stout, I matched her in December, 1852, for $500 a side, to trot, mile heats, three in five, with Centreville, to wagons of 250lbs. The mare had been let up, and had had no fast work for three or four weeks. She had, however, been jogged. Centreville was held to be very nearly or quite the best weight-puller we had at that time, and some endeavored to dissuade me from starting the little mare. It was 100 to 70 on the horse at the start. As soon as the word was given, Flora went with such a rush that she was over herself on the turn, and lost a good many lengths before she settled to work; but at the quarter-pole she had recovered her stroke, and she soon overhauled Centreville, and gave him a sight of a fast stern-chase. Joel Conkling drove him; and, finding that he could not come up with Flora, he took him in hand, and just dropped into the distance. The mare won the heat with great ease in 2m. 42s. The heat was a good one; and Flora had trotted so fast after her break that everybody could see she was mistress of the weight. Odds of 100 to 60 was forthwith laid upon her; and she won the second and third heats in 2m. 46s. and 2m. 44s.

Considering the time of year, the state of the ground, and the fact that she was not in reality in training, this was a performance of uncommon significance, and it added vastly to Flora's value. That winter she was sold to Mr. Boerum of Williamsburg, with an engagement to trot Young Dutchman for $1,000. The price paid for Flora was $4,000. She had, as was before related, been sold by George Perrin to his brother John for $575 in the previous spring. A great race very often adds immensely to the value of a horse, or rather, I should say, it vastly increases the price that the world is inclined to rate the horse at. Flora's is not the only instance I have known in which a trotter jumped from hundreds almost to thousands by reason of one performance. It sometimes happens that it is not the interest of the owners to let the horse be placed in a situation to do his best in public; and, again, a trainer of good observation and faith will sometimes be far ahead of the owner and of the public in his estimate of a horse.

Before the match between Flora and Young Dutchman came off, she went to Philadelphia to trot with Black Douglas, a young horse of great private reputation. They trotted mile heats, three in five, in harnesss, on the Hunting-park Course, April 23, the spring of 1853. The mare was big and lacked seasoning. The horse was fast, and beat her in three straight heats,— 2.35½, 2.30½, 2.35. This was a great performance for a green horse; but the little mare was forthwith matched to try the cause with him again on the 17th of the next month. Meantime she returned to New York for her meeting with Young Dutchman, which was to have come off on the Union Course on the 3d; but the Dutchman paid forfeit, not being up to the mark, and a match was made between Flora and Lady Brooks.

The latter was a good mare. Her friends were so fond of her, and there was so much bragging and boasting in regard to her speed and staying qualities, that 100 to 60 was laid against Flora. They trotted mile heats, three in five, at the Centreville, for $1,000, on the 4th of May. I liked the little mare well that day, and told my friends to take the odds to any amount. I knew a little of Lady Brooks myself; and, if there is one thing that a trainer and driver needs above all others except knowledge and skill, it is to turn an absolutely deaf ear to the boastings of his opponents. Flora won the race in three straight heats, — 2.31¼, 2.32, 2.33¼. They were all won with great ease; and not one of them was as fast as they all were to have been, according to what was proclaimed as to the capability of Lady Brooks. In this race Flora had fine speed. One of the half-miles was trotted in 1.13, and I took her in hand. She was now eight years old, very sound, of good constitution, a capital feeder, and was all the time improving. I say all the time improving; for, though she had been beaten by Black Douglas, I was satisfied that she would give a good account of him at their next meeting on the 17th. I had not driven her in her first trot with Douglas; but this time I went on with her. She suited the amateurs and trotting-men so well when she was hitched up, and I warmed her previous to the start, that she was backed at 100 to 80. The

Douglas was of no comparative account to her that day. She won in three heats, — 2.32½, 2.35, 2.31¼. Another match was made between them to trot on Long Island on the 30th of June; but, before that came off, Flora had a very hard race, and, if luck as well as her own speed and thorough game had not stood her friend, it is a question whether she would not have been beaten.

At that time, Mr. F. J. Nodine of Brooklyn owned two very fine young mares, as well as Centreville, who had been beaten by Flora in 1852. This horse Centreville was a dark-brown gelding, nearly sixteen hands high. When he trotted against Flora, Mr. Nodine, who was a very good and experienced driver, was asked to drive him a heat. He complied, and liked the horse so well that he bought him after the race. In 1853, he was quite successful with him. He got forfeits from Gray Medoc and Beggar Boy; and he beat Black Douglas to wagons in five heats, of which the time was 2.34, 2.32, 2.35, 2.33, 2.32. He also beat the Douglas in harness; and here again they had five heats of it, of which the time was 2.30½, 2.32, 2.32½, 2.33, 2.33½. As Flora had recently defeated these horses, she must have stood high in the estimation of Mr. Nodine; but, for all that, he matched one of the young mares he had against her.

The mare in question was Highland Maid. She was bred in Orange County, and foaled in 1847; consequently she was but six years old when she met the redoubtable Flora Temple. Highland Maid was exceedingly well-bred. Her sire was Saltram, a horse by Kentucky Whip out of a Gray-Messenger mare; and her dam was a flea-bitten gray mare of the Messenger blood. It follows that Highland Maid was inbred to Messenger. Her own color was dark bay, with a star in the forehead, and a little white in the heels behind. She stood about fifteen hands and half an inch high, and was low at the withers. She was, indeed, remarkable for her great height behind, as compared to her forehand; and this formation, with her immense loin, which was one of the strongest and best that ever was seen, tended greatly to give her the long, fast, and powerful stroke of which she was capable. She had a great reaching stride, gathered quick, and went with her head low. Her first race after Mr. Nodine got her was against Lady Vernon, a dapple-gray mare belonging to Jacob Somerindyke. She was afterwards sent to California. Highland Maid beat her in three heats, the time of which was 2.34¾, 2.36, 2.32½.

The matches between Highland Maid and Flora Temple were in harness and to wagons. The first was trotted on the Centreville Course, June 15, 1853. The race created a great deal of interest, and much money was laid. It was said that Highland Maid had been tried, and found to be amazingly fast. I have since been told that the time of her mile-trial, a week before the race, was 2m. 18s. The day was very fine, — a real June day, bright and warm, but not too hot for pleasure. The crowd at the course was immense: a greater attendance has seldom been seen there, if there ever was. Mr. Nodine drove Highland Maid, and I drove Flora. I took the lead in the first heat, and kept it round the turn nearly to the quarter-pole; then Highland Maid passed me, and I was never afterwards able to head her. She won the heat in 2m. 29s., and both seemed to me to be doing about all they were capable of.

The second heat was very similar to the first, but faster. Flora and I took the lead again for nearly a quarter of a mile, and then Highland Maid came on with an irresistible stroke and passed us. I pushed her all I could; and, though she won it in 2m. 27s., I thought I detected signs of her tiring. The mare was young. She had trotted but one race before. She had a trick of pacing; and I hoped to tire her out, and make her change her gait in the next heat. The odds was now very heavy upon her. In the third heat we went away together at a tremendous pace, and, upon the turn, the wheels of the sulkies hit. The spokes flew, and Highland Maid went up, and came down into a pace. It was near the half-mile before Mr. Nodine got her settled to trot again. When he did so, she went very fast, and it looked as though she might save her distance. But she was tiring. At the head of the stretch, she broke again, fell a-pacing, and was distanced in 2m. 32½s.

A great row followed. Some of those who had lost their money accused Nodine of throwing the race, and threatened him with violence. He intended to claim foul driving against me, but could not get near the judges' stand, by reason of the clamors and threats of those who had lost their money on Highland Maid. His claim would not have been allowed, I think; and Flora would have beaten Highland Maid that day, even if she had saved her distance in the third heat. It was, however, very unjust to charge Mr. Nodine with throwing the race. The truth is, that the mare tired, and, when tired, went into a pace as soon as she was forced hard. I have had them do just the same with me when the race seemed to be all but won. However, the charges of those who had lost money, and the prejudices of the public, very few of whom knew the rights of it, prevailed upon Mr. Nodine to get George Spicer to drive Highland Maid in the wagon-race. It came off on the Centreville Course, June 28, only two days before Flora trotted her third match with Black Douglas. I thought Flora a better mare that day than I had ever seen her before. Her races, and the work she had undergone, had done her good. It was always one of her great qualities that she would train on and get better,-when thoroughly hardened, towards the middle and close of the season. This is one of the most valuable qualities that a trotting-horse can have. The greatest excellence in trotting, as I observed at the beginning of this work, is only to be reached through much labor and cultivation. Now, if strong work at a few sharp races overdoes a horse and knocks him off, it is a great, almost an insurmountable, obstacle to his attaining the greatest excellence, even in speed for a mile.

When I got into the wagon to drive Flora against Highland Maid, I was confident that I had the bottom and resolute game of one of the best little mares in the world to rely upon, and consequently I determined to force the pace. We went away together with a grand rush, and, on the turn, Highland Maid broke. Spicer got Highland Maid to her trot again, and I kept the pace strong. It was a good heat. The Maid was unable to collar Flora, who won it by two lengths in 2m. 28s. That was much the best time that had then been made. The fastest time to wagon previously was 2m. 31s. This heat in 2m. 28s. was three seconds better. It is true that Flora afterwards wiped that out, and went three seconds better still; and also true that George Wilkes has since equalled her wagon-time,—2m. 25s. I will even state my confident belief that Dexter can beat that quite handily; but, nevertheless, we must remember that this race with Highland Maid was thirteen years ago, and, at the time, it was esteemed a wonderful performance.

In the second heat, Flora did not do so well. She broke and lost a deal of ground at the outset. Highland Maid won the heat very handily in 2m. 32s. The third heat was a very severe one. Soon after we got the word, Flora changed her leg, and tried to get up; but I was on the watch, and nailed her in time. We went head and head to the quarter. At the half-mile, there was not much difference. On the lower turn, I got half a length the best of it; but somehow or another, and I could not tell just how, Flora broke there and then, and Highland Maid showed me the back of her wagon. But, when Flora got down again, she made a very hot rush, and up the stretch she gained on Highland Maid. Seeing that she was honest, and would stand it, I gave her a good cut with the whip as we neared the score. She darted on to Highland Maid; and they struggled home together, making it a dead heat in 2m. 32s.

The fourth heat was unfavorable to us. Flora broke twice. The other mare trotted steadily, and won easily in 2m. 33s.

The next heat was another good one, being trotted from end to end. Flora took the lead at the start, was never headed, and won in 2m. 31½s.; but Highland Maid trotted exceedingly well, and hung on all round the lower turn in a very game manner. But she was younger than Flora, and not so well seasoned. She was now tired. In the sixth heat Flora took the lead from the start, was never headed, and won easily in 2m. 35s. The race did not seem to have much effect upon Flora Temple. Two days after it, she beat Black Douglas easily in 2m. 32s., 2m. 32s., 2m. 36s. It was otherwise with Highland Maid. She was not herself for some time afterwards; and some are of opinion that she never altogether recovered from its effects. This mare was very highly bred, very finely put together, and very fast. But she was an unlucky mare. She was afterwards matched with Gray Eddy, and lost by hitting her knee. After that wagon-race, Flora was deemed the mistress of any thing out in that way of going.

XXXII.

Flora Temple and Tacony. — Description of Tacony. — Flora, Green-Mountain Maid, and Lady Vernon. — Description of Green-Mountain Maid. — Flora and Rhode Island. — Flora goes to New Orleans, comes back, and is purchased by Mr. Pettee. —Flora and Mac. — Flora and Jack Waters. — Flora and Sontag. — Flora's Match Twenty Miles to Wagon. — Flora and Know-Nothing. — Description of Know-Nothing, afterwards Lancet. — Flora and Lady Franklin. — Flora and Chicago Jack. — Flora, Frank Forrester, Chicago Jack, and Miller's Damsel.

AS soon as Flora had defeated Highland Maid and Black Douglas, she was matched against Tacony, mile heats, three in five, in harness, the race to come off on the 14th of July, over the Union Course. Tacony was a roan gelding, bred in Canada. His reputation was high, but more particularly as a saddle-horse. He had trotted two consecutive heats, that way of going, against Mac, in 2m. 25½s. each. The match created a vast amount of interest. The betting ran high, and it was about even. The little mare had not made such fast time as Tacony: but the heat of 2m. 28s. to wagon was thought to be as good as 2m. 25½s. under saddle; and, besides this, the game and bottom exhibited by Flora in her race of five desperate heats with Highland Maid, and then in her contest with Black Douglas only two days thereafter, had inspired her friends and admirers with very great and reasonable confidence.

The attendance at the course was large, and the mare had a trifle the call in the betting. I thought well of her, although she did not exhibit as much of her dash and devil in scoring as I had sometimes experienced. The result convinced me that she was not quite up to the mark. The gelding was an uncommon good horse that day, and he won it in three heats. The first heat was a close and desperate struggle. Tacony lead about a length to the quarter, where the mare got to his girths. She staid there for half a mile, both of them doing their best, as near as might be. At the head of the stretch we were close together. Tacony gained from thence to the draw-gate, where he led two lengths. But the mare answered my call, and darted to his head. It was the signal for a great shout from the crowd; and, just at that moment, up she went. Tacony won it by a neck in 2m. 28s. The second heat was faster, closer, and harder still; but he won it in 2m. 27s. The third heat was another desperate struggle; and, though Flora was defeated, it was only by a short head in 2m. 29s.

Before the day was altogether done, we matched the horses again, two-mile heats in harness, to trot in five days. I did not think that Flora had been quite at her best that day; and, though it had been a hard, up-hill struggle for her, it was my opinion that she would recover from the effects of it quite as soon as Tacony would. To be sure, she had been beaten, while he had won; but, when horses trot three very close heats, it takes as much out of the winner as it does out of the loser, provided the loser possesses that game-principle, which, instead of being discouraged by defeat, rather is incited to put the matter to a further issue and avenge it. She was then, and remained to the last, a wonderful mare to "come again."

I liked her on the day of the two-mile race, and she won it easily in two heats, — 4m. 59s., 5m. 1s. This was the best two-mile time that had then been made. Soon after that race, I went with Flora to Saratoga, where she beat Tacony, mile heats, three in five, in harness, in 2m. 32s., 2m. 31s., 2m. 32s., on the 26th of July. The track was heavy. On the 30th we were at it again, two-mile heats in harness; and she beat the roan horse in 5m. 4s., 5m. 10½s. We then went on to Rochester, where Tacony beat Flora, mile heats in harness, but was himself defeated three days afterwards, to wagons, in three heats. Utica was the next place; and there Flora beat him in a capital race of three straight heats, — 2.33½, 2.27, 2.28½. The mare beat him again at Saratoga, and at Philadelphia in September. She then returned home, and remained until October. On the 15th of that month she was at Philadelphia again, there to contend with Green-Mountain Maid and Lady Vernon, at mile heats, three in five, in harness, for a purse of $1,000.

Green-Mountain Maid was a mare of the Messenger blood on the sire's side. She was bred in the Green Mountains of Vermont, and was got by the famous horse Harris's Hambletonian (also called Vermont Hambletonian), a grandson of Messenger. It is not known what her dam was. Green-Mountain Maid herself was a chestnut, fifteen three inches scant, very long in the body, with strong, powerful limbs and large quarters. Her shoulders were very flat and oblique, running right back to the saddle. She belonged to Mr. F. J. Nodine, who purchased her and brought her to Brooklyn in the fall of 1851, when she was five years old. She was entered in six or seven purses and stakes the next year; and what she didn't win, she received forfeit for. At the Centreville Course, in the following year, she beat Lady Brooks in four heats to wagons. The best time was 2m. 36s. It was on the 18th of April. Three days afterwards she beat Kemble Jackson, in a desperate race of five heats to wagons. She took the first and second; he got the third; the fourth was dead; and she won the fifth. Time, 2.47, 2.50, 2.34, 2.36, 2.50.

The race at Philadelphia resulted in a victory for Flora. She won easily in 2.33, 2.33½, 2.33¾. But at Rochester, on the 1st of November, Green-Mountain Maid succeeded in reversing the verdict. They trotted five heats; and the big chestnut mare got the first, third, and fifth. The time was 2.40, 2.35, 2.35, 2.36, 2.38. The two mares then went to Cincinnati, and I did not accompany Flora. At that place, on the 20th of November, she beat Green-Mountain Maid and Rhode Island, and afterwards beat the latter to wagons. She and Rhode Island then went on down the Ohio River to Louisville, where she beat him again. There the little mare embarked on one of the fine steamers which ran on the Ohio below the falls and down the Mississippi to New Orleans, where she and Green-Mountain Maid met early in January, and had two races, one in harness, the other to wagons. Neither of these races was very fast. Although the mare finished in January at New Orleans, her races there must be reckoned as part of her performances in 1863. In that year she trotted twenty-one races, and, out of the whole number, won seventeen. She also beat all the horses that beat her, and beat them more times than they defeated her.

On the return of the mare to New York, she was purchased by D. L. Pettee, Esq., who was then, and continues to be, one of the ablest and most highly respected of those distinguished gentlemen in the city and vicinity of New York who have had a worthy pride in the possession of fast horses. He at that time also owned Lady Brooks; and these mares he drove at Newport during the season of 1864, at that celebrated seaside resort. When he returned home, he suffered me to match Flora against the famous brown gelding Mac, for $1,000, mile heats, three in five, in harness. This Mac was very famous for his many contests with Tacony. They were very close together when in condition; but Mac had a little the best of the roan, in my judgment, until he was injured by over-driving, and got "the thumps." Mac was about fifteen two, and came originally from Maine. He was of the Maine-Messenger blood. John McArdle owned him. He had twice defeated Lady Suffolk, and, when matched with Flora, was thought as good as any thing out. But the mare beat him with great ease in three heats. Time, 2.31¾, 2.32, 2.33. That race was on the 5th of October.

On the 18th of the same month, Flora trotted a match for

$2,000, mile heats, three in five, in harness, against Jack Waters. This Jack Waters was a bay gelding by Old Abdallah. He was about fifteen two, — a long-tailed horse. He belonged to Mr. Ben Prince, and afterwards went to California. Jack was very fast, but he was a delicate-constitutioned horse; whereas Flora was steel and whalebone, and nothing could make her give out. They trotted on the Centreville Course, and she beat him in three heats with ease. Time, 2,33. 2,39. 2,37..

Flora Temple now changed hands again. Mr. James Irving bough ther, and intended to use her solely for trotting-races. But, like her former owner, he found the demands of business incompatible with his projected operations, and sold her to Jas. McMann. Her first appearance after she became the property of Mr. McMann was at the Union Course, on the 7th of May, 1855, in a match for $2,000, mile heats, three in five, against the famous mare Sontag. It was to wagons and drivers of 300lbs. Sontag was a gray mare by Vermont Hambletonian, who was also called Harris's Hambletonian. He was a grandson of Messenger, and stood in the same relation to him that Abdallah did, but not by the same line. The latter came through Mambrino; Harris's Hambletonian through the Hambletonian, of whom I have heard that he was the horse bred by Gen. Coles, of this Island, and run by him as Hambletonian. Of course all these horses preceded the Hambletonian of our day, for whom the name seems to have been adopted from the other branch of the Messenger family. None of them are related, except through distant collaterals, to the English horse Hambletonian, who beat Diamond in one of the greatest matches that ever was run in England, over the Beacon Course. But in one point they all resemble him, — they were large, strong, bony horses, and so was he; so much so, indeed, that the jockey who rode little Diamond exclaimed, as I have heard, "This looks like a race between a mare and her sucking colt."

Vermont Hambletonian was the sire of some capital trotters besides Sontag. Green-Mountain Maid, Gray Vermont, True John, and other noted horses, proceeded from him. Sontag was about fifteen three, — a long-tailed mare. When she first came to New York, at five years old or thereabouts (it is not always very easy to tell their ages precisely some time afterwards), she was a pacer.

In this race against Flora, William Whelan drove the big gray mare, and Warren Peabody drove Flora. Sontag won it in three heats. Time, 2.31, 2.33, 2.35. Flora was next matched to trot twenty miles within an hour, to a wagon, for $5,000. The only horse that had ever trotted twenty miles in an hour at all was Trustee, and his performance was in harness; therefore I do not think this was a good match for the little mare. She lost it. At the end of the eighth mile, she threw a shoe and cut herself; and, at the end of the twelfth mile, she was drawn. The truth is, that, in dogging along mile after mile for twenty times round the course, many horses not half as good as Flora Temple could do what she could not. I do not mean to say that she might not, under some conditions, have trotted twenty miles in an hour; but that kind of going on, in a tread-mill sort of way, was not her strong point.

That same year, Lady Fulton, a mare much inferior to Flora, trotted twenty miles in an hour; and the lunatic sort of horse Captain McGowan has since done it.

Flora took a trip to Boston after her race against time, and there went a match for $3,000, over the Cambridge Course, with the black gelding Know-Nothing, who was afterwards more famous as Lancet, and who is now turned out in John I. Snediker's pasture, just beyond the trees. Know-Nothing is said to have been a son of Vermont Black Hawk. He did not look much like that stock then, and he looks less like them now. He was and is a very long horse, fifteen three in height, with a long tail. There is a wiry, blood-like look about him, not without an indication of temper. His rump is steep, his hips are wide and ragged, and he was always a very rapid goer. The race against Flora was mile heats in harness. She beat him in two heats, over a heavy track, in 2.37, 2.43. That was on the 26th of June. When Flora came home, another match was made between her and Sontag, to be trotted on the 6th of July, over the Union Course. It was two-mile heats to wagons, for $2,000. This was the first time of my driving Flora that year. She won easily in two heats, — 5.07, 5.27. Flora's next race was against Lady Franklin, who was then in my hands.

She was a roan mare from Maine, about fourteen three, with a long tail. Her pedigree was not known. A man named Hayes brought her here, and offered to sell her to Sim Hoagland for $1,200. Sim took her to the course, drove her a mile in 2m. 36s., and repeated her at precisely the same rate. He would of course have bought her; but it happened that Capt. Yeaton, who had an interest in her, had come on the course during the trial with some others, and had caught her time in the repeating-mile. When Sim learned this, he did not want her. Her match against Flora was two-mile heats to wagons, for $2,000. They trotted over the Centreville, Sept. 11. Flora won it in two heats, — 5.12½, 5.11½. After her victory over Lady Franklin on the 11th of September, Flora trotted mile heats in harness, three in five, on the 17th, against Chicago Jack and Mac, and won it easily in three heats. Time, 2.29½., 2.31½, 2.34.

In the next race in which she was engaged, I had Flora on my side again. It was two-mile heats to wagons, extra-weight, — wagons and drivers 275lbs. There were four engaged,— Flora herself, Frank Forrester, Chicago Jack, and Miller's Damsel. The bay gelding Frank Forrester, who was since called Ike Cook, was got by Abdallah (the old horse), while he stood in Kentucky. Chicago Jack was a bay gelding, fifteen hands, two inches scant. He belonged to Gen. Dunham, and was a stylish, up-headed horse. Miller's Damsel was a chestnut mare, with three white legs and a blaze in the face. She belonged to Conkling Carl. Her sire was Emmons's Jackson, a son of old Andrew Jackson. Of these four, Flora and Frank Forrester were the only ones that appeared on the 20th of September. I had no trouble in winning it with Flora in 5.15½, 5.17½.

On the 10th of October, Frank Forrester paid forfeit to Flora in a match for $2,000, over the Union Course. On the 17th, she went a match against Hero the pacer, for $2,000, over the Centreville, two-mile heats, she in harness, the pacer to wagon. The mare won this in three heats. Hero got the first, and she the second and third. Time, 4.59, 4.57, 5.21½. This ended Flora's exploits in 1855.

XXXIII.

The Time-Test. — Saddle-Horses. — Riders of Trotters. — Mace, Murphy, and Doble. — Flora and Lancet. — Trusting to Trials. — Flora and Tacony — Flora distances him in 2m. 24½s. — The True Explanation of that Heat. — Caution to Young Drivers.

IN the year 1856, Flora lay by without a match until towards the last of June. There were not many horses likely to dispute the palm of superiority with her; for, although she had not then made the best time on record, she had defeated so many good ones, and had won races from those whose time excelled hers with such ease, that in every thing but the time-test she was already at the head of the trotting-turf. Time, no doubt, is a very good test, as far as it goes; but it is not the only test. There commonly has to be a conjunction of favorable circumstances in order to enable a horse or horses to make extraordinary time. Therefore, when it is found that one who has not made such time can beat those who have, race after race, all of them being apparently in good condition, a reasonable presumption is raised that the trotter in question will, at no distant day, beat the time at the head of the record, as well as the horses who made it. At this period, — the summer of 1856, — I had for some time entertained the conviction that Flora Temple would surpass all that Lady Suffolk and Tacony had done under saddle by making faster time in harness. Every thing indicated such a result; but I was not then prepared to say that we should see it done that year. Her first match in 1856 was with Chicago Jack, the horse mentioned in the last chapter as belonging to Gen. Dunham, a very worthy and enterprising man, known East and West. In the spring, Jack had met and defeated Know-Nothing, who was now called Lancet, in a race at Boston, under saddle. There were four heats in it, and two of them were trotted in 2.27½.

. The match between Flora Temple and Jack was mile heats, three in five, for $1,000; he under saddle, and she in harness. When a horse is clever under the saddle, it is a better and faster way of going than in harness; yet there are many horses as fast in harness as they are under the saddle, and some a good deal faster. There are, however, but few that would not have been faster under saddle than in harness, provided they had had a good share of saddle-work during that period of breaking and formation which is necessarily extended in the trotting-horse. We very often, now-a-days, see horses trot fast in harness and to wagon, that never have a saddle on their backs, and that are never ridden, except at walking-exercise or to the blacksmith-shop. The presumption is, that these horses would have been faster under saddle than they are in harness, if they had been accustomed to trot under the saddle. At the same time, there are horses whose make and character is such that saddle-work does not suit them. They have, commonly, weak backs and bad shoulders; and the weight on their backs tires them behind, and runs them into the ground forward.

There may, however, be a perfectly-shaped horse so far as the eye can perceive, and yet he will not trot as well under the saddle as in harness. A great want of steadiness is sometimes found in horses under the saddle, whose speed in that way of going is very great; and the reason is, I believe, that the horse is not ridden sufficiently to become thoroughly at home in that way of going. Of late years the great, almost the only, object of desire, in regard to a trotter, has been that he should be fast in harness. The saddle has been neglected, but it is now coming into its use again. Dan Mace, John Murphy, and Budd Doble have given specimens of saddle-horsemanship which remind the old frequenters of the trotting-turf of the days when my uncle, George Woodruff, used to ride against Peter Whelan, or of those races in which I used to ride against William Whelan and others. Flora herself never was a saddle-mare; and yet I think no man can look over her, and point out any defect of conformation as the reason why. It must have been, in her case, a want of education under the saddle, and that deficiency was greatly to be regretted.

The race between her and Chicago Jack came off over the Centreville Course on the 24th of June. The mare was the favorite, and won easily in three straight heats of exactly 2m. 30s. each. The victory over Chicago Jack was not so much considered by the thoughtful as the fact that Flora trotted the second quarter of the last heat at the rate of 2m. 20s., and seemed to be going within herself.

Her next match was against Lancet, for $1,000 a side, — mile heats, three in five, in harness, made for the second of July. Flora had beaten the gelding with great ease, at Boston, the year before; but since then his friends had become exceedingly confident by reason of the time he had shown in a private trial. Now, such trials are useful enough as indicating what the horse may be expected to do under certain circumstances; and a first-rate trial affords very strong presumption that a trotter is in the course of improvement. But, in making matches, the public doings of the horse, unless he has been out of condition, or has been pulled, afford a far safer guide for his owner and trainer than trials do. To follow one particular trial is a will-o'-the-wisp sort of business, and people are thereby often led deep into boggy ground. The horse gets beat every heat in time that is not any thing like as good as the trial was; and then there is much marvel and lamentation, to say nothing of something stronger, over a result which the whole history of the turf, running as well as trotting, might have led us to expect. In this match, the public turned a deaf ear to all that was whispered about the wonderful trial, and wisely stuck to Flora, who had on so many notable occasions stuck to them. She was backed at four to one; and, when the time for starting came, Lancet paid forfeit. They then trotted for the gate-money; and the mare won it in 3 heats, 2m. 30½s., 2m. 30s., 2m. 29s.

After Lancet's race, Tacony came forward again to try conclusions with Flora. The race was mile heats, on the Union Course, July 22d, the roan under saddle and the little mare in harness. Tacony won the first heat in 2m. 31¾s.; but Flora took the second and third in 2m. 28s., 2m. 29¾s. Another match was now made between the mare and Lancet, for $1,000 a side, mile heats, three in five, he under saddle, and the mare in harness. This match was made for the Fashion Course, then new, and constructed for running-horses. The deep ground was a great disadvantage to Flora with the wheels behind her; and the gelding won it in three heats of 2m. 29s., 2m. 29s., 2m. 30s.

In old times, there used to be a way of fighting among boys, in which some youth, of uncommon handiness with the fists and hardiness of courage and endurance, would contend with two. They were never to be at him both at one time; but, as soon as one was knocked down or thrown, the other could rush in, and carry on the battle. This was called "one down and the other come on;" and the doings between Lancet, Tacony, and Flora Temple greatly resembled it. After the trial at the Fashion Course, it was Tacony's turn again. A match was made between him and Flora, in which she was to pull a wagon, and he was to go under saddle. This was very great odds for the mare to give, and the match was never trotted. A new one was made for $500 a side, to trot mile heats, three in five, on the Union Course, Sept. 2d, Tacony under saddle and the mare in harness.

The mare was a strong favorite in this race, odds of a hundred to thirty being laid upon her at the start. She fully justified the confidence of her backers; and I might dismiss the subject by saying that she distanced Tacony the first heat. But this was a very remarkable race, inasmuch as Flora surpassed in it any time that had been made before, either under saddle or otherwise. It was also the last race in which I drove her; and it was made a matter of accusation against me that I had distanced Tacony, and purposely exposed the fast time of which Flora Temple was capable. Impartial and intelligent people, as well as those who were interested, and so perhaps not quite impartial, believed this. It was so set down in the contemporaneous accounts of the press; and yet it was not true. I might have contradicted it through the "Spirit of the Times" at that period, but I did not do so; and many believe to this day that I purposely drove the mare to the full extent of her capacity on that occasion.

Now, nothing is further from the truth. I have never in my life lost a heat purposely that I could have won without what I deemed might be too great an effort for safety in the race; and I have never, on the other hand, exposed all that any horse was capable of, unless it was necessary. In the race between Flora and Tacony, the condition of the mare was very fine, and her speed very great. She darted away, and was soon in the lead some three or four lengths. I pulled her hard round the turn up the hill, and she was thirty-seven seconds in going to the quarter. On the second quarter, along the backstretch, she was under a strong pull all the way, and did it in 36s., the half mile being trotted in 1m. 13s. All this time the mare was well within herself, fully collected, and pulling very hard. She had trotted a second quarter in a third heat in June, when she was green, it being her first race that year, in thirty-five seconds. She was now well seasoned, in splendid speed and wind, and full of ardor and determination. She went into the third quarter, where there is a little descent, with such speed and resolution that I deemed it unsafe to pull her any harder than

I was doing. I could have pulled her back, as a matter of course, unless the bit or the reins had given way; but it was my judgment then, and is now, that, if I had done so, it would have been at great risk of tangling her all up, and perhaps causing her to hit herself. The mare was so full of resolution, and pulling so hard, that the only safe plan was to let her go, in a fair degree. I did so; and the consequence was, that she trotted the heat in 2m. 24½s., and Tacony was outside the distance-flag by a long way.

I have not entered into this explanation, years after the matter occurred, and when it has been by the public almost if not entirely forgotten, with a view to defend myself, but for another purpose, or rather two purposes. One of them is, to show that Flora Temple could then, upon that second day of September, 1856, have trotted a mile as fast as she ever afterwards trotted one on that course, which was 2m. 21s. I am quite confident that I could have driven her that day in that time. If I had made up my mind to drive her so as to expose all she knew, it is hardly credible that I should have held her back to the rate of 2m. 28s. to the mile for the first quarter, and 2m. 26s. to the mile for the first half. The truth is, that the mare was always under a good, strong pull from first to last; and there never was a rood, even in the last half-mile in 1m. 11½s., when she was at her best. She was, as a matter of course, as near her best as she could get with the strain I had upon her. But her mouth was wide-open all the way; and, if her ears were at any time laid flat back, it was because she was pulling with all her power, and not because she was trotting with all the speed of which she was capable.

As I have before intimated, I fully believe that I could have driven her that day in 2m. 21s.; and I think it probable that she might even have got home in 2m. 20s. The other purpose of this explanation was, a caution to young drivers against pulling trotters out of their stride when they are trotting very fast, and going up to the bit with uncommon force and resolution. A great deal of mischief may result from such a course. It hurts the temper; it destroys the steadiness; it tends to break up a good, lasting gait. There are other evils to be apprehended from such a course. I could name several trotters, of very great speed and power, who were prevented from reaching the excellence they might otherwise have attained, by that means. The horse is a very intelligent animal. His disposition is to do about his best when in company; and if he finds, that, whenever he is about to do his best, he is suddenly hauled and yanked so as to break up his stride and gait, he is not likely to forget that fact.

XXXIV.

Flora and Lancet. — The Morgan Horses. — Ethan Allen. — His Breeding. — His Produce. — Flora and Ethan Allen. — Flora's Winter-Quarters. — Flora and Rose of Washington. — Want of Condition sure to beat any thing. — Value of a race in Public to produce Condition.

IT is my belief, that, when Flora Temple distanced Tacony in 2m. 24½s., she had about reached her greatest excellence. It is true that she trotted faster afterwards upon the same course; and that race in which she beat Geo. M. Patchen, in three heats, was one of the very best she ever made. But, as I observed in the preceding chapter, she could have gone in 2m. 20s., or thereabouts, in the race with Tacony. She was then eleven years old, thoroughly matured, with a constitution that nothing could surpass, and none of her vigor at all impaired. She was younger at that time in strength and vigor than many colts are at three and four years old. She did not long remain idle; for a match was made between her and Lancet, for a thousand dollars a side, he to go under saddle and she in harness. The place was the Centreville Course; the day, the 30th of September.

It was made rain or shine; and the backers of the gelding found to their huge delight, when they got up in the morning, that it blew great guns and rained hard. This was very disadvantageous for Flora. The south side of Long Island is a very wet place in wet weather. The sea-mist comes up along with the gale and the rain, and sets every thing so much a-drip that it seems as if the island was afloat, and about to shove off into the bay. It was as bad a day for a race as ever was seen; and, when the little mare came on the course in her sulky, the wind seemed fit to catch her up, and bear her away over the tree-tops. The black gelding went sloshing along through the mud as if he liked it. The mare got off badly in the first heat, and lost about twenty lengths by a break. She was commonly a very good mare for mud; but, on this occasion, the wind and rain combined seemed to be too much for her. Lancet went to the half-mile in 1m. 11s., Flora trotted very fast after she got settled, but could not overtake Lancet, who won it easily in 2m. 28s. Odds of two to one was then laid upon Lancet, and there were many takers. The second heat was very close, but the gelding won by a head in 2m. 28s. Still Lancet had more in him, and, in the third heat, let out the links in such a manner that he trotted it in 2m. 25½s.

Considering the day and the state of the course, this was a performance of very great merit. It put Lancet, as a saddle-horse, up to Tacony and Lady Suffolk in regard to time; and ahead of them, in the consideration that the course was muddy and the wind strong. At this time, many thought than Lancet was the "coming horse," and believed that he would succeed in deposing Flora, and setting the trotting-crown upon his own brow. But I never thought so.

Another match was made between them, both to go in harness; and, as the proprietor of the Fashion Course added $1,500 to the stakes, it was agreed to trot on that course. The Lancet party believed that he would get through the new, deep ground better than Flora; but her friends relied upon her game and bottom to pull through. The mare was the favorite in the betting, and won the race very easily in three heats, the fastest of which was 2m. 31s. This was on the 8th of October.

Their next engagement was at Boston, where the little mare was always a great favorite. Nowhere in this country is there a better class of gentlemen taking interest in the contests of the trotting-turf than in the neighborhood of Boston. The Eastern States have also been a fine nursery for trotting-horses. The fine action of the Morgan breed, and their good tempers and sound constitutions, helped a great deal; but New England was still more largely indebted to the two sons of Messenger, — Hamiltonian and the Bush Messenger: I mean the one that went to Maine. There were, as I have been informed, several Bush Messengers. One of them was owned by Philo C. Bush, the race-horse man; but that was not the one that furnished Maine with good trotting-blood.

The race between Flora Temple and Lancet at Boston was witnessed by about thirty thousand people, it being at the Agricultural Fair. She won it in three heats, and the best of them was 2m. 36½s. It was to be regretted that Lancet was unable to make Flora do better on this occasion, as there was such a vast attendance. Just before that, the famous little horse Ethan Allen had added largely to his fame by beating Hiram Drew; and now a match was talked of between him and Flora Temple. He stood very high in the New-England States, because he was the chief representative of the Morgan line, and also the fastest stallion that had then been trained. Ethan Allen is a small but beautifully-built horse. He is a very rapid goer, and his action and style are as near perfection as can be conceived; but he always had a trifling objection to weight, and to a long distance. He was one of the early-maturing trotters; and his first race was with Smith Burr's Rose of Washington, at four years old. He beat the filly; but I have heard Mr. Burr declare that he afterwards found out that Ethan was a year older than she was. He was bred in the north part of this State by Joel Holcomb, who owned him, in conjunction with Mr. Roe, for some years. Mr. Roe has always said that he was got by Hill's Black Hawk; but many have stoutly maintained that his sire was a colt called Flying

Morgan. I have seen it stated in Herbert's book on the horse, that Ethan Allen was got by Morgan Black Hawk. Now, there never was any stallion called Morgan Black Hawk; but there was Hill's Black Hawk and Flying Morgan, who were different stallions on the same farm. Ethan's dam was a gray mare of the Messenger strain. He has been a very good, enduring little horse, and especially great for his knack at going with a running-mate.

The last appearance of Flora in public — that is, in a race; for she appeared since on the grand day at Peter Dubois' track, when all the famous trotters in these parts went up to be reviewed by Gen. Grant — was going against Ethan Allen and his mate Socks. Ethan Allen has been more successful at the stud than many people are willing to concede. His son Honest Allen is a fast trotter. The mare Young Pocahontas is a wonder. She is as beautiful as Ethan Allen was himself in his prime; and it is my opinion that the famous old pacing-mare has put her own staying stuff into the young one. I saw Young Pocahontas trot at Boston on the day that Mr. Bonner bought her, and liked her way of going very much. Then there is an uncommon good mare got by Ethan Allen, called Fanny Allen; and others I might mention.

But, to return to the match between Flora Temple and Ethan Allen: it was first set down to come off on the 28th of October, but the weather just before that was so bad that they put the race off until the 5th of November. The day was cold, and the wind gusty and raw; but nevertheless some thousands of people, including many ladies, attended to witness the contest between the handsome bay stallion and the beautiful bay mare. They were a well-matched and a very comely pair. Nothing could exceed the symmetry of form displayed by Ethan Allen some ten years ago. Flora Temple was a little more angular, but her points were amazingly strong and good. She was very powerful behind, with a splendid shoulder and long carcass. I pay no attention to the views of those who say that a trotter should be straight in the shoulder and short in the carcass. The best trotters that I have ever known were not "punched-up" horses, but the reverse. In length, the mare had the advantage of Ethan Allen: she was, in fact, a very long mare for her inches, and a large one too. She was the favorite in this race at long odds, and won it easily in 2m. 32½s., 2m. 36½s., pulled all the way. That finished her trotting for the year 1856.

She wintered at Holmdell, in the State of New Jersey, where Mr. Francis Morris breeds his race-horses. His trainer, Mr. Chas. Lloyd, used to have the mare every winter for some years; and capital care he bestowed upon her. She would come out all blooming in the spring, and be ready to trot a good stout race after a few brushes. It makes a great difference to the trainer whether a trotter has been wintered well, or merely suffered to get fat and lazy during the resting-months. But that time Flora was wintered, and summered too, in Jersey; for she remained at Holmdell until July, and, when matched, was brought over at a few days' notice to trot. Her opponent was Rose of Washington, the one bred by Smith Burr away down on the Island here, and beaten in her first race by Ethan Allen, at four years old. She was got by old Washington, and was now a good mare. She was not, however, good enough for Flora on equal terms; and so, when we made the match, we stipulated that the latter should pull a wagon. I knew that Rose was a good mare. I had beat Brown Dick a heat with her to wagon in 2m. 31½s. in May. Then, in June, she beat Tacony under saddle, in 2.30, 2.31, and had in the mean time, between those races, defeated O'Blenis, two-mile heats.

But, for all that, I would not have advised the matching of her against Flora, if I had not believed that condition could not but be in Rose's favor. She had trotted all the spring, had done plenty of work, and had performed well in public. She was seasoned, and fit for the exertion of all her powers. Flora was not fit to exert hers. In the nature of things she could not be. But still she was the favorite in the betting, and a capital chance was afforded to win money. It was a hundred to seventy-five on her; but she acted so in scoring, that Rose was backed at nearly even before we got the word. We got away together in the first heat; and Flora tried to head me, and take the pole. I was glad to see her rushing off as hard as she could go; for, in her condition, that was just the way for her to lose it. She got half a length ahead of Rose on the turn, and then went all to pieces. That burst had settled her. At the quarter, I led her a length, and, at the half-mile pole, was five or six in front. Rose won it easily in 2m. 30¾s.

The second heat was all one way: Rose won it easily in 2.39. Tallman then got in to drive Flora, at the importunity of those who had backed her at the long odds. But it made no difference who drove her: the evil was not in the driving, but in the want of condition in the mare. She trotted a quarter with Rose in the third heat pretty well, and then broke up, and disappeared from my view. I beat her about fifty yards in 2m. 37½s. It is almost unnecessary to say that it was not Flora Temple who was beaten that day by Rose of Washington. Flora, coming from Lloyd's hands after one of her usual winterings, could commonly trot with a short preparation — but she wanted some preparation. And there remained the fact that she had been at Holmdell not merely in the winter-season, but for above seven months. She was in no condition, and I knew it. With all her excellence, she was subject to the same laws of nature as other horses; and I have never had, or read, or heard of one that want of condition would not beat, if the opponent could only force the pace, and keep it strong. Charges were made by some, that Flora's owner had had her defeated on purpose; but they were very unjust. His only fault was overweening confidence in his own mare, and an underestimate of Rose. A match for a thousand dollars, Flora in harness and Rose under saddle, was still pending between the mares. The former race came off on the 8th of July; the second was on the 20th. Meantime, Flora had been doing good work, and had beat Belle of Portland two-mile heats. That race was, without doubt, of much service to her.

I think, that, when a trainer has a horse of fine pluck and good constitution, a race or two in public does as much or more than weeks of preparation towards the production of good condition. The bustle and the shouting, and the being brought into the midst of crowds of people, stirs the blood, and acts upon the nervous system; besides which, the race demands some sort of exertion that a trainer would not be apt to employ in the regular work. In regard to training, I ventrue to lay this down as a rule, that a good stout horse is never got to his best until he has been ridden or driven so as to be tired a few times. And here is the distinction between stout, aged horses and young colts. The latter should never be driven to the extent of getting tired: the former will never be got into their best condition until they have been tired often. But still the treatment, and the extent to which the work must be carried, will vary with each particular horse; and in this it is that the trainer must exercise judgment. If all horses were alike in character, health, constitution, and ability, precise rules could be laid down for training; for what had produced a good effect in one case would do so in all, if applied. But horses differ; no two are exactly alike: and therefore it is impossible to give any thing further than general rules, the right application of which to particular cases must be made by each man for himself. In the second race between Flora Temple and Rose of Washington, the former had come to her condition in some measure. She distanced Rose the first heat, in 2m. 31s.

XXXV.

Introduction of Hippodroming. — Flora, Lancet, Miller's Damsel, and Redbird. — Flora and Brown Dick. — Flora purchased by Mr. McDonald. — Hippodroming again. — Flora and Prince. — Flora and Ike Cook. — Flora and Reindeer. — The coming Horses, Princess and George M. Patchen.

AFTER the races between Flora Temple and Rose of Washington, an arrangement was entered into by means of which the former and Lancet travelled together, to trot for purses and divide the profits. It was a new sort of thing, and was expressively called "Hippodroming" by Mr. Wilkes. In spite of all that was said against the system, it has come more and more into fashion; and now there are lots of horses that go about the country every season, and exhibit under just such an arrangement. In the case of Flora, there was more excuse for it than there has been in some others. She could not at that time get a match on even terms, and was excluded from all the purses. Flora and Lancet began at Elmira on the 2d of September. I fully believe, that, in all her hippodroming (and she was hippodromed with a good deal), her owner and driver never threw away a heat with her. It is my opinion that there is a great deal more satisfaction in a real race than in one of these shows, in which no money is actually at stake between the horses. But the people have sanctioned the system; and these exhibitions draw immense crowds all over the country, from Maine to Missouri. The evil is, that horses who might otherwise be engaged in excellent races for money, part stakes and part purses, are practically withdrawn from these real competitions, and kept for the purpose of such exhibitions at fairs.

At Elmira, the sum of $900 was given, mile heats, to go as they pleased. The first was to have $500, the second $300, and the third $100. Flora Temple, Lancet, Miller's Damsel, and Redbird were entered; and it seemed pretty clear that the first and second prizes would be secured by the partnership, while there would be a struggle between Miller's Damsel and Redbird for the third money. Flora, Miller's Damsel, and Redbird went in harness, Lancet under saddle. Flora won in two heats, Lancet second, and Miller's Damsel third. Time, 2.28, 2.27. Three days afterwards, Sept. 5, they trotted again for $3,500 in the aggregate. It was mile heats, three in five, as they pleased; the first to have $2,000, the second $1,000, and the third $500. They went as before, and the result was the same. Flora won in three heats,—2.26½, 2.27, 2.25. Lancet was second in all of them, and Redbird third.

In these two days at Elmira, Flora and Lancet had earned $3,800, to be divided between them; and this was a good deal more than they could have gained in any other way. They had also done quite as much as the spectators had a right to expect; and, taken altogether, that was the best performance that had then been made. Some, indeed, believed that the time was inaccurate, or the track short; but these notions were never confirmed. Flora then went to Albany to trot a match for $2,000 with the gelding Brown Dick, mile heats, three in five. Brown Dick was a good horse, but not quite first-rate. He was a brown gelding, by a son of American Star, and had been owned by a business-man at Williamsburg, who used him in his heavy wagon. He all at once showed such speed that he was sent to Dan Pfifer, who brought him out, and made a fast and stout trotter of him. The race between Flora and him was trotted on Sept. 12; and the mare won it in three heats, the best of which was 2m. 30s.: but then the track was slow, and the turns bad.

Flora Temple and Lancet now went together again. They

appeared at Springfield, Massachusetts, Oct. 3, and divided the purse of $1,000; Flora being first in all three heats, and Lancet was under saddle. The fastest time was 2m. 32s. They then passed on to Hartford, Conn., where the prize was $1,000, mile heats, three in five, as they pleased. Lancet again went under saddle, and this time earned the honors of the day as well as his share of the money. In the first heat, the mare grabbed a shoe off, and Lancet came home first in 2m. 34s. Flora won the second in 2m. 29s.; but the probability is, that Lancet was pulled, as he won the third heat in 2m. 25s., and the fourth in 2m. 28s. The third heat of 2m. 25s. was the best that had then been made under saddle; and some thought it was better than Flora's 2m. 25s. at Elmira, because the Connecticut track was a half-mile, with short turns. But my opinion was different; for he was under saddle, in which way of going a horse can hug the pole, and make much shorter turns than is possible to one pulling a vehicle and driver behind. If Flora had trotted in 2m. 25s. at Hartford, it might have been reasonably held to be better than her heat at Elmira; but she did not do so.

It was also believed by many that Lancet could beat her any time when he was quite himself, and under saddle. But in this opinion I never concurred, because, after the race in which I distanced Tacony with her in 2m. 24½s., I was satisfied, that, when she was quite herself, she could trot in harness in 2m. 20s. on a good track. The season of 1857 was now at an end, and the mare went into winter-quarters. The system of dividing purses had been inaugurated, and it has since increased to an enormous extent. At first, when Flora travelled with Lancet and he went under saddle, and afterwards, when she, Princess, and other horses, went upon these sort of expeditions, there was some semblance of a race; but the proceedings between Dexter and Patchen's son from California have been of a farcical character. The stallion was unable to keep decent company with Dexter when the latter went any thing like his best rate; and, to satisfy the lookers-on, Doble was compelled to bid good-by to Eoff and the stallion in order to show a fast mile. For my part, I never liked the system, and have never had any thing to do with it; but if the people who pay for it, knowing what it is, are satisfied, I have neither the right nor the inclination to interfere.

In 1858, Flora did not trot on Long Island at all; and it is a question whether she trotted at more than one place that year where there was not some kind of dividing arrangement made with the horse that appeared with her. The first place at which she came out was the Chestnut-hill Park, Philadelphia. The purse was $1,000, mile heats, three in five, in harness; the date, June 16; and the other horse was Lancet. She won in 2.29, 2.31, 2.35. Before she trotted again, she had been purchased by Mr. William McDonald, a wealthy gentleman of Baltimore, for $8,000. The price of horses was not as great then as it has since become, and Flora Temple was worth all the money he paid for her. The change of ownership made no change in the system of management, as she remained in charge of her former owner, Mr. McMann. On the 22d of June, the Oxford-park Course, Philadelphia, gave a purse of $1,200, for which Flora and Lancet appeared. She won in three heats, — 2.31, 2.27½, 2.29¾. The two then went to the Central Course, Baltimore, and two races there (if they can be called races) resulted in just the same way. The mare was driven to win every heat; and this she did with great ease, as Lancet was no competitor for her in harness. After the second race at Baltimore, which was on the 8th of July, Flora lay by until October.

Many people were still under the delusion that Lancet could beat Flora, as the wonderful private time of the gelding continued to be talked about. I offered to match her against him for $5,000, provided I could get the mare; but

Mr. McMann declined to let me have her; and I dare say he knew, that, if I had got her, the Lancet party would not have made the match. She went to the West, and trotted with the chestnut gelding Prince, at Detroit, on the 2d of October. He was under Mr. McMann's control, as much as Flora was; and, if he had not been, he would have been no match for her. He was, indeed, a splendid horse for bottom, when I drove him against Hero the pacer, and beat him in two ten-mile races, as I have previously related; but he had not speed enough for Flora at mile heats.

From Detroit, Flora passed on to Chicago, to trot for a purse of $800, added to a stake of $500 each, half forfeit. The others engaged were Frank Forrester (now called Ike Cook), and the gelding Reindeer. It was mile heats, three in five, in harness. Reindeer was withdrawn, and Flora beat Ike Cook in three heats. The best time was 2m. 30½s., and the last heat 2m. 42s. On the 15th, at Kalamazoo, Flora and Prince appeared again, mile heats, and the result was the same as at Detroit. On the 27th, they went mile heats, three in five, at Sandusky, Ohio,—same result. Best time, 2m. 35s. On the 4th of November, she trotted for a purse of $500 against the gelding Reindeer, and beat him in three heats. Two of these, however, were in 2.28.

On the 25th of that month, Flora trotted for a purse at St. Louis, mile heats, three in five, in harness, against Reindeer, who had before paid forfeit to her, and who had been beaten by her at Adrian. Still he had made the best race with her that had been made that year, and had only been defeated by a throat-latch in the third heat in 2m. 28s. For the race at St. Louis, his trainer, Otis Dimmock, brought him out in excellent condition, while Flora was no doubt off. She acted badly, and lost the first heat in 2m. 34s. She was still backed at odds of 100 to 80. It can hardly be got into the heads of some people that horses are not always at about their best. Half the calculations made in England, so far as I can see, proceed upon the assumption that all the horses are always right. If they were, the turf-prophets could select the winners more often than they do. Flora was distanced in the second heat in 2.35s.

Two days afterwards, she was herself again, and beat Reindeer, two-mile heats, in harness, in 5m. 11½s., 5m. 17½s., over a very heavy track. One more race at mile heats, three in five, they had on the 2d of December. It was a stoutly-contested one of five heats. Reindeer won the first and second in 2.31½, 2.31¼; but Flora lasted the longest in the heavy ground, and took the third, fourth, and fifth in 2.30¾, 2.32½, 2.36¼. Her races that year with Reindeer were the only ones in which she was called upon to put forth her speed. He made her show the people of Adrian and St. Louis the worth of their money.

The next year, 1859, was the most arduous, the most eventful, and the most glorious, for her in all her history. She was now fourteen years old; and her labors and performances in that season show what an extraordinary good little mare she was. She then exalted herself to a height of fame that many believe will hardly ever be equalled; though my opinion is, and has been for some time, that Dexter, if he meets with no accident, will surpass, in harness and to wagon, all that she ever accomplished. I ventured to predict this some time ago, and it was published in "The Spirit of the Times." I still adhere to it. The opinion may be wrong, but it is mine. Time, as it goes along from year to year, and time as it is taken in the judges' stand when the winning horse comes to the score, will show. The amazing goodness of this little mare, fourteen years old, was, however, established beyond all cavil in 1859. She met better horses in that year than she had ever done before; for, whatever may be thought about Princess, she then first encountered George M. Patchen, the Jersey stallion, who was, beyond all doubt in my mind, the best horse that ever competed with her. Then, again, the distance she travelled was enormous; and the races she trotted numbered no less than twenty-three, all but one of which she won.

XXXVI.

Flora Temple and Ethan Allen. — Flora and Princess. — Description of Princess. — Her Driver, James Eoff. — His Artful Strategy, and inveterate Humbug. — Princess beats Flora Two-Mile Heats. — Flora wins, Mile-Heats, Three in Five. — The best previous Time beaten in all the Heats.

IT was in 1859 that the fame of Flora Temple reached its highest point. Her first race that season was with Ethan Allen, at the Fashion Course. It was on the 31st of May, for a purse of $2,000, mile heats, three in five, to wagons. The race between Ethan and mate, and Lantern and mate, in double harness, had greatly increased the reputation of the little bay stallion; but, in considering the dead heat of 2m. 24½s., there was not enough allowed for the part in it which belonged to the running-horse. This way of going had not then become familiar; and nearly all the merit of the performance was attributed to the trotter, when it ought to have been given to the runner, who pulled all the weight, and carried the trotter along with him. Ethan Allen has since trotted with a runner faster than 2m. 20s.; and, from what has been confided to me respecting his trials in that rig, he can do a great deal better than that.

For this race on the Fashion Course, the odds was on Flora. I drove the stallion, and felt satisfied that he would make Flora trot a great race; but, as it was plain that her condition was good, I had no great confidence of winning it. In the first heat we got away together, and the pace was strong. Ethan Allen was always very rapid to begin with. On the turn, the mare got up, but was caught by the time I was a length ahead. Tallman now steadied her with a pull; and, at the quarter, I led her two lengths and a half. At the half-mile, in 1m. 11s., Ethan had a length and a half of lead; but the mare was coming with uncommon speed and resolution. Gaining inch by inch, she collared him on the lower turn, and he made a skip. She led at the head of the stretch; but the little horse finished very gamely, and she beat him but a length in 2m. 25s., — the best mile that had ever been trotted to a wagon.

It was also the best mile that he ever trotted single; and though, having been defeated, he gets no record for it, it is just as much to be considered for his credit, in estimating his value as a stallion, as if he had won in 2m. 25¼s. The second and third heats were won by the mare. The time of each was 2m. 27½s. Flora thus, in the first race of the season, gave a sample of her mature powers. Darius Tallman drove her that day. The time she made remained unequalled for above five years; but, finally, George Wilkes made it in a second heat on the Union Course, when the track was not fast, and the weather was unfavorable for clear wind. It is just also to say, that, though Ethan Allen gained no money by that race with Flora, he added much to his fame.

On the 16th of June, Flora met a new and formidable competitor in the bay mare Princess. This mare had formerly been called Topsy, under which name she had trotted fast in the West. She was then taken to California, and became the property of Mr. Teakle, a gentleman of fine parts and enterprise, and high character. She had been brought from the Pacific side to New York by James Eoff, a very able trainer and driver, and generally thought to be as hardy and unscrupulous as any man in our profession. Princess was a mare of singular beauty and high quality, combined with strength. I do not know her pedigree: I have heard several different stories about it; but she showed blood, and must have had a good strain in her. Her temper was not of the best; and, though she had a great gift of speed, she was not steady enough to be always reliable. Her bottom was great. Before leaving California to come here, she twice beat Glencoe Chief, ten miles, to wagons; winning those races in 29m. 10¾s., and 29m. 16¼s. The first of these races was for the large amount of $36,500, and the second for $10,000. Her best mile in public had been 2m. 30s.; but I have heard that she went an amazingly fast mile to wagon in a trial with a pacing-horse, and that trial induced Mr. Teakle to bring her eastward again.

Eoff was a great master of humbug, and had got up so much mystery and speculation in regard to this mare that Flora's owner refused to match her. An arrangement was then entered into that they should trot three-mile heats and two-mile heats, to wagons, on the Eclipse Course, and divide the gate-money. It was given out that they were matched for $2,500 a side; but the truth is, that there was nothing at stake between them. They trotted the three-mile heats on the 16th of June, in the presence of a great crowd. Eoff had so worked upon the belief of many credulous people, that they actually laid on 7m. 30s., to wagon, which would have beaten Dutchman's time under saddle by two seconds and a half. Tallman drove Flora; and Eoff, Princess. The beauty and style of the latter were much admired; but the odds were upon the little mare who had won such a gallant race, a little more than a fortnight previous, from Ethan Allen. It was a hundred to twenty-five on her. Before they started, there came up a thunder-shower, which drenched thousands of people to the skin, and made the course slippery and bad. In the first heat, Princess took the lead, and kept it for nearly a mile; but Flora got to her head a few strides from the score, and they crossed it together in 2.37. Tallman made a waiting-race of it, and pulled Flora back three lengths; but, at the score again, the big mare only led her a length. The time of that mile was 2m. 40½s. Flora made a little skip on the turn, and Princess was three lengths ahead at the quarter. But now her time was come. The little mare made such a fine rush that she was at the head of Princess at the half-mile pole. She took the lead, and won with great ease by five lengths, in 7m. 54s., amidst great shouting.

Ten to one was now laid; and it was whispered about that Eoff would not let Princess win it. He very likely instigated the report himself; for it was a part of his tactics to make people believe that Princess could beat Flora, whenever it became his interest to let her do so. In the second heat, Flora took the lead. The first mile was 2.37½., the second 2.36½. In the third mile, Flora began to come back; and she pulled a shoe off, and cut her quarter. Half-way up the stretch, Flora broke and many believed that Eoff might then have passed her, and won the heat, if he had wanted to do so. Flora was in a hobble all the way home, and broke three times after she passed the drawgate; but Princess never got to her, and the little mare won it in 7m. 59½s. About nineteen out of twenty people believed that Eoff pulled Princess in the last heat, on purpose to lose it. But, if he had a mare that could have beaten Flora, the odds that day were very tempting. He told a plausible, and I am inclined to think a truthful, story. It was, that Princess was as tired as Flora was; that, if he had sent her ever so little at the finish, she would have broken up; and, as she is a bad breaker, that would have lost it. The truth, to my mind, is, that Princess never could beat Flora when the latter was at herself; and Eoff was, of all the men in America, the man who knew it best. Flora, however, was not at her best that day.

The charges against Eoff for pulling and losing, when he could have won, were so loud and general, that there was an investigation by the Union Jockey Club. Eoff appeared, and made his statement; but of all those who had declared, that, if the reins had broken, Princess could not have lost it, not one came forward to substantiate the charge. The after-experience of Princess and Flora showed that the former could not beat the latter when they were both right; and what has since been seen of Eoff's management of the California stallion (George M. Patchen, jun.) throws some light upon his doings with Princess. In spite of their experience in the Princess case, he persuaded the people that this stallion could beat Dexter whenever he wanted to let him do it; and many continued to believe so after it was palpable to any man of good judgment that the gelding could lose him in any race that they might go.

In a week after the race of three-mile heats to wagons, Flora and Princess trotted two-mile heats in harness. The betting opened at 100 to 70 on Flora; but, before they started, it was even. Tallman drove Flora again; and, in scoring, she seemed rank and wild. Princess, on the other hand, was quite steady; and, from all appearances, her race to wagon had done her good. They went away at a great rate; and, before Flora had got round the turn, she pulled a shoe off and cut her quarter: this gave Princess the lead. The latter trotted the first mile in 2m. 26s., but there was no daylight between her and Flora. On the turn, Flora broke. When she caught, she trotted very fast; and, making a swift and resolute dart to close with Princess on the back-stretch, she grabbed off her other fore-shoe, and cut her quarter badly. Princess won the heat easily in 5m. 2s., and might, no doubt, have trotted it considerably faster if she had been pressed in the second mile. It was ten to one on the California mare. Flora was a little lame when brought out for the second heat. Princess took the lead, kept it all the way, and won handily in 5m. 05s.

The general opinion was, that little Flora had her mistress, and that Princess could beat her anywhere. But the truth is, that people forgot the wonderful constitution and come-again qualities of Flora. While with all her speed, bottom, and fine way of going, Princess was an uncertain mare, and nothing like as reliable for a long campaign as Flora was. The news of this race created a great sensation all over the country; and I must here say, that, in spite of her defeat, many stuck to Flora, and contended that the verdict obtained by Princess would be reversed, with heavy costs and damages, when there was a new trial. On the 6th of August, after a good let-up for Flora to repair her injuries and grow out her quarters, these famous mares again appeared to dispute for victory. It was on the Eclipse Course, mile heats, three in five. Few that witnessed the doings of that memorable day will ever forget it. Princess was the favorite at 100 to 80, and everybody looked for a fast race; but few expected such heats as they saw. The crowd in attendance was very great, but there was not much betting.

I suppose ninety out of every hundred who were present expected to see Flora defeated. I confess that I thought Princess likely to win it; although I was satisfied, that, when at her best, Flora could trot in twenty in harness. The truth is, that Princess was a little over-rated. It is often the case, that when a trotter wins with great ease, especially if the one defeated is a famous one, a calculation is forthwith made in which it is assumed, not that the loser was "off," but that the winner is greatly superior. This assumption is commonly erroneous. Another wide-spread error lies at the bottom of it. In spite of all authority and experience to the contrary, people generally believe that a horse, if there is nothing apparently ailing him, is as good one day as another. This is not so; and mares, especially in the spring season, are still more uncertain. Flora was driven by James McMann in this race; and, as soon as she was brought out and set a-going, I could see that she felt well, and was in fine condition. She was full of life and spirit; and her muscle was greatly developed, without much flesh. She meant mischief. In the first heat, she had the inside. At the word she darted to the front, out-footed the Princess to the quarter in thirty-five seconds, and got a lead of about twenty yards. Flora did the half-mile in 1m. 10½s.; and

Princess must have trotted the second quarter very fast, for, at the pole, Flora's lead was only a length. Thus they went until half way up the home-stretch; when the frantic shout of thousands of her admirers inspired the little mare to one of her great rushes, and she won the heat by three lengths in 2m. 23½s. When the judges announced that the record was a second better than ever before, and that Flora was still the sovereign mistress of it, the people were nigh crazy with joy. There was no betting between the heats; and many yet believed that Eoff could win the race if he liked to do so.

Flora had a bad start in the second heat. She was a length and a half behind, and under a pull when the word was given; but she darted on to Princess with such a rush that she collared her before she was well at the turn, and up went the California mare. At the quarter-pole, in thirty-four seconds, Flora led six or seven lengths. At the half-mile, in 1m. 09s., her lead was not quite so great; but she kept all the daylight open to the score, and won by six lengths in 2m. 22s. It was a capital heat for Flora; and, though she afterwards beat it on this Island at the Union and Fashion Courses, she never surpassed it much, considering the bad start she had. I shall always contend that Flora's best heat was made on this Island. The Kalamazoo Course, on which she beat 2m. 20s., may have been a mile. It was certified as a mile, and it is too late now to go behind what the record says; but, if that was a mile, our Island courses are more than a mile, for they measure a mile one foot nearer the pole than that did. Besides, it is a well-known fact, that the Eclipse Course, now called the Centreville, is more than a mile. Even after this heat, some continued in the belief that Princess could have won it.

In the third heat, Flora took the lead, and went to the quarter in thirty-five seconds, three lengths ahead. Princess gained two lengths in the straight quarter, on the back-stretch, and yet Flora got to the half in 1m. 10s. The

California mare drew forward until she was head-and-head with Flora. It looked critical; but the big mare was at her best, and Flora had still a link to let out. McMann touched her with the whip, and away she went. At the head of the stretch, she had the best of it, and, lasting the longest, came home the winner by three lengths in 2m. 23½s.

There had never been any thing like such a trot before. The best previous time had been beaten by two seconds and a half, and it had been beaten in all the heats. Princess had established the fact, that she was an extraordinary mare; but Flora's glory and reputation had been restored. She had not only showed as much speed as Princess anywhere, but had beat her in the rushes at the beginning, and, in the desperate brushes afterwards, had lasted the longest. Still it is to be remembered that she had the pole to begin with; and it actually seemed as if she was as well aware of the advantage she derived from that fact as any man on the ground. The dart after Princess in the second heat, when Flora was behind at the start, appeared to be inspired by reasoning, as though she made up her mind to this effect: "If she gets the pole, she beats me!" The rejoicing caused by that victory of hers spread from the shores of the ocean where it was achieved to the distant States and Territories which lie beyond the Mississippi River; for this little mare had become a national character.

XXXVII.

Flora Temple and Princess again. — Flora wins Two-Mile Heats. — They go Hippodroming. — Flora trots in 2m. 21½s., with Ike Cook, at Cincinnati. — Her Performance at Kalamazoo. — 2m. 19¾s.

Flora Temple and Princess met again at the Eclipse Course, on the 16th of August, to trot two-mile heats in harness. In spite of Flora's grand performance on the 9th, many still believed that the California mare was able to beat her, especially at two-mile heats. This feeling was so general that Princess was the favorite at 100 to 80; but I think there was but very little betting at those rates, and the odds were more nominal than real. The mares were both in fine condition; and as the day and, track were good, a performance of uncommon speed was looked for. Those who expected it were not at all disappointed, as, before they went home, they saw the fastest two-mile heat that ever was trotted.

In the first heat, Princess had the best of the start; and they went away at a rapid gait, — a tremendous gait for a two-mile heat. The little mare gained inch by inch; and at the quarter, in 35s., Princess had but a neck and shoulder the best of it. At the half-mile, in 1m. 11¼s., Princess led a neck only. Soon after passing the pole they were head-and-head, and a most excellent neck-and-neck race followed all around the lower turn. As they swung into the stretch Flora led by a neck; but the California mare gained it on the straight work, and they were neck-and-neck again at the distance. At the shout of the people, as they came on thus, Flora made a dart ahead, and crossed the score a length in the lead in 2m. 23s. At the quarter-pole Flora's lead was two lengths, and this she carried to the half. So it continued round the lower turn. Princess was unable to close with Flora; but the latter had to keep the pace very strong to retain the lead. But, when they struck the home-stretch, the long struggle at such a great rate had settled the California mare, while Flora remained full of trot. Princess broke badly. Flora made a lightning rush at the shout that was set up, and Eoff had no great deal to spare in saving his distance. The time of the heat, trotted all the way without a skip or a break, and some of it at the rate of 2m. 20s. to the mile, was 4m. 50½s. It still remains the best two-mile heat that ever was trotted in harness. I never saw but one in any way of going to equal it; and that was when Dexter trotted his two miles to wagon in 4m. 56¼s., and jogged in from half way up the stretch.

After this heat in 4m. 50½s., Eoff complained that Flora crossed him on the turn in the second mile. The judges, however, held that she was far enough ahead to take the pole without compelling Princess to shorten her stride. McMann, in turn, claimed the race as well as the heat, because Princess, as he alleged, was distanced; but the truth was, there was no judge in the distance-stand, the distance-judge having got by mistake into the distance-stand for mile heats, three in five. The trotting of this heat had opened the eyes of those who had up to that time believed that the California mare would beat Flora whenever Eoff called upon her to do so. It was clear enough that, however fast she might have gone in California, in the trial with the pacer, she was at her best in the first mile of that heat, where Flora was a length ahead in 2m. 23s. It was equally plain that Flora had out-lasted as well as out-trotted Princess; and, the farther they went, the more evident her superiority became. There were plenty of betters now ready to lay a hundred to thirty on Flora.

In the second heat, Princess had the best of the start, and tock the pole from Flora before she had lead enough to justify her in doing so. On the lower turn, Flora got to her head, and another neck-and-neck struggle ensued. On the stretch, Flora got a little the best of it; and rushing on with great vigor when she felt herself among her shouting friends and admirers, she led a length and a half at the score in 2m. 24s. On the turn, Flora ran over a man who had no business to be there, and then broke; but just then Princess broke, and Flora was first down to her work. At the quarter, she led five lengths, and at the half-mile Princess was dead-beat and tired. The rest of the heat was no contest at all. Flora jogged out in 5m. 5s.; the second mile being trotted in 2m. 41s. The question of superiority between these beautiful and capital mares had now been fairly tested. It was found, that, while the California mare was second to no other but Flora, she certainly was second to her. The recent contest had removed all doubt. Although there was no money at stake between them, the drivers had done their best to win; and some, indeed, thought they had both done more than they had any right to do, in view of the rule against foul driving. These mares, while only trotting for gate-money, had showed the two finest trots that had then been witnessed; but still I am persuaded that the example then set, and since followed, of going hippodroming round the country to trot for gate-money, which was already appropriated and divided without any reference to which might win, was pernicious.

However, they set off on an excursion of that character, and first showed at Boston on the 23d of August, to some sixteen thousand people. It was mile heats, three in five, in harness, and Flora won in three heats, — 2m. 26½s. being the fastest, the others being 2m. 33s., and 2m. 34s. Upon the principle of making hay while the sun shone, they appeared at Saratoga on the 27th. Flora won again in three heats, the fastest of which was 2m. 30s. From Saratoga they went away down east to Portland, in Maine, and gave an exhibition there on the 1st of September. Flora won all the heats again, — the fastest, 2m. 26½s.

The next trot was at Suffolk Park, Philadelphia; and this was for a real purse given by the proprietor, and not for a share of the gate-money. It was the opening of that Park. It was on the 8th of September; and the purse was $1,500, mile heats, three in five, in harness. The day was fine, the expectation was great; and no less than twelve thousand people had come together to see the mighty mares. At the start, in the first heat, Flora rushed off at great speed, and Princess soon broke badly. While she was bobbing up and down, Flora opened a great gap, and could easily have distanced her; but McMann took a long pull and a strong pull, and let Princess come up, so as to make it look a little like a race. Flora won by three lengths: time, 2m. 41½s.

When that time was announced, there was a good deal of dissatisfaction expressed. The people hooted and groaned at Eoff, but it was not his fault. The mare had lost her fine turn of speed in a measure, and was becoming more and more unsteady. Flora had got her on the go-downwards, and was fast breaking her heart. However, the judges pacified the crowd, by announcing, that, if Princess did not win the next heat, I should drive her in the third. She made another bad break in the second heat, and was beat in 2m. 31s. I was then induced to drive her. I did not much like the arrangement; for my opinion was, that she had no more chance to beat Flora that day than I had to beat her and go a-foot: but, as the judges had quieted the threats of the crowd by means of this device, I consented. Flora took the lead at the start, trotted the heat in 2m. 23s., and Princess was distanced.

On the 10th, the mares trotted at Baltimore. The first heat Flora won in 2m. 29s.; the second in 2m. 31s.; the third she trotted in 2m. 22s.; and Eoff pulled Princess up at the half-mile pole, there being no semblance of a contest.

From Baltimore to Chicago the mares proceeded, and there gave an exhibition on the 16th of September. A bigger farce was never enacted anywhere. Flora won the first heat in 2m. 31s. In the second, she had to wait so long for Princess, by reason of her bad breaking, that the heat was 3m. 21s. The third heat Flora won in 2m. 26½s.

Flora next appeared at Muscatine, Io., her partner there being Ike Cook. It was mile heats, three in five, in harness. Flora won in three heats. These two then travelled to Cincinnati, and there trotted in what was advertised as a match for $1,000 a side. Flora won it in three heats, the last of them being trotted in 2m. 21½s. This beat the time made at the Eclipse Course and at Baltimore: but it is to be remembered that it was not trotted on Mr. Cassady's old Queen-City Course, but on a new one; and there is good reason to believe that it measured a little short. I have heard from good authority that it was not then a full mile. But the people did not know that fact; and the news that the little mare was gradually coming down towards 2m. 20s., created much interest all over the country.

Expectation was rife in regard to her. And now she was about to make her fastest heat. It was on the 15th of October, at Kalamazoo, in Michigan, that she appeared, to trot with Princess and a horse named Honest Anse. The people of the famous oak-openings country have always manifested much fondness and liberality towards trotters. They gave a purse of $2,000, mile heats, three in five, in harness. Flora Temple, Princess, and Honest Anse appeared to trot for it. The first heat was just about fast enough to warm Flora up. In the second, Honest Anse made her trot fast for three-quarters of a mile: he then shut up, and she won it in 2m. 22½s. He was then withdrawn, and Flora and Princess started for the third heat. The little mare went clean away from Princess; did the first half in 1m. 9s., and trotted the heat in 2m. 19¾s. The news created very great excitement; and many believed that the course was short.

These were, in fact, more than half right; for, upon its being measured, it was found necessary to get four feet from the pole to make it a mile; while our Island tracks all measure a little more than a mile three feet from the pole. Therefore the Kalamazoo Course, at that time, was not as long as the Union or Eclipse Course. Still it was but a trifle short. Every track, however, ought to be full measure; and it is a greatly-mistaken policy to have any course short, be it ever so little.

XXXVIII.

Flora Temple and George M. Patchen. — Description of Patchen. — His Pedigree. — Patchen's Early Performances. — Dan Mace as a Driver and Rider. — Flora and Ethan Allen. — Flora and Patchen again. — The best Race ever made by Flora, and the best a Stallion ever made.

FLORA TEMPLE, after her grand exploit at Kalamazoo, went to Cleveland, where she beat Princess with great ease and in poor time; and then, at Cuyahoga Falls, on the 28th of October, she beat Ike Cook. They had four heats of it: the second was a dead heat. The time was slow in all of them. At Buffalo, on the 2d of November, Flora beat Ike Cook in three heats, the best of which was 2m. 23½s. On the 5th, Flora, Ike Cook, and Belle of Saratoga went three-quarter-mile heats in harness; and Flora won it in three heats. On the 11th, Flora and Ike Cook trotted at St. Catharine's, Canada; and the mare won in three heats. That may be said to have been the last of Flora Temple's hippodroming, at least for a season.

She was brought to New York, and entered for a purse of $1,000, given by the Union Course. It was mile heats, three in five: the mare was to go in harness, while her only competitor was to go under saddle. This competitor was the famous stallion George M. Patchen, who had not been very long on the turf, but had already proved himself to be fast and lasting, and good in every way of going, either under saddle, in harness, or to wagon. He was a powerful brown horse, that had been foaled on the farm of W. H. Sickles, which is about half-way between Keyport and

Freehold, N.J. The mare that dropped him belonged to Mr. Carman of Westchester County. She had been sent to Mr. Sickles to be wintered; and it was not thought she was in foal, though she had been covered: in fact, Mr. Carman told Mr. Sickles, that, if she was in foal, he might have the produce. That produce was Patchen. He was above sixteen hands high, with great strength and much bone. He was coarse about the head, and heavy in the carcass; but though he was what you might call a plain horse, his points were uncommonly strong and good, and his action was capital.

He had good blood in him: for he was got by Cassius M. Clay, who was by old Henry Clay; and his dam was by a young horse who was own brother to Trustee the trotter. So here was the Bashaw blood through Andrew Jackson, the Messenger blood also through him, the blood of imported Trustee, and the blood of the famous trotting-mare Fanny Pullen, who was herself a high-bred trotting-mare. Some have doubted whether the sire of Patchen's dam was own brother to Trustee the twenty-miler; but, after inquiry, I have reason to believe so. Her sire was a three-year-old colt, by imported Trustee, out of Fanny Pullen. Patchen's dam was probably the only foal he ever got; for he was soon made a gelding, and was driven for many years by a gentleman in Westchester County. He was himself a fast and stout trotter.

In 1858, Patchen was matched against Ethan Allen, mile heats, three in five, to 100lb. wagons. The little horse distanced the big one in 2m. 28s. But, while Flora was upon her exhibitions in the West with Princess, Patchen had performed on Long Island and at Philadelphia with great success and distinction. He had been sold, in whole or in part, to John Buckley, and was trained and driven by Darius Tallman. He had that season beaten such horses as Brown Dick and Lancet; had trotted two heats in harness in one race in 2m. 26¼s., and 2m. 26½s.; and, in another race, he had gone in 2m. 25¼s. under the saddle. He was, therefore, no mean opponent for the very best.

The day for this trot was the 21st of November. It was a cold, raw day, with a strong wind blowing; and the course, as is almost always the case so late in the season, was heavy. James McMann drove the little mare; and Dan Mace, a rider and driver of uncommon resolution and ability, was on the stallion. Mace is one of the best drivers that we have; but, according to my notion, his horses break more than trotters ought to do. I think it should be the aim of the trainer and driver to keep the horse at or near his best on a trot; to teach him to stay there when going fast; and to depend upon his steady-trotting powers, instead of using him to relieve himself three or four times in every mile by getting up. But, in a race, Mace is an opponent that needs watching. He is very resolute, and the horses he handles know it. His judgment is good, at times when judgment is absolutely required, which is just when some people lose it. And, besides all that, he knows enough to wait until his time has come, when he has the right sort of horse. The races he won in that way with Buffalo Prince — five or six, and I think, once or twice, seven heats — were very creditable to him; and it is no more than proper that I should say so. But, with all his skill as a driver, I think he was, as a rider, equally in the right place. His style is not quite as elegant as is sometimes seen; but he seems to grow out of his horse, and to squeeze him with a clip of the knees like the gripe of a vice. His hand upon the bridle is light and delicate until the horse needs help to finish; and then he takes hold of his head with a power that seems to be almost irresistible, and fairly launches him over the score. He, as I have said, was upon George M. Patchen at the first of his meetings with Flora Temple; and he afterwards rode General Butler, when he beat Patchen under saddle, and was compelled to go in 2m. 21s. to do it.

There were not many at the Union Course when Flora

and Patchen came out to trot, for the day was very unpleasant. In the first heat, Patchen took the lead, and was two lengths in front at the quarter. On the back-stretch he broke, and Flora went by him; but he trotted fast, and, after a long brush, got to her head again at the drawgate. He did not, however, succeed in keeping to his trot, but broke again; and she won in 2m. 28s. In the second heat, they trotted very fast; the stallion going like a whirlwind in places, but not with the steadiness of the mare. Her even stroke, and fine dash at the conclusion, won it in 2m. 23s. The third was a tremendous heat. Flora was first over the score by half a length, in 2m. 24s.; but the heat was given to the stallion, because Flora broke near home, and had crossed him when she ought not to have done so. It may be doubted whether a strict construction of the rules would not have warranted the distancing of her; but it is probable the judges based their decision on the break, and not on the crossing.

They came up for another heat, and went away at great speed without the word. It was getting dark; and, in spite of the recall, they kept on. Flora come out ahead; but the judges had not given the word, and declared it no heat. The race was postponed until the following day, but was never trotted out. On the 24th of November, it being Thanksgiving Day, Flora Temple and Ethan Allen trotted for a purse of $1,500, mile heats, three in five, in harness. Flora got off on a hobble, broke at the turn, and lost the first heat in 2m. 27s. The second heat was a good one. The stallion was out-trotted for the first half-mile, and Flora took the pole; but he got to her head as they swung into the straight work, and, for a moment, looked like winning it. He was, however, unable to maintain the pace, and broke. She won that heat in 2m. 26¼s., and took the third and fourth in 2m. 27s., 2m. 29¾. They had not yet done with her that winter; for, on the first of December, she trotted mile heats, three in five, in harness, against Ethan Allen, at Baltimore, and beat him in 2m. 27½s., 2m. 26¼s., 2m. 25½s.

It seemed now, that, after the downfall of Princess, and the way in which Flora had finished up her long and arduous campaign of 1859, she would remain at ease, the acknowledged Queen and Mistress of the Trotting-turf. But this was not the case. It was found that the Jersey stallion, George M. Patchen, was an improving horse; and, in the spring of 1860, he was matched against her for $1,000, mile heats, three in five, in harness, over the Union Course. It came off on the 6th of June. The race created a great deal of interest, and the betting ran high. The friends of Patchen were sanguine. On the 16th of May, he had defeated Ethan Allen on the Union Course in harness in 2m. 25s., 2m. 24s., 2m. 29s.; and on the 23d, had beaten Ethan Allen to wagons in 2m. 26¼s., 2m. 27s., 2m. 31s. Still, the memory of what Flora had done would hang in the minds of the people; and, prior to the day, she was backed at 100 to 80. The day was as fine as could be wished, and there was an immense crowd present. The horses looked as well as they could look. James McMann drove Flora, and Tallman did the same for Patchen. Before the start, there was a change in the betting, and Patchen was backed at odds of 100 to 80.

The stallion had the pole. In scoring for the first heat, he seemed to have the foot of Flora, and went flying by the stand ahead of her, as many as five or six times, before they got the word. The start was even; but Flora soon made a skip, and the stallion got the lead: but the mare caught, and, going on with uncommon resolution, headed him, and led a length at the quarter in 35s. On the straight work, she drew away a little more; but the stallion now made a great burst of speed, and she broke. At the half-mile, in 1m. 11s., he had a lead of a length, and soon increased it to two lengths; but, upon the turn, the mare squared herself, drew up to him, and came into the stretch with him. The struggle home, was one of the fastest and closest things that ever was seen. They came on neck-and-neck at an amazing rate; and within three strides of home, it seemed to be a dead heat. McMann, at the very last, struck Flora sharply with the whip, let go of her head, and with one desperate effort she was first, by a throat-latch, in 2m. 21s., the best time that we had then seen on the Island. The last half-mile had been trotted in 1m. 10s., and was a neck-and-neck race nearly all the way.

In the second heat, Flora was two lengths ahead at the quarter-pole; and Patchen breaking on the back-stretch, her lead was three lengths at the half-mile. On the lower turn he closed the daylight; and another very hard, close struggle up the home-stretch, ended in his defeat by only a neck in 2m. 24s. Tallman made an appeal after this heat, alleging that McMann had driven foul, by swerving out, and compelling him to go to the extreme outside. The judges disagreed; but the majority overruled the objection, much to the delight of the largest number of the people present. Many, however, believed, and still believe, that if the appeal had been made for her in a like state of the case, and if it had been allowed, there would have been quite as much hallooing.

In the third heat they got off well together. On the turn she led slightly, being on the inside, and at the quarter, in 36s., she led him nearly a length. He now made a wonderful effort, and trotted one of the best quarters that I have ever seen. He was nearly a length behind at the quarter-pole in 36s.; at the half-mile pole in 1m. 10s. he led. Therefore, he trotted this, the second quarter in the third heat, in better than 34s. On the lower turn, he led two lengths. But the mare now gathered herself up for one of her rushes, and closed with him. Up the stretch it was again, close and hot. But she had a little the best of it, and at the very last pinch he broke. She won in 2m. 21½s. I consider this the best race that Flora Temple ever made; and as the stallion was so little behind her that the difference could not be appreciated by timing, it shows what a remarkable and excellent horse he also was. No other stallion has ever made as good a race as he made that day.

XXXIX.

Flora Temple and Patchen, Two-mile Heats. — Flora and Patchen at Philadelphia. — Outside Interference.

ON the 12th of June, Flora Temple and George M. Patchen trotted two-mile heats in harness, at the Union Course. The capital race made by the stallion at mile heats emboldened some to back him; but the general public considered the little mare as invincible. She was the favorite at long odds: two to one was current, and in many instances a hundred to forty was laid; but there was nothing to justify such odds as this. Flora had only beaten the stallion in the mile-race by the most desperate of efforts, and in unparalleled time. It was true that she was known to be a good stayer; but his reputation for sticking close and coming again was also great. He was a horse that would blow so hard after an arduous heat, that one would think he was distressed: but he relieved himself quickly in that matter; and I have no doubt his heart was large, and his lungs sound and strong. He was now controlled by Mr. Joseph Hall of Rochester; but Tallman still trained and drove him well. The expectation of the people was, that amazing time would be made in this race. They had become so used to the cutting-down of old Time by Flora, just as he cuts down all things with his swinging scythe, that they looked for what was extremely improbable, — a heat better than that in which the little mare beat Princess in 4m. 50½s. Many bets were laid that a heat would be made in 4m. 50s. A considerable number of men went as low as 4m. 48s., and some put the time down to 4m. 46s.

They both seemed very fit; and, in scoring, Patchen's stride was particularly bold and commanding. The mare was fast too; but I rather fancied that she was somewhat short and hurried in her action that day. At the start in the first heat, Patchen, having the pole, drew a length ahead at the quarter, and had increased his lead to two lengths at the half-mile in 1m. 12s. Flora trailed him, hugging close to the inside. He kept the pace very strong, making the second half-mile in 1m. 11s., and thus doing the first mile in 2m. 23s. Flora still kept close behind, trailing. On the back-stretch, the stallion broke, and Flora passed him. He made another break; and, on the lower turn, she led him four lengths: but the pull that Tallman took on this turn greatly restored his horse, and Flora herself was tiring. When they reached the straight side to come home, the big, pounding stroke of the stallion came closer and closer, and finally away went Flora in a break. The stallion got the lead, and trotted over the score a length ahead of the little mare, she being on the run. The time of it was 4m. 58¼s.

In the second heat there was an even start. At the quarter, Patchen led but a neck in 38s.; but on the straight work he trotted amazingly fast, and passed the half-mile over a length ahead in 1m. 12s. Flora now trailed close to the inside, and unable to get through unless he should swerve out, or make a bad break; in which latter case she might have gone round him. As they came on inside of the distance, he broke; but the mare was in the pocket, and not in a situation to take advantage of it, and keep him bothered by going right to his head. The consequence was, that the stallion caught again, settled to his trot, and passed the score in the lead in 2m. 25s. I have always thought that there was an error in judgment made by the driver of Flora that day; but it is quite likely that the stallion would have defeated her under any circumstances; for, well as she looked outwardly, she was not quite up to the mark. Patchen now increased his lead. At the half-mile pole, he was two lengths and a half ahead, and she was tired and beat. He won it very easily in 4m. 57½s. A great deal of money was lost and won on this race.

Two matches were made, to be trotted at Suffolk Park, Philadelphia, the first, mile heats, three in five; the second, two-mile heats. The first of them was trotted on the 4th of July. Flora was the favorite at 100 to 70. The race was the fastest and best that ever was trotted at Philadelphia. In fact, few ever surpassed it anywhere. In the first heat, Flora was half a length ahead at the quarter, in 34½s. Just before they reached the half-mile, Patchen got to her head, and even showed in front for a moment; but she was going too fast for an endeavor to pass her to be safe, and in making such an effort the stallion broke up. She led at the half-mile in 1m. 09½s., and opened a gap. He afterwards closed it; and, on the straight work, coming home, got to her shoulder. But she had a link in; and, when she let it out, he broke again. She won in 2m. 22½s.

In the second heat they trotted nearly neck and neck to the quarter in 35¼s. Flora led a trifle there. On the back-stretch he out-trotted her, and led half a length; but just before they got to the half-mile pole she collared him again, and made the pole in 1m. 10¼s. Then she broke, and he took the lead; then he was so hard pressed in his effort to maintain it, that he broke, and she was once more in advance. At the head of the stretch, they were nearly neck and neck, and doing their very best. It need not be said that their best trotting, neck and neck, at the rate of about 2m. 20s. to the mile, was very fine. It is a spectacle which has very seldom been seen, except in the races between Flora and George M. Patchen; for they were the only two that came together capable of doing it, heat after heat. There had not been another horse that had been so close to Flora Temple herself in speed, in ability to stay a distance, and in apparent endurance and capacity to keep at it race after race, as George M. Patchen. The finish now was very fine.

Half-way up, when she led him only a neck, he broke, and away she went ahead above a length; but he soon caught, and rushed at her again with such speed and resolution that he was at the girths when she crossed the score in 2m. 21¾s. Before they trotted the third heat, there was a great storm of rain, and the track became very muddy. Some held that this was favorable to the stallion, but I could never see why. Flora was good in all sorts of going; and I do not believe that the ability to go fast in mud depends upon size. Yet people said, "He is a big, strong horse, and that helps him to get through mud." Now, her action was better calculated for heavy going than his was; and the shape and size of her feet were as near perfection for mud or hard road, rain or shine, as any I ever saw. At the first quarter of the third heat, they were together in 37s. Just before they got to the half-mile, Flora broke; at the half-mile, in 1m. 17½s., he led. When the mare settled, she gradually drew towards him, carried him to a break on the home-stretch, and won in 2m. 37½s.

On the 10th of July, Flora and Patchen trotted two-mile heats at Suffolk Park. Previous to the race, the stallion was sold to Mr. Waltermire, of New York, who afterwards was the sole owner of him to the day of his death. The odds were a hundred to seventy on Flora Temple. Before the race there was a dispute, and Tallman refused to start. It caused a delay until six o'clock in the evening, and prejudiced many people against the horse. When they came on the course, the odds on the mare advanced to as much as $100 to $40. The stallion out-scored Flora, and it was some time before they got the word. He had the best of it by a length when the judges gave the start; and, going fast before Flora got well at work, he led three lengths at the quarter in 35½s., and the same distance at the half-mile in 1m. 10s. The stallion now made a skip, but was quickly and neatly caught by Tallman, and lost nothing. On the home-stretch the mare gained on him; but he was first over the score in 2m. 22s. After going by the stand he increased his lead, and at the half-mile pole had three lengths the best of it. They came home in the same position; and the stallion won the heat in 4m. 51½s., which is the best two miles in harness that ever was trotted except Flora's 4m 50½s.

The layers of the odds now got alarmed, and 100 to 40 was laid upon the stallion. In scoring for the second heat, Patchen broke just before they reached the stand, and some outsider called "Go!" They went on, believing it to be a start; but, on coming round to the stand again, the judges informed them that the word was not given. Thereupon Tallman, who was behind, pulled up; but McMann kept on, and jogged round. A great row ensued, in which the judges were threatened with summary violence if they did not award the race there and then to Flora Temple; but being men of knowledge and firmness, they disregarded all this, and declared that no heat at all. They were quite right. The officious attempt to give a word by an outsider I have often seen, and it is a great nuisance. In the first place, it is an insult to the ability and impartiality of the gentlemen who have been selected to judge the race. In the next place, it is likely to confuse the drivers. Therefore, anybody who does it ought to be expelled from the course.

In the second heat, the mare took the lead, and led a little at the half-mile in 1m. 14½s. She then broke and lost a little, but trotted fast on the home-stretch, and got to his wheel, when he was broken up by the crowd, who pressed upon him with that intent. Flora was three lengths in the lead at the score in 2m. 28s. In the second mile, he trotted well, but made a couple of little breaks. At the head of the stretch, Flora's lead was three lengths, but the stallion now began to close with her. She was tired, and, in spite of McMann's whip, Patchen came fast and hard upon her; and now there was an outrage such as was seldom seen upon a race-course. Just as Patchen was getting the best of it, a band of men ran out at him, and threw clubs and hats in his face. In consequence, he broke, swerved behind Flora's sulky, and she was first at the score in 5m. 1½s.

Patchen was then withdrawn, and Flora was declared the winner; but the decision, to my mind, was unsatisfactory. If the horse had not been interfered with, it is probable that he would have won that second heat. It is quite true, that he was not interfered with by Flora or by her driver; but he was by her outside backers. Therefore, the judges would have been justified, I think, in declaring that there had not been a fair race; that it was out of their power to have a fair race; and that, this being so, the whole affair should end there and then in a draw. The best way to discourage rioting and roguery upon our race-courses is to take care that the guilty parties shall never secure their sole object, the plunder. As long as they are permitted to get and hold the money, they will care but little for what people say to them in the newspapers, or otherwise.

XL.

Flora Temple and Patchen again. — A Dishonored Check. — Appeal to aid Decision of the Judges. — Flora and Brown Dick. — Flora and Ethan Allen. — Flora and Patchen again. — Flora against Dutchman's Time.

ON the second day of August, in the hottest time of the year, and on a very warm, drowsy day, Flora Temple and Patchen came together again. It was mile heats, three in five, for $500, and seventy-five per cent of the gate-money to be divided between them. They both looked well, and Flora was the favorite at 100 to 80. The Philadelphia squabbles were not yet quite over. McMann held a check for $500, which had been put up against his $500 at Philadelphia in the first race there. Since the race, payment of it had been stopped; and he now asked the judges to require it to be made good before Patchen was allowed to start. This was resisted by Waltermire, upon the ground that he was not responsible for acts done by Hall of Rochester, who had now no interest whatever in the stallion. But, in answer to this, James McMann replied, that the match he had made and won was made with Tallman, who appeared here again with the horse. The judges decided that they could not interfere, and I think they were right. It is probable James McMann knew that Hall's check was staked against his money; and, if he did not, he waived his right to object to it, when he received it as part of the stakes. The judges then could not prevent Patchen from starting, so far as I can see. Hall's check had been accepted as payment by McMann; and it was not Tallman's fault that it was dishonored. But, nevertheless, McMann was fully entitled to the money; and it is to be hoped that Hall was compelled to pay. After having got $20,000 for the horse, which was said to be his price, this stopping of the check was small business.

The race now on hand was not as good as that which was witnessed when they came together on the same course the first time that year. That was a race, the like of which I have never quite seen for speed, obstinacy of contest, and close finish. This in August was very fast also; but the mare won with more ease. When they met early in June, it was her first race that season; while Patchen's trots with Ethan Allen had served to sharpen up and season him. Besides that consideration, there is another. This was her fifth race with him that year, and all of them had been very fast. Now, about four races with Flora was enough to take a little of the fine edge off any horse that ever trotted with her, if the pace was strong. It took more to get Patchen down completely within her power, than it had ever done with any former horse; but, if the process was slow, it was sure, as we shall presently see. In the first heat of this race at the Union, they started well together, after scoring four or five times, in which Patchen, as usual, displayed great speed on the straight work. On the turn, his inside place gave him a little advantage, and the mare made a skip. McMann caught her on the jump; but he led a length and a half at the half-mile pole in 1m. 11s. This lead was maintained all round the lower turn and somewhat increased on the stretch. At the draw-gate, James called upon the little mare, and she appeared to collect herself for one of her grand rushes; but she did not get the right stroke, and tangled all up, so that he won in 2m. 23½s., and she ran over the score a couple of lengths behind him.

It was now a 100 to 40 on Patchen. He seemed somewhat distressed, but he was a horse that got over his blowing in an admirable manner. After some scoring, McMann rather caught Tallman napping; and, Flora getting up to one of her rapid bursts of speed, she headed the stallion at the score, and got the word to her advantage. She seemed determined, now that she was ahead, to keep there; and by very fast and resolute trotting, she dropped him behind, so that she led four lengths at the quarter. At the half-mile, in 1m. 11s., he got closer to her, and he gained slowly on the lower turn. In the stretch he was near enough to her to be dangerous; and, as she made a skip, it looked so. But James caught her again at the instant of time, and on she came. In the endeavor to collar her the stallion broke, tired, and Flora won by three lengths in 2m. 22½s.

In the third heat they got away together at a great rate, and the stallion soon broke. He lost four lengths by it. On the second quarter they trotted very fast, — about thirty-four seconds being the time. At the half-mile, she was leading three lengths and a half. On the lower turn, he got closer, and they came up the stretch with little daylight between; but before they got home, he broke, and she won in 2m. 23½s., by four lengths. This was very great trotting; and though Patchen was surely being defeated, and was the worse off the further he went, he certainly made a good, game fight for it. In the last heat, Flora led all the way, except for a stride or two at the start, and this she won in 2m. 25¾s. Take away their own race in June, and this in August was the best that had ever been witnessed on the Union Course. Patchen never made such another in harness; and, as he went on with her in her customary tour that fall, she took more and more of the steel out of him, just as she had formerly done out of Princess and all the others that ventured on a long campaign against her.

After this race Flora went to Fonda, and beat Brown Dick, mile heats, three in five, in harness, in three heats. On the 28th of the same month she met Geo. M. Patchen at Boston, at the Franklin Course, for a purse of $1,500, mile heats, three in five, in harness. The mare won in four heats, the second being a dead heat; and the best time was 2m. 28½s. On the 15th of September, she was in the oak-opening country again, among her friends and admirers at Kalamazoo. At that place, on the 15th of September, she beat Ethan Allen for the purse of $2,000, mile heats, three in five, in harness. Flora won in three straight heats, the best of which was the last — 2m. 23s.

On and about the 24th of September, there was a great gathering of turfmen in New York. The four-mile heat sweepstakes then pending to be run on the Fashion Course, in which Planet, Congaree, and Daniel Boone were engaged, had brought gentlemen here from all over the Union, — from Virginia and Maryland and the Carolinas; from Alabama, Louisana, and Mississippi; from Kentucky and Tennesee; and from the great rising States of the North-west. That race did not amount to much: for Daniel Boone hit himself at exercise, and was unable to start; and Congaree was not in condition; so the Virginian stable, the chief owner of which was Major Thomas Doswell, a man entitled to great respect, obtained a very easy triumph.

The day before the race was run, I had the pleasure of entertaining many of the turfmen at my house, as they had come over to the south side of the Island to see Flora Temple and Patchen trot two mile heats, in harness, on the Centreville Course. The mare was the favorite at about a hundred to sixty. Patchen had been resting since their trot at Boston; while Flora had been to Michigan and back, and had defeated Ethan Allen. Nevertheless, she was the favorite at these long odds, and her condition was the best; yet she was just upon the point of being overmarked by so much work and travel. On the day before she had tired at her work, and nothing but her wonderful capacity of coming round quickly made her fit to trot the next day. At the start in the first heat, Patchen took the lead; and at the half-mile pole, in 1m. 11s., he was two lengths and a half ahead of her. She now began to close with him, and they trotted very finely to the end of the mile. At the score, in 2m. 23., her head was at his wheel. On the back-stretch she got to his head and he broke, whereupon Flora got a lead of three lengths. On the lower turn he made another break; but, even after that, trotted so well that Flora did not win it easily. They were both whipped on the stretch. She won by a couple of lengths in 4m. 55¼s.

This was almost five seconds more than she had beaten Princess in; and I conclude that Flora was not at her best. There was apparently nothing in the weather or the track to cause her to require more time; and yet she had to be whipped to get the second mile out of her in 2m. 32¼.; but one can never tell precisely what fast time depends upon, and this makes time an uncertain test. It could not have been the first mile in 2m. 23s. that made them quit in the second; for they had both gone a first mile as fast in a two-mile heat, and had not quit in the second mile. My opinion is, that neither of them was quite up to the mark that day; and I give it here, because I attribute her defeat in the attempt to beat Dutchman's time, three days afterwards, to the fact that she was stale and not at her best. In this two-mile race with Patchen, she won the second heat in 5m.

On the 27th, she was brought out again in a match against time for $500 a side, to beat Dutchman's three-mile time under saddle. This was 7m. 32½s.; the four-mile running-time of Fashion. It is unnecessary to say much about Dutchman's time here, except to state that it was not all he was capable of, by any means. I have said, in a previous chapter, that I could have ridden him that day ever so much better than 7m. 30s., — from 7m. 26s., to 7m. 28s.; therefore, I should not consider it a very wonderful thing to have a horse come out and beat 7m. 32½s. in harness. It is true that no horse has ever done it; but I have driven three that I consider were quite capable of doing it, and one of them is now. I allude to Dexter, who, in my opinion, would stand a good chance to beat it, and pull a wagon. The others were Flora Temple and General Butler. Patchen could perhaps have done it when he was at his best; and I have no doubt John Morgan could. To accomplish this feat, a horse must be fast and stout, and his or her condition must be as near perfect as may be. He must have a great deal of speed; for no horse can stay three miles except by keeping well within himself. He must be stout and honest; for a weak-constitutioned or faint-hearted one will be sure to quit before he has finished the job. He must be about the best pitch of condition; for, if defective at all in this, the trial would be more hopeless than if he was lacking in one of the other particulars.

Now, we knew that Flora had plenty of speed, and good bottom; but, considering her race with Patchen three days before, it was not probable that she was at or near her best pitch of condition; but a great many people never took that into consideration at all, and she was backed at two to one. James McMann drove her. I was one of the judges. At the start she went off at good speed, but was not altogether as steady as her backers might have wished; for she broke twice in the first half-mile, which was trotted in 1m. 14½s. The first mile was made in 2m. 30¼s., which was a winning rate, with a second and a half to spare. The pace was now forced too much. She trotted the next half-mile at the rate of 2m. 25s. to the mile, and the whole mile was 2m. 27¼s. This gave her a large margin for the third mile, but left her with little or nothing to do it with. She had trotted the two miles in 4m. 57½s., and now she had only to beat 2m. 35s. in the last mile to win; but this she could not do. She broke badly in the first part of the third mile, and her time in it was 2m. 36¼s. Her whole time was 7m. 33¾s. It was now mooted whether she could start again that day, and we decided that she could; but this is not to be taken as a general precedent. I am now satisfied that when there is a race against time, a failure in one trial beats the horse, unless it has been stipulated that there shall be more than one. Flora tried again, but was 7m. 43½s. in the second trial. It was urged, that as the Centerville Course was more than a mile, Flora should be allowed the excess three times over, which might have brought her within the time; but we held that we could not allow it to her. This question was debated for some time, and was finally left to Mr. Wilkes, who decided that we had not been in error, — that as the backer of Flora took the track for a mile when he made the match, selected the Centreville to trot on, he could not be allowed for its overmeasure.

XLI.

Flora Temple and George M. Patchen on a Tour. — Flora and Widow Machree. — Description of Widow Machree. — Flora and Princess again. — Flora and John Morgan. — Breeding of John Morgan. — Description of him.

AFTER the failure of Flora to beat Dutchman's time, she started out upon a tour with George M. Patchen, upon much the same principles as those which controlled in her campaign with Princess. They were at Elmira on the 3d of October, and, according to the published programme, trotted for a purse of $2,000; but, if anybody paid it, a fool and his money then parted, for the mare won in three heats, and the best time was 2m. 30s. It seems probable that Tallman and the owner of the stallion had come to the conviction that he could not beat Flora that season, and had made up their minds to earn his share of the gate-money as easily as might be. On the 17th, they were at Watertown; and here there was a good race between them. The track was heavy. In the first heat, Flora led all the way by two lengths, and won in 2m. 28s. In the second heat they went away together, and she had a little lead for three-quaters of a mile. But the stallion was close to her; and he made it so hot on the homestretch that she broke, and he won in 2m. 26s. But the little mare was not to be beaten in the race, for she won the third and fourth heats in 2m. 26s., 2m. 25s.

They passed on to Rochester, and there had another race of four heats. The stallion won the first, and the mare secured the other three. The time was 2m. 29s., 2m. 29s.

2m. 28s., 2m. 30s. On the 27th of October they were at Geneva, and trotted on a heavy course. Flora won the first heat in 2m. 32s. In the second, she was defeated in 2m. 28s. In the third, she beat the stallion in 2m. 29s. But in the fourth heat she was distanced. On the 31st, they reached Corning; and there the mare won in three heats, with 2m. 31s. the best, the track being very heavy.

That was the last time that Flora and Patchen trotted together, I believe. There was much talk the following spring about matching them, and one or two meetings were held at the office of "The Spirit of the Times," for the purpose of coming to some definite agreement. But they could not come to terms. Mr. Waltermire and Tallman declared that McMann was afraid to trot the mare against Patchen any more. But the truth is, that James was quietly laying back to entice them into an offer to trot for a large amount of money, and finally offered to trot Flora against him any race they could name in harness or to wagon, for a large amount. But by this time Mr. Waltermire had made up his mind to let Patchen go to the stud. I do not think that he could have balanced the books with her if he had tried again; for events afterwards showed that she was quite as good as ever, if not better. But he had stood a longer and stouter struggle with her than any other trotter had done. He beat her more heats than any other horse; and most of the heats in which she beat him were very fast and close. He met her, too, at the golden prime of her life, when she had just reached the full maturity of her extraordinary power.

When every thing is considered, I am under the impression that Patchen was the best horse that Flora Temple ever contended with, and that, therefore, their names must go down linked together as those of the best mare and the best stallion that have yet appeared. On the other hand, James McMann has a leaning to the opinion that the very best horse she ever met was the Chestnut from Kentucky, first called Medoc, and afterwards John Morgan. Now, it is true, as we shall presently see, that he made her put forth all her powers to beat him, especially at two-mile heats. But Patchen did this more than once, and actually beat her two-mile heats as well. Moreover, it did him no perceptible harm; for he was still very fast and very stout when he was trained again to trot with General Butler, after having been at the stud: while, as regards John Morgan, the race appeared to upset him. It "cooked his mutton," as the saying is, and he never was as good again. With this, which Patchen well deserved, I leave him.

But Flora's work in 1860 was not ended when she had done with Patchen. James McMann would make hay when the sun did not shine as well as when it did; and so, a purse being offered down at Danbury, in Connecticut, on the 15th of November, he took Flora there to trot for it. The attachment of James to Flora was very great. He gloried in her, and often reproved the boys for giving her nick-names, other than the one he fondly applied to her which was DOLLY; but it must be confessed that he kept her busy, and at it early and late. Her opponent at Danbury was the Widow Machree, a mare that bade fair at one time to win a place only second to that of Flora herself, and would have done it, in my opinion, if her legs had been as good as her pluck and her constitution were. The Widow was a low, wiry chestnut, with all the hard, condensed quality of a thoroughbred. She had great speed, she was capital before a wagon, she was as game a mare as any that I remember; but she was light in the bone below the knee, and her fore legs went early. The truth is, however, that, with proper care and judicious management, they might have lasted a good deal longer. She was one of the daughters of that famous horse American Star, of whom I have spoken in prior chapters.

At Danbury, the mud was deep and heavy, and the weather bleak and cold, as it commonly is in New

England in the middle of November. Flora Temple and Widow Machree trotted a tremendous race. The former won it in three heats, and the fastest was 2m. 30s.; the third was 2m. 33s. This, in the state of the ground and the weather, was justly considered amazing. The Widow is no longer on the course, but has been bred to Hambletonian, by whom she has had three sons, all said to be fine colts. It is the same cross that produced Dexter; and, in my judgment, there is none better. The stallion gives the size and bone, which many of the Star mares somewhat lack; while they supply a style of action that cannot be surpassed, and an amount of pluck and gameness that never was exceeded.

In the year 1861, Flora made her first appearance, on the 21st of May, at the Fashion Course. Her opponent was the mare Princess, who had been for some time in retirement. She was now thought to be in fine condition, and had trotted so well in private, that many thought she would stand a good chance to defeat Flora, who had just come up from Charles Lloyd's, in Jersey. The Fashion Course had lately come under control of a new club, composed of such gentlemen as Mr. Pettee, Mr. Genet, Shephard F. Knapp, Morgan L. Mott, etc. The club offered a purse of $500, mile heats, three in five, to wagon, for Flora and Princess. The latter went wrong just before the race, being sore in the fore-feet. Flora won in three heats, and the time was slow.

It now seemed difficult for Flora to get further engagements; but at length a new candidate for the highest honors of the turf was brought on from the West to trot against her. It was the chestnut-gelding Medoc, or John Morgan, a Kentucky horse, and, I think, the best trotter that has yet been produced there. He was the result of a cross between a trotting-stallion and a thoroughbred, or nearly thoroughbred, mare. His sire was Pilot, jun., a son of old Pilot the pacer. His dam was by the race-horse Medoc, who, being a son of American Eclipse, inherited the Messenger blood through the famous Miller's Damsel. This latter was out of an imported mare by Pot-8-os, who was the best son of English Eclipse, and one of the fastest and stoutest running-horses that ever was trained.

John Morgan was a golden chestnut, with a white foot and a blaze in the face. He was sixteen hands high, a powerful horse, with great bone, and fine, bold action. He was worked, and worked hard, even when two years old; and at four he was put through such a preparation as his owner, Mr. Bradley, gave to the running-horses. In my opinion, his early and severe handling was a great evil. It did not prevent him from displaying wonderful speed and bottom; but it cut his career very short, to what it might otherwise have been. If this horse had not been trained and trotted until he was four or five years old, he might have gone on improving so as to beat Flora herself. He was a very stout horse, as well as very fast. No distance seemed too long for him. He was trained and driven in Kentucky by his owner, who had never trained and driven any other trotting-horse.

After having won two and three mile heats in Kentucky, he was sold to Mr. George Bockius and James Turner, for $6,000 or $7,000. They brought him to New York, and matched him to trot three races against Flora; mile heats three in five, two-mile heats, and three-mile heats, in harness. The races were trotted on the Centreville Course, the first, mile heats, three in five, was on the 13th of June. Very few thought that he could beat Flora at mile heats, and the bettting was 100 to 20 on her before the start. Still his fine, bold action, as he came up the home-stretch, seemingly with the power of a locomotive, greatly impressed the gentlemen who were present. Turner drove him, and the horse was a little too powerful for him. He pulled strong, and had run away once or twice. Turner had been sick; and, though a man of great natural courage, he was a little nervous.

In the first heat they went away level, and the quarter was trotted in 34s., Flora having a lead of two lengths. She did not increase her lead, and the time at the half-mile pole was 1m. 10½s. He now drew towards her, and at the head of the stretch was at her wheel. A good race home followed; and, if Turner had been able to keep up his pull, it would have been a near thing. The chestnut broke inside the draw-gate, but caught his trot well; and Flora only beat him a length and a half in 2m. 24½s.

In scoring for the next heat, Flora came up behind several times, and finally the gelding threw one of his shoes. It was replaced; but, when they got the word, he made a wild break just as he neared the place where he threw it, and Flora took a lead of four or five lengths. He broke again on the back-stretch, and the mare won the heat with ease in 2m. 26s. The third heat was very much like the second. Turner was tired, and could not stand the pull of the horse. His gait was so bold and his stroke so long, that he could not keep up to it, without putting considerable weight on the bit. He broke again soon after they got the word, and lost ground that he could never make up. She won the heat in 2m. 28½s. The friends of John Morgan were somewhat disappointed, but they still thought that he would do better on another occasion. In this they were quite right; for, as we shall presently see, he made her trot the best two-mile race in harness that she, or any other horse, ever made.

XLII.

Flora Temple and John Morgan.—The Fastest Two-mile Race that had been trotted.—Remarks upon the Race.—The Three-mile-Heat Race.—Flora against Ethan Allen and a Running-Mate.—Flora before Gen. Grant.—The Widow Machree.

ON the 11th of June, Flora Temple and John Morgan had their second meeting at the Centreville Course, to trot two-mile heats in harness. It was a most beautiful day, warm and bright, with the atmosphere of that genial and active sort that the lungs and chest seem to expand at its approach to take plenty in. The attendance was not as large as it would have been if the people had known what a contest was about to take place; for, in all Flora's career, she never made quite such another race as she was compelled to do on this occasion. When she appeared upon the course, she looked a little thinner than usual; and she speedily warmed up to a little damp sweat upon the neck. It was understood that for a day or two she had not been feeding as greedily as she usually did. In common, she was a very voracious feeder. This might have led to the supposition that she was just a little over-marked; but her eye was bright, her coat sleek and glossy, and her nostril expanded like the mouth of a trumpet. Therefore I concluded that she had just reached the finest condition to which she could, in all probability, attain.

It is well known to horsemen who are close observers, that, though a horse cannot make a great race when decidedly off the feed, some of the finest efforts that ever were made, and some of the greatest successes that ever were won, came just as the horse was beginning to get dainty, and to pick and nibble at the oats. This, I have no doubt, was the case with Flora. John Morgan looked all the better for his race at mile heats; and as he came up the home-stretch, in warming up, it was with a boldness and power of stroke that seemed to indicate uncommon confidence and resolution. There was but little betting, and that little was at three to one on Flora Temple. The horse was driven by Turner, who, not from any lack of skill, but for want of bodily strength, was likely to give out before the trotter did. The style of the horse was of that sort which requires a good strong pull to support him, especially when he tried to keep up his great stroke in going round the turns. If he could have had a chance at Flora, two miles straight away, on a good dirt-road, it is my belief he would have beaten her.

In the first heat, they went away well together; but he seemed to hang on the turn, while she made one of her electric rushes, and took the pole from him. She went on to the half-mile, with a lead of two lengths, in 1m. 12½s. The chestnut began to close with her on the lower turn; and, at the head of the stretch, he was at her wheel. Here he lay coming up the stretch, on which he made a little skip, but caught well. The mile was trotted in 2m. 27s., the mare being a length ahead at the score. Again, in rounding this upper turn, he lost some ground, but on the back-stretch made it up, and placed his head at her wheel. On the lower turn, he got to her quarters; but, when they had swung into the home-stretch, her inside place brought her a length ahead of him. Turner now called upon him; and, the work being straight ahead, he answered with such an effort that he gained upon her inch by inch. It was a very fine spectacle. At the distance he had got to her head, and it looked as though he would win it. But the little mare was not yet all out. McMann shook the whip over her; and, the crowd setting up a shout, she made a desperate effort, and, getting her nose in front of him again, she managed to keep it there in spite of all his efforts, and won by a head. It was one of the finest finishes that I remember to have seen, when the big horse began to out-trot her up the stretch, and she, making a grand rally as she saw his smoking nostril, succeeded in just beating him out. The time was 4m. 55½s.

Between the heats they both showed that their condition was good, and that they were good-winded ones. In the second heat they started even; but Flora was the quickest beginner, and began to draw ahead at the turn. Turner, indeed, was afraid to let his horse out at first, for fear that he might break. The little mare went on until she was three lengths ahead of him; but when he got well settled into his stroke, on the back-stretch, he began to overhaul her. At the half-mile, in 1m. 12½s., he was an open length behind her, and at the head of the stretch had shut up the daylight. The first mile was 2m. 26s., Flora leading a length and a half. He lost a little on the turn, as usual; but on the back-stretch he trotted in magnificent style, and showed a truly great rate of speed for the sixth quarter of a two-mile heat. At the half-mile pole, he was at her quarters, and his head reached her flank. McMann set up a yell at her, or perhaps at him, and he broke. But he caught in fine style, and, losing but little, dashed on after her. At the head of the stretch she led a length; but now the chestnut came on, and made another resolute and most determined effort to get the heat. He gained upon her inch by inch, until at the distance she was but a neck in front. McMann put the whip on to Miss Flora, and Turner held John Morgan to his brush with all his might. But it lasted a little too long. He broke close at home, and she won the heat in 4m. 52½s.

When the heats are put together, it will be found that this was the fastest two-mile race in harness that ever was trotted; and it shows conclusively that John Morgan was a tremendous horse. He had not had that gradual, patient development which I contend is best for a trotter, if not absolutely necessary to make a first-rate one. Instead of that, he had been knocked about at two years old, and at four was put through a preparation like that which running-horses receive, by a man who was notorious as a hard worker. Yet, as we have seen, he compelled Flora to do a greater thing in the beating of him than she had been called upon to perform in the conquering of Princess and George M. Patchen. He only lost the race, in my opinion, because Flora was a quicker beginner than he was, and her driver had recourse to the cunning tactics of rushing off with her so as to get the pole, and then "waiting in front." I think John Morgan should have forced the pace more in the first heat, after he got well into his stroke. Both the heats were so close at the finish, that a very little change would have made the result different; and in both heats he showed the most speed in the last quarter of a mile. In the first, she was a length ahead of him when they entered that quarter, and only beat him out by a head. His reputation for stoutness was very great; and, if he had forced Flora more in the mile and three-quarters preceding, he might have lasted the longest, and so have won it. Altogether, it was a very extraordinary trot.

On the 18th, they met again, at three-mile heats, and the odds were 100 to 40 on the mare. The reputation of John Morgan as a three-mile horse had been very great; but then it was to be remembered that he had not before encountered any trotter that could carry him at any thing like the rate of Flora Temple. Moreover, we have seen that she was such a thorough campaigner, that no horse had been found able to keep at the same relative place with her in a series of races as he began with. Lancet, Princess, and Patchen had all proved this fact, that, the further they pursued their contest with her, the easier they were defeated. John Morgan, great horse and good stayer as he was, proved no exception, and was the last of her illustrious victims. The two-mile race had taken a great deal out of him. He was not at his best on the day of the three-mile race; and, what is more, he never again came back to it.

At the start, he had the inside, but broke, and she took the pole. The first mile was trotted in 2m. 29s., the mare being a length ahead at the end of it. On the turn, she increased her lead; but, on the back-stretch, he got to her quarters. She finished the second mile, which was trotted in 2m. 27s., with him at her quarters, and on the turn he got to her head. They went neck-and-neck for a short time, and then the chestnut broke; but Turner caught him, and Flora soon after broke. While she was up he took the lead, and this was the first time he had ever obtained it in their races. But at the half-mile pole she was with him again, and able to make a stout struggle for victory, while his powder was burned out. He died away to nothing after she passed him, and Flora actually walked in, — time 7m. 47s. I have no doubt that he hit himself in the last half-mile, for he broke three or four times in coming up the home-stretch. He had always had a strong liability to hit himself from over action; and, after his races with her, it got to be a good deal stronger. She won the second heat of the three-mile race in 7m. 48s.

He was afterwards matched with her again, but hit himself in his work and paid forfeit. I think, that, in John Morgan, the material out of which one of the finest trotters that our country ever produced might have been made was partly ruined by overwork at an early age. It is quite true that the horse's power and breeding, and Bradley's forcing-system, produced a wonder; but it was a marvel of very short duration to what we might have witnessed if he had been handled as Flora Temple and Dexter were in their early years.

It now appeared to be absolutely certain that there was not a horse in the country who could contend with Flora, on even terms, with any hope of success. She was the mistress of them all. Therefore it seemed to be probable that she would get a period of repose. But, though one horse could not beat her, two might; and Joel Holkam, who had control of Ethan Allen, had found, that, assisted by a running-mate, he could trot in double harness at an immense rate of speed. Flora met Ethan Allen and his running-mate Socks for the first time on the Union Course, July 15. Flora went to a wagon.

I shall not describe these races at any length, because I do not consider them trotting-races; and I have my doubts whether the system of training a horse to trot by means of having a runner hitched up with him to pull the weight is a good one. I know that by such means some moderate horses may be made to do what appears to be a very remarkable feat; and this makes me think that the system may be deceptive and mischievous. The truth seems to be, that, in that way of going, it is the running-horse that furnishes the moving-power. The trotter is almost as literally pulled along as the man who drives and the wagon are. The team beat Flora the first race in three heats, — 2m. 22½s., 2m. 22s., 2m. 23¾s. But inasmuch as the team only beat the mare by a short length, in 2m. 22s., it appears that she never made a winning-heat to wagon as good as she showed then. On the 25th, they met again, on the Fashion Course, Flora in harness. The team won the first heat in 2m. 21¼s., and was distanced in the second heat, because Ethan, as well as Socks, ran for more than half a mile. A viler and more disgraceful transaction was never witnessed than this affair; and it is greatly to be regretted that the judges did not declare the bets off, and so defeat the ends of the promoters.

On the 8th of August, they met again on the Union Course; and this time the team was driven by a man who never threw a race, in my judgment, — the late lamented Horace Jones, who was drowned in the Delaware River. The consequence was, that they won easily in three heats, —

2m. 24¾s., 2m. 22s., 2m. 22¼s. Once more they met, and this time Joel Holkam drove them himself. They won again in three heats, and in the fastest equalled Flora Temple's time in harness at Kalamazoo, — 2m. 19¾s. She was only defeated by a head in this fast heat.

After this, Flora was seized by some officious persons, and an attempt was made to confiscate her; but the Government ordered her to be restored to Mr. McDonald, and, when she was given up to him, he took her to Baltimore. There she remaind until his death. She was then purchased by Mr. A. Welsh, a gentleman of wealth, residing at Chestnut Hills, Philadelphia. She was again put in work; and it created a great sensation when she was entered in two purses on the Fashion Course, in the name of Mr. George Wilkes.

When these entries were made, that was done which ought to have been done before. She was sent to McMann again. If James had had her from the first day that she was put to work again, and had gone at her with his cautious, gradual method, it is not unlikely that she would have stood a preparation, and trotted those races among horses of a generation that was foaled after her name was great. The last time Flora appeared on a public occasion was when Gen. Grant reviewed the great trotters at the Dubois track. She showed well on that day; but, soon after, her hind legs filled, and she had to be let up. If she had been trained on in 1862 and the following years, instead of laying idle so long, she might, perhaps, have continued to improve. Her speed had come to her gradually; and though it may be said she was then too old to get any better, I am unable to perceive that she must necessarily have reached her best in the fall of 1861, when she last trotted. She had certainly been gaining a little up to that time; and why should we conclude that she had then ceased to gain? Her constitution was wonderfully good. She was a younger mare in the fall of 1861, in regard to health and vigor, than thousands who had not numbered half her years.

I have previously stated that the Widow Machree was a speedy mare and an all-day trotter; and, as I have always considered her among the most reliable and gamest trotting-horses that I had ever driven, I will give a sketch of her performances while in my stable and under my observation. She was first called Mary Hoyt. In the spring of 1859, she was purchased by Capt. Isaiah Rynders of New York, of James W. Hoyt of Middletown, Orange County. After driving her on the road a short time, he matched her against John J. Kelly's bay mare, to trot two miles and repeat, to wagons, over the Union Course, in the month of August following, for $1,700. Her name was then changed from Mary Hoyt to Widow Machree. After the match was made, Mr. Kelly proposed to make it pay or play; which was accepted, and the money put up. A considerable amount was betted the same way before the race came off. Horace Jones, Alderman Compton, and others, backed the Kelly mare; Capt. Rynders backed the Widow. The Widow was sent to my stable to be trained for the race.

I knew nothing of her qualities, except that I had heard she was a good, game mare; and the captain knew about as much as I did. After I had worked her about three weeks, we gave her a trial to a wagon, a mile and repeat. I did not drive her to the top of her speed the first mile; but I found I was behind a trotter of no ordinary capacity, and one that did not give back in the home-stretch. The second mile she was timed, and made 2.34; which was much better than we expected. We did not time her again until within a week before the race. We gave her the trial a week before the race, two miles to a wagon.

She made the first mile in 2.35; and then I urged her a little more, and she came round the second mile in 2.33: so I was informed by Mr. Rynders, who held the watch. I could have driven her faster than that; but this was fast enough to win the match without much trouble. The race came off at the appointed time; but it was not much of a contest, as the bay mare was not in good fix.

We got the word. I took the lead; and the bay mare n.ver got alongside of me after we went a hundred yards: in fact, the gait was nothing more than a good exercise for the Widow. I think the time was 5.30. After the two-mile race, the Widow was left in my charge. She had two or three forfeits paid to her. I worked her moderately, and she grew fleshy very quick; being at all times a good feeder.

In the fall following the race in August, I entered the Widow Machree and Frank Temple in a double-team trotting-race. The first time I hooked up the Widow and Frank Temple together, I drove round the Union Course inside of 2.40. I had entered the Widow for a purse that was offered to be trotted the day after the race with the double teams at Boston. The day before the race, I put them on board the steamer. We had a stormy night; and the horses got wet, and took cold. Frank Temple was a little off his feed next day: not so with the Widow; she was a little stiff, but took her feed eagerly.

We took the cars early in the morning, and arrived at Boston in good time. Three teams put in their appearance, — A. Carpenter's, William Whelan's, and my own. I took the lead, and kept it easily, and could have distanced the other teams.

I noticed in this heat that Frank Temple did not act in his usual prompt and vigorous style; and this I told to Capt. Rynders. Thereupon he cautioned his friends not to bet long odds. They had been offering ten to one. In the second heat, I again took the lead without much trouble. Frank, however, tired after going half a mile, and the Widow had to do all the work herself in the last quarter; but we won the heat. Frank Temple was evidently out of fix, and showed distress. Still I thought we should manage to pull through; for the Widow was great at a desperate pinch, and Frank himself was a very gallant little horse. Capt. Rynders, however, feared defeat, as Carpenter's team seemed very fresh and well.

In the third heat, I got a very bad start, being two lengths behind. Carpenter's team, Telemachus and Nellie Holcomb, took the lead, and finally won the race. But the unflinching game and bottom of the Widow in the losing heats, the third, fourth, and fifth, created great admiration, and made her a host of friends. As for Frank Temple, he did all he could in his condition; and neither man nor horse can do more. The time of the five heats was 2.55, 2.50½, 2.42, 2.44½, 2.44. Whelan's team was distanced in the third heat.

When we took the team to their stable that night, I thought neither of them would be able to trot again that year. In the morning, I found the Widow laying down and eating hay. She was so stiff that she could not get up without our help. We thought she had trotted her last race; and the captain said he would sell her for $500; but, when she was on her feet, she went at her oats, and cleaned the manger, while we rubbed her fore legs with warm lotions. After this she was walked for an hour.

The proprietor of the course said that the people would be greatly disappointed if she did not start in the race in the afternoon, and requested that she might be led by the stand that her unfitness might be seen. When the time for the race came, I took her to the track, and drove her past the stand in a sulky. She could hardly put one foot before the other. The other horses, Draco, Somerville, Lady Spurr, and Ephraim Smooth appeared. I had jogged the mare round, and was about to take her off, when I noticed that she pricked up her ears at sight of the other horses, and acted as though she'd warm up and get limber. I then told the captain that I thought she might do better than we expected if started. He said I was crazy, but finally told me to do as I pleased, adding that he knew she would be distanced in the first heat. For all that, I resolved to start her; and, as the day was cold and windy, I jogged her round again.

The first heat was won by Draco in 2.38½; but I was second, although I had been run into by Ephraim Smooth, whose wheel took the hair off one of the mare's legs. The second heat was won by Draco in 2.41½, and I was second again, Lady Spurr and Ephraim Smooth both distanced. The latter ran into the mare, upset her sulky and herself, and she fell with her neck over Dan Mace's body. Ephraim also spilt his own driver, and ran off with the sulky upside down. When Mace's sulky was upset, I was close behind him, and lost nearly a hundred yards. I had to call upon the Widow to get inside the distance; and the way she answered let me know that her dead-game quality had triumphed over her infirmity, and that she was all the time "a-coming." I sent her along, and got second place.

Between the heats she was blanketted close and kept moving, except while her legs were being rubbed with lotion. In the third heat, we got off well; and Draco and the Widow went neck-and-neck to the quarter. The mare then began to show in front: but Holcomb let the stallion break and ease himself by a few jumps; and this expedient, being several times repeated, Draco was ahead in turning into the stretch. But the steady stroke of the mare overhauled him at the distance; and, in spite of another break and run, she beat him out by a neck in 2m. 39½s. The stallion was second, and Somerville third.

In the fourth heat, I had the pole, which was a great advantage, as it was a half-mile track. The mare took the lead, and kept it, although Draco made a good game struggle. The time was 2m. 34½s.

In the fifth heat, Draco made a desperate race of it for half a mile, hanging at the mare's wheel all the way. It was at the rate of about 2m. 30s.; but after that he fell off, and I took the Widow in hand. She could have trotted out in 2m. 30s. if there had been any thing to force her. As it was, the time was 2m. 39s.

In those five heats, the Widow Machree never broke. Considering her arduous race of the day before, and the state of her legs when we brought her to the course, it was one of the most splendid exhibitions of unflinching game and strong bottom that was ever seen. The Widow's pluck was always so good, that she was counted a real "do or die" mare. That race at Boston was the last she trotted with me.

XLIII.

The King of the Trotters, Dexter. — Description and breeding of him. — His Purchase by Mr. George Alley. — His History prior to his coming to me.— His First and Second Trials. — Dexter's First Race. — He beats Stonewall Jackson, Lady Collins, and Gen. Grant. — Dexter and Doty's Mare. — Dexter, Shark, and Lady Shannon. — Dexter, Shark, and Hambletonian. — Dexter hits himself, and is drawn.— Evil of much Scoring.— Dexter's Trial in November, 2m. 23¼s.

AT one time it was my intention to have said nothing about any horse that was still upon the turf; and, if I had carried that resolution out, it would have shut out any remarks concerning the prime favorite of my latter day, Dexter: but so many gentlemen have urged, and, indeed, demanded, that I should give a sketch of so famous a horse, that I finally determined to comply. Dexter is a brown gelding, very rich in color, with four white legs, and a blaze in the face. He is fifteen hands and an inch high, and is what we call "a big-little one." He is long for his inches, deep through the heart, and very powerful in the stifles, loins, and quarters. He has a good head, neck, and eye, capital oblique shoulders, and good legs and feet. There is all over him a very resolute and workmanlike look, and his quality does not at all belie it. This horse was bred by Mr. Jonathan Hawkins of Montgomery, Orange County, N.Y. He was got by Hambletonian out of a little black mare by American Star, and she was out of Shark's dam. The pedigree of the latter is not known; but this much is certain, that she was a good road-mare, of great bottom, and with a very sound, tough constitution. She lived to be very old. At one time a story was got up to the effect that Dexter was got by Harry Clay, but there was no truth in it. He was foaled in 1858, and was not held in much favor for some time. His white legs and the blaze set people against him. I have no doubt the old saw, —

> "One white leg, inspect him;
> Two white legs, reject him;
> Three white legs, sell him to your foes;
> Four white legs, feed him to the crows!" —

was often quoted by people who saw this colt in the field at Mr. Hawkins's. In the June of 1862, Mr. George Alley went up to Orange County to look at him. That gentleman has long been known as one of the best and most sagacious judges of trotting-horses to be found among the merchants and business men of New York. He had heard of this colt from Mr James Jacks, another very good judge of a trotter among our business men. At that time the colt was not broken. They had had harness on him two or three times the preceding winter; but he had slipped on the ice, and hurt one of his-hind legs, so that they did not persevere with him. At that time, too, he had never had any grain fed to him : his feed had been hay and grass from the time he was weaned.

Mr. Alley found him in one of Mr. Hawkins's fields; and, being full of grass, he did not show well when started up and made to trot; but afterwards they drove him out into the road, and there sent him backwards and forwards, loose. Mr. Alley, and Mr. Felter who was with him, then perceived that the action of the four-year-old was of the squarest and finest character. The former purchased him for $400, and had him sent down to his place at New Rochelle. Here he bitted and drove him, until he left home in the fall to go to Philadelphia for a short time. He then sent the colt to John Mingo, the breaker, at Flushing; and with John he remained about two months.

Mr. Alley then had him home again, and drove him himself until the roads got bad. He still kept him at New Rochelle, intending to drive him to a sleigh when the snow fell; but there was no sleighing that winter until February, and the very first day that Dexter was hitched to a sleigh an accident befel him. He has never had any vicious ways; but he has always been a high-strung, nervous, determined horse. No sooner did he come with the sleigh on to a bare piece of ground, than he made a jump (he jumps like a cat), and the whiffletree broke, the neck-yoke came off the pole, and he got loose. Mr. Alley then sent him here, not to me, but to Pelham John, who had him in hand two months.

That spring Mr. Alley moved to Islip, and drove Dexter again. In June he had him to a Boston wagon with C springs. It was only meant to carry one, but Mr. Alley had a friend in with him. Dexter made a shying jump away from some pea-straw that lay in a heap near the road, the wagon slewed, the gentlemen fell out, Dexter ran home to his stable. That fall, in the month of September, he being then five years old, Dexter was sent to me to be trained a little. After a short time, I sent him a trial to a wagon in 2m. 42s. This was the first trial he ever had. In a week after that we tried him a mile in harness, and he went in 2m. 31¼s. Here was indication of great speed when it should be developed, in course of time; and, as he trotted the last halves of these miles as fast as he did the first, I set him down at once as possessed of bottom worthy of his breeding. Mr. Alley and I immediately concluded that in Dexter we had got hold of an extraordinary young horse.

Soon after that he fell lame behind, as we supposed from kicking in the stall. Ordinarily he was no kicker nor no biter. As his lameness did not leave him, Mr. Alley took him to Islip, and drove him a little; but it was of no service, and he was turned out for about six weeks. He was taken up again on the 1st of December, and Mr. Alley drove him that winter in double-harness, along with the mare Baby Bell. It seemed now that his accidents were all over, for with the mare he went steady and well that winter. In the spring he was entered in a number of the purses given by the proprietors of the Fashion and Union Courses, and at the proper time was sent to me to be trained. I soon found out what sort of a horse he was. His constitution was fine; his temper was good; he was a good feeder, not a glutton, nor a great eater of hay, but with a healthy appetite and digestive powers that would always consume about twelve quarts of oats a day; and that is enough for any horse in training. Hence I looked forward with great confidence to a successful career for this young horse.

Dexter made his first race on the 4th of May, 1864, at the Fashion Course, for a purse of $100. There were twelve entries to this race, and four started. The starters were Dexter, Stonewall Jackson of New York (a fast bay gelding who had been very successful that spring), the chestnut-mare Lady Collins, and Gen. Grant (a brown gelding). This horse had been a pacer. He trotted now, and trotted exceedingly fast, but he was very unsteady. The public thought Stonewall Jackson nearly sure to win it; but when we got over to the Fashion Course, and put the money upon Dexter, he became the favorite at the rate of six to four. Still, I dare say that no one but Mr. Alley and myself suspected and believed that the curtain was about to draw up upon the greatest trotter, taken for all-in-all, that has ever appeared.

The race was the usual mile heats, three in five, in harness. We got off in the first heat, and I took the lead with Dexter. At the half-mile, in 1m. 13¼s., Dexter had a good lead, and was going quite within himself. The others could not get near him. He won by half a dozen lengths, jogging out in 2m. 33s. Stonewall Jackson was second, the Lady third, and Grant distanced. The other heats were similar to the first. Dexter was never headed in the race, and won all the heats very easily. The second and third were 2m. 36s. and 2m. 34¼s. Two days afterwards, Dexter trotted again. This was at the Union Course, mile heats, three in five, in harness. Lady Collins went against him. He won in three heats easily,—2m. 34½s., 2m. 36s., 2m. 37½s.

Previous to the first race, I had put the muzzle on Dexter, as we commonly do with trotting-horses in training, especially just before the race; but I now discovered that there was no occasion for it, and after that he was never muzzled, and had all the hay he wanted. I have said, in prior chapters of this work, that no rules can be laid down as absolute guides for training horses, because horses differ so much in constitution. Dexter was a good, moderate feeder, but would not stuff himself full of hay, or eat his litter. Other horses I have had that could not be kept in condition and wind without being usually muzzled in their training.

On the 13th of May, Dexter trotted again, at the Union Course, against Doty's bay mare, to wagons. He won the first two heats in 2m. 36¼s., 2m. 39s. and then she was drawn. On the 18th, at the Fashion Course, he trotted mile heats, three in five, in harness, with Lady Shannon, a gray mare, in the hands of Robert Walker, and the bay gelding Shark, who was in Dan Mace's care. This horse belonged to Mr. Jacks then. He was by Hambletonian, out of the old mare that was the dam of Dexter's dam. So they were closely related. Shark had had a trial on the Union Course with a running-horse, and was said to have gone fast. He had some backers, but Dexter was the favorite. In the first heat Dexter took the lead, and was three lengths ahead at the half-mile pole in 1m. 15¼s.; Shark was second. Dexter made a skip on the home-stretch, but won it easily in 2m. 33s.; Shark second. In the second heat, the gray mare was nearly head-and-head with Dexter at the quarter; but she broke on the back-stretch, and he had a lead of three lengths at the half-mile in 1m. 15¼s. Shark was second there. They could not stand the pace; and Dexter won it in a mere jog in 2m. 32¼s. In the third heat, the little horse took the lead again, and, at the half-mile pole, led the gray mare three lengths in 1m. 13s. On the Flushing-end of the course he was full of trot, and I let him go along. He increased his lead. On the home-stretch, I took him in hand, and he jogged out in 2m. 30s. This race was for a purse of $200, and a stake of $50 each.

Dexter had now, in the course of two weeks, trotted four races, in which there were eleven heats. In none of these heats had the little horse been headed. People began to say, "Hiram Woodruff has got hold of another Ripton;" but I had a trotting-mare in my stable then who made a great stride forward. On the 1st of June, Lady Emma beat May Queen and Dan Mace at the Union Course in such time and such easy style, that she was forthwith classed with the best trotters, and there she remained until her death late last fall.

Misfortune was now close at hand for Dexter, but not in any grave shape. On the 3d of June he trotted mile heats, three in five, to wagons, on the Fashion Course, with Shark and another son of Hambletonian, called after the old horse. Horace Jones had him: Ad. Carpenter drove Shark. There was an immense deal of scoring, — more than there ought ever to be. Above ten times we came up without getting the word: when we did get it, Dexter broke. Shark took the lead, Hambletonian second. At the half-mile, in 1m. 18½s., I had passed Hambletonian, and had got to the quarters of Shark: at the head of the stretch I had nearly collared him; but, just in the straight, Dexter hit his knee, and broke up. Shark won it in 2m. 36s., and Hambletonian was second. I then drew my horse, as he had given himself a pretty hard wipe. He had been backed at five to one at the start; and it seemed a hard case for the layers of the odds. Some people blamed me. It w.is a hard case for the backers of Dexter, and for his owner and me too; and they should have blamed those in authority, who stood up and saw a very valuable young horse, and a great public favorite, compelled to score above twelve times. I say this, if others can beat me in a race, let them do it; but do not give them a chance to beat me before the race begins, by "double-banking" me in scoring. The scoring for the first heat is no part of the race, for a horse or horses can pay forfeit after it; yet we often see a good horse prevented from winning by two or three scoring against him alternately, while one stays behind each time and hinders a start. This is a game for which a remedy ought to be found. This is the way Dan Mace with Commodore Vanderbilt, and Jim Eoff with Gen. Butler, beat me and Lady Emma at the Union Course.

Dexter's knee swelled a good deal; and I advised Mr. Alley, after we had reduced it, to take him home to Islip, and let him run out for a couple of months. He did so. He then took him up, and drove him until the 1st of October. Dexter then came back to me. After two week's work, in which he went well, I gave him a trial. He went in 2m. 29s., and I knew that he was every day a-coming. I then said to Mr. Alley, that the horse was improving every day, and that I thought in about two weeks he would be likely to show us something worth seeing "to a man up a tree." But it was three weeks before the trial came off, and it was a damp, cloudy day in November. There was not much wind, however, and the track was hard. Mr. Shepherd F. Knapp and Mr. Alley were present, and they timed him. I knew all the way round that Dexter was doing a great thing. I had hardly ever then, if ever, except in the cases of Flora Temple and the gray mare Peerless that belongs to Mr. Bonner, seen such a stroke kept up from end to end. When I turned and came back, I lifted up my hand, and said to the gentlemen, "Oh, what a horse!"

"What do you think you made?" said they.

"Not worse than 2m. 24s." I answered.

"It was just 2m. 23¼s.," said they; and I was satisfied.

This was speed enough for a six-year old horse, in his first season of trotting. He remained with me until the 1st of December, and then he went to Mr. Alley's, at Islip, to be wintered. His blankets were gradually taken from him; and he passed the cold weather without clothing, in a good box, with a paddock to run in during the day.

XLIV.

Dexter's Three-Mile Heats — Match with Stonewall Jackson of Hartford. — Description of Stonewall. — Dexter and Gen. Butler. — Dexter and Lady Thorn. — Description of Lady Thorn. — The Three-Mile-Heat Race under Saddle. — Dexter and Gen. Butler under Saddle. — Dexter, Butler, and George Wilkes. — Dexter against Time, to beat 2m. 19s.

AFTER the trial I described in the last chapter, I was pretty well convinced that this young horse, Dexter, was as good a one as had ever come into my hands. Here was a young horse that had never had a quart of oats until he was more than four years old. In his first season, and with very little handling, — for it is to be remembered that he was turned out from June to October, — he had trotted a trial in 2m. 23¼s., and had finished in masterly style. My opinion of him was so high, that during the winter I matched him to go three-mile heats against a horse that had great fame just then, and was thought by many to be invincible for a long distance. This horse was Stonewall Jackson of Hartford, who had beat Shark with great ease after the race in which Dexter hit himself. After I made this match, some of my friends thought I had been imprudent and overweeningly confident. The Hartford party, who had the other horse, certainly thought so too. It was to trot a race of three-mile heats, to go as they pleased, on the Fashion Course, June 26, — rain or shine. The stake was $2,500 a side, half forfeit.

When I came to talk to Mr. Alley about it, I found that he was not much in favor of letting Dexter trot. He said that he was but a young horse, was not seasoned, and that he believed three-mile heats might be too long for him against such a horse as Stonewall Jackson of Hartford. This latter was a bay horse, with two white legs and a blaze. He was nearly thoroughbred, was very fast and lasting, and a good saddle-horse; but he had a temper, and had bolted once or twice. The upshot of the conversation with Mr. Alley was, that I went and offered a large sum to get out of the match. The other parties refused to take any thing less than the whole of the forfeit, and that I was sure not to pay before the day of the race, if then.

Meantime, Dexter was entered in two of the Fashion purses, with Flora Temple, Gen. Butler, and Lady Emma. One of these was mile heats, three in five, in harness; the other mile heats, three in five, to wagons. The first of them was trotted on the 2d of June. The starters were Dexter and Gen. Butler. Dexter won it easily in three heats; time, 2m. 26¾s., 2m. 26¼s., 2m. 24½s. The day before, Lady Thorn had defeated Frank Vernon and Stonewall Jackson of New York, at the Union Course, and had gone in 2m. 21½s.; and now Dexter and the Lady were matched.

This match was for a thousand a side, mile heats, three in five, in harness. Lady Thorn was a fine, high-bred mare from Kentucky, got by Mambrino Chief, and with another cross of the Messenger blood through American Eclipse. She belonged to Mr. Relf of Philadelphia. I knew she was fast, but I thought the little horse could just about beat her. The race was made to be trotted over the Union Course on Friday, June 9, good day and track. It caused great interest, and my house was crowded to its utmost capacity at dinner-time. Before the time came to go to the course, a great storm came up from the south-east, and soon there was much rain. After it ceased, I and one or two others walked over to the course, and found it too muddy and slippery to trot. The race was postponed until the following Monday. This was rather unfortunate for Dexter. He was very fine indeed that morning, but went off a little before Monday. The fact is, that he is a horse of remarkably quick intelligence. He knew that there was a race on hand just as well as I did, and that knowledge kept him excited until after it was over.

The mare was the favorite at 100 to 70, and her party exhibited great confidence. A vast deal of money had been laid, but these bets were off by reason of the postponement. On the Monday, she was backed at the same rate. When we got the word, we went away at a great rate. At the quarter pole, in 35s., she was a neck a-head. Dexter broke, and lost two lengths. She led that space at the half-mile, in 1m. 9¾. On the lower turn, the little horse gained on her, but broke before he had collared her. He broke again on the stretch; and I found it was of no use to persevere with him for that heat, so she jogged it out in 2m. 24s. It was now three to one on the mare. She won the second heat by a length in 2m. 26½. In the third heat, the mare led to the middle of the back-stretch, where Dexter pinched her and she broke; but she caught before Dexter had opened daylight, and he broke, and fell two lengths behind. She led that much at the half-mile pole. On the lower turn, he out-trotted her, and she broke. He led her on the stretch, where she broke again, and he jogged out in 2m. 27s.; but it was not his day, and she jogged out the fourth heat in 2m. 26½s.

Dexter had won one race and had lost one in his second season, and his engagement at three-mile heats was nigh at hand. Mr. Alley, upon further consideration, had not only told me that the horse should trot, but had taken half the race. When the day came, it was very wet, and the course was more like a canal than a race-course. We offered to postpone it, but they would not agree. Stonewall Jackson was backed at two to one. This odds was tempting to those who knew that Dexter was a splendid horse under the saddle, and had been ridden a good deal by John Murphy. He rode in the race, and Mace rode Stonewall Jackson. In the first heat, Dexter broke twice in the first quarter, and lost a great deal. Stonewall was never headed, and won by almost a distance in 8m. 2½. The betting was now 100 to 40. Our party took these odds freely. There was at that time a prevailing notion that Dexter was not as good a stayer as Stonewall Jackson. The reverse was true. The latter was greatly tired after the heat, while the brown horse did not mind it at all.

In the second heat, Stonewall took the lead, but was deprived thereof, and broke badly. On the back-stretch he got to the front again, but was very unsteady. Before they reached the head of the home-stretch Dexter had the lead; and it was now good-by to Mace. Dexter went on through the mud with his fine, square stroke, splashing away, seemingly as much at his ease as a duck in a horse-pond. Stonewall, on the contrary, was all abroad, and never in a settled trot. Dexter came in alone in 8m. 5s. It was now four to one on Dexter, who looked, after these two heats, as though he could trot all day. The race was practically won. They started Stonewall again; but Dexter took the lead at the outset, was never headed, and won just as he pleased in 8m. 9½s. Money had been laid before the race that Dutchman's time would be beaten; and it might have been, had the weather been good and the track fast. It is not prudent to lay on fast time in a race made to go "rain or shine."

Dexter's fall racing-season commenced with a match under the saddle, mile heats, three in five, against Gen. Butler, for $2,000. They trotted at the Fashion Course, on the 7th of September. Dexter won it easily in three heats — 2m. 26½s., 2m. 24½s., 2m. 22½s. He was ridden by John Murphy. On the 21st of the same month, Dexter trotted with Gen. Butler and George Wilkes, mile heats, three in five, in harness, for a purse of $1,000, at the Fashion Course. He won in three straight heats, the fastest of which was 2m. 25s. Butler was second in this race, the stallion having been drawn after the second heat.

Dexter's next engagement was that famous one against Time, in which the latter was backed against him at $5,000 to $1,000. Mr. Alley undertook that he should beat 2m. 19s., and took the bet twice over. The horse was to be allowed three trials if he required as many. He was also matched two races with Gen. Butler, to wagon, one of them mile heats, three in five, and the other two-mile heats. These were to be trotted in October, after the time-race should be determined. Dexter was never better than during his preparation for this time-race. He was already in condition, and it did not take a great deal of work to keep him there. I had to see that he did not make new flesh, and that was about all that was required. We did not give him a high trial, but contented ourselves with the knowledge that he had his speed, and was in order.

At first, the betting was at nearly as heavy odds as the main stake; but afterwards no more than three to one could be obtained. We felt a good deal of confidence; for I relied upon the thorough bottom he had always shown in finishing, even from his very first trial, when he came into my hands the fall that he was five years old. My opinion, declared before the race to a confidential friend, was, that he could perform the feat, even if he made a break; and I thought that if he had every thing in his favor, and rated right through as he might possibly do, he would just about trot the mile in 2m. 15s., or 2m. 16s. We had once thought of selecting the Centreville Course for this race; but it was finally deemed better to take the Fashion Course. On the evening before the race, things looked favorable, but the track was dry and lumpy. Mr. Crocheron went to work with his usual energy, and gave it a good watering. After this it was brushed.

There was considerable wind on Tuesday morning; but we waited until well on into the afternoon, when it went down, till it was somewhat calm. This was what I had hoped and expected. Many years of experience of the weather of this Island, and habits of observation in a great deal of out-door life, in races, working trotters, fishing, and otherwise, had led me to conclude, that, as the tide was that afternoon, the wind would abate about three or four o'clock. Prior to that, we had had the half-mile pole removed. It cast a shadow across the course, and Dexter had sometimes jumped over it. He was in his box in charge of Peter Conover, whom he always liked well, and who liked him well, until about half-past three.

We then took him on to the course, and I gave Murphy his final instructions. They were, that he should hold him within himself the first half-mile, let him *come* round the Flushing end, and, when he got into the straight side coming home, call upon him for his best rate. Pace is a difficult thing to estimate; but Murphy, for so young a man, is a very good judge of the rate he is going at. Still, it was not effected just as we had intended it should be, and we could hardly expect that it would be. The wisest and best-laid plans are often difficult to carry out. Johnny Murphy mounted, and jogged around to warm the horse up. The judges in the stand were Mr. James Jacks, Mr. F. Howard, and Mr. S. Truesdell. These gentlemen are well known as competent timers and impartial men. Nobody in this country ever questioned the decision they rendered as to the time Dexter took to trot the mile; but the French and English do not to this day fully believe that the horse did it. It is so opposed to all their notions of trotting-speed, that they cannot put full faith in it.*

After having jogged Dexter round, Murphy set him a-going, and sent him along by the stand, but not for the word. On the turn he made such a break as would have defeated him in that trial, if he had received the word; but I did not care about that at all. I could see that his speed was

* They have had another year, and a surpassing of that performance, since Hiram dictated the above; but they remain incredulous.

enormous. He was chock-full of fire and devil, and, if any thing, a little too eager.

When he got the word, Murphy steadied him nicely, and he went to the quarter in 34s. This would win, and he was well within himself. The next quarter was a little faster than I wanted, as they made the time at the half-mile 1m. 6½s., giving 32½s. for the second quarter; but it may have varied a small trifle from this, as the half-mile pole was down. Everybody was saying he will do it easy, when he broke half-way along the Flushing end. He caught well. I have heard people maintain that he did not lose by that break, as if a horse can break when trotting better than a twenty gait and catch again without losing. It is true that he may run fast enough and far enough to make up for it; but Dexter did not do so. When he broke, the people cried, "He can't do it this time." But he settled well; and, when he came on to the home-stretch, he had a fine burst in. I was up towards there, and sung out to Johnny, as he came by me, "Cut him loose: you'll do it yet!" Then Johnny clucked to him, and he went away like an arrow from the bow, true and straight, and with immense resolution and power of stroke. I knew he must do it if he did not break before he got to the score, and up I tossed my hat into the air. I never felt happier in all my life. The time given by the judges was 2m. 18¼s.: the outsiders made it somewhat less. Murphy rode this race with nerve, judgment, and skill. He went faster in the second quarter than he thought he was going; but, after the break, he rode it to perfection. Most lads would have gone all to pieces, and taken the horse along with them, after that crisis; but Johnny was cool and judgmatical. He collected and steadied his horse, and brought him on to the stretch exactly as I told him to bring him, — in wind and heart for a grand rally. To stand behind and see him go, after Murphy clucked to him and moved his bit, was the finest thing I ever saw in all my life.

XLV.

Dexter and Butler to Wagons, Mile Heats. — Two Mile-Heats to Wagons. — The Best ever made. — Remarks upon the Race. — Dexter at Astoria. — Eoff and George M. Patchen, Jun. — Dexter offered for Sale. — Dexter and George M. Patchen. Jun. — Eoff's Strategy.

IN a week after the time-race, Dexter trotted his first wagon-match with Gen. Butler. It was mile heats, three in five, for $1,000 a side. Gen. Butler had always been a remarkably good wagon-horse: his wagon-time was, in fact, as good as any he had made in harness; and one of the best races ever witnessed was that in which he beat the gray horse Rockingham in five heats on the Fashion Course. The third heat in that race, which was the first heat that Butler won, was very fast; but the fourth was still faster, — 2m. 27s. if my memory serves me. This race with Gen. Butler was the first appearance of Dexter to wagon since the race in which he hit himself the previous year. The public did not know that he was a good wagon-horse; but my idea was, that his excellence was as great to wagon as in harness and under the saddle. Dexter was a little thin and tucked up when we took him over to the Fashion to trot this race. He had done a great deal of work during the season, and some thought him stale; but he was not stale. He was, though, thoroughly seasoned and hardened; and every bit of flesh and muscle about his frame was nearly as solid as so much brass. In the first heat, Butler had the pole; and, as I did not want to spend about half an hour in scoring with him, I took the word a length and a half behind. I gained on him a little in the first quarter, which was 37s.; then Dexter got into his stroke and trotted very fast. They were head-and-head at the half-mile, and that quarter was 34½s. We went on neck-and-neck until Butler broke, and I took the lead. The black horse made another break before we entered the stretch. Half-way up I took Dexter in hand, and this enabled Butler to get within a length and a half of him at the score. The time was 2m. 27¼s.

They now offered ten to one on Dexter, but nobody took it. Butler had two lengths the start of us, and Dexter broke on the turn, and lost three lengths more. The black horse was thus five lengths ahead at the quarter in 37s. Dexter was now settled, and began to overhaul the "Contraband," just as a custom-house official overhauls a smuggler—provided he isn't bribed. At the half-mile, Butler's lead was reduced to a length, and on the Flushing turn I passed him: at the head of the stretch I had a slight lead, but in the straight side he came with a fine rush, and got even with me; but he did not pass Dexter, and, being pressed to his utmost, he broke three or four lengths from the score, and ran over it. In the third heat, I took the word a couple of lengths behind and; at the quarter, in 38s., Butler's lead was only a length. Dexter continued to gain, and trotted this quarter so fast that at the half-mile he was head-and-head with Butler, in 1m. 14s. We went as near neck-and-neck as might be till nearly the head of the stretch, where Dexter broke. In turning into the straight side Butler had a strong lead; but I collected the brown horse, and he gained so that at the distance Butler's lead was reduced to a length. It was necessary to get this length and a little more to win; and this was not very easy to do, for Butler was trotting very fast. There was not a better finisher on the trotting-turf than Butler, except Dexter himself; and the struggle was close and fast: but Dexter beat him by a neck and shoulders in 2m. 29s.

Darius Tallman drove Butler in this race, and drove him

well. He is one of the hardest horses to drive that there is about here, for he will not bear enough of a pull to help him when he needs help. I believe I drove him in the first race he ever made, which was against Lady Suffolk, — not the old mare, but a gray mare belonging to Mr. Genet.

On the 27th of October, Dexter and Butler trotted their second match to wagons, on the Fashion Course. It was two-mile heats, and certainly was the best two-mile wagon-race that ever was made. Dexter had done well since the mile-heat race. He looked somewhat gaunt, but his coat lay right, his eye was bright, and he was full of spirit; but, as I knew that Gen. Butler was a very formidable two-mile wagon-horse, I thought the odds laid on Dexter (100 to 40) were too great. The black horse had trotted the fastest two-mile heat to a wagon that was ever known. I had seen him do it, and knew that it was well done. It was when he trotted the matches with George M. Patchen, and Dan Mace drove him in it. I recollect somebody saying to Mace, as he came along with his lead after weighing, "You have got cotton in Butler's ears to-day." Upon which I remarked, "I shall put cotton in mine when anybody comes along hereafter to talk down this horse."

I considered that the odds of 100 to 40 on Dexter against such a horse was too great; but I had great confidence, nevertheless, that Dexter would beat him. My opinion had always been, that Dexter was quite as remarkable for staying-power as he was for speed; and here was a race in which staying-power was sure to be in demand. It was at the close of a long and arduous season, in which Dexter had trotted many races, and had won them all but one. It was late in the year, and the day was not calculated for a very fast race. The clouds hung low and dark, and the wind came from the eastward, keen and salty. There were many time-bets, and the marks ranged from 5m. 3s. to 5m. 5s. I suppose there was not a man on the course who thought five minutes would be beaten. The company was large. It would have been much smaller if Mr. Alley's friends and acquaintances had not come out to see his wonderful little horse trot once more that fall, in which he had made himself so famous. There were also a number of Western gentlemen and some of the most eminent merchants of New York on the ground. Tallman drove Butler again, and I drove Dexter.

After scoring a couple of times, in which Butler broke and ran, we got the word, he having a small lead. He soon broke; and, when he caught his trot again, he was two lengths and a half ahead. I saw thus early that Tallman did not mean to lose that day for want of a little running. He led, with a break or two here and there, after which he would catch and trot very fast, half-way round the Flushing end. There I passed him, and came on to the straight side with a little lead. At the stand, in 2m. 30½s., I took the pole, and went on with the lead; Dexter drew away from Butler, and led two lengths and a half at the half-mile pole. He was going as steady as a clock; and, as it was not worth while to pull him back to Butler, I let him keep up his stroke until we got on the straight side. There was a great gap between us, and I jogged the little horse out in 5m. ¾s. The time, and the ease with which it was done, amazed everybody but me. My uncle, George Woodruff, was there; and says he to me, "Why, Hi., this is a wonderful horse for bottom! He seemed as if he would have kept up that rate for another mile!"

"Well," said I, "it's my firm belief that he could, and more too, though that would beat Dutchman's time."

It was ten to one on Dexter now. At the start I was three or four lengths behind, and did not rightly know that it was a start, until I had called out to Mr. Crocheron, who stood at the turn inside the rails, "Is it a word?" says I.

"Yes, it is; go along, old man!" says Joe. Well, I did go along; and at the half-mile pole Dexter had nearly got to

Butler's wheel. Turning into the Flushing end, Butler broke, and Dexter went on in front. I had not intended to take the lead in this first mile; but the little horse was so full of go, and pulled with such resolution, that I thought it safest to let him go ahead. He went the mile in 2m. 28s. Butler, with some running, was within three lengths of him at the score. The little horse went on with a stroke that was marvellous for power and precision. It was as strong and as regular as when he started; and it was a perfect joy to sit behind him in that fourth mile, and find that he was going faster and better than in any former portion of the race. At the half-mile, I had lost sight of Butler; and, from that out, the little horse and I had it all to ourselves. A hundred yards from home I got him down to a slow jog, and thus we jogged out in 4m. 56¼s. There was a good deal of excitement when the time was given out. Mr. Dexter Bradford, after whom the horse was named, came to me with Mr. Alley and Mr. Foster. The latter said, "This horse, in my judgment, considering where he was when he got the word, and how he jogged out, could in this heat to a wagon have equalled Flora Temple's 4m. 50½s. in harness." "You little rascal," said I, for I was well pleased, "I told you, before people thought much of him, that this was the King of the World. I don't know that he could have come out in 4m. 50½s., but I could have driven him three or four seconds faster than I did." I have considered all the circumstances over since, and I am quite sure that I could have brought him home in 4m. 52s. or 4m. 53s.

Now, I wish to point out that in this race Dexter showed the perfection of trotting. He was never in the least flurried or disturbed; he never made a break; and his speed was very equally distributed over the ground. In the first heat, his second mile was just a quarter of a second faster than his first. In the second heat, his second mile was a quarter of a second slower than his first; but it would have been faster if I had wanted it to be. He did the last hundred yards in a mere dog-trot. The day was not favorable; and the second was his great heat. This shows the bottom of the horse. If the first heat had been a slow one, we might have looked for a better; but it was fast, much faster than any body expected. And then to go and beat that by four seconds and a half, with such a start as he took and such an outcome, was truly wonderful.

While Dexter had been achieving the great feats which I have related, Mr. Alley was living at Astoria, and the horse was taken there to be wintered. A little paddock and box were constructed for him on the sheltered slope of a hill looking towards the south-east, and thus protected from the north-west winds. Peter Conover went with him to look after him; and there he ran out of doors all winter, without clothing. He had a good many visitors there; and gentlemen from the West often went up to Astoria with Capt. Longstreet, on the Sylvan Stream, for the express purpose of seeing him. Towards the close of that winter, the horse being then eight years old, Mr. Foster, who was always one of his greatest admirers, came to me, and told me that he thought he had grown since the fall. He seemed to think it almost impossible that it should be so; but I told him I had no doubt his idea was correct.

It is never to be forgotten, in connection with this horse, that he was not subject to the early-forcing process. He had no oats to eat until he was four years and a month old; and he did not trot until he was six. Now, I have heard some express the opinion that he would have been a better horse if he had had grain early. For my part, I can hardly conceive of a better trotting-horse than Dexter; for he has all the qualities and gifts that a good trotter can have. He is amazingly fast, and he is as stout as he is fast; he is good under the saddle, good in harness, and good to wagon; he is good on a hard track, and good in the mud; finally, he is a grand campaigner. His last race in this hard season just gone by was, as we have seen, his best. Such another two-mile-heat race to wagons was never seen before, and has never been seen since. But, if a horse is wanted to stand training and trotting at three or four years old, I admit that he must be fed and forced young.

Before the next spring came, Eoff had arrived from California with the brown stallion George M. Patchen, jun., and had begun to throw out hints that he was Dexter's master. At that time it was thought Mr. Teakle owned the California stallion; but this was not the case. He was, however, part owner of Dexter; and Eoff had driven Princess for him when he owned her. At my birth-day dinner on the 22d of February, there was a considerable celebration. My friends mustered very strong. The Long-Island breeders of game-fowl fought a main of cocks as a part of the sports of the day, and after dinner we all got warm and merry. Finally, Eoff began to say what he would do with Patchen. He would trot him three miles, and this and that, against Dexter. At last I got rather excited, and, encouraged by Oliver Marshall and Foster, offered to back Dexter against his horse, three-mile heats, Dexter to pull a wagon, and he to go in harness, for five thousand dollars a side.

At first Eoff pretended that he would make it; but when I stated the proviso, that the owners of Dexter must let me have him or it was no match, he objected to the proviso. Up to that time, some had thought that Eoff would have Dexter; but, when he objected to the proviso, I immediately discovered that Mr. Alley still had sole control of the horse, and that Eoff was afraid he would let me have him for that match. In due season, Peter Conover brought him back to me, and he was put in work. Mr. Alley soon after decided to sell him; and in "Wilkes' Spirit of the Times," of April 14, 1866, he was advertised to be sold on the Union Course, by auction, on the 9th of May. When he was put up, the first bidder was John Morrissey, who offered $11,000: that was before he was elected to Congress, you know! Then William Saunders, a very good, sagacious horseman, offered $13,000. Mr. Pettee advanced $500 on that, and then I jogged Dexter around again; then Saunders offered $13,750: but Mr. Alley did not want to sell him for that; so Mr. Pettee went on and bid $14,000, at which price he was bought in for his owner.

Soon after that, Mr. Isaac Anderson of Chicago offered to give $15,000 for the horse, provided I would go to Chicago to drive him; but it did not suit me to go so far away. At the same time, Saunders wanted him very much; and I challenged with him for three races, three-mile heats, under saddle, in harness, and to wagon. Meantime, Dexter got a little sore; and when Saunders came over to my stable intending to buy him, to keep the Chicago man from getting him, he was so lame that William lost his resolution.

Eoff's California stallion made a brilliant opening, and defeated Vanderbilt in such style that many people protested that Dexter's time was come, and that the big horse could beat 2m. 20s. Eoff kept this humbug alive by his artful way of talk and action. Mr. Crocheron, in the month of May, advertised a purse of $2,000, mile heats, three in five, in harness; the winner to have $1,200, the second $500, and the third $300, if there was a third. This purse closed at the Fashion Course on the 1st of June, after the race between Commodore Vanderbilt and Stonewall Jackson, which was won by the Commodore in three heats. The entries to the $2,000 purse were Dexter, Geo. M. Patchen, jun., Commodore Vanderbilt, and Gen. Butler. The race was to be trotted on the 28th of June. As soon as the entries were announced from the stand, Eoff coolly challenged any horse in the world to trot mile heats, three in five, and two-mile heats in harness. Mr. Relf was not there, and Dan Pfifer said nothing for Lady Thorn; so, with my consent, Oliver Marshall took it up for Dexter, as to the mile-heat race. The days named by Eoff were the 15th and 22d of June. I thought it best to trot Dexter but one race prior to the great purse. On the 15th, this match was trotted on the Fashion Course. The number of people present was immense, and it was a great pity that such a concourse should have gathered together to be sorely disappointed.

Dexter, I knew, was not half himself. He was sore and lame, and his lameness had kept him in a state of nervous irritability. This put Mr. Eoff in a very tight place. He must beat Dexter; — and he had a strong suspicion that he could not do it, even lame as he was, — or the people might discover that the California stallion was not the horse they believed him to be. A man of less courage and artfulness than Eoff would have been in a regular dilemma; but he hit upon an expedient which enabled him to keep up the humbug of his horse's ability to beat Dexter. He managed in such a way that people thought he threw the race. This maintained the character of the horse; and as for Eoff's own character, it was in keeping with that.

But the truth is, that he made his horse do all he could; and in the third heat he was clucking to him all along the back-stretch. Dexter won it in three heats: time, 2m. 29½s., 2m. 28¾s., 2m. 27½s. The day before, George Wilkes had defeated Lady Thorn to wagons at the Union Course in 2m. 27s., 2m. 25s., 2m. 25¾s; but, for all that, Eoff was anxious to match the California stallion against him. It was a part of his system. If the match was not accepted, it added to the notoriety of his horse. If it was, his share of the gate-money would greatly exceed what he lost; and he would either make the people believe that he threw it, or invent some plausible reason why he was beaten. Besides, as he knew that he was quite sure to be beaten by such horses as Dexter and George Wilkes, he had almost a certainty in bets that he might procure to be laid upon them and against George M. Patchen, jun. The mainstay of the whole thing was the keeping up of the fabulous reputation of that horse.

XLVI.

Dexter sold to George Trussel. — Dexter, Gen. Butler, and Commodore Vanderbilt. — Dexter goes to Budd Doble. — Dexter and George M. Patchen at Philadelphia.

THE last race in which I drove Dexter was for the purse of $2,000, mile heats, three in five, in harness; the second to have $500 out of the purse if three started, and the third $300 if four started. It was originally fixed to come off on the 28th of June; but the wretched display made by the California stallion in his match with Dexter (alluded to in the preceding chapter) had disgusted so many people, and so disheartened Mr. Crocheron, that he resolved to postpone it until the 2d of July. Before the race, Dexter had been disposed of by Mr. Alley to a gentleman from Chicago. It was not, however, to Mr. Anderson, but to Mr. George Trussell, with whom Mr. Fawsett had an interest, either at that time or very soon afterwards. The price they paid was $14,000. It was not large, considering the powers and achievements of the horse, taking into account what his winnings had amounted to the preceding year, and keeping in view the large prizes and brilliant prospects held out all over the country for the best trotter on the turf. The idea that he was not the best trotter had long ceased to trouble me: but many still held that Lady Thorn was his equal in some points; and there were people who believed and maintained that the California stallion was sure to beat him as soon as it suited Eoff's book to let him do so.

This infatuation remained for months, when events had

made it palpable to all but the wilfully blind that Dexter could lose the stallion in any way of going that trotting-horses go. The stallion did not appear in this race; Eoff believing, no doubt, that he had a much better chance to win with Gen. Butler. He had, to give him due credit, brought Butler into magnificent condition; and his patient, skilful handling of the horse in driving was very fine. All that party over at the Fashion were full of confidence that Butler would win it; and they took the odds of 100 to 40 on Dexter to a large amount, and laid 60 to 40 on Butler against Commodore Vanderbilt. There was one consideration which no doubt largely influenced the Butler party in taking the odds; that was, that Dexter had not been just himself that year. Eoff affected to doubt it, but he knew it well enough. The trouble was in the horse's feet, which kept him continually on the fret through soreness. That had, no doubt, some effect on the price at which he was sold; for, if he had been clearly all right forward, there were scores of men who would have given $15,000 for him.

My own opinion was, that the trouble was merely of a temporary nature; but every man of much experience with horses knows that a great deal of vagueness and uncertainty, not to say contradiction, has long existed, even among the most advanced veterinarians, in regard to lameness in the fore-feet. There was a chance, that, instead of getting better, he would get worse, and have disease of a chronic character. The chance was remote; but it existed, and had prevented William Saunders and some other good horsemen from buying him. When we took him on the course on the 2d of July, he looked exceedingly well bodily, but he had not been going well. He was limping a little, pulling a little on one rein, and was prevented from letting loose in his usual limber and determined manner by the soreness. If he had not got better during the race, he could not have won it: but he did get better, as we shall presently see; and his immense pluck and bottom enabled him to add another to those performances which had already made him one of the boasts of this country and one of the wonders of the outer world.

The start was not soon got, for Butler and Vanderbilt broke often in scoring. I did not, however, mind this to-day; because I knew, that, whatever they might think of the staying-power of Gen. Butler, I had the real sticker when the pace was very strong. The question was, whether Dexter would warm up, and regain the ability to cut loose. In the earlier part of this work, I related how I won a great race with Ripton, when he was stiff and lame; and that race came into my head as I scored time after time with Eoff and with Vanderbilt. When the word was given, Vanderbilt broke, and Dexter took the lead: Butler lay next me at the quarter-pole, two lengths behind. At the middle of the back-stretch, Dexter wanted to get up; but I succeeded in keeping him to his trot, and at the half-mile he led two lengths in 1m. 13½s. Butler got his nose to my wheel at the head of the home-stretch, and soon after broke: but he caught, and trotted very fast, and Dexter broke, and lost it in 2m. 28s.

There was a good deal more scoring before we started for the second heat; and, while it was going on, Eoff offered to lay 500 to 400 that Butler won. The start was a good one, and we went together in close order. At the quarter-pole, Dexter's nose was at Butler's haunches, and the Commodore was at my horse's shoulder: so we went to the half-mile, but not without a skip or two. The time here was 1m. 13½s. On the Flushing end, Butler drew away a little, and Dexter broke on the home-stretch. Vanderbilt took the inside position, and tried hard for the heat, John Lovett laying on the whip; but he broke, and Butler won in 2m. 27s.; Dexter second.

They now laid ten to one on Butler. Some of the stanch friends and admirers of the little horse came to me, and bemoaned that they had lived to see the day when it was ten to one on Butler against Dexter, and they dared not take the odds. I did not encourage them to bet; but I said to Mr. Alley and Mr. Foster, "The race is not lost, and won't be till it's won: there's a chance yet, mind you, with this horse." That was because I knew his invincible game and thorough bottom, if he could once manage to get his speed. I kept him on the move between heats; for to suffer him to cool slowly down to torpor and stiffness again was to lose it to a certainty.

We had another good start. On the turn, Butler led a length, and the Commodore was neck-and-neck with me. The Commodore was trotting fast; and I took a good pull on Dexter, to let the former take a tussle with Butler. At it they went, these commanders of the land and sea; and past the quarter-pole the Commodore reached Butler's shoulder. I was a couple of lengths behind. The Commodore now broke, and went all to pieces; and Dexter, well settled, began to close accounts with Butler. We gained inch by inch; and at the half-mile pole, in 1m. 13½s., Eoff did not have to look much over his shoulder to see the white face and wicked eye that was after him. Half-way round the Flushing end, Dexter was at Butler's girths, and at the head of the stretch had got forward to his shoulder. It was now or never. We came along the straight side head-to-head. Butler trotted well, and Eoff drove him with fine art; but Dexter lasted the longest in the brush at their best. Inside the distance, Butler broke, and Dexter won in 2m. 27¼s.

There was a good deal of excitement now, but little betting. Sim Hoagland came to me, and said, "Hiram, you've got 'em." I thought I had too; but I knew that Butler would make a desperate fight to the end. So it proved. In the fourth heat, we went away neck-and-neck; while Vanderbilt was outpaced, soon broke, and was out of it. At the quarter in 37s., Dexter and Butler were side by side. Dexter then got a neck in front, and thus we went to the half-mile pole. I did not wish to leave Eoff. With him under my eye on the outside, I had him just where I wanted him; and I thought to myself, "*When* you get the pole away from me, you'll have won it." Half-way round the Flushing end, we were neck-and-neck again. Butler then broke, and Dexter took a lead of a length. Up the home-stretch, Eoff and the black horse tried all they knew, and made a gallant fight for it; but Dexter was getting better and better. I could feel his stroke growing bolder and firmer the farther he went. Half-way up, Butler broke, and Dexter won it in the splendid time of 2m. 24½s.

Many of those who had laid wild odds on Butler after the second heat looked as if they felt sick at the stomach when they heard the time given out, and saw Dexter move briskly away, as limber as an eel, and full of the devil again. As Vanderbilt had been distanced in the fourth heat, the only starters in the fifth were Dexter and Butler. It was 100 to 60 on the brown horse. We went away head-and-head, and fast. On the turn Butler broke, but caught readily and trotted fast. At the quarter in 37¾s., he was at Dexter's shoulder. They went away very fast along the back-stretch; for they got to the half-mile in 1m. 12¼s., neck-and-neck. This made the eighteenth quarter in the race better than 35s.; and the rate at which they trotted the nineteenth and twentieth quarters shows what gluttons they were, especially Dexter, who never made a break in his winning-heats. We went from the half-mile pole to the head of the stretch neck-and-neck, and at a great rate; but Butler could not stand the pressure any further, and he broke, and I got the lead. Butler made another effort, but broke again, and Dexter won it easily in 2m. 24¼s. This was the fastest heat in the race, and the fastest fifth heat that ever was trotted. When we consider that it followed the fastest fourth heat that had been trotted, we shall be enabled to appreciate its value. I think that in this race Dexter displayed as much constancy, courage, and unflinching game as any horse ever did in any race that I remember. He struggled against difficulties, and contended with pain, until finally he overcame his bodily ailments by means of a dauntless spirit, and defeated a very formidable adversary, upon whom 100 to 10 had been going a-begging.

As I have before remarked, this was the last race for which I prepared him, or in which I drove him. What I have hitherto said about him I knew of my own knowledge. Concerning his career after this, I shall have to proceed upon the reports of his public performances, and what I have gathered from those who witnessed them. When he left my stable, Peter Conover went with him; and that was no small advantage to the horse and his owner. Mr. Trussell selected for his future trainer and driver Budd Doble, a young man of high character, good intelligence, and much experience of horses for his years. He had been among trotters from the time that he was a little boy, his father being a trainer and driver; and Budd himself was everywhere esteemed as one of the very best riders in the country. It was very soon understood that Doble would have to drive and ride against Eoff, for a hippodroming expedition between Dexter and the California stallion had been agreed upon.

The first place they visited was Philadelphia; but, prior to that, Dan Pfifer published a letter in "The Spirit of the Times," offering to make a match with Toronto Chief against either Dexter or Butler, to be trotted under saddle early in July. The response to this was an offer from the owners of Dexter and Butler to make up a stake of $1,000 with Toronto Chief, to trot mile heats, three in five, and go as they pleased, about the 18th of July. This race was afterwards brought about.

The trot at Philadelphia was on the 9th of July, and, as advertised, for a purse $2,000. Whether the parties agreed to divide equally, or what share Eoff and his horse were to have, I do not know, and we need not inquire. Everybody knows that the terms were fixed beforehand upon which

Eoff consented to trot with Dexter; for, though some continued to think that the big brown horse could beat the little one, his trainer and driver was quite certain that he could not. The race was on the Suffolk-park Course. Two to one was laid upon Dexter, whose race of the Monday previous of five heats had done him a great deal of good. I concluded that it had done so before he left my place to go on to Philadelphia; and the event proved that it was so.

In the first heat, Dexter took the lead, and kept it. He won in 2m. 26½s. In the second, the little horse broke in the first quarter, and the big one got a lead of four or five lengths; but then Dexter out-trotted him all the way, and won by three lengths in 2m. 25s. In the third heat, Dexter took the lead, went to the half-mile in 1m. 10s., four or five lengths ahead, and continued to drop the California horse as he went on. On the home-stretch, Dexter made a break, but won the heat by six lengths in 2m. 23½s. That made the fastest heat that had been won in harness, except those of Flora Temple. I had looked for it that season, but not quite so soon after the five heats on the Fashion, in which the fifth was 2m. 24¼. It had been my conviction for a long period, as my trusted friends know, that Dexter would reform the record from top to bottom, and beat Flora Temple's time in harness and to wagon, just as he had beat the best saddle-time. It was, however, a question with me how Eoff could have been within six lengths at the finish of this heat in 2m. 23½s., unless the course was uncommonly fast, or something else. But perhaps the six lengths were ten or twelve. Afterwards, when these horses travelled the country together, and Dexter made better and better time, it used to be a matter of remark among a few of us, that Eoff was never distanced; but at last I heard an explanation hazarded, which I believe to have been the truth. The parties being all in together, none of them could afford to have a part of the concern disgraced; and the judges were probably given to understand, that, in order to see Dexter do his best, they must agree to see nothing else. As for the rest of the people, their eyes were all on Dexter, and none of them knew or cared where Eoff's horse was at the finish. I cannot otherwise imagine how Dexter could trot so fast as he often did afterwards, without distancing the California horse.

XLVII.

Dexter, Gen. Butler, and Toronto Chief under Saddle. — Dexter and Geo. M. Patchen, Jun., at Avon Springs. — The Track Short. — Short Track no Record. — Dexter, Patchen, Jun., and Rolla Golddust at Buffalo. — Dexter and Butler under Saddle. — Dexter trots in 2m. 18s. — Dexter, Patchen, Jun., and Butler at Cleveland. — Dexter and Patchen, Jun., at Detroit. — Dexter and Patchen, Jun., at Chicago. — Dexter and Butler under Saddle. — Dexter and Patchen at Milwaukee. — Same at Adrian, Toledo, Kalamazoo, and Wheeling. — Dexter and Magoozler the Pacer at Pittsburg.

THE sweepstakes of $1,000 each, in which Dexter, Gen. Butler, and Toronto Chief were engaged, was trotted on Fashion Course, on the 19th of July. After his race at Philadelphia, on the 9th, Doble brought Dexter back to the Island, and gave him a little saddle-work, to fit him for this race, which was mile heats, three in five, under saddle. He went so fast, and appeared to be so well, that he was the favorite over both the others. He was ridden by Doble, while Eoff rode Butler, and Johnny Murphy was upon Toronto Chief. In the first heat, Dexter broke, and was ten lengths behind at the quarter; but he made up the gap, and won in 2m. 24¼s. This heat warmed him to his work. He soon took the lead in the second heat, was never headed, and won easily by five or six lengths in 2m. 19s. Butler was second. The third heat was won very easily in 2m. 22s., although he broke near the quarter-pole, and lost a deal of ground. At the half-mile pole, he was fifteen lengths behind Toronto Chief, who was leading; but, on the Flushing end, Dexter cut loose in earnest, and trotted the third quarter in 33s., which brought him up to Toronto Chief at the head of the stretch. He then came away, and won with great ease by five lengths. Butler was second, and the time was 2m. 22s.

Dexter and Patchen now started on a tour to the West. The people of that section, especially those of Buffalo, Cleveland, and Chicago, had offered larger purses than had ever before been given to trotters; and the fact that Dexter then made his first appearance in those cities enabled the associations to realize the money they gave. He was, beyond all question, the great source of attraction. A fair number of people would have assembled to see Butler, Patchen, jun., and the other trotters, who moved upon what a poetical friend of mine terms "The path of empire;" but the vast crowds who appeared in such multitudes as even to surpass our greatest day on the Island came out to see Dexter. It was a hippodrome arrangement, so far as he was concerned, because none of the others had a ghost of a chance to beat him as long as he remained well.

But the people did not mind that. It rather added to their enthusiasm when they found that he was not only the best of the strangers, but so much the best that there was no comparison. I had long held to that opinion, as also did Mr. Alley, Mr. Pettee, and Mr. Foster, and now nearly everybody who stayed at home coincided in it. I did, however, see one gentleman lay a bet with Mr. Crocheron, that Geo. M. Patchen, jun., would beat Dexter a race before they came home again; but some time afterward, I heard the same gentleman trying to convince Uncle Joe, that it was the latter who had backed the California horse. So, while we were fishing for horse-mackerel and sheeps-head in the waters of our bays on the south side, the great trotters, with the exception of George Wilkes, Lady Thorn, and Lady Emma, put out to reap the rich harvest of the West. The first place they trotted at was Avon Springs, where a purse of $1,000 was given. The track was a half-mile one, and unfortunately a trifle short. The first heat was close but slow. Dexter won in 2m 31½s. In the second heat, Dexter went clean away from the stallion, and trotted the first round in 1m. 9s. He came home in 2m. 21s.; but, as it was afterwards found that the course was a little short, "The Spirit of the Times" wisely decided that it should not make a record.

It is of great importance that short tracks should be discouraged. Very often they are short by accident, as this at Avon Springs was; but I fear they have been sometimes purposely constructed short, with a view to deceive and swindle purchasers of horses. Hence, Mr. Bonner and some other gentlemen, when going to see horses on some tracks, have prudently carried surveyors' chains in their carpet-bags.

From Avon Springs, Doble passed on with Dexter to Buffalo, and there trotted him on the third day of the great meeting for the large purse. The race was mile heats, three in five, in harness. The whole value of the purse was $5,750. Of this sum the winner was to have $4,000; the second, $1,000; the third, $500; and the fourth, if there was a fourth, $250. But there were but three starters, Dexter, George M. Patchen, jun., and Rolla Golddust. The latter was a fine, rangy gelding, bred by Mr. Dorsey, near Louisville, got by his stallion Golddust, out of a high-bred mare. He was the best of a lot of young trotters brought here by Mr. Dorsey and my brother William Woodruff, who then trained for him, and I think him a horse of a good deal of promise. But, in this race at Buffalo, he was last in all the heats. Dexter won with great ease in 2m. 27¼s., 2m. 29s., 2m. 25s.

This was no great things to see for $5,500, and the twenty thousand people who were present went away rather discontented. On the fifth day, Dexter trotted again, and this time it was under saddle. It was against Gen. Butler, mile heats, three in five, for an extra purse of $1,500. In the first heat, Dexter forced the pace, and won by twenty lengths in 2m. 21½s. Dan Mace was now put on Butler; but the horse was not as he had been when he beat George

M. Patchen in 2m. 21s., and Dexter won again in 2m. 26s. The people began to be disappointed; and feeling how generously the Association had behaved, and how much the assemblage would like to see a fast heat, Mr. Joseph Hall of New York persuaded Mr. Trussell and Doble to let the little horse do something like his best. Doble averred that the track was not altogether good, and that the dense crowd on the stretch might break him up; but he said, with Mr. Trussell's consent, that, if he was level and well settled at the half-mile pole, he would let him come the last half fast. This just happened. He trotted the first quarter in 35½s., the second in 34½s., and came home the last half-mile in 1m. 8s. From all that I have heard, I believe that the course was not near as good as the Fashion Course, and therefore his performance was one of great value. But it was no more than might have been looked for. The preceding year, I had rated him as good for a mile, under saddle, in 2m. 16s.; and, if the Buffalo Course was 2s. slow, his performance was equal to 2m. 16s.

At Cleveland, Dexter trotted on the fourth day of the meeting, Aug. 25, for a purse of $2,000, of which the second horse was to have $300, and the third $200. His competitors were Patchen, jun., and Gen. Butler. The latter was now in charge of William McKeever, who was afterwards killed at Chicago, while driving him in a heat after dark against Cooley. He was a young man that I knew well, and a very honest and worthy young man. We deplored his death very much when the news reached us on the Island. This race at Cleveland was mile heats, three in five, in harness. The course was heavy; and Dexter won very easily in three straight heats, in the thirties.

The next place of action was at the city on the strait between Lakes Erie and St. Clair, — Detroit. Patchen, jun., went against Dexter in harness, and, as usual, was easily defeated in three straight heats. The time was 2m. 24¾s.,

2m. 26¼s., 2m. 23¼s. Chicago was the next place; and there Dexter and Patchen trotted in harness, on the 5th of September, for a purse of $5,000, of which the second horse was to have $1,000. Dexter won the first heat in the thirties; and, when the time was announced, the crowd grew turbulent, and began to hoot and yell. Thereupon Mr. Trussell and Doble made up their minds that it was better not to wait for Eoff and the stallion. In the next heat, Dexter went on, and trotted it virtually alone in 2m. 24s. This restored good humor; and, when he completed the third heat in 2m. 23s., the people of that part of Illinois perceived what sort of a horse he was.

But his only defeat that year was now at hand. On the 8th of September, he trotted against Gen. Butler under saddle. The course was very bad going, and the cinder slack of which the track was composed flew up and hit him at every stride. He won the first heat in 2m. 33½s. Butler won the next two in 2m. 27s. and 2m. 26½s., and then Dexter was drawn. The track was no doubt bad; but the horse must have been very much off, because the going was as good for him as it was for Butler, who beat him. He came again quickly; for in a week, at Milwaukee, he beat Patchen, jun., in great style, in harness, in three straight heats,—time, 2m. 24¼s., 2m. 22½s., 2m. 29s. Patchen was said to be forty yards behind in the fast heat; but, as his time was taken as 2m. 29s. in his fastest heat, I think he must have been eighty yards behind, instead of forty.

In another week, McKeever was killed at Chicago, while driving against Cooley; and that was a heavy blow and great discouragement to trotting in that neighborhood. On the same day that this tragedy occurred at Chicago, Dexter beat Patchen, jun., in three heats at Adrian, Mich.; time, 2m. 32s., 2m. 27½s., 2m. 31½s. Toledo was the next place at which Dexter and Patchen appeared. Dexter won again in three heats,—2m. 32s., 2m. 22¼s., 2m. 31s. The farce of pretending that there was a race between the stallion and the little horse was now too broad even for Eoff; so, with the amazing coolness which is one of his characteristics, he told the people, before the word was given, that he was not trotting against Dexter. I think this was rather unnecessary, considering that the people of North-western Ohio are commonly accounted as smart as their neighbors. This affair at Toledo was on the 28th of September.

They went on to Kalamazoo, and trotted for a premium of $2,000, with an extra $500 if Flora Temple's time on that course was beaten. The first heat was slow, — 2m. 27s.; but the second and third were fast, — 2m. 21¾s., 2m. 21¼s. This did not beat Flora's time; but, as the course was not as good as when she trotted, it was deemed to be a performance of sufficient merit to receive the extra $500. On the 12th of October, they trotted at Wheeling, West Virginia. It was the old ten-times-told tale. Dexter won as he pleased, and the fastest heat was 2m. 26½s. They now went on to Pittsburg, and appeared with a pacer called Magoozler. The pacer beat Dexter the first heat in 2m. 22¾s.; but the little horse outlasted him, and won the second, third, and fourth heats in 2m. 21¾s., 2m. 23¾s., 2m. 32s. It was on the 21st of October. After this the horses were brought back to the eastward of the Mountains.

XLVIII.

Dexter, Polly Ann the Pacer, and Patchen, Jun., at Philadelphia. — Dexter, Silas Rich, and Patchen, Jun., at Baltimore. — Dexter under Saddle against Time. — Dexter and Silas Rich at Washington. — Dexter's Performances that Year considered. — Integrity and Capacity of Budd Doble. — No Reason to believe that Dexter then reached his best. — His fine Points. — Dexter compared to Peerless. — The Auburn Horse. — Grand Combination of Qualities in Dexter.

ON the 29th of October, Dexter trotted at Philadelphia, on Point-Breeze Park, against Polly Ann a pacer, and George M. Patchen, jun. It was mile heats, three in five, in harness. The day was unfavorable, as it was blowing a strong gale of wind at the time. Dexter won in three heats: time 2m. 23½s., 2m. 27s., 2m. 28s. On the 14th of November, Dexter, Silas Rich, and George M. Patchen trotted at Baltimore, on the Herring-run Course, where the Maryland Horse-Fair was held. It was mile heats, three in five, in harness, and Dexter won in three straight heats, — 2m. 31s., 2m. 21¾s., 2m. 25¾s. Silas Rich was second in all the heats. On the 17th of November, that being the last day of the Maryland fair, Dexter trotted under saddle against time. Gen. Grant acted as one of the judges. Doble rode Dexter, and young Dimmock went with him on a runner to force the pace. The track and weather were both unfavorable; for the ground was heavy, and the wind blew high. In the first trial, Dexter made a bad break at the quarter, and his mile was no better than 2m. 27¼s. In the second trial, he trotted the first half-mile in 1m. 9s., but broke badly in the third quarter, and the time of the mile was 2m. 24½s.

I think it was very bad policy for the owners of Dexter to start him in this time-race. The horse had already made such time under the saddle, — in his match the year before on the Fashion, and at Buffalo this year, — that to have him come back from that great record should have been avoided. Yet it was perfectly certain, one would have thought, that on such a course and in such weather he could not get anywhere near his best mark of 2m. 18s. In going against another horse, it mattered very little what the time was, because it would be assumed that Dexter could have gone faster if it had been requisite for him to do so. But, in going against time, Dexter was really trotting against himself, as his time was much the best time that had ever been made Now, to start Dexter on a bad track and on a bad day against Dexter on a good track and good day was not wise. Yet this was virtually what was done at Baltimore.

The little horse was now taken to Washington, where he appeared upon the National Course on the 20th of November, mile heats, three in five, in harness, against Silas Rich. The company was very distinguished. Sir Frederick Bruce the English Minister, and the Marquis de Montholon the French Minister, were present. Gen. Grant was one of the judges. The first heat was slow, — 2m. 30s. In the second heat, Doble cut loose from Silas Rich, and made the mile in 2m. 21$\frac{1}{2}$s. The third heat was 2m. 27$\frac{3}{4}$s.

This concluded as good a year's performance as there is to be found in the records of trotting-horses; and the mile at Washington in 2m. 21$\frac{1}{2}$s., late in the month of November, shows that after the thousands of miles Dexter had travelled, and the many arduous performances he had been called upon to make, he was fully as good as, if not better than, he had been at any time during the season. He was of course drawn very fine, and reduced to a mere frame of bone and muscle, pretty much as he had been when he finished the doings of the year 1865 by beating Gen. Butler two-mile heats to wagon.

He is passing this winter at Baltimore, under the charge of Peter Conover; and, from all that Doble tells me, he is likely to come out fine in the spring. It is unnecessary to recapitulate his performances since he left my stable. I believe I have given them all; and it occurs to me that I ought to call public attention to the integrity and capacity with which Doble has trained and driven him. The owners of Dexter were fortunate in selecting this young man for the post; and the public were fortunate that some people did not get hold of the horse, and use him for the purpose of plundering the people.

Great as the achievements of Dexter have been, I can see no reason to believe that he has yet reached his highest development. It is a long time now since I took Mr. Foster to his box, and pointing out his very remarkable shape,— the wicked head, the game-cock throttle, the immense depth over the heart, the flat, oblique shoulder laid back clean under the saddle, the strong back, the mighty haunches, square and as big as those of a cart-horse, and the good, wiry legs,—predicted to him that here stood the future Lord of the Trotting-World. That prediction has not yet been wholly fulfilled, but my faith in its accomplishment is not at all shaken. He has not yet beaten the 2m. 19¾s. in harness of Flora Temple; nor has he beat the 2m. 25s. to wagon which stands to her credit and to the credit of George Wilkes; but I can see no reason to doubt that to do both these things is clearly within his capacity. The 2m. 21½s. at Washington City, on the 20th day of November, seems to me to proclaim that Dexter is still improving, and may be expected to surpass the grand doings of 1866, by those we may reasonably look for in the year which has just begun.*

Some people imagine that the strong point in Dexter is

* Hiram died in the middle of March, 1867; and therefore the grass had not grown upon his grave when these predictions in regard to Dexter had been fulfilled.

his great speed, but I have never thought so. When I matched him three-mile heats against Stonewall Jackson, in the early part of his career, I was fully convinced that he was a horse of fine game and hard bottom. I have had horses as fast as he is for a brush; but I have never had another that could maintain a great rate so far, and come again in repeating heats, making the last the best. I think the gray mare Peerless, who is closely related to Dexter, as she was by American Star out of a mare in the Messenger line, was as fast as he is. The breeding of Peerless was much the same as his in blood, but reversed in the sexes. She was the produce of Star and a mare of Messenger descent. He was the produce of a Messenger horse in the male line and a Star mare. I do not mean to say that Peerless could equal Dexter's saddle-rate, but I think that to wagons they would be very close together, if she is as good as she once was; but, as Dexter appears to be steadily improving, he will probably attain to a rate of speed in harness and to wagon such as we have never yet seen.

I had a horse in my stable late last fall that I am satisfied was then as fast as Dexter; and I think it quite likely that he was a little faster. I allude to Mr. Bonner's big chestnut gelding, the Auburn Horse. He certainly carried me faster than I had ever before ridden behind a trotter, and he went away from Lady Thorn with the greatest ease. The Auburn Horse had just come right, and got to feeling well after having been out of sorts for some time. His speed and resolute way of going had soon made a strong impression upon my mind; and I told my friends Oliver Marshall and Foster that if I could have him to trot a race, I thought I could put a mark up so high that it would take a long time to wipe it out. That is my opinion now, and the readers of this work have a right to know it. Yet it does not follow that the Auburn Horse is equal to Dexter, though he might trot a mile in harness faster.

When we look at the grand combination of excellent

qualities with which Dexter is gifted, it is at least probable that no other given horse possesses them. One may have his speed without his bottom; another may have speed and bottom for a race or two, but be quite unable to stand the long campaign of a journey of two thousand miles, with trots nearly every week, and sometimes two or three in a week. A third may be a fine harness and wagon horse, but of no account under saddle. A fourth may be fast under saddle, but come back about ten seconds when in harness or to wagon; and a fifth may go along finely until he strikes the mud, or feels weight behind him, either of which stops him. But all the most desirable characteristics Dexter possesses. What any trotting-horse can do, at any reasonable distance, or in any way of going, he can do.

I think the Auburn Horse might trot faster than Dexter can do in harness; but I should not feel at all confident of winning a race with him against Dexter. I know the thorough bottom of the little horse, and I have never tested that of the big one. There is no reason why I should not say here what I have already said to some of my friends: therefore I give it as my opinion, that, when the Auburn Horse is all right, I can drive him a mile in 2m. 18s. in harness. That would win a heat from Dexter, I think, but it would not win a race; and, if the Auburn Horse came back much in the second or third heat, the little one would probably split the heats, and finally win the race. Of course this is all speculation, as Mr. Bonner will not trot any of his horses in a race; but having had both the horses, and having driven them on various occasions when they were both feeling fine and trotting very fast, I have formed the opinion that the Auburn Horse can trot as fast in harness as Dexter himself can.

Some may think that my prejudices lean a little against Dexter, now that he is no longer in my hands; but I do not think they do. One thing is certain; and that is, that I believed in him before anybody else did, except Mr. Alley, and pronounced him the best trotting-horse in the world, or that had ever been in the world, to Mr. Foster, at a time when the majority of people would have said that I was crazy, if they had heard me. There has been a constant improvement going on in the trotting-horse. The trotters are much better bred than they used to be, and that has had much effect. The courses, sulkies, and wagons have also been improved. Our best horses have generally been close together in rate. There was but a shade of difference between Flora Temple and George M. Patchen, and her and John Morgan, except in this, that, though they were close up to her head in one or two races, they were unable to follow her along, and campaign with her. But considering what Dexter has done, keeping in mind the fact that he seems to be steadily improving in his rate in harness, and not forgetting that he could certainly trot under saddle in 2m. 15s. a year ago last fall, I am sometimes led to the belief that he may some day, not only beat Flora's best time in harness, but open a gap that will look very wide to those who come next.

XLIX.

On Driving.—Difficulty of laying down Rules.—Importance of a Sensitive Mouth.—The Bit proper for a Colt.—Much Use of "Bitting" Apparatus Mischievous.—The Bits in Cold Weather to be warmed before Use.—A light. Fine Hand required.—Pulling to be avoided.—Gentleness and Firmness.—The Horse to be harnessed so as to be at Ease.—Dead Pull an Evil.—Proper Position of the Driver.—The Shift of the Bit.—How to hold the Reins.—Severe Bits bad.

IT is of course very difficult to lay down rules for driving trotting-horses; for a great deal depends upon the character and disposition of the horse in hand, and much depends upon the method which may have been followed by those who broke him. It very often happens that the driver will have to spend some time in undoing and repairing the mischievous effects of the bad driving to which the horse has been subjected. The colt ought to be bitted and broken, so that he shall have a lively, sensitive mouth, and be ready to answer to a light, neat touch upon the rein. The bit for a colt should not be of great size and thickness. A bar of moderate size, rather fine than thick, is what I have always preferred. Such a bit is sooner felt, and the colt keeps his head up, and does not bear down steadily upon it. With a big bar-bit in his mouth, he is much more likely to hang on it, by which means the mouth is often made hard and callous. This is, of all things, to be avoided.

It is also my opinion that colts do not require as much bitting as they are commonly subjected to; and the bitting-apparatus ought not to be kept on them very long at one time, for this is what causes sore mouths, and they result in hard, unfeeling ones. If a big, heavy bit is used in bitting, and it is kept in the colt's mouth long at a time, he will soon begin to hug down upon it, and the probability of his having a good mouth for driving is lost. It will become hard and tough, and he will fall into a habit of always bearing the weight of his head upon the bit. There is another thing I will mention here, to which more attention ought to be paid. Bits are often kept in places to which the frost penetrates in very cold weather. The bits become frosted; and, without a thought of what he is doing, the man claps a frosted steel bit into the horse's mouth. The consequence is a sore mouth, just about as certainly as if the bit had been nearly at a red heat; and then the man bothers his brains to find out what caused it. If he had put the frozen bit into his own mouth, it would have brought the inner skin of the lips away with it, and then he would have felt the mischief. In very cold weather, take your bits to the fire, and be sure that there is no frost in the steel when the bit is placed in your horse's mouth.

Now we will return to the colt. When you come to drive him, it should be with a light, firm hand. The reins should be handled nicely and gently. The driver can manage the colt without any jerking or pulling and hauling, if he keeps cool, thinks of what he is about, and uses proper care and patience. The mouth is now fine and sensitive; and it ought to be kept so, because this is the great organ of communication between a good driver and the trotter, when he is cultivated and improved into a fast horse.. What you want the trotter to do when he is at speed is to be got into him through his mouth. You may encourage him by speaking to him, or sting him into a greater effort with the whip; but neither of these is half as good as the play upon the reins, with which you let him know what you want through his lively, sensitive mouth. You are then to keep in constant mind the necessity of not impairing the colt's mouth by rough handling of the reins. If you pull and lug at the bit, the colt, in his efforts to resist what hurts him, will very soon pull too, for he will find out that this numbs and deadens the jaws; but this is at the expense of ruination to the mouth. It will become hard and insensible; and the first and largest part of the mischief which goes towards the making of a hard puller is done.

When you begin to drive the colt, you must find out what sort of bit suits him best. This is matter of experimental trial. Use both bars and snaffles, all easy; and by feel of hand, and observation of the way in which the colt carries his head, you will soon be able to ascertain which bit suits him best. The nicety of your touch as driver should correspond to the lively sensibility of the colt's mouth. A bad-tempered, hasty man will very soon spoil a good-tempered young horse. The use of the whip ought, as a general rule, to be avoided. In some cases, it must be used; but it should never be brought into play when the horse does not know what it is for. A slap with the whip, which almost makes the colt jump out of the harness, is often immediately followed by a powerful snatch on the reins to pull him back again. Both of these are as bad as bad can be. Sore mouths, bad tempers, and broken gaits, are the almost inevitable results of such handling. On the other hand, if the colt has been well broken, and has a good lively mouth, and the driver handles the reins skilfully and thoughtfully, the colt will soon learn to understand every move of the hand, and to answer it. From this it follows that you ought to make no move with the bit without a definite object. When you feel an impulse to do something with the reins without knowing what you are to do it *for*, don't do it at all. Such moves only fool the horse. Everybody admits that a very hard-pulling horse is a nuisance; and everybody knows that some horses will pull if they are to trot, and will not extend themselves without a strong pull: but, even in regard to these, it is not well to keep up a steady, rigid pull all the time. I say, rather pull for a space, and then ease off, not suddenly, but gradually, and by this means they will not pull quite so hard, and will trot faster. It is not natural for horses to pull hard. Some there are, of uncommon ardor and determination, that will pull in company; but more are made hard-pullers by faulty handling when young, which has deadened their mouths.

In order that a fast horse should be under circumstances to do his best, he should be as much at his ease in his harness and general rig as possible. If he is not, he is placed at almost as much disadvantage as if sore or stiff, or suffering from some bodily ailment. You may see horses brought out of the stable to trot with a very tight check to keep their heads up, and a tight martingale to keep it down. Such a horse is in irons; and when to this is added a dead drag at the reins, and no movement of the bit from end to end, I cannot see how he should do his best. People talk about a steady, bracing pull; but, in my opinion, that is not the right way to drive a trotter. There is a great difference between letting go of your horse's head, and keeping up one dull, deadening pull all the time. The race-horse riders practise what is called a bracing pull; and, a great many times, I have seen their horses tire under it without ever running their best. The steady pull choked them. The pull should be sufficient to feel the mouth, and give some support and assistance, so as to give the horse confidence to get up to his stride. More than that is mischievous. To keep the mouth alive, the bit must be shifted a little occasionally. But this is not to be done by a pull of the hand on the rein. A mere half-turn of the wrist, or less than half a turn, by which the thumb is elevated and the little finger lowered, is sufficient to shift the bit, keep the mouth sensitive, and rouse the horse.

The reins are to be steadily held with both hands while this play with the wrist is made; and it is, of course, only to be done with one wrist at a time. The hands should be well down; and the driver ought not to sit all of a heap, with his head forward. Neither should he lean back, with his bodily weight on the reins, which, in that case, are made a sort of stay for him. He should be upright; and what pulling he must do should be done by the muscular force of the arms. The head and the arms are what a good driver uses; but some have their arms straight out, and pull by means of putting the dead weight of their bodies on the reins. If, instead of lying back, and putting their bodily weight on the reins, with which latter they take a turn round their hands, drivers would depend upon their muscular strength, they could let up on the pull, graduate it, and so ease the horse from time to time instantaneously. The driver who depends upon the arms has command of the horse: he who substitutes bodily weight with the reins wrapped round his hands, has not half command of the horse, or of himself either; and, if the horse is a puller, he will soon take command of the driver. The reason of it is, that there is no intermission of the exertion, no let up, either for man or horse. Besides, in that way of driving, it is impossible to give those movements to the bit which seem to refresh and stimulate the horse so much. When a horse has been taught the significance of this movement of the bit, the shift by the turn of the wrist, he will never fail to answer it, even though he should seem to be at the top of his speed. The moment he feels this little move of the bit in his sensitive mouth, he will collect himself, and make another spurt; and the value of this way of driving is, that the horse is not likely to break when thus called upon, while a high-strung, generous horse, if called upon for a final effort with a whip, is as likely to break the moment it falls on him as not. I have won many a very close heat by practising this movement, and therefore I have no hesitation in recommending it. It is not difficult to acquire, and the horse soon comes to know what it means.

Let us come now to the way of taking hold of the reins. A wrap around the hand, such as running-horse riders take, is clumsy and bad. I do not know whether many people take hold of the reins as I do, or not. Perhaps not. Sim. Hoagland is the only one who takes hold precisely as I do, so far as I have observed. When we have been jogging horses together at early morning, we have often talked over these matters; and, whether our way was the best way or not, we could never see any other that suited us half as well.

I will try to explain how I hold the reins: I could show it in two seconds. Take, first, the right-hand rein. This, coming from the bit, passes between the little finger and the third finger, over the little finger, then under the other three fingers, and up over the thumb. The left-hand rein is held in the left hand exactly in the same way; but the bight of the slack of the reins is also held between the thumb and forefinger of the left hand. This gives more substance in that hand; but, if it is found inconvenient to have it there by those who have small hands, it may be dropped altogether. A firm grasp on each rein, with the backs of the hands up, and without any wrap, is thus obtained. It is a great point in driving to be able to shift the reach — that is, the length of the hold you take — without for an instant letting go of the horse's head. With this way of holding the reins, it is easily done. If I want to shorten the hold on the left-hand rein (the near rein), I take hold of that rein just behind the left hand with the thumb and forefinger of the right hand, and steady it. This is very easily done; and it does not interfere at all with the command of the off rein with the right hand. The near rein being thus steadied behind the left hand, I slide that hand forward on the rein, which is kept over the little finger, under the other three fingers, and over the thumb all the time, and then shut the grasp again on the new reach. A shift with the right hand is made just in the same way, by taking hold and steadying the rein behind that hand with the thumb and forefinger of the left hand.

I have often observed, that, with other methods of holding the reins, there was great difficulty in shifting the reach. The driver tries to do it; but, for an instant, he has let go of the horse's head on one side altogether, and broken his stride. When this is found to be the case, the dead pull all the time is adopted; and this spoils the freedom and elasticity of the horse's stride, and chokes his wind. I do not intend this to be taken as instruction for professional drivers. Every driver has a way of his own; and some of them have very good ways, for, as I have taken occasion to state before, they drive well. But what I have set down above may be of service to gentlemen who drive their own horses, and to those young men who, having as yet no settled method of their own, may think it well enough to try that which I have found to answer. Another word about bits. I am opposed to the use of severe bits, and complicated things of that sort. Some of the inventors of such things say that I am prejudiced; but I don't think I am. If a man has a horse that cannot be driven with a bar-bit or a snaffle, he may as well sell him, except it is a very exceptional case. Where are these kinds of severe complicated bits most in use? Why, in England; five hundred or a thousand of them are used there to one that is used here: and where do the horses trot the best? These bits are mostly invented by men who have had no practical experience whatever as to what sort of driving a fast trotter requires to keep his gait square and bold, and induce him to do his best when it is called for. When a horse has a good mouth, — and a bad one is almost always the fault of bad breaking and driving, — the easier the bit you use, the better he will act for you, and the more speed he will show you.

L.

Of Breaking in Trotting. — A gaining Break. — Snatching to be avoided. — How to catch the Horse to his Trot. — Nature of the catching Pull. — The Horse to be steadied when he has caught. — A Break sometimes desirable. — How to bring it about. — Confidence of the Horse in his Driver. — Sagacity of Horses. — To prevent a Break. — Signs of one coming.

IN the consideration of the art of driving a trotting-horse, another important part is that of breaking. As a general rule, breaking is to be avoided rather than encouraged and promoted; though there are times when a trotter may be broken with advantage to his speed and staying-power in the latter part of the work. There is, however, no horse but will break sometimes, and that when he is not tired; for the steadiest and stoutest of trotters may break through a false step. When you are educating a horse for the purpose of making a trotter of him, you must endeavor to shape his action in his breaks. Just as it depended whether you should make a puller of him by your way of driving in his educational period, so it depends whether you shall teach him to make a gaining break, — which is to say, to lose nothing in space, and gain something by change of muscular action, — or whether you shall suffer him to become a bad, losing breaker. In the one case, nothing is actually lost by a break; in the other, you drop behind largely, often so far that it cannot be made up.

Then, when the horse is being formed for a trotter, he is not to be suddenly snatched at when he breaks: if he is, he will contract a habit of dropping back in his harness, and almost coming to a stand-still as soon as he breaks. You will see some of our fastest trotters do this. In order to avoid it, let the horse, when being formed for a trotter, take a good lōpe or two when he makes a break before you try to catch him. Should you find, that, without being pulled, he has a tendency to come back into the breeching when he breaks, touch him with the whip at such times, and teach him, that, whatever else he may do, his main business is to go right ahead all the time until you pull him up. In catching a horse in a break, the driver must do it principally with one rein. Some chiefly use the off rein, some the near rein. It is not material which, except in this, that some horses catch more readily and easily on one than on the other. This, as regards any particular horse, is only found out by observation and trial. It is always to be done with one rein. A dead pull on both reins will not bring a horse to his trot; but, if his head be pulled slightly round to one side and upwards, he will grab for his trot immediately.

The movement of the reins to be somewhat like that which is effected by the turn of the wrist, in shifting the bit, to keep the mouth lively and call for another effort when the trotter is doing about his best. There is, however, more pull on one rein; for, in the shift, the action is merely momentary, besides which in the catch there is to be a yielding of the other rein. The driver is not by any means to let go of the head with one hand, while trying to catch the horse in a break with the other; but he must give with the opposite hand just about as much as the horse's head must come to one side to catch his trot. The catching pull is not to be a yanking, jerking pull: if it is, the horse will sheer off, and lose a great deal by the swerve, — perhaps cross, or run into somebody. It is to be a quick, firm, but not violent movement. To do it well, and to learn to do it just at the right time, will be worth your while; and practice will enable you to learn it if you will follow these directions.

By making the horse understand that he is not to come back in his breaks, and by learning how to catch him readily and get him going on with his trot right forward, he will be made a lively breaker, and you will have gained a very great point in the art of driving. Some horses eventually learn to catch their trot with their head straight and their noses out; but this can only be said of few. When the horse has caught after a break, cool nerve and steadiness are wanted on the part of the driver. If the latter is in too much of a hurry, and lets go of the horse's head as soon as he lands on a trot, a double break is commonly the result. It is necessary to steady the horse when he has caught, and to see him settled down square to his trot before you ease off to him, and call for speed. When you do ease off, it should be gradually, so that he may get up to the length and quickness of his stroke by degrees, instead of trying to do so by a convulsive effort.

This, in my opinion, is the method the driver should adopt to teach the horse to be lively in his breaks, and to catch well. I do not call this teaching them to break. There is a great difference in principle between the two things. I have long heard that a driver has no business to teach a horse to break. The thing to be got into the horse is to trot fast and maintain his trot for a mile or two miles, if he is a stout and honest horse, without any break at all: but as I have shown in prior chapters, and in the beginning of this chapter, there are times when a horse will break; and then it makes a vast difference whether his break shall be lively, and he shall catch well, or whether it shall be dead into the ground or up into the air, bobbing about like a ship in a ground swell, with no wind to steady her. Therefore, distinguish the difference between teaching your horse to break, which is mischievous and to be avoided, and teaching him to break lively, with a free forward movement, and to catch well when he does break.

Sometimes a driver of good judgment will break his horse

on purpose, but this is not in a process of teaching him to break well. It is at a pinch, when he sees that the horse is becoming lifeless and dull in action, and beginning to dwell in his stroke. A good lively break at such a time will often revive the horse amazingly, and therefore it ought to be forthwith put in practice. There are two ways of doing this. If the horse is a quick one, hit him with the whip across the buttocks, and, as you do so, let go of his head. He will break with a good forward bound; and, as you will have made him break at your own time, you will be all ready to catch him. The other method is by a sudden snatch on one rein, which will throw him out of his stride and break him. The former of these two methods is to be preferred where the horse can be broken by the cut with the whip, and the accompanying let-go; but though this breaking up on purpose is sometimes useful, and even necessary in a tight place, beware of doing it often. If you practise in this way on your horse to learn how to do it yourself, and see how nicely you can break him up and catch him, you will teach him to break as a habit, and confirm him in it. Many good horses have thus been spoiled.

There is another thing of which you should beware, and it is a thing that is often done: when your horse breaks, do not go under him with the whip. If you do so, the horse will become scared, and will not know what to do. This uncertainty, and the fear of the whip, will keep him all the time in danger of a break. He is afraid: expecting the whip, expecting to break, having no knowledge of what his driver wants him to do, and no confidence in any settled and understood purpose in him as a driver, what can the horse be expected to do? Confidence between the trotting-horse and his driver is of the utmost importance: it is all in all. Some men inspire it readily, so that a horse will take hold and do all he knows the first time the man drives him. For another man the same horse will not trot a yard. The truth is, that the horse is a very knowing, sagacious creature, much more so than he gets credit for. If a driver has no settled system of his own, or if he is rash or severe without cause, it is not likely that confidence will be inspired in the horse, even in a long time. Especially is this the case when the horse is punished without his knowing what it is for.

In nine cases out of ten, a horse punished without his knowing what for is punished for his driver's fault, not for his own. Confidence cannot grow in such circumstances. If you observe two good trotters who have been accustomed to work together in double harness, you will see what speed and steadiness follow from confidence in each other. Each knows that he or she can depend upon the mate to keep up the stroke, and maintain the even pull and level action. It is of just as much importance that the single-harness horse should understand and have confidence in his driver, as it is for a double-harness horse to know the power and ways of his mate. Unless this sort of mutual understanding can be established between the driver and the horse, the latter can never be relied upon to do his best. The readiest way to produce it is to use him gently but firmly, and to accustom him to the system of telegraphing to him by means of the reins in your hand and the bit in his mouth. The whip is to be kept very much in the background while you are cultivating confidence in your horse. It is more likely to prove an obstacle than an aid.

I now come to the last critical point in this matter, — when the horse is tired, and inclined to break. In a long brush, you will often have reason to look for an attempt to break, and it will generally be in circumstances when the horse must not be suffered to do it. There are times, as I have shown, when, with a tired horse, a break may be brought on with advantage; but there are others when all will be lost if a break occurs. To prevent it, give the shift with the bit when you perceive that he begins to tire, and soon renew it; this will revive and rouse him, and take his mind off the break which he has felt he was about to make. The signs of a coming break will be discovered by watching the head and ears of the horse. The attention of the driver ought always to be fixed upon the head of his horse. Many a heat is lost by neglect of this matter. A driver is seen coming up the stretch a length or a length and a half ahead. Both the horses are tired, but the leading one could win. The driver, however, when he gets where the carriages are, turns his head to look at the ladies, or to see whether they are looking at him. Just then the horse gives a twitch with his ears; the driver don't see it; up flies the trotter, and the ugly man behind keeps his horse square, and wins by a neck.

THE END.

APPENDIX.

DEXTER IN 1867–68.

If the author of the foregoing work had lived another year, he would unquestionably have continued the sketch of Dexter down to the period of that horse's retirement from the public trotting-turf, when he was purchased by Mr. Bonner, in the summer of 1867. To supplement that sketch, by a few brief observations upon the most excellent of Dexter's performances in that year, now devolves upon the editor. The horse was wintered at Baltimore, and did well. In the spring of 1867, a challenge was published in "The Spirit of the Times," from Mr. C. P. Relf, the owner of the celebrated mare Lady Thorn, offering to trot her mile heats, three in five, and two-mile heats in harness, and the same races to wagons, against any horse in the world. The challenge was accepted for Dexter, and the matches were made to trot on the Fashion Course.

Before these matches came off, Dexter trotted for a purse at Middletown, Orange County, on the 16th of May, against Goldsmith Maid. He beat her very easily; and this early appearance convinced those who saw him trot that he retained all his speed.

The matches between Dexter and Lady Thorn were for two thousand dollars each. The first of them, mile heats, three in five, in harness, came off at the Fashion Course on the 28th of May.

A great deal of public interest had been excited, and there was an immense gathering of people to see the race. When the matches were first made, the betting was about 60 to 40 on Dexter; but, as his performances of the previous season were called to mind and discussed, he became a stronger favorite, and, just before they started, he was backed at 100 to 50. He was driven by Budd Doble, while the mare was handled by Dan Pfifer. In the first heat, Dexter took the lead at the start, was never headed, and won by two lengths in 2m. 24s. In the second heat, Dexter also took the lead, and was ahead of the mare a length at the half-mile in 1m. 12s. The pace was then improved, and was very fast to the head of the stretch. There the mare was called upon to "head him or die;" and, being unable to stand the increased rate necessary, she made a bad break, and he distanced her in 2m. 22s.

The next race between Dexter and Lady Thorn, mile heats, three in five, to wagons, was trotted on the 7th of June. The public had now come to the conclusion that no living horse could beat Dexter if he was in good condition; and 100 to 20 was laid on him. The first heat in this race was slow. The mare broke twice, and Dexter was held back for her. He won in 2m. 32s. But, in the second heat, there was one of the finest displays of fast and powerful trotting that has ever been witnessed. They went away together, and at the quarter pole Dexter led half a length. At the half-mile, he was a length ahead. He held the mare at his wheel to the head of the stretch, and from thence a desperate struggle ensued. Lady Thorn surpassed any thing that had been done prior to that to wagon; but Dexter beat her by half a length in 2m. 24s. This beat the best time before made to wagon by one second. Flora Temple and George Wilkes had both trotted previously in 2m. 25s. The third heat was another fine one, especially in appearance. Dexter was pulled back so as to just keep the mare well extended, and beat her half a length in 2m. 28s.

On the 14th of June, Dexter and the mare had another meeting at the Fashion, and trotted two-mile heats in harness. It was a good race and fast. Dexter won the first heat by two lengths in 4m. 51s. This was within half a second of the best two miles ever made in harness, which was 4m. 50½s., by Flora Temple. Dexter then won the second heat in 5m. 01½s.

Before this race of two-mile heats in harness, another engagement had been made for Dexter. He was matched to trot in harness against Ethan Allen and a running-mate in double harness. The terms of it were for two thousand dollars, mile heats, three in five, to come off on the 21st of June. Six years before, Ethan Allen and his running-mate Socks had trotted in 2m. 19¾s. It had been lately found, that, in Dan Mace's hands, Ethan was capable of going faster than that in the like rig. He had now for a running-mate a young thoroughbred mare, called Charlotte F. She was got by imported Scythian, out of Blackbird's dam by imported Ainderby; and Mace had taught her to run so evenly, and with such power of stroke, that she carried the old stallion along by the breeching at an enormous rate. On the 29th of May, Ethan Allen and his mare went against Brown George and his runner, and beat them in three heats. The third was trotted in 2m. 19s. This led to the match with Dexter.

On the 21st of June, an immense crowd assembled at the Fashion Course to see the race. The team paid forfeit, Charlotte F. having strained a tendon. But a new match was made for five hundred dollars a side, and they came up to the post. The runner substituted for the mare was the one that had gone with Brown George, a black gelding, captured in the war. The betting was two to one on Dexter.

In the first heat, he had the pole. They went off at amazing speed, and at the quarter the double team led two lengths in 32s. They maintained the rate, and went to the half-mile in 1m. 04s., three lengths ahead. They were four lengths in the lead at the head of the stretch, and won by five lengths in 2m. 15s. A wonderful performance it was all round, but especially for Dexter, who trotted singly, and pulled his own vehicle and driver. He unquestionably beat 2m. 17s.

The betting was even, it being thought that the team would give out before the end of three heats, while it was pretty well known that Dexter would "stick." Soon after they got the word in the second heat, the stallion broke. Dexter led a length on the turn, where he was trotting close to the outside. He took the pole before he reached the quarter, and went on with the lead to the half-mile, where his time was 1m. 06s. But now the runner and the trotter had got to his wheel, having come through the straight work of the back-stretch at a very high rate of speed. The pace was so hot that Ethan broke on the Flushing turn; but, when he caught, the runner whirled him along at such a rate that they overhauled Dexter, and beat him by three lengths in 2m. 16s. Dexter must have trotted this heat in 2m. 17s. or 2m. 17¼s.: and it affords the most notable example of constancy and courage that ever was seen; for, after he had trotted the first half-mile in the amazing time of 1m. 06s., and had kept the lead for three-quarters of a mile, he never left his feet when the team, like a storm, came rushing by, but trotted out to the end in 2m. 17s., or thereabouts. The team won the third heat in 2m. 19s.

The trotting of Dexter in this race settled three things in the minds of thoughtful and reasoning people: first, that, high as his powers had been estimated, they had been underrated; second, that no trotter going on equal terms with him had any chance to beat him, barring accidents; third, that a race between a trotter in single harness, and another trotter in double harness with a running-mate, was no fair match. The conclusion was, that the running-horse beat Dexter.

On Saturday, June 29, Dexter and Lady Thorn trotted their last race on the Fashion Course,—two-mile heats to wagons. The horse was fine-drawn and wiry, from the effect of his desperate exertions against the double team; but he was in no wise stale, for his eye was bright, his coat sleek, and his spirit eager. Ten to one was laid on Dexter before the start; and he won with great ease in two heats, — 5m. 01s., 5m. 09s.

He had an engagement on hand with Ethan Allen and Charlotte F., for the Fourth of July. It was to go mile heats, three in five, on the half-mile track at Morristown, N.J. The track was not calculated for a very fast race; but yet the team was compelled to go in 2m. 20$\frac{1}{2}$s., 2m. 20$\frac{1}{4}$s., and 2m. 20s., to beat Dexter. Some maintained at the time, that, considering the nature of the course, this was quite as good a race as the one at the Fashion.

Dexter now met Lady Thorn for the last time. On the 10th of July, they trotted mile heats, three in five, in harness, at Trenton, N.J. Dexter won in three heats. The last was fast, — 2m. 20$\frac{1}{2}$s. The track was sandy, deep, and heavy; and it was now clearly perceived that the hour for surpassing Flora Temple's crowning heat — 2m. 19$\frac{3}{4}$s. — was close at hand.

On the 16th of July, Dexter was at Albany, and there trotted against Brown George and running-mate on the Island-park Course. Brown George was not much of a trotter by himself; but, with the aid of a good running-mate, he could put in three heats very fast. Inferior as he was to Ethan Allen in that and in every other way of going, he could still, with his running-mate, beat any horse in the country save Dexter. But Dexter he could not beat. The little wonder won in three heats, — 2m. 22s., 2m. 20$\frac{1}{2}$s., 2m. 20$\frac{1}{2}$s. The great fact which had so often been insisted upon by the admirers of Dexter was now being made manifest to the dullest mind; viz., that his deep bottom, and immense constitutional power of standing fast work, enabled him to improve under a course of travelling and racing which would have upset, and for the time ruined, any other trotter in existence.

Dexter beat Brown George and running-mate in three heats at Providence on the 26th of July, and then, going on to Boston, surpassed any thing that had ever before been done by a trotter. It was on the 30th; and he went in harness against Brown George and running-mate on the Riverside-park Course. The track is a half-mile one. The fame of Dexter, and the speed of his recent exploits, drew together an immense multitude. The fences and stands broke down; and it was with difficulty that the course could be kept clear for the horses. Dexter won the first heat easily, in 2m. 21¾s. The second was fast and close. In the first quarter, George made one little break, and Dexter led at the half-mile, in 1m. 10s. The last half-mile was stoutly contested. Fast as Dexter was going, the runner and the trotter drew towards him, and at length headed him. But the little horse then made himself up for a finishing struggle. He again got even with the team, and, passing them in the straight work, came home full of power and trot in 2m. 19s. The best time of Flora had now been beaten! Dexter won the third heat in 2m. 21¼s. Let it be remembered that this was on a half-mile track; and then let us look at the figures, — 2m. 21¾s., 2m. 19s., 2m. 21¼s. They are so forcible and eloquent that no more need be said. This is not one fast heat out of three, but three fast heats in succession. Yet there was good reason to expect it after the races against Ethan Allen and mate, and from the known almost-everlasting capacity of Dexter to improve under plenty of strong work.

It is unnecessary, in this place, to notice any further performances made by Dexter on the trotting-turf, except that in which he went against time at Buffalo. There is little doubt of the fact that the negotiations between Mr. Bonner and Mr. Fawcett for his purchase and sale had been virtually concluded soon after he went against Ethan Allen and running-mate on the Fashion Course. But, be that as it may, on the 14th of August, at Buffalo, Mr. Bonner and Mr. Fawcett being both present, Dexter was engaged by Doble to beat his own time on the Riverside Park at Boston. The famous little horse was brought out and warmed up. Doble then intimated to the judges that he should drive one round as preparatory. The horse went to the quarter in 34s., to the half-mile in 1m. 10s, and trotted in 2m. 21½s. This was a great deal faster than Doble had intended to drive him; and, indeed, most of the people thought that it was a real effort and failure. After being scraped and cooled out, Dexter was again harnessed, and brought on the course at four o'clock. With him there came Ben Mace and the thoroughbred mare Charlotte F., who had aided Ethan Allen at Morristown. She was under saddle, Mace riding; and it was his office to lay at Dexter's quarters, to keep up his emulation and determination to conquer. A little jog or two, and then the trotter in harness, and the runner under saddle, went up the stretch, and came along for the word. As Dexter was seen to be going very square and well, it was given. The pace was fast. He trotted the first quarter in 33¼s., made the half-mile in 1m. 07s., and came home in 2m. 17¼s., in good wind, and with a stroke of commanding power. This performance capped the climax of his fame, so far as public trotting in races is concerned. The sale to Mr. Bonner was made known, and also the condition that Dexter was not to be delivered until after he had fulfilled an existing engagement at Chicago. The price was thirty-three thousand dollars; and considering the income he had earned, and might have continued to earn, by trotting in public, Dexter was one of the cheapest horses that ever was sold. He was not only a means of wealth, but of distinction, to Mr. Fawcett.

Although the time Dexter made at Buffalo, 2m. 17¼s., capped the climax of his fame, it was not the full measure of his capacity. He had steadily improved up to that date, and there is no reason to believe that he then attained the greatest excellence of which he was capable. He *has* improved since he came into the possession of Mr. Bonner; and facts warrant the belief, that he will some day, when he is at the pitch of condition, and other things are favorable, trot a mile in harness several seconds faster than 2m. 17¼s. In estimating his present powers, it is material to consider the fact that the Buffalo Course was slow when Dexter made his fast time there. During that week many fast horses trotted over it, and only one of them made a heat as fast as 2m. 30s. It has since been drained, and otherwise improved, and is now fast. My own opinion is, that Dexter can now go in less than 2m. 20s. any day and every day that he may be called upon to do so when he is fit to trot and the course is good. If that is correct, his regular rate is such that he must be capable of an effort so enormous, that he may, and probably will, far surpass his feat at Buffalo, and again make "limping Time toil after him in vain."

CHARLES J. FOSTER

it thoroughly, and follow what is set down, he may, with good sense and plenty of practice, come in time to train and drive as well as I do.

Yours truly, D. MACE.

From Hiram Woodruff's legitimate successor, Dan Pfifer.

CYPRESS HILLS, L. I., Oct. 31, 1868.

CHAS. J. FOSTER, Esq.—*Sir:* Hiram Woodruff's book is sure to be of very great service to the young men of the country who have got young horses. I have read it through more than once. People who have horses should read it carefully, and follow the directions set down for the treatment, feeding, training, and driving of trotters. It makes me remember old times, when I read the story of Ripton, for I was with Hiram then.

Yours truly, D. PFIFER.

Wilkes's Spirit of the Times.

This book has been put before the public in a very handsome and complete style, by Messrs. J. B. Ford & Co., of this city, and we observe from our exchanges that it is receiving handsome notices from the press. The estimation in which we hold it is well known to our readers. We believe it to be *the most practical and instructive book that ever was published concerning the trotting horse;* and those who own or take care of horses of other descriptions may buy and read it with a great deal of profit. Besides all this, it is a work of great interest.

Mr. Bonner's New-York Ledger.

Hiram Woodruff was the great trainer of his day; but, by his unsullied integrity and unequaled capacity, he rose above his profession. No man could ever say of him that he had his price. Indeed, it is the universal testimony of all who knew him—friends and foes—that his integrity was absolutely unassailable. In this work, which has been ably, carefully, and judiciously edited by his faithful friend, Mr. Charles J. Foster, are recorded for the benefit of the public at large, his life-long experiences; his sayings and doings; his authoritative views on almost every thing pertaining to the horse. *It is a book for which every man who owns a horse ought to subscribe. The information which it contains is worth ten times its cost;* and we hope, for the sake of the widow who owns the copyright, that the sales may, at least, reach one hundred thousand copies.

New-York Herald.

The author of this work stood at the head of his profession as a trainer and driver of the trotting horse. . . . . The book under consideration is the matured result of forty years' labor on the part of the author in developing the speed and endurance of the trotter, and his method of training and driving is accepted by turfmen as the perfection of that art. This method is fully set forth in this volume, accompanied with abundant illustrations of its correctness by the track performances of many of our most celebrated trotting horses. To horsemen in particular the book will be found especially attractive and of great value. *It will become a standard authority on the subject of which it treats.*

New-York Times.

This book will become the manual of the roadsters. Woodruff was king of the horse-trainers, and the *rationale* of his system shows that he was a man of excellent judgment, while his many successes on the course furnish the best commentary on his modes of equine management. The book is calculated to be a very popular one, for every one who drives a nag in harness will have the ambition to read it, and it has an excellent narrative style. Indeed, if this was the style of Mr. Woodruff himself, he must have been as clever in his talk with men as in his management of horses. The book is handsomely got up, with a well-executed portrait of the late New-York Mareschal and Master of Horse.

New-York Tribune.

This is a masterly treatise by the master of his profession—the ripened product of forty years' experience in handling, training, riding, and driving the Trotting Horse. There is no book like it in any language on the subject of which it treats. It is accepted as authority by the owners of racing trotters, and of fast roadsters. Its publication has been hailed by gentlemen as critically appreciative as Robert Bonner, and by trainers and drivers as distinguished as Sim Hoagland, Dan Mace, and Dan Pfifer. The book is unquestionably one of great value. For in America and England the development of the horse has long been considered second only in importance to the development of man. This work contains the results of forty years' uninterrupted labor in bringing the trotter up to the highest speed and the greatest endurance of which he is capable. Before we read it we had seen with curious surprise very hearty commendation of it and eulogy of its author in the leading Presbyterian, Baptist, and Methodist journals. No wonder, for Hiram Woodruff's system is based on the law of love.

Brick Pomeroy's Democrat.

Hiram Woodruff, a life-like portrait of whom adorns the book, of course needs no introduction to any American who cares any thing about horses. His life was one continued benefit to that noble animal, one prolonged and successful effort to improve its condition, speed, and usefulness to man. His memory is that of a man proverbially honorable and of unapproached excellence in his calling. What Hiram Woodruff did *not* know about horses, and particularly the training of good colts and the driving of trotting horses, is hardly worth the knowing. What he *did* know, he has put into this book.

The (N. Y.) Liberal Christian, (Unitarian.)

We have a decided distaste for every thing connected with horse-racing, and when the *Trotting Horse of America* was put into our hands the book dropped of its own weight on to the table. Ashamed of this prejudice, we took it up, and soon found ourselves reading at full pace about the way colts should be raised, and horses trained, and racers cared for, and the breed improved. . . . In reading the book we were struck with the analogy between the scientific treatment of the horse and the best treatment of the human being. . . . What a pity parents and teachers would not learn wisdom from the horse-trainer! . . . The book gives us a higher estimate of the horse, and what a proper care and training can make him, but increases our contempt for those who abuse and maltreat an animal that has so many good qualities, and is capable of so much service and so much suffering.

Springfield (Mass.) Republican.

A capital book is *The Trotting Horse of America*, by that most famous of whips—or, as the Greeks, with more appreciation of driving, called them, reinholders — Hiram Woodruff. Half of the manly virtues belong to the man mounted. Almost all conquerors and great rulers have been fond of the chase and fond of the horse; and it is no accident, but comes out of a real congeniality between a strong, brave, resolute man, and a powerful, fleet, and high-spirited horse. The volume before us contains the best results of Woodruff's large observation and matured judgment, in regard to the breaking, feeding, and training of horses. It is full of shrewd remarks and sound rules. Those who know nothing about a horse, or not much, will be surprised at the amount of information and the variety of directions contained; and to see how truly the care and handling of the horse rise to the dignity of a science.

Boston Watchman and Reflector, (Baptist.)

One may read and study this book with profit, for it was written by a man who loved the horse, knew hi peculiarities, and from the experience of years, utters words of wisdom as to the best way of training and driving the noblest animal ever given to man for service. *The advice, the suggestions, the rules given in the book are invaluable.* If we owned a "stable," we would make our grooms study it; if we were a Vermont farmer, each son should have a copy, for, while it is specially devoted to trotting horses, the work contains valuable information for every man who owns or drives a horse.

N. Y. Examiner and Chronicle, (Baptist.)

"The Woodruffs" seem to have been horsemen and horse-trainers for generations, and the "reminiscences" of the most celebrated of the family are *full of piquancy and attraction, as well as of information useful to all who own horses.* The author is another evidence of the truth that only those who *love* horses can manage horses, and the *mere* groom is never a good horseman.

Chicago Evening Journal.

The mass of information which it contains is not easily accessible in any other form, and will prove immensely acceptable to those whose inclinations are with the turf and whatever concerns its heroes and heroines.

Boston Traveller.

The volume embraces a wonderful amount of information on its subject, admirably prepared and presented, and *really leaving little more to be desired on that subject*, till the passage of years shall have furnished new illustrations of it. Mr. Foster has edited the work well and discreetly, and the biographical sketch he gives of Mr. Woodruff is a model piece of writing; and Mr. Wilkes gives an introductory sketch of the great trainer that is worthy of his strong and lively pen. A striking portrait of Mr. Woodruff adorns the volume, which is got up in very elegant style.

Worcester Spy.

Mr. Woodruff, whose experience and observation for forty years have prepared him to discuss this subject in the best manner, has given us a book that all interested in trotting horses will be likely to study. It has the indorsement of George Wilkes and Robert Bonner, and is undoubtedly *the best book on the subject that has ever been written.*

Boston Post.

A volume which, from the glance we have given it, we should say was worthy the experience of a man who did more than any one else to raise the standard of our fast horses.

Philadelphia Press.

It may be characterized, briefly but emphatically, as the best, because the most practical and "knowledgeable" book upon trotting-horses ever printed.

Boston Advertiser.

A book thoroughly unique in its way.

Boston Journal.

A valuable volume for reference.

American Agriculturist.

This is the title of a very neat 12mo volume. . . . It was published in chapters in *Wilkes's Spirit of the Times*, and now, as soon after the death of the famous trainer as possible, it is given to the public, and will be found of great interest to all who love a good horse. The first eleven chapters, together with others scattered through the book, are chiefly instructive on handling, feeding, training, etc. Others are reminiscences of the trotting turf, told in a very pleasant way. It contains 412 pages, with a portrait of the author, and will no doubt meet, and worthily, with a very extensive sale.

Boston Cultivator.

While this book was written by one preëminently skilled in his art, and especially designed for all interested in the breeding, training, as well as all else that relates to the horse, it can not fail of being attractive to the general reader. . . . We therefore commend it as *deserving a place in all public libraries, and especially so to the notice of Farmers' Clubs*, wherever they have been organized.

St. Louis Democrat.

Every thing desirable to be known of the famous trotters is found in these pages, with suggestions and instructions for rearing stock, breaking, or rather "educating" colts, and full details of practical experience. It is accompanied by a sketch and portrait of Woodruff, and *will be sought for by every owner, breeder, or lover of the horse in the land.*

Catholic World, (Monthly.)

It is one of those rare books which, while got up for a special purpose, and seemingly suited to the few, overleaps the narrow limits apparently prescribed, and *attracts to itself the favorable notice of the entire community.*

The American Farmer.

It is the most complete work of the kind, and possesses all the fascination of a novel, even to others than horsemen.

Working Farmer.

We commend the work under consideration to farmers in all sections of the country. It is calculated to do great good, and to teach them many things about the horse which they probably do not but ought to know.

The Nation.

The record of his experience and suggestions constitutes, therefore, a valuable accession to our knowledge, and will prove to be of *standard authority among the most skillful.* The graphic style of his descriptions, the vivid pictures he draws of the breeding and education of his favorites, and the reminiscences he recalls of incidents on the turf, form a work of great merit. . . . Those who are desirous to form an accurate idea of the characteristics of the trotting-horse, for their benefit as riders or drivers, *can not find any other work in our language so replete with useful information*, interesting hints, and readable anecdotes. Hiram Woodruff is now dead, and it will be many a year before we shall look upon his equal in his line of business.

N. Y. Evening Post.

While, as the work of an enthusiastic horseman, and with a true purpose, a large part of the book is made up of "reminiscences of the trotting turf," there is a vast deal else exhibiting the grasp of a master in the art of training and caring for the animals he so profoundly appreciated. It is, then, not only by lovers of the horse that this book will be valued. It contains a store of observation and suggestion *valuable to every man who owns horses either for trotting or draught.*

LIFE OF JESUS, THE CHRIST.

BY

HENRY WARD BEECHER.

THE Publishers of this forthcoming work find it necessary—on account of the intense and abiding interest aroused all over the land by their announcement that the greatest living religious teacher was engaged upon so important a theme—to make some answer to the constant inquiries concerning the book. Germany, France, England—all have their schools both of orthodoxy and of skepticism, no two of which occupy the same ground or help each other in dealing with the popular mind in the different countries; and none of which is properly adapted to the wants of religious thinkers in America. This must be the work of an American—and of a completely representative American.

It is with full confidence in the attainment of this result that the publishers of the "Life of Jesus, the Christ," to which great work Mr. BEECHER is now constantly and earnestly devoting his abundant energies, are preparing for its issuance in a manner worthy the public expectancy, the universal interest in the subject, and the repute of the author.

The work is to be issued in two styles. It will be first published in a full octavo volume of about 800 pages. This, although called the "Plain Edition," will be illustrated with several valuable engravings. First, with four superb Maps, constructed expressly for this work from the very latest data, including the great English, Dutch, and French governmental surveys of Palestine, the present explorations of Jerusalem itself by Lieut. WARREN, Royal Engineers, and every attainable source of exact geographical and topographical information. These are engraved on copper and on stone (printed in two tints) by COLTON, the famous map-maker and publisher. The other illustrations are a Frontispiece, "Head of Christ," restored, painted, and engraved on steel by the renowned American engraver, WM. E. MARSHALL, from a photograph of LEONARDO DA VINCI's rapidly decaying masterpiece in Milan, "The Last Supper"—a really grand work of the engraver's art; and a beautiful Steel-plate Title-page, containing a Vignette of Bethlehem, engraved by R. HINSHELWOOD, of the Continental Bank-Note Company.

The other style will be in royal octavo size, richly illustrated. It will contain the Frontispiece, Title-page, and Maps mentioned above, a series of twenty large full-page wood-engravings, and from fifty to seventy-five smaller cuts printed in the text.

The whole series are from *new and original drawings never before published,* having been designed expressly for this work after sketches taken directly from the places represented. They are a new and full illustration of localities, people, and customs among the scenes of our Lord's earthly labors, and, as artistic productions, are believed to be superior to any thing before published on that subject. They are engraved by W. J. LINTON, the celebrated wood-engraver, now resident in New-York, universally acknowledged to be the first master of his art, and his brother, H. D. LINTON, long well known and highly esteemed in Paris.

The maps were constructed and the illustrations designed by A. L. RAWSON, an artist for years resident in the Holy Land, and thoroughly conversant with its features. The drawings on wood are from the artistic pencil of HARRY FENN. The work will be printed at the University Press, Cambridge, Mass., by WELCH, BIGELOW & Co.

Concerning the date of publication, more particular information will be given through the newspaper press in due time. It may be said, however, that the book will not be ready for canvassing by subscription agents (in which manner alone it is to be sold) before the month of May next.

J. B. FORD & CO., PUBLISHERS,

164 NASSAU STREET, PRINTING-HOUSE SQUARE, NEW-YORK.

SCHOOL BOOKS.

I. PRINCIPLES OF DOMESTIC SCIENCE: As applied to the Duties and Pleasures of Home. A Text-Book for Young Ladies in Schools, Seminaries, and Colleges. By CATHARINE E. BEECHER and HARRIET BEECHER STOWE.

A compact 12mo volume of 390 pages; profusely illustrated; well printed, and bound in neat and substantial style. Price, $2.00.

Prepared with a view to assist in training young women for the distinctive duties which inevitably come upon them in household life, this volume should find an honored place in every institution devoted to feminine education. Very many topics of vital importance in the regulation of the household receive thorough treatment. The book has been made with especial reference to the duties, cares, and pleasures of *the family* as being the place where, whatever the political developments of the future, Woman, from her very nature, of body and of spirit, will find her most engrossing occupation.

The New York *Tribune* says: "This book is a whole library of sound suggestion, important information, exhortation, and reproof. Indeed, almost every small, every-day perplexity finds its help and answer here." It is the text for a fresh and important study for young women.

II. HISTORY of the STATE OF NEW YORK. From the Date of the Discovery and Settlements on Manhattan Island to the Present Time. A Text-Book for High Schools, Academies, and Colleges. By S. S. RANDALL, Superintendent of Public Education in New York City. 12mo vol., 396 pages. Illustrated. Price, $1.75.

The author, for many years intimately connected with the management of our Public Schools, has written with *a full knowledge of what was needed*, and the result is a clear, compendious, and admirable digest of all the important events in the life of New York, down to the year 1870.

Extract from the Author's Preface.

"So far as I am aware, the compilation now presented to the public is the first attempt at providing for our elementary and higher institutions of learning a separate History of the State of New York. Many of the most important events in that history are, it is true, contained in the current school histories of the United States; necessarily, however, greatly abridged and condensed. It has seemed to me, and others interested in the work of popular education, that some attempt should be made to supply this deficiency by presenting within a convenient compass the prominent outlines of those interesting details which have rendered our own 'Empire State' so conspicuous in the history of the great American Republic."

☞ ***Single copies of the above will be mailed, post-paid, to Teachers, on receipt of half the retail price.***

MISCELLANEOUS.

I. THE OVERTURE OF ANGELS. By HENRY WARD BEECHER. Illustrated by HARRY FENN. 12mo. Tinted paper, Extra Cloth, gilt. Price, $2.50.

This exquisite Book is a chapter from Mr. BEECHER's great work, the "Life of Jesus, the Christ." It is a series of pictures, in the author's happiest style, of the Angelic Appearances, — giving a beautiful and characteristically interesting treatment of all the events recorded in the Gospels, as occurring about the period of the Nativity of Our Lord. The charming style in which the book is written, the poetic imagery and beauty of sentiment with which it abounds, the delicate and tender treatment of Mary's experience of motherhood, the vivid pictures of the manners and customs of the Orient in that day, — indeed, all its parts and features, are characterized by the peculiar strength and spiritual beauty which Mr. BEECHER brings to whatever subject he touches.

II. BEECHER'S SERMONS: First Series. September, 1868, to March, 1869.

Embellished with a new Steel Portrait of Mr. BEECHER, — the best likeness of him ever published, and a superb piece of engraving. 8vo. 438 pp. Price, Extra Cloth, $2.50; Half Morocco or Half Calf, $5.00.

III. BEECHER'S SERMONS: Second Series. March to September, 1869.

Illustrated with a large and effective engraving, giving a fine view of the INTERIOR OF PLYMOUTH CHURCH. 8vo. 451 pp. Price, Extra Cloth, $2.50; Half Morocco or Half Calf, $5.00.

Mr. BEECHER's discourses need no new commendation. Their freshness and originality of method in presenting the old familiar truths, their felicity of illustration, their aptness, skill, and impressiveness, make them interesting to readers of every class and of every religious denomination.

The two volumes above mentioned, containing Mr. ELLINWOOD's masterly and complete phonographic reports, are portions of a course, one of which is to be issued every six months.

IV. LECTURE-ROOM TALKS. A Series of Familiar Discourses on Themes of Christian Experience. By HENRY WARD BEECHER. Phonographically reported by T. J. ELLINWOOD. 12mo. Extra cloth. Price, $1.75.

These "Talks" are the well-known and delightful expositions of Scripture and extempore remarks made at prayer-meetings, and on similar occasions, in the familiar and free intercourse of Mr. BEECHER with his own people.

☞ *These books for sale everywhere, or sent, post-paid, upon receipt of price by the Publishers.*

V. THE MINES OF THE WEST. A full Statistical Account of the Mineral Development of the Pacific States and Territories, for the Year 1868, with Sixteen Illustrations; and a Treatise on the **Relation of Governments to Mining,** with Delineation of the Legal and Practical Mining Systems of all Countries from early Ages to the present Time. By ROSSITER W. RAYMOND, Ph. D., United States Commissioner of Mining Statistics. 8vo. Extra cloth, $1.75.

"Mr. Raymond's conclusions, the well-weighed convictions of an acute observer and practical mineralogist, will carry with them great weight." — *Round Table.*

"Well worthy the attention of the general public." — *Philadephia Post.*

"It has attracted marked attention by its clearness of statement and the broad, scientific view which it presents of the whole subject of mining, in its relation to legislation." — *New York Commercial Advertiser.*

VI. THE TROTTING HORSE OF AMERICA: How to Train and Drive him. With Reminiscences of the Trotting Turf. The Results of the Author's Forty Years' Experience and Unequalled Skill in Training and Driving, together with a Store of interesting Matter concerning celebrated American Horses. By HIRAM WOODRUFF. Edited by CHARLES J. FOSTER, of *Wilkes's Spirit of the Times.*

12mo. 412 pp. With splendid steel-plate portrait of Hiram Woodruff. Price, Extra Cloth, $2.25; Half Calf, $4.00.

HIRAM WOODRUFF may almost be said to have been the creator of our distinctively national animal, the Trotter. The value of this record of his experience, and these suggestions of his skill, cannot, therefore, be doubted as a standard authority in the technicalities of which he treats; while his book is attractive to the general reader, useful to the seeker for practical advice, and worth the perusal of all who would be well informed upon the history of one of America's most characteristic developments.

ROBERT BONNER, who owns the fastest horses in the world, says: "*It is a book for which every man who owns a horse ought to subscribe. The information which u contains is worth ten times its cost.*"

IN PRESS.

VII. MATERNITY: A Popular Treatise for Young Married Women in their New Sphere as Wives and Mothers. By TULLIO SUZZARA VERDI, A. M., M. D. 12mo. 425 pages. Extra Cloth, $2.00.

Concerning Pregnancy, its symptoms, its disorders and their relief; Labor and its necessities and helps; Infants and the daily care of them; Children's Diseases, their prevention and treatment, Accidents; Poisons and their Antidotes; Medicines, their preparation and administration; the Physical and Moral Training of Boys and Girls; Marriage; General Suggestions to Parents.

☞ *These books for sale everywhere, or sent, post-paid, upon receipt of price by the Publishers.*

www.ingramcontent.com/pod-product-compliance
Lightning Source LLC
LaVergne TN
LVHW021200120826
845150LV00011B/1206
* 9 7 8 1 4 2 5 5 4 6 4 1 0 *